NEW TIMES

NEW TIMES

The Changing Face of Politics in the 1990s

edited by
Stuart Hall
and
Martin Jacques

LAWRENCE & WISHART
in association with Marxism Today
LONDON

Lawrence & Wishart Limited
144a Old South Lambeth Road
London SW8 1XX

This edition first published 1989

Photoset in Norfolk by
Art Services, Norwich
Printed and bound in Great Britain by
Short Run Press, Exeter

To my mum, Dorothy Jacques,
from whom I learnt so much.
She always looked to the future,
never fearful of change,
always a woman of new times.

Contents

V POLITICAL CULTURE

VI THE SHAPE OF THINGS TO COME

Preface

This book is a compilation of essays, for the most part reprinted from *Marxism Today*, some as they first appeared, others adapted to varying degrees.

Two of these essays appeared in 1985: Göran Therborn, 'The Two-Thirds, One-Third Society' (June) which is based on an extract from *Why Some People Are More Unemployed Than Others* (Verso 1985), and Robin Murray, 'Benetton Britain' (November). Frank Mort, 'The Politics of Consumption' was substantially revised from an article written with Nicholas Green (May 1988). Tom Nairn, 'Tartan Power' (June 1988) is a revised version of an address made at the launch of The Campaign for a Welsh Assembly (November 1988). David Marquand, 'Beyond Left and Right: The Need for a New Politics' appeared in July 1988.

All other essays from *Marxism Today* were first published between October 1988 with the 'launch' of the New Times project and September 1989. From the 'New Times' issue in October 1988 we have included: Rosalind Brunt, 'The Politics of Identity'; Stuart Hall, 'The Meaning of New Times'; Charlie Leadbeater, 'Power to the Person'; Robin Murray, 'Fordism and Post-Fordism'; and John Urry, 'The End of Organised Capitalism'. Other essays published since are: David Held, 'The Decline of the Nation State' and Geoff Mulgan, 'The Power of the Weak' (December 1988); Dick Hebdige, 'After the Masses' (January 1989); Göran Therborn, 'Vorsprung Durch Rethink' (February 1989); Sarah Benton, 'The Decline of the Party', Geoff Mulgan, 'The Changing Shape of the City' and Fred Steward, 'Green Times' (March 1989); Neal Ascherson, 'Eastern Europe on the Move', Martin Jacques, 'Britain and Europe', David Marquand, 'The Irresistible Tide of Europeanisation' and Gwyn A Williams, 'The Onward March of the Small Nation' (April 1989); Charlie Leadbeater, 'Thatcherism and Progress' Stuart Hall and David Held, 'Citizens and Citizenship' (June 1989); Gareth Stedman Jones, 'The Crisis of Communism' (July 1989); David Edgar, 'Novel Approaches: A Tale for New Times' (August 1989); Geoff Mulgan, 'Uncertainty, Reversibility and

Variety' (September 1989).

There are three pieces which are reprinted from other publications: Beatrix Campbell, 'New Times Towns', based on her series 'Campbell's Kingdom' which first appeared in *The Guardian* (August and September 1989); Paul Hirst, 'After Henry' based on the piece of the same title which appeared in *New Statesman and Society* (21 July 1989); Michael Rustin, 'The Trouble with New Times' based on 'The Politics of Post-Fordism' which appeared in *New Left Review*, 175 (June/July). There are also three extracts here from *The Manifesto for New Times*, published in June 1989: 'The New Times', 'Paths to Renewal' and 'Realignment of Politics'. *The Manifesto* was written by Beatrix Campbell, Marian Darke, Tricia Davis, David Green, Joanna de Groot, Ron Halverson, Steve Hart, Martin Jacques, Charlie Leadbeater, Bert Pearce, Jeff Rodrigues, Mhairi Stewart and Nina Temple, and was subsequently amended by the Communist Party executive committee.

The editors would like to thank the Barry Amiel Memorial Trust for their financial support for the *Marxism Today* seminar in May 1988 which gave birth to the New Times project and Mauro Andreini and staff at Gavorrano town hall for various technical assistance.

Introduction

Stuart Hall and Martin Jacques

The 'New Times' project began with a seminar in May 1988 organised by the *Marxism Today* editorial board. It was not at that stage a formed project at all. What triggered it off was a sense around *MT* of the need to move on, to develop the magazine's political project beyond the analysis of Thatcherism and the crisis of the Left. Above all, it represented the felt need to address the future of the Left more directly, from a position rooted in an analysis of present and emergent tendencies in our society. The seminar itself was a mixed event, part coherent, part incoherent, exciting and frustrating in about equal measure. Old arguments and new perspectives jostled with one another. However, out of it emerged the 'New Times' issue of *Marxism Today* in October 1988 and the related debates in subsequent issues of the magazine. This was the moment when it began to come together, acquire coherence. It no longer felt simply like a collection of disparate, interesting ideas. It began to connect with a series of parallel debates going on in other circles. It began to feel like something new — in fact, a project.

We use the word 'project' advisedly. 'New Times' is not, and was never intended to be, a position. Some critics have sought to interpret 'New Times' as a new line, an orthodoxy. This is to misunderstand what is involved. It is no such thing. The object is to make better sense of the world, and, on that basis, to realign the Left with that new world.

The 'New Times' argument is that the world has changed, not just incrementally but qualitatively, that Britain and other advanced capitalist societies are increasingly characterised by diversity, differentiation and fragmentation, rather that homogeneity, standardisation and the economies and organisations of scale which characterised modern mass society.

This is the essence of the so-called transition from 'Fordism', which defined the experience of modernity in the first two-thirds of the 20th century, to 'post-Fordism'. In economic terms, the central feature of the transition is the rise of 'flexible specialisation' in place of the old assembly-line world of mass production. It is this, above all, which is orchestrating and driving on the evolution of this new world. However, this must not be understood as exclusively an economic development, in the narrow sense. Just as Fordism represented, not simply a form of economic organisation but a whole culture — what Gramsci in 'Americanism and Fordism' called a new epoch of civilisation within advanced capitalism — so post-Fordism is also shorthand for a much wider and deeper social and cultural development. Thus many of the features of this new world have been long in the making and are best seen in areas apparently removed from what the Left has traditionally thought of as the 'point of production'. The changing position of women, inside and outside the paid labour force, is one such feature, which has over the years served to disrupt, if not entirely displace, the old distinctions between production and consumption, production and social reproduction.

The transition, then, is epochal — not in the sense of the classic transition from feudalism to capitalism, but as fundamental and far-reaching as, say, the transition in the closing stages of the 19th century from the 'entrepreneurial' to the advanced or organised stage within capitalism. The argument here is not that we have suddenly moved from one world to another — that has never been the nature of historical change at the level at which the concepts of Fordism and post-Fordism operate. Rather, it is suggested that, in the last decade or so, we have witnessed a qualitative change, which has shifted the centre of gravity of the society and the culture markedly and decisively in a new direction. There is nothing smooth, even or comprehensive about this shift; it operates with remarkable unevenness both within and across the advanced capitalist societies. Fordism is still alive and well in many places. So, by the way, are pre-Fordist forms. The point is that, despite these many lags and delays which complicate the picture and make definitive assessment difficult, post-Fordism is at the leading-edge of change, increasingly setting the tone of society and providing the dominant rhythm of cultural change.

One of the most difficult problems is to assess what stage we are at in this process — to recognise the changes, separating what is ephemeral from what is more fundamental, but at the same time not to exaggerate them. It would be quite wrong to see the world purely in post-Fordist terms, because this is certainly not the reality, in Britain or indeed anywhere. The first problem is the more serious — refusing to recognise the changes and how they transform the world in which the Left has to operate — and by far the more common one. For reasons which we cannot go into at length here, it is all too common for the Left, which emerges in one conjuncture, to become doctrinally fixed to that epoch, and to cling on to both the analysis and the organisational and programmatic forms which it gave rise to, long after its moment has passed. This is how a Left which is at the forefront of change in one era can become stuck and transformed into a conservative political force when history moves on.

But we also recognise the second problem — the temptation to exaggerate the new and to represent it one-sidedly, without taking full account of the enormous unevennesses and ambiguities that characterise the process of change. This is the fine line which the 'New Times' analysis is seeking to tread — and one of the difficulties with this book. We have focused here on the new, because that is what we are trying to understand. But, in so doing, we have inevitably played down the old. The lines of continuity are given rather less attention than the points of rupture. Here we can only signal our recognition of this danger, while defending our emphasis because of our central objective — to place the fact and novelty of the changes squarely on the agenda for the Left.

This raises a second problem with the 'New Times' project: not only do our critics read it as a new orthodoxy, they also tend to see it as a finished piece of work, comprehensive in scope and already complete, an analysis which covers all the ground and has either to be rejected or swallowed whole. You must take it or leave it. This is not our intention. On the contrary, 'New Times' is, by definition, 'work in progress'. We are only at the very beginning. Behind each of the elements in the 'New Times' analysis lies, in many instances, a developed specialist and theoretical literature with which, in the essays that follow, there is frequently only a limited engagement. Moreover, the analysis can only be developed and refined by debate, discussion and critique − which is why we reprint two critical reviews as an integral part of this volume.

Take the essays revised and reprinted in this book. They were, for the most part, originally published in *Marxism Today* over the course of a year, following the publication of the 'New Times' issue. They were stimulated by the initial sense of discovery and energy which that original intervention released and − to judge from political and journalistic comment from a variety of directions at the time − the impact it had. We might add to these essays the two more overtly political documents, *'Facing up to the Future'* and *'Manifesto for New Times'*, which were part of the same impulse. What must be clear to even the most casual reader are the many different emphases, approaches, ideas and positions taken by different authors in these various pieces of work. They contain many unresolved ambiguities and contradictions. No attempt has been made to smooth these out into a single, comprehensive or consensual position. In our view, that is exactly what 'work in progress' − a project of discovery − is all about.

The problem is that we on the Left are not used to working in such an open-ended manner. We are accustomed to dealing in certainties, with having some clear and reassuring idea of where we are likely to end up. The Left does not much like venturing into uncharted territory. It is filled with suspicion. And yet there is surely something odd about the Left − a political force committed to historical change and to a different future − only feeling comfortable on well trodden and familiar ground. At all events, the 'New Times' project is characterised by no such comfortable assumptions. Nor should it be, since they belong to an era when the Left slowly lost touch with change and the world outside of itself and, in many respects, became a culturally conservative force.

The Left's failure to move with the times has been evident for some while, a creeping phenomenon of the postwar era, but it was in the 1980s that the reality of the situation was revealed in all its drama. This was not least because the Left was faced with a new protagonist − one which it did not really understand, though always thought it did. It fought this new protagonist − Thatcherism − on old ground, with old ideas and old practices, on the basis of an old analysis and an old political agenda. It was akin to deploying the cavalry against the tanks − and had much the same, predictable result. The Left got splattered and dispersed. For a while it looked as if the Left had not simply lost a campaign, but that its time was up: not defeated by the enemy, but overtaken by history itself.

Actually, this was a too simple and over dramatic reading. It was not just that much of the Left had failed to understand the novelty and specificity of Thatcherism. What is more important is that it failed to distinguish adequately between Thatcherism and the way the world had changed – or, to put it another way, between Thatcherism and the world which Thatcherism claimed to represent and aspired to lead. The two were too easily conflated – a fault to which *Marxism Today* itself, which led the way in the analysis of Thatcherism, must also plead guilty. As a result, the Left failed to recognise the new ground or understand the new world that was being made. That new world and Thatcherism were seen as one and the same thing. The latter, as a consequence, looked omnipotent, as if it was in command of history.

Not least, 'New Times' is a project to prise Thatcherism and that world apart. What is clear is that Thatcherism has had a much stronger sense of the epochal changes than the Left, both in terms of the break-up of the old postwar settlement and the creation of a more fragmented and variegated society and culture. As a result, Thatcherism has sought to appropriate that new world for itself, ideologically ('socialism is dead', 'the market determines everything'), materially (giving it shape, a Thatcherite inflexion, through policy and practice), and culturally (the attempt to promulgate a new entrepreneurial culture).

In a similar way, the ambition of the 'New Times' project is not only to make sense of the new world – to appreciate the tendencies and limits of post-Fordism, to unravel the emergent postmodern culture, to understand the new identities and political subjects in society – but also to provide the parameters for a new politics of the Left, a politics beyond Thatcherism, which can give a progressive shape and inflexion to New Times. This, after all, is what is missing from the otherwise sophisticated current debates around post-Fordism, flexible specialisation and the even more ambiguous and treacherous reaches of post modernism, namely, the question of what can be made, politically, of these New Times by and for the Left.

No question could be of greater significance or urgency for the Left. Since the opening up of the 'New Times' debate, a number of new initiatives and policy documents have been launched by different sectors of the Left. For the most part, they represent a real attempt to engage with the new. Yet a powerful tendency is to struggle to get the surface details right, without making any serious, long-range, probing or fundamental analysis of where society is going. But this is to underestimate the scale of the changes and what they mean. The old visions of the Left have literally been overtaken by history. The orthodox political perspective, which for so long shaped the outlook of the centre-Left – Keynesianism – lies interred in the grave of Fordism. Communism in its 'actual-existing' forms is undergoing, at the same time, its own crisis, searching for a new road, as both Gorbachev and Tiananmen Square testify. Its statist and inflexible social, economic and political forms have been undermined, not only in competition with the West, but by its own species of Fordism – an obsession with quantity, the centralised plan, the masses, the suppression of variety, and the suffocating grip of centralism and authoritarianism. In whichever direction you turn, the Left faces a massive cultural crisis which demands a creative and bold engagement with New Times.

For much of the 1980s, it seemed as if the main danger was that the New Right would hijack New Times for itself. In the West it was the ascendant force: Reaganism in the US, Thatcherism in Britain, Chirac in France, Kohl in West Germany. At the beginning of the 1990s this now looks much less likely, above all when this broader international view is taken. But there is another lesser danger: that the Left will produce, in government, a brand of New Times which in practice does not amount to much more than a slightly cleaned-up, humanised version of that of the radical Right. Such would be the inevitable consequence of two things: a pragmatic adjustment by the Left to the collapse of its various previous visions and a failure to generate its own new historic project.

Nothing could be further from the spirit, purpose or ambition of this volume. The aim is not simply to understand New Times, but to generate a progressive perspective for them. Thatcherism represents a profoundly reactionary settlement for New Times. While it speaks the language of choice, freedom and autonomy,

Thatcherite society is increasingly characterised by inequality, division and authoritarianism. But it is also becoming clear that Thatcherism's conception of New Times is partial and inadequate, its guiding ideas are just not up to the task. It will not succeed in its long-term aim of hegemonising New Times for itself because they are much bigger, more profound, more epochal than it is. For while part of Thatcherism has been modernising, another part has always been regressive, organised around a view of Britain which is essentially backward-looking. From the perspective of New Times, Thatcherism increasingly appears as a weighty and powerful anachronism.

This is not to argue that New Times are necessarily and inevitably 'good times'. Unqualified optimism is as dangerous as an unthinking and unrelieved pessimism. Both fail to take the contradictory movement of history sufficiently into account. New Times, after all, is still new times for capitalism, which remains in place, untranscended in all its fundamental rhythms and tendencies. Capital is still deeply entrenched — in fact, more so, globally, than ever before. And the old inequalities associated with it remain, defining the life-experiences and limiting the hopes and aspirations of whole groups and classes of people, and whole communities. Alongside that the New Times are producing new social divisions, new forms of inequality and disempowerment, which overlay the old ones. What is called, on several occasions in this volume, the 'two-thirds, one-third society' appears to be a new pattern, almost as characteristic of New Times as flexible specialisation and social differentiation. Is such inequality endemic to New Times or only one possible scenario? Whatever the case, it is clear that the potential for inequality in a more variegated and heterogeneous society is greater not less.

Another feature of New Times is the proliferation of the sites of antagonism and resistance, and the appearance of new subjects, new social movements, new collective identities — an enlarged sphere for the operation of politics, and new constituencies for change. But these are not easy to organise into any single and cohesive collective political will. The very proliferation of new sites of social antagonism makes the prospect of constructing a unified counter-hegemonic force as the agency of progressive change, if anything, harder rather than easier. Moreover, because the spread and pace of change is so uneven, the problems of the kind of political strategy required to unify old and new constituencies of change — even when this is conceptualised as a multi-faceted political project — are profoundly complex. There is nothing remotely 'optimistic', in any simple sense, about New Times.

What the 'New Times' analysis does argue is that New Times has no necessary and inevitable political trajectory already inscribed in it. Its political future remains undecided, open-ended. Greater social inequality, an erosion rather than a deepening of democratic life and culture, could as well be the outcome of New Times, as a more optimistic result. Only a new political project for New Times can resolve these questions which are — as political questions for *Marxism Today* always are — matters of practice as well as of analysis. What is certain is that if the Left cannot win the struggle for New Times, more regressive and reactionary political forces certainly will.

The emergence of New Times is marked by extraordinary unevenness, and that unevenness is a global phenomenon. What is becoming evident by the day is that we are witnessing an extraordinary synchronisation of epochal change. The engine of this change may be located in the West, but its impact is global. Our discussion of New Times has so far concentrated largely on the national, on the nation state. Yet we already know that New Times is characterised by forces which transcend, and at the same time weaken, the nation state. This has consequences for the political prospects of the European Left, since neither its own future in the nation states of the West, nor the deep and profound problems of uneven development, backwardness and colonialism and the associated question of ethnic and racial difference, can be resolved within national boundaries. The growing globalisation of change, in markets and culture alike, is eroding the importance of national frontiers; and, by putting limits on the capacity of any one government to act nationally, outside of the international framework, it is changing the very terms on which the politics of the Left have so far been overwhelmingly conducted. Few countries of the West are so vulnerable to this radical new set of circumstances as a medium-sized, highly internationalised country, with an increasingly racially mixed and socially heterogeneous society, such as post-imperial Britain.

But the global character of New Times should not disguise the fact that the focus of its dynamic lies in the West. One of the major weaknesses of the 'New Times' analysis so far is that it has failed to assess what New Times means for those countries and peoples outside the perimeter of the West, whose whole pattern of development and forms of dependency continue to be governed and dominated by shifts and changes generated in the West over which they have no control and of which they are not, in any proper sense, the subjects. New Times could easily be the signal for yet another cycle of Western domination, economically and socially, rather than the beginnings of a new kind of settlement between the over-developed and the under-developed parts of the world.

This global picture of epochal change is not simply a product of the enormous process of internationalisation we have witnessed over the last decade or more. It is also a function of a parallel but separate development – the disintegration of the old communist world and the drawing to a close in the USSR of over seventy years of history. The leninist model of society – which provided the Left in industrialised countries and the Third World with an alternative model of social development – is historically exhausted. And the search for a way out of the crisis that now engulfs the East is underway. The problems are legion. And the outcome remains uncertain. Enormous energy and creativity, exemplified by Gorbachev and the forces around him, coexist with tendencies towards conservatism, closure, paralysis and destruction, as evidenced by the events in China. The old autarchic model of socialism has disintegrated. It cannot be rescued in its old form – though its passing could be long, difficult and dangerous. Some parts of the Left regard this with gloom and despair. Difficult as its evolution is likely to be, from the perspective of New Times it can only be regarded as a positive process; indeed, as one of the necessary, if not sufficient, conditions for a renewal of the Left, and thus an integral aspect of New Times. Not least of its consequences is the way it has undermined the bipolar world of postwar politics, bringing to an end the terrible stasis of the cold war divisions which have dominated the perspectives and prospects of the Left since the war.

It is impossible to make sense of New Times without taking into account all these extraordinary changes. Of course, they are not all part of 'all the same thing'. They do not necessarily and inevitably all belong to the same phenomenon. But they are all occurring in the same moment, though they have different origins and histories. And they are all reshaping the ground on which, for better or worse, the Left must operate. Thatcherism would have us believe that globalisation is simply a question of markets. But in this, Thatcherism is itself a victim of its own narrow, and narrow-minded, economism. The measure of the changes we are trying to signal in the essays collected in this volume lies precisely in their epochal character. It is not only a question of markets but also a crisis of nation states, and thus of national cultures and identities. These are all being subtly but profoundly reworked by New Times. It is a crisis in the way in which the world is socially organised and politically divided. Beyond that it is a crisis of the planet itself, requiring a new conception of the relationship between the human race and the planet earth. Globalisation suggests interdependence and co-operation on a new scale and in new forms, not simply competition based on narrow national and economic interests. New Times, in short, is about making a new world.

In this volume, we do not claim for a moment to have posed all the questions, let alone provided all the answers, to the puzzle of New Times. The book makes a beginning − that is all − in a number of different directions at once. It represents an attempt, from the Left, to outline some starting points, to provide a frame of reference, for understanding the new epoch which we are now entering; but its nature is still far from clear, and its political shape is still certainly far from being resolved or determined.

I New Times

From the Manifesto for New Times

The New Times

As we enter the 1990s Britain will be a capitalist society, riven with enormous inequalities in income, wealth and power, with key decisions taken by a minority of international financiers and industrialists. But it will be a different kind of capitalist society from Britain in the 1930s or 1950s. International capitalism is entering a distinctive phase of development. The signs are all around us.

The ownership of capital is more diverse than ever. Corporate bodies rather than powerful individuals or families play the dominant decision-making role. A greater share of our wealth is owned, indirectly, by working people, through pension funds and other institutions representing the collective product of working people, whose control is increasingly remote.

Robots and computers are familiar parts of our workplaces, just as satellite television will become familiar in our living rooms. Semi-skilled work in mighty manufacturing plants is in decline, while professional, new technology skilled jobs are growing, alongside part-time unskilled work in services. The rise of women's paid employment to more than 50 per cent of the workforce will create strong pressures for new relationships between paid employment and domestic work. So also will new political priorities which challenge the traditional settlement between patriarchal capital and patriarchal labour.

The products, skills and communities of old industrial areas – shipbuilding in Sunderland, newspaper production in Fleet Street – are being overtaken by new centres of economic growth – Telford, Crawley, Basingstoke – based on new technology, manufacturing and services. The City of London has become a hub in a 24-hour-a-day, computer-integrated, global financial system. Multinational manufacturers and business service companies are becoming more powerful as capitalism becomes more transnational in every dimension, and more intensive in advanced countries.

A profound ecological crisis will demand a search for international regulation of economic development and the environment. The recurrence of famine increasingly demands new solutions to the consequences of the destruction of the traditional economies in the southern hemisphere by the actions of governments and big business in the northern hemisphere.

The spreading impact of *perestroika* in the Soviet Union and the opening of European nations to one another offer an opportunity to create an era of more open, co-operative international relations.

Woven into the new times of the 1990s are changes which are inevitable, changes which are desirable, and changes which are neither. If Britain is to develop in a more democratic and sustainable way in the 1990s, we have to work with the grain of the new times, to enable society to develop in a more progressive way. Progressive forces in Britain need to realign, modernise, and contest the changes underway by offering an alternative vision of progress.

Socialists are yet to develop a radical, popular appeal for the 1990s because we do not yet confidently speak the language of the future. For much of the labour and democratic movement still rests upon a world which is fast disintegrating beneath its feet. It lives in the last house of a terrace which is slowly being demolished and redeveloped.

A Departing World

Two key developments laid the foundations for postwar British society. Firstly, the depression of the 1930s led industry to shift from the production methods inherited from the 19th century, based on coal and steam, to the new technologies based on electricity, oil and petrol. At Ford's Dagenham plant, opened in 1931, the company introduced the mass production methods which were to have a sweeping impact on much of the rest of industry. They became known as 'Fordism'. They left an indelible mark on the economy, workers, consumers and social life. These new methods were propelled by a concentration of ownership with a wave of mergers and acquisitions, which created what are now familiar household names like

ICI and GEC.

The second factor was the economic, social and political upheaval of the struggles against unemployment and fascism in the 1930s, which culminated during the second world war. Social aspirations, together with working class and democratic pressure bred by the war, propelled the Labour Party into power with a wide-ranging programme of social and economic reform – nationalisation, the creation of the National Health Service, the expansion of public education, an enormous council-house building programme, the introduction of a system of welfare benefits, and perhaps above all, a commitment to maintain full employment through Keynesian economic policies. These were the twin pillars of the postwar settlement: a modernising capitalism and a labour and democratic movement intent on social and economic reform.

The postwar settlement created a framework to meet both companies' demands for profitable markets and popular desires for rising living standards. The institutions of the postwar settlement were designed to contain struggles within manageable limits. It was not a single settlement. It was made up of several components, which became the focal point for conflict and arenas of struggle. For these settlements did not mark the end of conflict or struggle. Rather, they set the basic parameters for those conflicts, until these settlements themselves were beseiged.

The Settlements: Sites of Struggle

The economic core was an *industrial settlement*. Large manufacturing factories sucked in armies of mainly semi-skilled labour to work within a strictly regulated divison of labour on assembly lines, which pumped out largely standardised products. The large manufacturing plants, taking up the mass production methods of Fordism, were the leading edge of economic development, capitalist profitability and accumulation. They were also the leading edge for industrial struggle between increasingly well organised unions and employers over productivity and pay.

This industrial settlement was embraced within a wider *economic settlement*. Full employment gave the labour movement considerable strength in collective bargaining. It also meant companies could profit from a growing, protected national market. The full productivity gains of standardised, mass production could only be unleashed with a mass consumer market created by full employment and rising living standards. The balance between wages and profits, on the one hand, and the rate of taxation and public spending, on the other, was subject to continual conflict. But the power of big business was never seriously challenged or weakened.

The economic settlement was entwined with a *social settlement*. The establishment of the NHS represented an enormous advance, though weakened by the deal struck with the consultants, private drug companies and private practice. There were big advances in public education through the development of comprehensive education in schools and a greater access to higher education, but a significant private education sector remained. The televisions, fridges, vacuum cleaners and cars pumped out from the great factories transformed consumption and domestic work, creating the affluence of the postwar years. The expansion of public services, from broadcasting to the NHS, created a new politics of mass public consumption. Public-sector, white-collar service work expanded, and with it public sector unionism and industrial struggle within the state. While both employees and users of the public services were excluded from any real involvement in decision-making within them.

Running through these settlements was an unstable, contested and conservative *gender settlement* of relations between men and women. Women had filled the labour market during the war, struggling for adequate nursery provision and against union agreements which ensured their employment was temporary.

The patriarchal settlement between capital and labour was rehabilitated again after the second world war. Women were expelled from the labour market immediately after the war, and subsequently re-entered in the context of a new and rigid sexual division of labour, one in which women's lives more than ever moved between paid and unpaid labour, while men's remained largely unchanged: women's re-entry into the paid labour market was not matched by a transformation in men's relation to children, women or domesticity. To women's new postwar identity was added another – women became, *par excellence*, the focus of consumption. It was women who used the newly available domestic appliances. Their role as 'mothers' was promoted through ideological and cultural developments, including new popular theories of child development. And it was women as recipients of child benefit who became the vital link between state welfare and the family budget.

Society was also scored by an oppressive *racial settlement*, the assertion of white privilege and power against the Caribbean and Asian immigrants who were encouraged into the labour market of Great Britain in the 1950s and 1960s, but who were to face a widespread colour bar in jobs, homes and services. Black workers were abandoned to a racist culture which refused to make any accommodations to the black British. Most disastrously they were consigned to a racist housing market, which confined black people largely to the bomb-damaged inner cities. The postwar immigration rules were consistently racist, while discrimination was inscribed in all public practices from the labour market to the town hall.

The enormous development of industry, technology, and modern cities rested upon an implicit, exploitative *environmental settlement*. It was embedded in the industrialism of the big factory and the overpowering modernism of the tower block, and in the pollution from cars, power stations and chemical plants.

Postwar Britain had a distinctive political geography, with many key mass production companies congregated within a core region stretching northwards from the Midlands and on the outskirts of London. The imbalance of growth between these core regions and the peripheral areas around them promoted continual pressure for government policies to spread growth through regional policy. Within that *regional settlement*, workers and consumers massed within sprawling conurbations, in which slums were replaced by modern, functional housing, corner shops were overtaken by supermarkets, and the north-south divide persisted with cultural subordination and economic dependency of northern regions to the metropolitan south.

The postwar settlement also featured a *national settlement* in which the interests of the people of Wales and Scotland were subordinated to English interests.

The situation in Northern Ireland has constituted the most intractable problem facing all British governments. Partition and the failure to recognise the Irish people's right to self-determination meant that just as Britain spent the opening years of the century with a crisis over Ireland, it faces the closing years in the same situation. No British government over the past twenty years has offered a perspective for ending that crisis.

The frame for these settlements was a *party political settlement*, commonly referred to as a political consensus, between the Labour Party and the Conservative Party. This political settlement, the product of progressive struggle over many years, represented an enormous political advance over the prewar period. But it was a settlement which also served to limit the degree of economic and social advance and disappointed millions who aspired to more radical reforms in key areas. Thus, for example, public ownerhip was restricted in the main to loss-making industries such as steel and coal (once massive compensation and other charges were met), and took a highly conservative form with no effective participation by either workers or consumers. The Left within the labour movement campaigned and argued for policies to move beyond those settlements by radicalising them, but was for the most part defeated.

The progressive peak of that political settlement was the immediate postwar period, but far from being renovated and renewed, in later years the political settlementt ossified. The radical energy of the Labour Party in 1945 had been largely dissipated thirty years later and the reforming zeal of the immediate postwar period slowly gave way to the miserable pragmatism of the Callaghan era. If the gains of 1945 had been taken as a first step in a determined struggle to reduce, step by step, the power of capital, and empower working-class people, there could have been a different outcome.

These settlements within Britain were enveloped with an *international settlement*. It was founded upon the industrial economic and military power of the United States, the cold war arms race, the regulation of the international economy through the Bretton Woods currency system and the spreading neo-colonialism of the United States multinationals to Europe, Africa, Latin America and Asia.

Britain's distinctive position in this international order had a crucial bearing upon its development. It was already one of the most multinational economies in the West, with substantial American investment. In the face of independence struggles and the rapid disintegration of the British Empire it clung for as long as possible to its imperial legacy, which provided manufacturing industry with protected markets to disguise its weakness. It attempted to modernise its world role through nuclear weapons. This was the source of one of the most potent contradictions of the postwar settlement — the combination of an extremely internationalised economy, and a xenophobic sense of self-importance which did not match the reality of Britain's decline.

The labour and democratic movement was a parent to these settlements. But it was also a child of them. It was a movement committed to social and economic reforms. But it was also committed to the central state, the electoral priorities of the Labour Party's institutionalised politics and the demands of male, manufacturing unions from the factories and conurbations of Fordism. It largely co-operated in the conservative gender and racial settlement, it tacitly accepted the national settlements within the UK and was wedded to an ideal of progress which did not question the industrialism which exploited nature and the modernism which created the tower block.

The Slow Disintegration

In the 1970s those interlocking, contested settlements began to break apart, provoking a tumultuous economic, social and political crisis at the end of the decade. We are living with the way that crisis was resolved. It was not an accidental, cyclical or short-lived crisis. The roof finally fell in on the society built after the war. For it was a structural crisis, created by long-run weaknesses which were exposed by crises of the 1970s.

The industrial and economic settlements broke apart because the modernising investment of British capital at home did not match developments abroad. Slowly rising unemployment and inflation, falling productivity and profitability threw into doubt the ability of Keynesian economic policies to keep the economy at full employment.

Faltering growth intensified industrial conflict. Constraints on public expenditure, and the ill-fated mixture of monetarism and incomes policy concocted by the Callaghan government produced strikes in both the private and public sectors. And the reaction in the labour movement, a regression to sectionalist and syndicalist forms of resistance, mirrored the government's retreat from renovation.

This intensifying conflict within the United Kingdom combined with international upheavals which served to destabilise all advanced economies. American hegemony was fatally undermined by the defeat in Vietnam and the collapse of the Bretton Woods international economic agreements. Anti-war and peace movements challenged both the expansion of neo-colonialism and the modernisation of the cold war. The Opec oil price increases and the rise in international competition, particularly from Japanese manufacturers, undermined the western economies.

The social upheavals of the late 1960s, centred on the first generation of the postwar welfare state, the beneficiaries of higher living standards, better health and improved educational opportunities spawned new aspirations for social, individual and sexual liberation, which could not be contained within the mores of respectable postwar society. An increasingly assertive youth culture culminated with the punk assault on respectable sensibilities in the 1970s.

The legitimacy of the conservative gender settlement was increasingly challenged by an insurgent women's movement, the continued rise in women's employment, greater access to education, the introduction of the pill and more liberal legislation on divorce which gave women more control over childbirth and marriage. The abortion and divorce laws and the availability of relatively reliable forms of contraception – a historic moment in women's quest for control over their own bodies – implicitly acknowledged and contributed to the increasing instability of the patriachal family.

The women's liberation movement challenged the sexual division of labour, politicised sexual and domestic violence as expressions of a culture of sexual domination and thus challenged the ideologies of state agencies, from the police to housing authorities, for their patriarchal practices.

The conflict over the racial settlement became more open and intense, with an open embracing of racist politics by sections of the Conservative Party alongside the rise of the National Front. Successive immigration bills and racist policing, rather than protection for black communities, were challenged by anti-fascist and anti-racist movements.The poor quality and management of mass council housing, and generally the remoteness of Labour in local government from its electorate, led to mounting criticism. Community politics was born from the demands of people struggling to humanise ghastly urban social environments and gain a greater say in decision-making over their own lives.

The destruction of swathes of British cities by motorways and speculative developments which privatised − and brutalised − vast tracts of the public realm, exacerbated the housing crisis in the new and the old slums. Elsewhere in Europe mounting concern at the effects of industrialism, militarism and modernism on the social and ecological environment gave rise to green movements. The postwar settlements had survived by creating a framework to contain social conflict. But by the 1970s they began bursting at the seams.

The Path From the Crisis

The crisis of the 1970s provoked two fundamental developments which are shaping our times.

Firstly, there was a political struggle to coalesce discontent with the decaying postwar settlement and the impotence of the Keynesian, social democratic state. It was a struggle the labour and democratic movement lost.

The Right in the labour movement pushed an increasingly autocratic, visionless agenda which paved the way for conservative developments in education, the erosion of trade union rights and monetarist economic policies. But the Left of the movement was trapped by a complacency that the movement's future was guaranteed by history. Although the Left participated in broad social movements − for instance, anti-nuclear campaigns − and although it developed new ideas − for instance, the alternative economic strategy − it did not offer a popular, modernising perspective, to coalesce disenchantment with the postwar settlement behind a new phase of socialist development.

The labour movement failed to move as society had developed. It was caught defending a discredited past when it should have captured hopes for the future. Thatcherism rose to power on the back of the exhaustion of the postwar social-democratic project, with an authoritarian but populist agenda to dismantle the rusting infrastructure of the postwar settlement.

But there was a second, equally important factor at work, which made it much more likely that Thatcherism would succeed: capitalism's search for a successor to the regime of accumulation developed in the 1930s. As Mrs Thatcher was struggling against opposition in the early 1980s, to pave the way for a radical shift to the right, so multinational companies were in search of new production methods, to raise productivity and profitability in the face of intensifying international competition.

It is these large companies in search of a secure position within increasingly global markets which are the key forces reorganising the UK economy. It is their response to international competitive pressures which is driving crucial changes in the technology people work with, the structure of industry, the ownership of companies, the location of investment and consumption patterns.

A Second Dual Revolution

The postwar settlement was created by the confluence of the economic restructuring of the 1930s, and the popular impetus for social democratic reforms, which cemented the institutions of the full-employment welfare state.

The 1980s have been shaped by a different dual revolution: the confluence of Thatcherism's radical right-wing politics with an international wave of capitalist restructuring. Thatcherism has both facilitated that restructuring and been propelled by it. Thatcherism's regressive modernisation is only one path to the future. Its terms for creating the new times will be challenged by other social forces with a different vision of the future.

The New Times

Britain will still be an advanced capitalist society, with key decisions taken in the boardrooms of powerful multinational companies in Detroit, Tokyo or Seoul. But it will be markedly different from the capitalism of the postwar settlement. For its component settlements are being dismantled and remade. What emerges will be the outcome of industrial, social and political struggle.

At the industrial heart of the new times will be production based on a shift to information technology and microelectronics. New technology allows more intensive automation and its extension from large to smaller companies, pulling together the shopfloor and the office, the design loft and the showroom. It allows production to be both more flexible, automated and integrated.

These changes are not confined to manufacturing. Banks and building societies propelled by fiercer competition in more international markets are also using information technology to innovate new services and products. It is seeping into the public sector and local authorities.

Work is being re-organised around new technology. Traditional demarcation lines between blue and white collar, skilled and unskilled, are being torn down in the wake of massive redundancies in manufacturing. In future, work in manufacturing will be about flexible team-working within much smaller, more skilled workforces. Services will continue to provide the main source of new jobs, fuelling the continued rise of women's part-time employment which will be at the core of the 1990s economy.

Combined with persistent mass unemployment, these changes are creating deeper divisions within the workforce. There will be more professional, highly-skilled technicians' jobs, but also more low-skill, low-wage, low-technology jobs. The economy will be marked by a division between core full-time workers in large companies and the growing number of part-timers in small subcontractors, between those in employment and the long-term unemployed.

Traditional bases for union organisation are declining. The rise in unemployment, extensive corporate restructuring and the government's anti-trade union laws, allowed more assertive managers to marginalise unions. Collective bargaining is no longer about regulating an industrial machine. It is about setting the terms for widespread restructuring of work.

These developments amount to a structural change in the economy. The economic and industrial settlements, which were at the centre of industrial conflict in the postwar settlement, are being superseded. This upheaval in the industrial and economic core of modern capitalism is one of the forces which is replacing the postwar social settlement with greater social fragmentation, diversity and polarisation.

The television industry is the sharpest example of how new technology, multinational restructuring and government legislation combine to produce more fragmented conditions of work and consumption. In the 1990s, multinational media groups will use the new satellite technologies to create European television stations. Their rise has been facilitated by the government's ideological and legislative attack on the institutions and ethos of the public-service broadcasting system established after the war.

National union agreements are being broken up. Programme production will be largely devolved to a sea of small sub-contractors, employing technicians on short-term contracts lasting anything from three weeks to six months.

The family crowded around a black and white television was one of the images of the 1950s. Their counterparts in the 1990s will be switching between a swarm of European commercial stations. One of the most important acts of mass consumption, which is vital to the quality of information in a modern democracy, will have been completely transformed.

But restructuring is promoting far more savage forms of social polarisation. A very small and very rich minority has done extremely well. But in general Britain is becoming a two-thirds, one-third society, with a growing gulf between the majority itself, highly differentiated, leading relatively comfortable lives; and the one-third trapped in poverty. The rise in home ownership in the 1980s means many working-class families will become property inheritors for the first time in the 1990s. But homelessness has grown to record levels.

The welfare state is increasingly ill-equipped to cope with high unemployment and the growth in the number of single-parent families, who are faced with the continuing privatisation of childcare and are unsupported by collective responsibility for the cost and care of children. At the same time the growth of women's employment could fundamentally undermine the legitimacy of conservative assumptions about work and welfare: that workers are men, earning for families in which women would be available to care for children, the elderly and the sick.

These social developments are creating enormous pressure for established institutions, from the family to the welfare state, to be refashioned in the new times.

A new political map is taking shape. The regions and cities of postwar industry, which bred so much of the labour movement's culture, are in decline. The concentration of newspaper production in Fleet Street in London has been dispersed to new technology printing sites, with smaller, more tightly controlled workforces. Up and down the country docks are being redeveloped into yuppie housing and retail space.

The poles of the political map of the 1990s will be the politics of race and the underclass in the inner city, and the growth of new industrial regions such as the M4 corridor, and within them growth towns like Swindon and Basingstoke. The labour movement is present in these towns. But it is not central to the spirit emerging within them, in the way that it was in Sheffield in the early part of the century or Coventry during the heyday of engineering.

The local politics of the new town has become a key site for conflict between international capital and the community. All cities, from Bridgend to Dundee and Skelmersdale, are in search of foreign investment to attract an international growth sector to their industrial estates. The competition has been intensified by government regional policy and the constraints on local authorities' abilities to plan economic development.

A vital part of this new political geography is the resurgence of nationalism in Scotland and Wales in response to Thatcherism's authoritarianism, and the disproportionate costs of restructuring they have borne.

The next decade will also be shaped by the environmental crisis bequeathed by Fordism: from the social environmental crisis of congested, polluted conurbations, and the classic product of the postwar period — the car — to the global crisis of the greenhouse effect.

The international settlement which enveloped British postwar capitalism will be dismantled in the 1990s. The two-dimensional world of superpower conflict is giving way to a more complex set of international relations. The Japanese, South Korean and Far Eastern companies will continue to disorganise the western economies, which will also be reshaped by the European integration programme. Eastern and Western Europe are likely to become more open to one another as India and China take on much more significant world economic and political roles.

Resolving Britain's position within this new international order
will be a key task of the 1990s.

Politics and New Times

Much of postwar capitalism mirrored the mass production
methods which were at its industrial heart. They became known
as Fordism. In the new times, the industrial core of the economy
is being transformed into what we call 'post-Fordism'. This does
not mean that mass production will disappear. It does mean that
in both manufacturing and services, production and work is
taking on more flexible, diverse, fragmentary forms. Bargaining
between workers and employers will also take on new forms to
match the new conditions. Post-Fordism does not describe the
whole economy but the leading edge of the most competitive
modernising companies.

These changes in the industrial and economic organisation of
capitalism are not determining all the changes which are shaping
the new times. International, social and cultural forces are at
work independently of changes in production. Post-Fordism is at
the economic and industrial core of the new times, but it does
not encompass and define all aspects of the new times.

The 1990s will see myriad political and social struggles. But in
essence they will come down to a single question: on whose
terms will this new era be moulded? Thatcherism's attempt to
facilitate a 'conservative modernisation' will create privatisation,
polarisation, fragmentation, public squalor and authoritarianism
in the new times. Its grip will only be broken by a progressive
movement gathered around the aspirations bred by the new
times.

There are powerful social currents which offer an alternative
path to modernisation which is more just, democratic, humane
and sustainable. For on each of the central issues facing society
in the new times, powerful progressive forces are developing.
These movements do not necessarily share the same interests,
nor do they possess properties which unite them spontaneously.
But they do move to a similar rhythm:

— The green movement's response to the environmental crisis
with a challenge to current economic priorities;

– The optimism that the internationalisation of the economy may be matched by a new era of more co-operative international relations, symbolised by changes in Soviet foreign policy;

– The mounting moral and political opposition to the savage inequalities Thatcherism is creating;

– Women's challenge to the traditional demarcation lines between domestic work, welfare and waged work, which will be consolidated by women's expanding presence in the labour market and the political domain;

– The widespread concern over Thatcherism's authoritarian transformation of the state;

– Nationalism's challenge to authoritarian centralism;

– Increasing doubt that the government's economic policies are capable of fully modernising the economy, through investment in research and development, training and skills.

These are not formal policies or parties. They are moods, currents and forces in society. They can trace their lineage to discontent with the postwar settlement as clearly as Thatcherism. They could offer an alternative vision of modernisation which is as credible and potentially more popular than Thatcherism's.

For these forces are in the grain of the new times. They stem from popular social aspirations. They offer the prospect of a new wave of progressive social and economic development in the 1990s.

Robin Murray

Fordism and Post-Fordism

During the first two centuries of the industrial revolution the focus of employment shifted from the farm to the factory. It is now shifting once more, from the factory to the office and the shop. A third of Britain's paid labour force now works in offices. A third of the value of national output is in the distribution sector. Meanwhile 2.5 million jobs have been lost in British manufacturing since 1960. If the Ford plants at Halewood and Dagenham represented late industrialism, Centrepoint and Habitat are the symbols of a new age.

The Right portrayed the growth of services as a portent of a post-industrial society with growing individualism, a weakened state and a multiplicity of markets. I want to argue that it reflects a deeper change in the production process. It is one that affects manufacturing and agriculture as well as services, and has implications for the way in which we think about socialist alternatives. I see this as a shift from the dominant form of 20th-century production, known as Fordism, to a new form, post-Fordism.

Fordism is an industrial era whose secret is to be found in the mass production systems pioneered by Henry Ford. These systems were based on four principles from which all else followed:

a) products were standardised; this meant that each part and each task could also be standardised. Unlike craft production – where each part had to be specially designed, made and fitted – for a run of mass-produced cars, the same headlight could be fitted to the same model in the same way.

b) if tasks are the same, then some can be mechanised; thus mass production plants developed special-purpose machinery for each model, much of which could not be switched from product to product.

c) those tasks which remained were subject to scientific management or Taylorism, whereby any task was broken down into its component parts, redesigned by work-study specialists on time-and-motion principles, who then instructed manual workers on how the job should be done.

d) flowline replaced nodal assembly, so that instead of workers moving to and from the product (the node), the product flowed past the workers.

Ford did not invent these principles. What he did was to combine them in the production of a complex commodity, which undercut craft-made cars as decisively as the handloom weavers had been undercut in the 1830s. Ford's Model T sold for less than a tenth of the price of a craft-built car in the US in 1916, and he took 50 per cent of the market.

This revolutionary production system was to transform sector after sector during the 20th century, from processed food to furniture, clothes, cookers, and even ships after the second world war. The economies came from the scale of production, for although mass production might be more costly to set up because of the purpose-built machinery, once in place the cost of an extra unit was discontinuously cheap.

Many of the structures of Fordism followed from this tension between high fixed costs and low variable ones, and the consequent drive for volume. First, as Ford himself emphasised, mass production presupposes mass consumption. Consumers must be willing to buy standardised products. Mass advertising played a central part in establishing a mass consumption norm. So did the provision of the infrastructure of consumption – housing and roads. To ensure that the road system dominated over rail, General Motors, Standard Oil and Firestone Tyres bought up and then dismantled the electric trolley and transit systems in 44 urban areas.

Second, Fordism was linked to a system of protected national markets, which allowed the mass producers to recoup their fixed costs at home and compete on the basis of marginal costs on the world market, or through the replication of existing models via foreign investment.

Third, mass producers were particularly vulnerable to sudden falls in demand. Ford unsuccessfully tried to offset the effect of the 1930s depression by raising wages. Instalment credit,

Keynesian demand and monetary management, and new wage and welfare systems were all more effective in stabilising the markets for mass producers in the postwar period. HP and the dole cheque became as much the symbols of the Fordist age as the tower block and the motorway.

The mass producers not only faced the hazard of changes in consumption. With production concentrated in large factories they were also vulnerable to the new 'mass worker' they had created. Like Taylorism, mass production had taken the skill out of work, it fragmented tasks into a set of repetitive movements, and erected a rigid division between mental and manual labour. It treated human beings as interchangeable parts of a machine, paid according to the job they did rather than who they were.

The result was high labour turnover, shopfloor resistance, and strikes. The mass producers in turn sought constant new reservoirs of labour, particularly from groups facing discrimination, from rural areas and from less developed regions abroad. The contractual core of Taylorism — higher wages in return for managerial control of production — still applied, and a system of industrial unions grew up to bargain over these wage levels. In the USA, and to an extent the UK, a national system of wage bargaining developed in the postwar period, centred on high-profile car industry negotiations, that linked wage rises to productivity growth, and then set wage standards for other large-scale producers and the state. It was a system of collective bargaining that has been described as implementing a Keynesian incomes policy without a Keynesian state. As long as the new labour reservoirs could be tapped, it was a system that held together the distinct wage relation of Fordism.

Taylorism was also characteristic of the structure of management and supplier relations. Fordist bureaucracies are fiercely hierarchical, with links between the divisions and departments being made through the centre rather than at the base. Planning is done by specialists; rulebooks and guidelines are issued for lower management to carry out. If you enter a Ford factory in any part of the world, you will find its layout, materials, even the position of its Coca Cola machines, all similar, set up as they are on the basis of a massive construction manual drawn up in Detroit. Managers themselves complain of deskilling and the lack of room for initiative, as do suppliers who are confined to producing blueprints at a low margin price.

These threads − of production and consumption, of the semi-skilled worker and collective bargaining, of a managed national market and centralised organisation − together make up the fabric of Fordism. They have given rise to an economic culture which extends beyond the complex assembly industries, to agriculture, the service industries and parts of the state. It is marked by its commitment to scale and the standard product (whether it is a Mars bar or an episode of *Dallas*); by a competitive strategy based on cost reduction; by authoritarian relations, centralised planning, and a rigid organisation built round exclusive job descriptions.

These structures and their culture are often equated with industrialism, and regarded as an inevitable part of the modern age. I am suggesting that they are linked to a particular form of industrialism, one that developed in the late 19th century and reached its most dynamic expression in the postwar boom. Its impact can be felt not just in the economy, but in politics (in the mass party) and in much broader cultural fields − whether American football, or classical ballet (Diaghilev was a Taylorist in dance), industrial design or modern architecture. The technological *hubris* of this outlook, its Faustian bargain of dictatorship in production in exchange for mass consumption, and above all its destructiveness in the name of progress and the economy of time, all this places Fordism at the centre of modernism.

Why we need to understand these deep structures of Fordism is that they are embedded, too, in traditional socialist economics. Soviet-type planning is the apogee of Fordism. Lenin embraced Taylor and the stopwatch. Soviet industrialisation was centred on the construction of giant plants, the majority of them based on western mass-production technology. So deep is the idea of scale burnt into Soviet economics that there is a hairdresser's in Moscow with 120 barbers' chairs. The focus of Soviet production is on volume and because of its lack of consumer discipline it has caricatured certain features of western mass production, notably a hoarding of stocks, and inadequate quality control.

In social-democratic thinking state planning has a more modest place. But in the writings of Fabian economists in the 1930s, as in the Morrisonian model of the public corporation, and Labour's postwar policies, we see the same emphasis on centralist planning, scale, Taylorist technology, and hierarchical organisation. The image of planning was the railway timetable, the goal of planning was stable demand and cost-reduction. In the welfare state, the idea of the standard product was given a democratic interpretation as the universal service to meet basic needs, and although in Thatcher's Britain this formulation is still important, it effectively forecloses the issue of varied public services and user choice. The shadow of Fordism haunts us even in the terms in which we oppose it.

The Break-up of Fordism

Fordism as a vision − both left and right − had always been challenged, on the shopfloor, in the political party, the seminar room and the studio. In 1968 this challenge exploded in Europe and the USA. It was a cultural as much as an industrial revolt, attacking the central principles of Fordism, its definitions of work and consumption, its shaping of towns and its overriding of nature.

From that time we can see a fracturing of the foundations of predictability on which Fordism was based. Demand became more volatile and fragmented. Productivity growth fell as the result of workplace resistance. The decline in profit drove down investment. Exchange rates were fluctuating, oil prices rose and in 1974 came the greatest slump the West had had since the 1930s.

The consensus response was a Keynesian one, to restore profitability through a managed increase in demand and an incomes policy. For monetarism the route to profitability went through the weakening of labour, a cut in state spending and a reclaiming of the public sector for private accumulation. Economists and politicians were re-fighting the battles of the last slump. Private capital on the other hand was dealing with the present one. It was using new technology and new production principles to make Fordism flexible, and in doing so stood much of the old culture on its head.

In Britain, the groundwork for the new system was laid not in manufacturing but in retailing. Since the 1950s, retailers had been using computers to transform the distribution system. All mass producers have the problem of forecasting demand. If they produce too little they lose market share. If they produce too much, they are left with stocks, which are costly to hold, or have to be sold at a discount. Retailers face this problem not just for a few products, but for thousands. Their answer has been to develop information and supply systems which allow them to order supplies to coincide with demand. Every evening Sainsbury's receives details of the sales of all 12,000 lines from each of its shops; these are turned into orders for warehouse deliveries for the coming night, and replacement production for the following day. With computerised control of stocks in the shop, transport networks, automatic loading and unloading, Sainsbury's flow-line make-to-order system has conquered the Fordist problem of stocks.

They have also overcome the limits of the mass product. For, in contrast to the discount stores which are confined to a few, fast-selling items, Sainsbury's, like the new wave of high street shops, can handle ranges of products geared to segments of the market. Market niching has become the slogan of the high street. Market researchers break down market by age (youth, young adults, 'grey power'), by household types (dinkies, single-gender couples, one-parent families), by income, occupation, housing and, increasingly, by locality. They analyse 'lifestyles', correlating consumption patterns across commodities, from food to clothing, and health to holidays.

The point of this new anthropology of consumption is to target both product and shops to particular segments. Burton's − once a mass producer with generalised retail outlets − has changed in the 1980s to being a niche market retailer with a team of anthropologists, a group of segmented stores − Top Shop, Top Man, Dorothy Perkins, Principles and Burton's itself − and now has no manufacturing plants of its own. Conran's Storehouse group − Habitat, Heals, Mothercare, Richards and BHS − all geared to different groups, offers not only clothes, but furniture and furnishings, in other words entire lifestyles. At the heart of Conran's organisation in London is what amounts to a factory of 150 designers, with collages of different lifestyles on the wall, Bold Primary, Orchid, mid-Atlantic and the Cottage Garden.

In all these shops the emphasis has shifted from the manufacturer's economies of scale to the retailer's economies of scope. The economies come from offering an integrated range from which customers choose their own basket of products. There is also an economy of innovation, for the modern retail systems allow new product ideas to be tested in practice, through shop sales, and the successful ones then to be ordered for wider distribution. Innovation has become a leading edge of the new competition. Product life has become shorter, for fashion goods and consumer durables.

A centrepiece of this new retailing is design. Designers produce the innovations. They shape the lifestyles. They design the shops, which are described as 'stages' for the act of shopping. There are now 29,000 people working in design consultancies in the UK, which have sales of £1,600 million per annum. They are the engineers of designer capitalism. With market researchers they have steered the high street from being retailers of goods to retailers of style.

These changes are a response to, and a means of shaping, the shift from mass consumption. Instead of keeping up with the Joneses there has been a move to be different from the Joneses. Many of these differences are vertical, intended to confirm status and class. But some are horizontal centred and round group identities, linked to age, or region or ethnicity. In spite of the fact that basic needs are still unmet, the high street does offer a new variety and creativity in consumption which the Left's puritan tradition should also address. Whatever our responses, the revolution in retailing reflects new principles of production, a new pluralism of products and a new importance for innovation. As such it marks a shift to a post-Fordist age.

There have been parallel shifts in manufacturing, not least in response to the retailers' just-in-time system of ordering. In some sectors where the manufacturers are a little more than subcontractors to the retailers, their flexibility has been achieved at the expense of labour. In others, capital itself has suffered, as furniture retailers like MFI squeeze their suppliers, driving down prices, limiting design, and thereby destroying much of the mass-production furniture industry during the downturns.

But the most successful manufacturing regions have been ones which have linked flexible manufacturing systems, with innovative organisation and an emphasis on 'customisation' design and quality. Part of the flexibility has been achieved through new technology, and the introduction of programmable machines which can switch from product to product with little manual resetting and downtime. Benetton's automatic dyeing plant, for example, allows it to change its colours in time with demand. In the car industry, whereas General Motors took nine hours to change the dyes on its presses in the early 1980s, Toyota have lowered the time to two minutes, and have cut the average lot size of body parts from 5,000 to 500 in the process. The line, in short, has become flexible. Instead of using purpose-built machines to make standard products, flexible automation uses general-purpose machines to produce a variety of products.

Japanisation

Manufacturers have also been adopting the retailers' answer to stocks. The pioneer is Toyota which stands to the new era as Ford did to the old. Toyoda, the founder of Toyota, inspired by a visit to an American supermarket, applied the just-in-time system to his component suppliers, ordering on the basis of his daily production plans, and getting the components delivered right beside the line. Most of Toyota's components are still produced on the same day as they are assembled.

Toyoda's prime principle of the elimination of wasteful practices meant going beyond the problem of stocks. His firm has used design and materials technology to simplify complex elements, cutting down the number of parts and operations. It adopted a zero-defect policy, developing machines which stopped automatically, when a fault occurred, as well as statistical quality control techniques. As in retailing, the complex web of processes, inside and outside the plant, were co-ordinated through computers, a process that economists have called systemation (in contrast to automation). The result of these practices is a discontinuous speed-up in what Marx called the circulation of capital. Toyota turns over its materials and products ten times more quickly than western car producers, saving material and energy in the process.

The key point about the Toyota system, however, is not so much that it speeds up the making of a car. It is in order to make these changes that it has adopted quite different methods of labour control and organisation. Toyoda saw that traditional Taylorism did not work. Central management had no access to all the information needed for continuous innovation. Quality could not be achieved with deskilled manual workers. Taylorism wasted what they called 'the gold in workers' heads'.

Toyota, and the Japanese more generally, having broken the

industrial unions in the 1950s, have developed a core of
multi-skilled workers whose tasks include not only manufacture
and maintenance, but the improvement of the products and
processes under their control. Each breakdown is seen as a
change for improvement. Even hourly-paid workers are trained
in statistical techniques and monitoring, and register and
interpret statistics to identify deviations from a norm − tasks
customarily reserved for management in Fordism. Quality circles
are a further way of tapping the ideas of the workforce. In
post-Fordism, the worker is designed to act as a computer as well
as a machine.

As a consequence the Taylorist contract changes. Workers
are no longer interchangeable. They gather experience. The
Japanese job-for-life and corporate welfare system provides
security. For the firm it secures an asset. Continuous training,
payment by seniority, a breakdown of job demarcations, are all
part of the Japanese core wage relation. The EETPU's lead in
embracing private pension schemes, BUPA, internal flexibility,
union-organised training and single-company unions are all
consistent with this path of post-Fordist industrial relations.

Not the least of the dangers of this path is that it further
hardens the divisions between the core and the peripheral
workforce. The cost of employing lifetime workers means an
incentive to subcontract all jobs not essential to the core. The
other side of the Japanese jobs-for-life is a majority of low-paid,
fragmented peripheral workers, facing an underfunded and
inadequate welfare state. The duality in the labour market, and
in the welfare economy, could be taken as a description of
Thatcherism. The point is that neither the EETPU's policy nor
that of Mrs Thatcher should read as purely political. There is a
material basis to both, rooted in changes in production.

There are parallel changes in corporate organisation. With
the revision of Taylorism, a layer of management has been
stripped away. Greater central control has allowed the
decentralisation of work. Day-to-day autonomy has been given
to work groups and plant managers. Teams linking departments
horizontally have replaced the rigid verticality of Fordist
bureaucracies.

It is only a short step from here to sub-contracting and
franchising. This is often simply a means of labour control. But
in engineering and light consumer industries, networks and

semi-independent firms have often proved more innovative than vertically integrated producers. A mark of post-Fordism is close two-way relations between customer and supplier, and between specialised producers in the same industry. Co-operative competition replaces the competition of the jungle. These new relationships within and between enterprises and on the shopfloor have made least headway in the countries in which Fordism took fullest root, the USA and the UK. Here firms have tried to match continental and Japanese flexibility through automation while retaining Fordist shopfloor, managerial and competitive relations.

Yet in spite of this we can see in this country a culture of post-Fordist capitalism emerging. Consumption has a new place. As for production the keyword is flexibility − of plant and machinery, as of products and labour. Emphasis shifts from scale to scope, and from cost to quality. Organisations are geared to respond to rather than regulate markets. They are seen as frameworks for learning as much as instruments of control. Their hierarchies are flatter and their structures more open. The guerrilla force takes over from the standing army. All this has liberated the centre from the tyranny of the immediate. Its task shifts from planning to strategy, and to the promotion of the instruments of post-Fordist control − systems, software, corporate culture and cash.

On the bookshelf, Peters and Waterman replace F W Taylor. In the theatre the audience is served lentils by the actors. At home Channel 4 takes its place beside ITV. Majorities are transformed into minorities, as we enter the age of proportional representation. And under the shadow of Chernobyl even Fordism's scientific modernism is being brought to book, as we realise there is more than one way up the technological mountain.

Not all these can be read off from the new production systems. Some are rooted in the popular opposition to Fordism. They represent an alternative version of post-Fordism, which flowered after 1968 in the community movements and the new craft trade unionism of alternative plans. Their organisational forms − networks, work-place democracy, co-operatives, the dissolving of the platform speaker into meetings in the round − have echoes in the new textbooks of management, indeed capital has been quick to take up progressive innovations for its own purposes. There are then many sources and contested versions of post-Fordist culture. What they share is a break with the era of Ford.

Post-Fordism is being introduced under the sway of the market and in accordance with the requirements of capital accumulation. It validates only what can command a place in the market; it cuts the labour force in two, and leaves large numbers without any work at all. Its prodigious productivity gains are ploughed back into yet further accumulation and the quickening consumption of symbols in the postmodern market place. In the UK, Thatcherism has strengthened the prevailing wind of the commodity economy, liberating the power of private purses and so fragmenting the social sphere.

To judge from Kamata's celebrated account, working for Toyota is hardly a step forward from working for Ford. As one British worker in a Japanese factory in the North-East of England put it, 'they want us to live for work, whereas we want to work to live'. Japanisation has no place in any modern *News From Nowhere*.

Yet post-Fordism has shaken the kaleidoscope of the economy, and exposed an old politics. We have to respond to its challenges and draw lessons from its systems.

Political Consequences of Post-Fordism

Firstly there is the question of consumption. How reluctant the Left has been to take this on, in spite of the fact that it is a sphere of unpaid production, and, as Gorz insists, one of creative activity. Which local council pays as much attention to its users as does the market research industry on behalf of commodities? Which bus or railway service cuts queues and speeds the traveller with as much care as retailers show to their just-in-time stocks? The perspective of consumption − so central to the early socialist movement − is emerging from under the tarpaulin of production: the effects of food additives and low-level radiation, of the air we breathe and surroundings we live in, the availability of childcare and community centres, or access to privatised city centres and transport geared to particular needs. These are issues of consumption, where the social and the human have been threatened by the market. In each case the market solutions have been contested by popular movements. Yet their causes and the relations of consumption have been given only walk-on parts in party programmes. They should now come to the centre of the stage.

Secondly, there is labour. Post-Fordism sees labour as the key asset of modern production. Rank Xerox is trying to change its accounting system so that machinery becomes a cost, and labour its fixed asset. The Japanese emphasise labour and learning. The Left should widen this reversal of Taylorism, and promote a discontinuous expansion of adult education inside and outside the workplace.

They should also provide an alternative to the new management of time. The conservative sociologist Daniel Bell sees the management of time as the key issue of post-industrial society. Post-Fordist capital is restructuring working time for its own convenience: with new shifts, split shifts, rostering, weekend working, and the regulation of labour, through part-time and casual contracts, to the daily and weekly cycles of work. Computer systems allow Tesco to manage more than 130 different types of labour contract in its large stores. These systems of employment and welfare legislation should be moulded for the benefit not the detriment of labour. The length of the working day, of the working week, and year, and lifetime, should be shaped to accommodate the many responsibilities and needs away from work.

The most pressing danger from post-Fordism, however, is the way it is widening the split between core and periphery in the labour market and the welfare system. The EETPU's building a fortress round the core is as divisive as Thatcherism itself. We need bridges across the divide, with trade unions representing core workers using their power to extend benefits to all, as IG Metall have been doing in Germany. A priority for any Labour government would be to put a floor under the labour market, and remove the discriminations faced by the low paid. The Liberals pursued such a policy in late 19th-century London. Labour should reintroduce it in late 20th-century Britain.

Underlying this split is the post-Fordist bargain which offers security in return for flexibility. Because of its cost Japanese capital restricts this bargain to the core; in the peripheral workforce flexibility is achieved through insecurity. Sweden has tried to widen the core bargain to the whole population with a policy of full employment, minimum incomes, extensive retraining programmes, and egalitarian income distribution. These are the two options, and Thatcherism favours the first.

Could Labour deliver the second? How real is a policy of full employment when the speed of technical change destroys jobs as rapidly as growth creates them? The question − as Sweden has shown − is one of distribution. There is the distribution of working time: the campaign for the 35 hour week and the redistribution of overtime should be at the centre of Labour policy in the 1990s. There is also the distribution of income and the incidence of tax. Lafontaine's idea of shifting tax from labour to energy is an interesting one. Equally important is the need to tax heavily the speculative gains from property, the rent from oil, and unearned and inherited income. Finally taxes will need to be raised on higher incomes, and should be argued for not only in terms of full employment, but in terms of the improvements to the caring services, the environment, and the social economy which the market of the 1980s has done so much to destroy. Full employment is possible. It should be based on detailed local plans, decentralised public services and full employment centres. It cannot be delivered from Westminster alone.

Thirdly, we need to learn from post-Fordism's organisational innovations, and apply them within our own public and political structures. Representative democracy within Fordist bureaucracies is not enough. What matters is the structure of the bureaucracy and its external relations. In the state this means redefining its role as strategist, as innovator, co-ordinator, and supporter of producers. In some cases the span of co-ordination needs to be extended (notably in integrating public transport and the movement of freight): in others production should be decentralised and the drive for scale reversed (the electricity industry, education and health have all suffered from over-centralised operations). Public services should move beyond the universal to the differentiated service. Nothing has been more outrageous than the attack on local government as loony leftist, when councils have sought to shape policies to the needs of groups facing discrimination. Capitalist retailers and market researchers make these distinctions in the pursuit of sales, and socialists should match them in pursuit of service. If greater user control and internal democracy were added to this, then we would be some way towards the dismantling of mass-produced administration, and the creation of a progressive and flexible state.

Lastly, there is private industry. In many sectors both industry and public policy are frozen in Fordism, even as the leading edge of competition has shifted from scale to product, and from costs to strategy. In spite of the restructuring that has taken place in the 1980s, largely at the expense of labour, manufacturing competitiveness continues to decline. By 1984 only five out of 34 major manufacturing sectors did not have a negative trade balance.

The Left's response to this decline has been couched largely in terms of macro policy: devaluing the pound, controlling wage levels and expanding investment. Industrial policy has taken second place, and centred on amalgamations and scale and the encouragement of new technology. This has been Labour's version of modernisation.

The fact remains that size has not secured competitiveness. Neither has a declining exchange rate with the yen, nor wage levels which have made the UK one of the cheap labour havens of Europe. The changes are much deeper than this.

An alternative needs to start not from plans but from strategies. Strategic capacity within British industry is thin, and even thinner in the state and the labour movement. Sector and enterprise strategies need to take on board the nature of the new competition, the centrality of skilled labour, the need for specialisation and quality, and for continuous innovation.

What public policy should do is to find ways of ensuring that the resultant restructuring takes account of social priorities: labour and educational reform is one part of this; industrial democracy another; environmental and energy saving a third; user concerns about quality and variety a fourth. Some of these will require new laws; others incentive schemes; others collective bargaining. They all need to be a part of strategic restructuring.

In each sector there will be giants barring the path towards such a programme. One will be the stock-market. A priority for a Labour government will be to reduce the stock-market's power to undermine long-term strategic investment (in this we need to follow the example of the Japanese). Another will be multinationals which dominate so may industrial and service sectors in the economy. The urgent task here is to form coalitions of states, unions and municipalities across the

European Community to press for common strategic alternatives at the European level. A third will be the retailers. In some cases retailers will be important allies in restructuring industry progressively (the co-op has a role here); in others the conduct of retailers is destructive, and a Labour government should take direct measures against them.

At the same time, Labour needs to develop a network of social industrial institutions, decentralised, innovative and entrepreneurial. For each sector and area there should be established one or more enterprise boards. They would be channels for long-term funds for new technology, for strategic support across a sector, for common services, and for initiatives and advice on the social priorities.

Public purchasing should be co-ordinated and used not just to provide protection in the old manner, but as supporters of the sectoral programme, as contributors to the improvement of quality, and as sources of ideas. New technology networks should also be set up, linking universities and polytechnics with the sectors and unions (this is an effective part of Dukakis's Massachusetts programme).

In short we need a new model of the public economy made up of a. honeycomb of decentralised, yet synthetic institutions, integrated by a common strategy, and intervening in the economy at the level of production rather than trying vainly to plan all from on high. The success of the Italian consortia, and the German industrial regions has been centrally dependent on such a network of municipal and regional government support.

A key role in taking forward this industrial programme should be played by the unions. Restructuring has put them on the defensive. They have found their power weakened and their position isolated. Few have had the resources to develop alternative strategies and build coalitions of communities and users around them. Yet this is now a priority if unions are to reclaim their position as spokespeople of an alternative economy rather than defenders of a sectional interest. Research departments should be expanded, and commissions given to external researchers. There should be joint commissions of members, and users and other related groups, as well as supportive local authorities. The production of the policy would itself be a form of democratic politics.

Mrs Thatcher has led an attack on the key institutions of Fordism: on manufacturing, on the centralised state, on industrial unions and on the national economy. She has opened up Britain to one version of post-Fordism, one that has strengthened the control of finance and international capital, has increased inequality and destroyed whole areas of collective life.

There is an alternative. It has grown up in the new movements, in the trade unions, and in local government over the past twenty years. It has broken through the bounds of the Left's Fordist inheritance, in culture, structure and economics. From it can develop – as is already happening in Europe – an alternative socialism adequate to the post-Fordist age.

Robin Murray

Benetton Britain:
The New Economic Order

---

*This was written in 1985 — before Thatcher's third term and the
Labour Party Policy Review, while the GLC still existed. But,
though the times have changed this essay remains an important
contribution to the popularisation of the notion of post-Fordism.*

If there is one economic lesson we should have learnt from the
last twenty years, it is the limits of Keynesian policy. Whether
in this country or abroad — in Spain, France, Greece or
Australia — social-democratic governments have come in on a
platform of expansionism and redistribution, only to traumatise
both their electorates and themselves by introducing cuts and
deflation. In this country such turning points occurred in 1966
and 1976. The general election of 1983 was a trauma of a
different kind, but with a similar lesson. Since then Labour has
fought monetarism with Keynesianism, and has lost both the
economic argument and elections.

In spite of this, Labour's current economic policy is still
predominantly in the Keynesian mould. Its main axes are
reflation, redistribution, and balance of payments control — in
short, the management of markets. A few Labour politicians may
still believe that such measures will restore full employment.
Most have lowered their sights to what they think Keynesian
orthodoxy can deliver. But in the movement as a whole there is a
deeper ache, a sense that what has happened to Mitterrand will
happen here. As a result, there is a real openness to new policies,
without any clear idea along which path a credible alternative
actually lies.

Part of the problem is that progressive alternatives to Labour
orthodoxy have shared a similar Keynesian outlook. Reflation

has been a common starting point. What has divided the Left and Right has been the extent of reflation and the severity of controls necessary to complement it. The size of the public sector borrowing requirement (PSBR) has become an index of economic progressiveness: the higher the braver. The larger the deficit, the more severe must be protection and exchange controls, and the more extensive the internal control of the economy. Around the Keynesian problematics of expanding demand and protecting the national economy there is a continuity which runs from the Alliance on the Right to virtually all versions of the alternative economic strategy on the Left.

Three Weaknesses

There are three weaknesses in this general approach. First, as Roy Hattersley himself is acutely aware, there will be balance of payments and inflationary pressures even with an injection of the £5 billion into the economy that he is currently proposing. With the collapse of so many sectors of British production, an increase in consumer demand and capital investment cannot but help draw in imports in the short and medium term – however severe the protection. To take a recent example from the Enterprise Board's work in London. The Board has been backing an attempt to move the leading electric bicycle design from prototype to mass production. It could find no firm remaining capable of manufacturing the frames in this country. The designer has turned instead to Italy and the USA.

Strategies of reflation aim to counter this problem by concentrating their short-run plans on activities with a low import content (like construction) or on labour-intensive projects (like job creation schemes). But there will still be import pressures when the new wages are spent and there will still be inflationary bottlenecks in sectors like construction. Taking London again: there are already skill shortages reported in the engineering and building trades, reflecting the departure of skilled labour from those industries and the decline in the number of apprentices to replace them. As with a person who has been starved, there are limits to which the British economy can be force-fed.

The key issue is under what conditions and at what speed 're-industrialisation' could take place. All the evidence we have from the GLC's firm and sectoral studies of the London economy is that many sectors are unlikely to recover, even with protection, without profound restructuring.

The second weakness of the Keynesian approach is that the power of any government to control the national economy through macro measures has been seriously eroded by the growth of multinationals and the openness of the British economy. In the late 1930s imports accounted for a tenth of the UK market for manufactures. Today the figure is nearer a third. Four-fifths of all UK exports are accounted for by multinationals, much of it transferred between affiliates within the same company. Industrial and banking multinationals also dominate flows on the foreign exchanges. Changes in tariffs and exchange rates do affect the pattern of multinational trade and investment, but in different ways and over different time periods than they did in the days of more integrated national economies.

The third, and perhaps the most significant weakness of Keynesianism, is that it has no direct purchase on the major economic issue of our time, which is the restructuring of production. The central fact of the present era of capitalism is that Fordist production (mass production of standardised goods, using specially designed machinery, production lines and a semi-skilled workforce) began to run out of steam in the 1960s. Its earlier spread had been the basis of the postwar boom, but, as markets became saturated, profit rates fell. Expansions of credit and government-financed consumer demand slowed down but did not reverse this process.

From Fordism to Neo-Fordism

The major counter-tendency has come from another quarter − the introduction of a quite new stage of capitalist production. In the USA it is referred to as 'flexible specialisation', in France as 'neo-Fordism'. It consists of applying computer technology not only to each stage of the production process, from design to retailing, but also to the integration of all stages of the process into a single co-ordinated system. As a result, the economies of scale of mass production can now be achieved on much smaller runs, whether small batch engineering products, or clothes, shoes, furniture and even books. Instead of Fordism's specialised machinery producing standardised products, we now have flexible, all-purpose machinery producing a variety of products. Computers have been applied to design, cutting down the waste of materials, and to stock control. Distribution has been revolutionised, as has the link between sales, production and innovation.

A good example of the 'new production' is that of the Italian clothing firm, Benetton. Their clothes are made by 11,500 workers in northern Italy, only 1,500 of whom work directly for Benetton. The rest are employed by sub-contractors in factories of 30 – 50 workers each. The clothes are sold through 2,000 tied retail outlets, all of them franchised. Benetton provide the designs, control material stocks, and orchestrate what is produced according to the computerised daily sales returns which flow back to their Italian headquarters from all parts of Europe. Similar systems are at the heart of the success in the UK of the 'new wave' clothiers − Burton's, Next and Richard Shops.

In industry after industry a parallel restructuring has been taking place. Japan has been the home base for the new production, together with West Germany, northern Italy and parts of the Scandinavian economy. The UK and the USA, mostly deeply bound into Fordism, have been slowest to respond (the car industry is a notable example), though the USA is now changing rapidly. Policies which are restricted to managing markets, providing finance, or merely changing formalised control, do not begin to address these issues. What is needed is for the labour movement to shift the whole focus of policy, from money and markets, to production. It is the crisis in production which is at the root of the world recession and the British slump, and it is the way in which the labour movement addresses restructuring which should be at the centre of economic debate.

The Japanisation Strategy

What are the alternatives? The first is a 'Japanisation' strategy which would aim to restructure industry in the interest of British-based capital. It would require a central restructuring institution − in the tradition of the Industrial Reorganisation Corporation, and on the scale of the Japanese planning ministry MITI. It would also need a source of long-term finance, as well as specific government policies of protection, research funding, and state support, that would be linked to the individual industrial plans and financial packages. There are traces of such a 'Japanisation' project in Alliance policies and in parts of Labour's economic programme. But in both cases industrial policy is obscured beneath the shadow of Keynesianism.

Socialists have been understandably wary of restructuring proposals along these lines. Such restructuring is merely another word for rationalisation, involving loss of jobs, and the undermining of labour's position in the workplace. It recalls the 'Mondist' movement in Britain of the 1920s and 1930s, which was concerned with the introduction of Fordist methods of production with the consent of the trade unions.

In the case of Japanese-type restructuring, the dangers go well beyond the workplace, as the Benetton example shows. For the establishment of single integrated systems of production and distribution has permitted the break-up of large factory complexes and the growth of a sub-contract and franchise economy. In Japan the resulting dualism is particulary sharp. On the one hand, there is a central core accounting for a third of the workforce (with the celebrated corporate welfare systems, high skill levels and jobs for life). On the other, there is a peripheral sub-contract and sweated economy, casualised, low-paid, weakly organised, and restricted to a grossly inadequate public welfare system.

We should certainly be suspicious of such trends. But we cannot ignore them. For already they are taking root in the British economy. Sub-contracting has expanded. So has franchising. Private welfare systems, from health to pensions to job security and even to housing, are growing as the welfare state is being run down. There is a deepening dualism in the labour market. The problem is that in the market sectors of the economy, the failure to match the new flexible production systems has meant the destruction of many of the manufacturing strongholds of the labour movement.

The point was brought home to us in London by the experience of one of the Greater London Enterprise Board's clothing factories. GLEB bought it from the receiver, re-equipped it, and improved the plant lay-out and the flow of work. The company slowly raised wages, and has been developing an enterprise plan. But when it bid for one public contract, it found itself undercut by quotations which were from 18 – 36 per cent below its own direct labour and material costs. Initially, GLEB thought that the competitors must have been relabelling imports from south-east Asia. But they found that their rivals had set up flexible systems in this country, linking design, production, distribution and sales. The lower bids reflected the large increases in efficiency that resulted.

Differences of this magnitude are common in other industries. Ford Europe, for example, found that their Japanese associate, Mazda, was able to produce an Escort in Japan £1,000 per car cheaper than Ford. A top-level Ford management team were astonished when they discovered that only 10 per cent of the difference could be accounted for by labour factors (wages, running along the line and so on). 90 per cent was due to factors of flexible specialisation.

Another Path?

Such findings show up the futility − even from capital's point of view − of the present government's cheap labour solution. But they also pose as great a problem to the Left as did Fordism to the Bolsheviks after 1917. What policy should socialists adopt towards the most advanced forms of capitalist technology? Lenin's answer was to embrace the principles of Fordism and scientific management. Trotsky argued along similar lines, that if socialism failed to adopt the most modern technology and narrow the gap between domestic and world prices then, at some point, internal political opposition would emerge, arguing for imports. Hence he supported and organised the massive import of western technology as a means of restructuring Soviet manufacturing on Fordist lines. Henry Ford's largest tractor plant in the world was built in the Soviet Union.

All socialist countries have faced the force of the world market. However strong the protection, a Labour government would face it here. This means we cannot avoid having a policy on restructuring. If we do not have such a policy, the market and its managers will settle it for us. Some version of Japanisation will take further hold of the British economy, with British factories being increasingly confined to the periphery − as subcontractors, assemblers, finishers − the screwdriver plants of the world economy.

But while agreeing with Lenin and Trotsky that we cannot ignore foreign technology, the question we must pose is whether there is an alternative path of restructuring to that offered by the Japanese model. Can we have restructuring in the interests of labour rather than of capital? Can we take over the advantages of new computer systems of production without the deskilling, fragmentation, and dualism that goes with it? Can we talk of a strategy of alternative production?

I believe we can, though its outlines are hazy. In this, as in so many other fields, Brecht's maxim 'Truth is in concrete' applies. Our answers will necessarily be in the details of particular sectors. Take retailing, for example. The modern superstores, hypermarkets and out-of-town shopping centres have pioneered the new principles of flexible specialisation. But they have done it in such a way as to destroy local shops. They have made access to shopping harder for the immobile and for those without cars. They have followed a policy of employing casual, part-time, largely female labour, and have failed − in the food sector − to transform the nutritional quality of food and its conditions of production, in line with their extraordinary advances in systems of physical distribution and stock control. The conditions and wages in meat product factories in London, for example, are atrocious.

The transformation of retailing need not be like this. The technology could be developed to bring the advantages of the supermarket to local corner shops. There is wide scope for improvements in food quality, and in the provision of fresh food using the 'just-in-time' systems of stock control. Supermarkets could provide creches and independent nutritional advice centres. Many of these policies may conflict with the market. They do not conflict with need.

Or take software. The computer programmes that are written to control the new systems of production are geared to control labour rather than emancipate it. There is no necessity in this. Busworkers in Leeds, for example, found that computerised bus schedules could be rewritten (with the help of a friendly programmer) in a way in which was just as efficient in time terms, but which took into account their own (and the passengers') needs in a quite different way. Professor Rosenbrock's human-centred lathe and automatic factory systems − designed to extend traditional engineering skills rather than dispense with them — provide another example.

Britain has great strength in programming. But the private software economy is about to be swamped by US mass-produced programmes. Software, like retailing, is one of the new commanding heights of the present phase of capitalism. Its effects have already gone deep into market production. The next phase of expansion is to be directed at public services. It is therefore critical, in terms of a strategy of alternative production, that a public software capacity is secured to develop the alternative computer programmes on which the advances in production will be based.

Some Lessons Learnt

I have given examples of how computer systems can be applied in the interests of need rather than merely of profit. But their implications go beyond this. If, for instance, such systems are developed for the furniture industry, and if they are applied in plants under social control, then those plants will have a competitive advantage. It is this advantage which will give scope for those things that have been driven out by the market economy: adequate wages, training, full access for women and for black people (in all industry where the workforce is still almost entirely white and male), designs that take into account those needs which have no power in the market (like those of the disabled), planned imports from progressive Third World countries that are desperate for foreign exchange. The scope will be wide, too, for an extension of real control by the workforce. I say 'real' as well as 'formal' since real control requires the development of confidence and strategic skills, and this takes time, resources and groups of support workers.

All these we have been trying to put into practise, in conjunction with the trade unions, through the Enterprise Board in London and the GLC. In one factory, one thing will work, but not in another. We have learnt as much from the failures as from the successes. But there are four overall conclusions:

(a) there is enormous scope for public intervention in the restructuring of production. Many sectors in which medium-sized firms are significant have been or are being destroyed by imports, and have shown themselves quite incapable of innovating on the scale required. In sectors where large, multinational firms predominate, some have found it difficult to escape from their Fordist traditions. In others, particularly those involved in military production, there is an appalling waste of technological capacity which could be applied to civil markets and to social need. Local enterprise boards cannot take on these giants, though councils have supported trade unionists in pressing for alternative plans. It is here that a National Enterprise Board – committed to a strategy of alternative production – is needed.

(b) the main constraint in extending public intervention is people: people who have managerial skills (to turn round a factory, for example) and who, at the same time, are sympathetic with the strategy. Because of a lack of such staff, the enterprise boards have often been forced into joint ventures with private owners. For GLEB at least, the relationship has again and again been unsatisfactory, compared to those cases where there has been full, or majority, municipal control.

(c) there is a need for new systems of investment appraisal and social accounting. These must shift the emphasis from short-term financial return, to the longer-term questions of the product, its relative strength with respect to other products and the extent to which it can meet non-market, as well as market, needs. As the Japanese have found, restructuring of any kind often takes a long time. They have geared their institutions and methods of assessment accordingly.

(d) the robustness of the strategy depends above all on the involvement of the workforce. Strategic plans have been developed not by economists divorced from production, but by researchers in conjunction with those working in the industry, who again and again have provided a level of deep knowledge, and a sense of what practicably could be.

The enterprise boards have intervened in market sectors. What local councils have also been sharply aware of is that there are restructuring issues – usually on a much larger scale – in public services themselves. As with market production, there are clear alternatives in restructuring. Some of them are not confined to issues of flexible specialisation. In energy, for instance, there is a choice between nuclear power, on the one hand, and conservation on the other. This cannot be settled on financial grounds, but rather on the basis of employment, ecology, and political considerations. With London Transport, on the other hand, the battle between the alternatives did involve questions of how new systems were put into practice (as well as fares). The growing strength of the progressive alternative led to the government 'nationalising' LT. Similarly with cable − which will provide the basic infrastructure for the electronic era − there are wide options about how fibre optics will be introduced and controlled.

In each of these cases restructuring is taking place. There is no one way in which it has to happen. The alternatives have very different implications for labour, and the choice that exists cannot be settled by comparing rates of return. It is rather a question of social and political choices. There are even some cases where the options which are desirable socially are greatly superior on narrow cost grounds as well (preventive health care, for example).

A Strategy of Alternative Production

My argument then is this. The present economic crisis should be seen first and foremost as a crisis of restructuring. It is a restructuring which is taking place at great cost. The priority for the Left should be to intervene in this restructuring in order to change its course. This requires detailed popular planning, sector-by-sector and firm-by-firm, and the development of a material capacity for intervention at a national, as well as a local, level. This is what I mean by a strategy of alternative production.

There are implications for political as well as economic strategy in all this. Policies which enter from the Keynesian end, or from the end of abstract systems of control, concentrate the mind on the need to take state power. For it is the state which can alter the interest rate, and taxation, and who owns what. Part of the problem with this is that, for many people, it all seems abstract and far away from their immediate abilities to act for themselves.

An alternative production approach is different. It starts from where people are: the particular plant, or shop, or office; the kind of food on sale at the local supermarket or the programme on television. Not only can alternative plans start from there, but something can almost always be done. It will be limited and difficult, but will have that one overwhelming political virtue of practicality. And the limits, soon felt, lead to new connections, more general demands and to detailed practical policies which only a progressive government can deliver. Instead of the state being seen as the 'great deliverer' and the focus of power, it becomes the supporter of initiatives begun and fought for elsewhere by trade unionists, communities and municipalities. And, paradoxically enough, a movement developed in this way provides a stronger, not a weaker, foundation from which a progressive government can build.

I say all this not as a litany of wishes, but as a reflection of what has happened over the last fifteen years. That great flowering of local alternative action in the 1970s, through a myriad of community papers, women's groups, trade-union support units, peace groups, legal advice centres, tenants' groups, trade-union branches, and combine committees, all these have been the basis for a change in municipal politics. In London it came first at the level of boroughs, and then in 1981, at the GLC. And the GLC in its turn, like other councils, has tried to see itself as giving strength to, and not merely drawing strength from, the innumerable groups from which it sprung.

What is now possible is for all this to be extended to the national level. In the field of economic strategy, groups of local authorities have already got together to produce national alternatives for the clothing industry, for Ford's, for steel, cable television and combined heat and power. Each has the detail and the organised suppport necessary to make a strategy of national industrial intervention a serious possibility.

The development of national company and sectoral plans is, I think, the most urgent task for the next two years. It is only when these are in hand that the Keynesian measures, left or right, will become credible and capable of supporting a programme of progressive restructuring. Without such plans, the Keynesian interlude will be short-lived, and will do nothing to protect British labour from the gathering embrace of 'Japanisation' and all that follows in its wake.

Fred Steward

Green Times

One of the most positive and encouraging developments in the present period of New Right ascendancy is the emergence of green politics as the focus for a creative and engaging opposition. This success has been achieved by a diverse movement with little formal political power yet a compelling capacity to influence the political agenda. In Britain, in spite of its growing support shown in the 1989 Euro-election, it remains unrepresented at parliamentary level. Yet the prime minister feels obliged to treat it with respect rather than contempt. In Brazil local landowners feel confident enough to kill the union organiser and rainforest champion Chico Mendes, yet internationally politicians compete to express their outrage. Why does green politics have such a purchase while its status remains limited in terms of established political and economic power?

What is it that the greens express which makes them in tune with those same new times in which the Right has flourished and the Left has foundered? There are many dimensions to the green outlook which relate to different aspects of the changing economic and cultural context. Care is needed to avoid one-sided interpretations. One of the features of the new times appears to be the offer of new opportunities for social diversity and individual choice. Does this relate to the emergence of green politics in any significant way?

Some dimensions of green politics do indeed express aspects of change in which issues of individuality, diversity and choice figure very strongly. Personal responsibility for the consequences of one's actions is a prominent theme on matters ranging from recycling newspapers to the purchase of fur coats. Decentralisation of economic power is expressed in relation to self-sufficiency and emphasis on small-scale local enterprise. Choice of new patterns of work and consumption for individual satisfaction and self-realisation are central to the green outlook. These aspects appear to reflect those broader economic and cultural shifts which in general have been appropriated by the Right.

Yet these issues represent only part of the green picture. In addition there is a striking renewal of collectivism, universalism and social purpose. The individual is seen in the context of a global identity, the human species. The ecology of the planet is given a primary status which informs all policy issues. Interdependence and sustainability set the terms for individual and social choice. The future of the planet is a fate shared by all and is hence the over-riding focus for common purpose and action. The rise of green politics therefore also represents a pattern of change in which collective identity and universal values assume a new status and significance.

These two contrasting dimensions are both of fundamental importance to an understanding of current processes of change and an assessment of new political potentialities. Analysis must embrace the dynamic of their interrelationship, and not privilege one over the other. Individuality and choice cannot be dismissed as peripheral to a new social purpose. Universal moral aspirations cannot be consigned to the conformist dustbin of bureaucratic industrialism. The reality is that both of these elements are present in the new context and the Left has been outflanked by political currents engaging with both. The Right has captured the terrain of economic modernisation and consumer choice. The greens now hold the high ground of grand moral vision and all-embracing social transformation.

The political options for the Left are neither a 'realism' based on accommodation with a selfish individualism nor a new fundamentalism reinstating benevolent centralism. Instead we need to combine the collective and the individual, common purpose and personal choice, in a new way. The greens offer some valuable insights into the possibilities. Both their agenda and their style are vital pointers to important new features of the social landscape.

At the heart of green concerns is the threat of environmental destruction. Implicit in this concern is the suggestion of a qualitative leap in the impact of industrial development, expanding consumption and technological change. Does this perception signify a new epoch in the environmental impact of the economy and technology? Most schemes for periodising industrial change concentrate on work and the production process rather than on its environmental effects. Environmental impact in itself is hardly new. Economic change throughout history has had such effects. The rise of mass production carried with it a range of substantial and negative environmental effects. Air pollution from smoke, river pollution from toxic effluent, exhaustion of mineral and energy resources, despoliation of landscape through over-exploitation, all took their toll. Such destructive consequences were gross and manifest, yet in general were limited geographically and over time. Effects were usually confined within national boundaries and were evident within a short space of time. Causality was direct and immediate.

The postwar period has been marked by two striking developments concerning geography and time. The globalisation of industry and technology has dramatically increased our capacity for affecting the planetary biosphere. This is a consequence both of the scale of production and consumption and the speed of diffusion of technology into the world market. Product innovations ranging from motor cars to aerosol cans have global repercussions. In addition new technologies like nuclear power embody features which transcend national boundaries in the event of catastrophe. Human capacity to affect the planetary environment appears to have reached a new level. Accompanying this has often been an increased difficulty in ascertaining the relationship between cause and effect. Consequences are expressed way beyond both the workers in the industry and the direct consumers of its products. A local event like a nuclear plant melt-down has an impact across the world through the radiation released. Individual consumption decisions on the use of aerosols containing CFCs can affect planet-wide systems such as the ozone layer. Environmental impacts become increasingly cumulative and indirect. They are expressed over new and unpredictable time spans. Actions which in the past appeared sustainable, for example the use of the oceans as a source of food or a destiny for wastes, may reach critical thresholds for the survival of species like seals and whales. Events in the present, such as burning fossil fuels and deforestation, could have dramatic consequences for future generations through the greenhouse effect. On all of these issues the evidence is contested yet the potential threat is one of unprecedented enormity.

The new epoch carries with it new problems of handling uncertainty and exercising political power. These have engendered a crisis in the structures of regulation and representation characteristic of the earlier order. The rise of mass production was accompanied by social pressure in response to environmental impacts which led to reasonably effective regulation. This occurred through the political and legal channels of the nation state. The Clean Air Acts got rid of the London smogs, planning legislation controlled the balance between town and country. Such national legislation was accompanied by the growth of administrative structures in which rationality and expertise were deemed the province of the professional, and social interests were confined to indirect representation. It was the era of the standing expert committee in which consensus was based on detachment and reason. Partisanship and explicit values were seen as introducing emotion and irrationality into a political process that would best succeed without them. Regulation was essentially a form of negative control over immediate and overt risks.

The new features of environmental concern have challenged these established political forms. There are serious limits to the capacity of national sovereignty to deal with threats to the environment. Priority needs to be given to new international and supranational forums for the resolution of such issues. Interdependence at a global level has to inform the international agenda. The growth of uncertainty and conflict between experts as to the severity of environmental risk has led to a recognition of the limits of rationality alone and an enhanced status for explicit values. There is widespread dissatisfaction with existing structures premised on professional exclusiveness and expert consensus. Instead there is pressure for an acknowledgement of uncertainty, for explicit representation of diversity in the regulatory process, and for a positive commitment to pre-empting indirect and subtle threats. All of these are expressed in proposals to facilitate direct expression of public interest groups and encourage a more open contestation of the values underlying environmental decisions.

The power of green politics is that it has responded to these changed circumstances and articulated a political philosophy and practice in a novel and imaginative way. This has been expressed by the emergence of a new political culture which embraces a notion of individual responsibility along with one of collective strategy. The new green organisations of the 1970s such as Friends of the Earth, Greenpeace and the green parties embody this culture and have shown a unique capacity to bridge the gulf between transformative politics and the reality of existing political institutions. At the individual level people have shown the capacity to change their habits and make new choices about personal consumption.

The green consumer is no longer an eccentric but a growing and sought-after market segment. Regulatory agencies have been stimulated into action through effective use of established channels of expert evidence and media briefings. The culture is both eclectic and integrative, individualist and collective. Demands are made equally on personal lifestyle, government action and industrial management. Criticisms of the inadequacy of bureaucratic rationality are accompanied by skilful use of expertise and reason in the presentation of arguments which affirm explicit environmental values.

The openness and effectiveness of this political style is clearly underpinned by a clarity of common purposes. It is the combination of these elements which begs analysis. The timeliness of its practice is matched by a resonance for its philosophy. What is it that fosters a receptiveness to a new 'world-outlook' at the same time as reinforcing a commitment to choice and diversity. What ideas and values lie at its root?

Green thinking draws on a clear moral stance which is both a radical challenge to the existing order yet in tune with the times. There are two central values to the green outlook and these inform a range of green social and economic policies as well as specifically environmental issues. One of the core values is an emphasis on the importance of qualitative as opposed to quantitative objectives as a measure of social progress. The quality of life expressed through health and environment takes precedence over the quantity of material wealth. The wholesomeness of air, food and water are more central than the size of the pay packet. The beauty of the environment overrides the growth in GNP. Job satisfaction and the fulfilment of mixing work and leisure to personal taste are considered more important than restoration of conventional full employment. The other core value concerns the primacy of nature over

society. Human goals of all kinds are seen as dependent on the
integrity and diversity of the biosphere. As a result a politics
concerned solely with the position of different social groups or
the relationship between human beings, however radical, is seen
as implicitly subordinating nature, the source of life, to a
secondary position.

It is these core values which inform a series of alternative
policies to the prevailing 'industrialism' of both Right and Left.
The bureaucratic productionist structures of the past are unable
to pursue these values. Neither are macro-economic policies
confined to quantitative redistribution. 'Socialist modernisation'
conceived in terms of conventional economic goals such as
increased competitiveness of a national economy, does not
address such questions even if it embraces new democratic forms
on the path to these goals. The new scope for choice between
technological options must be adopted not simply as a better
route to the fulfilment of diverse consumer needs but as enabling
an environmentally viable path to be followed. A reassessment is
needed of the fundamental objectives of a democratic economy,
and the adoption of broad strategic goals embodying the
principles of quality of life and primacy of nature.

The exercise of choice within such a strategic framework is to
be made not by centralised institutions, however benevolent, but
through a decentralised economic and political system relying on
active individual consent by citizens. Such an approach has often
appeared individualistic and utopian, neglecting the realities of
power and the need for firm central direction. Yet there is little
doubt that such views now seem more timely, and strike a more
serious popular note than before. A decade ago suggestions that
wind, wave and sun were serious options for energy policy were
ridiculed. Now they receive public money and scientific
attention. Concern over food processing and additives was seen
for many years as the preserve of the crank. Now consumer
pressure has put it at the centre of political attention.

Two important factors have contributed to this change. They
concern technology and knowledge. Firstly, the new information
technology makes it possible to combine decentralised activities
within a wider, even global, strategy to a degree hitherto
inconceivable. The capacity to handle complex information with
great speed enables an interactive flow between centre and
locality, producer and consumer, organisation and individual. It

becomes more feasible if such a technical path is chosen to combine central purpose with individual choice. Secondly, there is a spread of education and access to knowledge via the mass media and international communications technology. This has opened a global perspective to the individual which was inaccessible to previous generations. The consequences of technological change have therefore been double-edged. Although human power to affect the planet has been unleashed, the capacity for local control of technology and the economy has been enhanced. These two factors have combined to make the phrase 'think global, act local' actual rather than rhetorical.

Green Politics and Tradition

The local dimension of a politics that embraces the global and the individual is expressed in a new emphasis on 'community'. This encompasses a desire for a smaller, more human scale of economic organisation and social activity. It also embodies a powerful sense of tradition and the maintenance of links with the past. This identification with cultural continuity has been prominent in the recent debates on the built environment which reflect the urban dimension to green politics. Prince Charles has been a prominent exponent of a desire shared by many environmentalists for a smaller scale to our immediate environment and for the preservation of tradition and identity through buildings to blend with the past. The arguments surrounding this are often trapped in inappropriately rigid categories. Classical and modernist architects readily wield the traditional philosophies of conservatism or progress to legitimate their choice. In the TV series *Visions of Britain*, the classicist rested his case on conservative philosopher Roger Scruton's explanation of why change was a bad thing, and the modernist quoted Marx and Freud to show that change was good. Yet the intent of the emphasis on community and continuity is not to narrow horizons or seek to remain static. Instead intimacy and heritage are seen as legitimate values within a global and dynamic perspective.

'Nature' and 'tradition' are two values that are central to the green philosophy and represent a challenge to modernism. Modernism's philosophy rested on the virtues of 'technology' and 'change' both of which were enthusiastically embraced by the Left in its vision of social progress. The epoch of Fordist industrialism was accompanied by the rise of modernism and the Left. The new times are accompanied by a challenge to those values expressed in the rise of the greens. Does such a challenge represent a return to the reactionary or romantic ideals of an even earlier era? There seems no *a priori* reason why it should be linked to political conservatism. Choice over future paths of economic and technological change could give greater weight to nature and community without denying the value of human technical endeavour or succumbing to social stasis. The new times are an opportunity for the elaboration and assertion of such values in the context of material progress and social and personal liberation.

A synthesis of a new type is required rather than simply offering modifications confined within a narrow framework of modernism. The categories of 'technology' and 'change' have indeed changed. The category of 'technology' has rightly been shown to have shifted from process to product, standardisation to differentiation, production to consumption. That of 'change' has been transformed to accommodate social diversity rather than homogeneity, strategy rather than planning, consumer choice rather than state ownership. But whatever the importance of these insights, they need to be accompanied by a re-evaluation of the fundamental objectives of political change prompted by the values of green politics.

The Green and the Left

The relationship between the green perspective and that of the Left remains a problematic one. Too many on the Left still see the ideals and culture of the greens as a risky departure from the rationality and progress that they hold dear. Yet in reality these new aspirations challenge the one-sided interpretation of the older values made by both Right and Left within the industrialist order. The successful combination of 'greening' and 'modernisation' is a formidable challenge. A settlement is needed between the progressive forces for industrial modernisation and those for environmental protection. Common ground between these political forces has to be identified and articulated. It requires a new synthesis of political objectives. These have often been in conflict and Thatcherism strives to sustain their opposition to each other. Only through such a synthesis can the polarisation between industrialism and environmentalism be replaced with an ecologically sensitive modernisation strategy. It will embrace a number of central features.

The first is a recognition that ecological objectives have to be pursued both through government *regulation* and consumer choice. There is neither a simple statist or market solution. The avoidance of new environmental risks will involve greater social regulation and control of business activities. The scale of these problems will require the use of the law to intervene in private business decisions to achieve a broader common purpose.

At the same time there needs to be a new ethic of personal responsibility. Consumer choice, expressed through the market, for environment-friendly products is a necessary accompaniment to regulation. Such a social change of attitudes and objectives cannot simply be legislated for. It rests on a broader cultural and ethical shift in individual behaviour. It can certainly be assisted by encouragement through information and facilities addressed to the individual. At local level this could involve local authorities providing the appropriate infrastructure.

Responsiveness to environmental issues through local and decentralised decision-making requires shifts in perceptions of the individual's relationship to the environment. Only in this way can conflicting roles of residents, consumers and workers, as seen in cases like Sellafield in Cumbria, be resolved.

The second feature concerns the contrasting economic objectives of *sustainability* and *competitiveness*. Economic decisions will have to incorporate new environmental criteria in addition to traditional measures of product and output. These criteria concern the consequences of economic and technological choices for nature. Options like nuclear power, which carry the risk, however small, of catastrophic environmental impacts, should be avoided wherever possible. Choices should be resource conserving rather than resource depleting: energy policy should be concerned with saving energy and using renewable sources as well as the provision of conventional generating capacity. Qualitative objectives for economic performance such as human satisfaction and environmental preservation are needed in addition to quantitative measures of GNP.

At the same time the enhancement of quality of life also depends on the development of a technologically advanced and internationally competitive economy. Without such a material basis, options for quality of life will be enormously restricted. There are tensions evident between these two goals of sustainability and competitiveness, and a mixed strategy, with different priorities for different industrial sectors, will form the basis for such a settlement. The relationship between the industrially developed countries and the Third World, between north and south, must also figure in this equation. The industrial and technological development of poorer countries must be promoted with regard both to the improvement of material standards and to ecological viability.

The third feature concerns a new relationship between popular movements and *professional* experts in the assessment and control of environmental risks. The changing nature of environmental threats means that anticipation of uncertain risks becomes more important than action based on proof of past harm. This will require an enhanced role for popular environmental interests to represent explicit ecological values in the political process. Decisions will give greater weight to caution in the face of uncertainty and the rights of future generations. This will involve a change in the dominance of expert and the professional in this field of political decision, and a broadening out of the traditionally narrow rationality applied to environmental risks. At the same time the complexity of new global risks will offer new challenges for science and knowledge in the analysis of such issues and the uncovering of obscure and unexpected paths for the causation of environmental harm. The role of the professional will be more enhanced, but as part of a more broadly representative political process. New types of political institution will be needed to combine these popular and professional forces.

The fourth feature concerns the objectives of *conservation* and *progress*, of stability and change. The enhanced status of nature requires a more positive view of the importance of continuity and conservation. At the same time the notion of social and technological progress needs to be enriched and developed. Innovation must remain a central feature of progress, but it will address a wider range of technological options and environmental objectives. The new times of post-Fordism offer greater scope for technological choice, and information technology offers new opportunities for both social pluralism and environmental harmony.

The achievement of such a new synthesis, both in terms of political analysis and of a new policy agenda, is the central challenge of the new times. An affinity between the new analysis of the Left and the practice of the greens could contribute to realising the opportunities, rather than the threats, of the times ahead.

Dick Hebdige

After the Masses

Few people — whatever their political persuasion — looking at
Britain in the 1980s would deny that we are living in new times.
The crucial question is how far are the long-term global shifts in
cultural, political and economic life mapped out under the
heading of new times intrinsically connected to the rise of the
Right? One way of opening up this question — if only to present
a 'worst case' scenario — is to see how these same shifts have
been interpreted in recent debates on postmodernism.

The wide currency of this term over the last few years in
Mediaville may alienate many readers. For some it may seem
that the word has become too baggy or trendy or annexed by the
Right to be of use. Others will protest that they never got the
hang of modernism (or its relevance for the Left) let alone
*post*modernism. After all, what have the design of buildings or
pop videos or the fate of the novel or the current obsession with
advertising, packaging and style got to do with the real political
issues of the day ? For others on the Left — perhaps those who
are closer to the debates themselves — the resistance to the idea
not just of postmodernism but more importantly of
post*modernity* — suggests a reaction against that sense of an
ending that hangs over so much currently fashionable theorising.
After riding out all those arguments about post-industrialism
and the end of ideology in the 1960s here we are again
confronted with another version of apocalypse.

This refusal of apocalyptic thinking runs right to the core of
what the contemporary Left's about. It's a matter of principle,
identity and faith. If the multiple factions that make up the Left
have any common identity then it is one which is rooted in a
powerful sense of modernity as a condition in which all
traditional 'truths' and 'absolute' values, all 'natural' social roles
and 'essential' meanings are open to challenge and to change. If

the Left has any unifying faith then it is the conviction that history is neither god-given nor predetermined but is there to be actively made and remade in a process of collective struggle by men and women freed from the chains of ignorance and fear. What can a theory of *post*modernism or *post*modernity have to say to people whose collective identity and political will are so deeply wedded to the sense of radical possibility opened up by modern times? To talk about the temporary fusion of the heady promises of modernity and capitalism is one thing. It's to say that the vanguard of the Left has been left behind for *now*. New times demand new strategies for change. On the other hand to use a term like *post*modernity is to say that the motor of history has run down, that there is no united front along which the Left can advance, that there is no authority or rationality in accordance with which it can proceed. It is, in other words, to give up the ghost.

There is a great deal more at issue here than questions of 'style'. To appreciate just how much is at stake we have, from the start, to mark out a distinction between theories of post*modernism* which address a sense of crisis in the ways culture in the West is organised, produced and thought about, and those more general theories of post*modernity* which directly challenge the principles of hope, critique and practice on which Left politics have always been built. We may or may not care about the role of art and design in contemporary culture but we can't afford to ignore the larger crisis provoked by the severance − so evident throughout the world today, not just in 'Thatcher's Britain' − of the link between modernity and progress. We have to think *through* that historic crisis even if we find it easier to reject the claim that history nowadays is finished, or that it is, as Jean Baudrillard puts it, a 'toy' or a 'game'. A game what's more, that he insists the Left has lost.

The idea that 'the dream is over' is hardly a new one − it forms one of the pressures against which socialism has always sought to make itself. But at the same time one of the ways in which socialism has been renewed in the past has been by actively engaging with those forces which have set out to consign it to the 'rubbish heap of history'. If the engagement with theories of postmodernity and postmodernism is to be fruitful − dialectical rather than defensive − then it has to be acknowledged from the start that such theories pose a challenge to the Left's ambition to 'change the world' because they question the belief in rationality and progress which direct and underpin the Left's project(s). Those challenges have to be squarely faced if we are to move beyond them to understand the dynamics of new times.

Before looking at postmodernity, we have to consider the era it supposedly replaces. Marshall Berman sets out in his book *All That Is Solid Melts Into Air* to provide a sketch of modern times by tracing out the connections between three terms. Firstly *modernisation* refers to the economic, social and technological innovations associated with the rise of capitalism. Secondly *modernity* describes the radically transformed character of life under capitalism most clearly visible in the great European and American cities of the 19th and early 20th centuries. Lastly, there is *modernism* − the answering wave of experimental movements in the arts linked again to the capitalist metropolitan centres. Together these radical modernist innovations, from symbolism and cubism to surrealism and stream-of-consciousness writing, set out to articulate the experience of modernity. The terms of this engagement with modern life were always critical, whether modernists were rejecting 'mass culture', negating bourgeois norms and values or seeking to align themselves with progressive social forces. In the case of the International Style of modern architecture and the Bauhaus ideals of industrial design (the so-called 'machine aesthetic') the ambition was to merge with the modernisation process itself in order literally to build a better world founded on rational principles (eg, 'form follows function').

But it's precisely this equation between modernity, progress and rationality that has itself been brought into question in the 'postmodern' era. At the core of this question lies the 'legitimation crisis'. If modernity is a condition in which 'all that's solid melts into air' then all the old institutions and centres of authority − from religion to royalty − which guaranteed stability and continuity in earlier epochs and more traditional societies are prone to crisis and contestation. If ideals like truth and justice are not underwritten by divine authority then how is authority to be guaranteed? If all values are flattened out beneath exchange then how are true and lasting values to be established? One of the quests within modernity has been to find ways of resisting this tendency towards the relativisation of all values and claims to power by grounding knowledge and legitimating authority so that they are placed beyond question.

According to the French philosopher, Jean- Francois Lyotard, this 'legitimation crisis' has been solved through the invention of what he calls 'the great meta-narratives' of the modern period. By this he means all those overarching belief systems originating in the Enlightenment — from the belief in rationality, science and causality to the faith in human emancipation, progress and the class struggle. These great stories have been used over what he calls the past 'two sanguinary centuries' to legitimate everything from war, revolution, nuclear arsenals and concentration camps to social engineering, Taylorism, Fordist production models and the gulag. The collapse of faith in these meta-narratives heralds what Lyotard calls the 'post-modern condition'. None of the 'centres of authority' legitimated by these collapsed meta-narratives — including that essential 'holding operation', the modern nation state — survives the transition into new times, at least as the latter are defined in postmodern theory.

What replaces them for the American marxist critic, Fredric Jameson, is the universal 'logic' of the market. For Jameson, the global spread of capital has meant that all such centres are either destroyed or have been made over and absorbed by the interlocking cultural and economic systems that make up 'late capitalism'. In the process the political and cultural maps of the modern period have been redrawn so that the old oppositions — science versus art, fact versus fiction, Left versus Right, high culture versus low culture, mass culture versus 'progressive' modern art and so on — no longer hold. In the postmodern world no values prove 'timeless', 'authentic' or ' oppositional' forever when absolutely everything from the price of pickled mushrooms on a Polish street corner to definitions of desirable art in the West moves with the market.

At the same time, the 'radical' nature of modernism has been called into question in two ways. First, modern art is no longer marginal or oppositional: the 'masterpieces' of the modern 'tradition' now fetch astronomical prices at auctions and sit comfortably within the gallery system, and university and polytechnic arts curricula; TV ads routinely use all the shock effects of modern art. Second, as part of a process of critical review, the canon of High Modernism has been brought to book for its 'Eurocentrism', its 'masculinist' stress on transgression and transformation, its downgrading of everything that doesn't fall within its definition of what's important, women's art, domestic culture and reproduction, black and Third World art, 'bourgeois' and 'socialist' realism, peasant and working-class white, 'mass' culture, middle-brow and high culture, non-metropolitan culture etc. Far from being 'progressive', it's condemned for its partriarchal values, its aggressive change-the-world heroism, its colonialist plundering of 'primitive' Third World art. But you don't even need the benefit of hindsight to see that any link between modernisation, modernism and utopia is no longer tenable. That link has been dramatically broken − and not just in capitalist societies.

The violence that can flow from the fusion of centralised power structures, Fordist production models, aggressive modernisation and a debased version of Modern Movement architectural principles is nowhere more apparent than in Romania today where the seventy-year-old Ceausescu is engaged in a village-levelling exercise described by the Helsinki Federation for Human Rights as 'cultural genocide'. The destruction of minority ethnic Hungarian and Saxon cultures in Transylvania and the 'rationalisation' (eradication) of the informal peasant economy on which rural Romanians depend, are two of the consequences of Ceausescu's transplantation of the inhabitants of over 7,000 villages to concrete 'agro-industrial complexes', complete with huge communal kitchens and washrooms. Modernism here involves a tyrannical obliteration of difference. Nowhere is the Faustian link between a patriarchal gerontocracy and willed violence towards organically grown 'archaic' cultural forms more clearly visible than in Ceausescu's crazy plan to wrench 'his' country into the Stalin era before he dies. As the rest of the Eastern bloc confronts the centripetal forces of *perestroika* and the public expression of formerly suppressed ethnic-cultural divisions and nationalist demands, Ceausescu, the ailing 'father', is attempting in the face of international opposition, to exert absolute mastery over the future by turning Romania into a concentration camp.

The contention within a lot of postmodernism that today there is no centre is not just a gesture of solidarity with these excluded, repressed or exterminated 'others'. It demands a review of priorities and a rethinking of terms like 'representation' and 'power' at so fundamental a level that any description of the crisis of the Left that doesn't take it seriously just will not be productive. But the contention also has specific ramifications at both the macro and the micro levels within theories of postmodernism and postmodernity. For Jameson it indicates the end of locality altogether as the multinational character of the late late show of capitalism reduces everything to its own image. The implication here is that we'll soon be able to watch *Dallas* or eat a Big Mac in any part of the inhabited world.

At the same time, the point where we 'experience' all this and make sense of it as individuals has allegedly been made over too. The 'sovereign subject' – central to Enlightenment models of rationality, science and the individual – is itself 'de-centred' from the throne of authority. It's de-centred in theory by the *new* 'sciences' – psychoanalysis and marxism. But in the 20th century it's also de-centred *practically* in the West by the rise of mass consumption and advertising. As the 'consumption economy' has developed, so the value of commodities is seen to derive less from the laws of economic exchange governing the market or from the ability of products to satisfy primary needs as from the way they function *culturally* as *signs* within coded systems of exchange.

This provides the key for the critique of the marxist theory of value put forward by the French champion of postmodernity, Jean Baudrillard. For Baudrillard, the distinction between 'real' and 'false' needs upon which marxist economics is based collapses as consumption becomes *primarily* about individuals and groups using commodities like a language to mark out taste and status *differences* between themselves. In his later work, commodities and signs are seen to merge completely as the opposition between what things look like and what's really going on begins to dissolve in the 'hyper-reality' of the media age. This process – what he calls 'implosion of the real' – supposedly displaces all models of rational critique. It is no longer possible for us to see through the appearance of, for instance, a 'free market' to the structuring 'real relations' underneath (eg, class conflict and the expropriation by capital of surplus value). Instead, signs begin increasingly to take on a life of their own referring not to a real world outside themselves but to their own 'reality' − the system that produces the signs.

It's at this point that Baudrillard grafts a global theory of postmodernity onto a global theory of cultural postmodern*ism* to produce a scenario which is well and truly apocalyptic − 'fatal', to use Baudrillard's word. In this world of surfaces TV takes over from the real as the place where real things happen only if they're screened (real things here include profits made on the screen of computer terminals by dealers juggling prices on the international money and commodity futures markets). In such a thoroughly *imaged* universe − the world of Reagan-Gorbachev photocalls, Thatcher visits to Gdansk and HRH's *Vision of Britain* − 'politics' becomes largely an adjunct of PR and showbiz even when the etiquette is breached (eg, the attack on a newscaster on air by lesbian activists to publicise opposition to Clause 28). Rational critique and the will to change the world are replaced by what he calls the 'ecstasy of communication' − a state characterised by 'banal seduction' and 'mindless fascination' where any kind of judgement − not just artistic but moral and political − becomes impossible.

Clearly a great deal more is at stake in the apocalypse laid out by Baudrillard than a shift in the mode of production. But it's also clear that he offers a kind of picture of *some* of the changes that make up new times.

However much we want to resist the chilly extremism of this kind of analysis, it's clear that the 'information revolution' has implications far beyond the extension of financial services and the further diminution of our civil rights. The sheer volume and variety of information may conceal the fact that the shifts are qualitative as well as quantitative. One result of the print boom for instance, associated with desk-top publishing, Wapping and the end of hot-metal trade unionism, is that more and more publications compete for advertising revenue tied to increasingly fragmented and specialised markets. Manic competition at the bottom end of the tabloid market has led editors to abandon the distinction between entertainment and information, as TV soap gossip crowds out 'hard news' on the front pages. Although the tendency isn't new, in recent years it's been intensified to the point where hype creates its own 'reality' so that some of the dailies now carry the 'Aliens From Outer Space' stories pioneered in the notorious *Sunday Sport*.

What sense would an orthodox left analysis make of this

decline of standards ? It would probably begin by mentioning the circulation war, perhaps citing American precedents. It might go on to condemn the 'Aliens Turned Our Son Into An Olive' style of story as degraded entertainment, even as part of the ideology of authoritarian populism in which all 'aliens' (gay men, the loony Left, black youths, the IRA, acid house fans etc,) are defined as a threat to the 'family of the nation', as part of the unassimilable enemy within.

But such analyses would be inadequate insofar as they remain tied to an outmoded 'economy of truth'. They fail to acknowledge how far the ground has shifted. For what is also at stake in such mutations of the codes of journalism is the whole 'information order' upon which meaningful debates over issues of this kind rely. The survival of the public realm − a forum of debate where conflicting interests and ideologies struggle to define reality − in turn depends upon the public's ability to discriminate *in the last analysis* between what is true and what isn't. If the generalised scepticism towards mainstream media reportage moves beyond issues of 'fact' and interpretation − (what happened when, where and why and what does it mean?) − to question the line between truth and lies itself then the whole 'economy of truth' collapses.

The idea of a verifiable information order, however precarious and shifting, however subject to negotiation and contestation by competing ideologies, does not survive the transition to this version of new times. After all, it's not as if anybody is really being asked to believe in aliens. Instead they are being invited to relinquish the right to believe in the verifiability of public truths *per se*. Such a stretching of the codes of journalistic licence beyond the limits established in the early days of the mass-circulation press may free the readers from any obligation to believe in the bourgeois myth of disinterested truth by offering itself as a kind of joke in which the reader is invited to participate (the 'joke' is how low can we go?), but its potential dangers are also pretty clear: today aliens from Mars kidnap joggers, yesterday Auschwitz didn't happen, tomorrow who cares what happens? Here the so-called 'depthlessness' of the postmodern era extends beyond the integration of signs and commodities into saleable 'lifestyle packages', beyond the tendency of the media to feed more and more greedily off each other, to affect the very function and status of information itself.

It may be that the Left will have to dig deep to find strategies capable of coping with the apparent 'depthlessness' of new times versions of the 'public realm'.

It is easy to see why postmodernism has been characterised as an intellectual gloss for Thatcherism – an invitation issued by people who should know better to give up, lie back and enjoy. Yet in some of their founding premises and points of focus, theories of postmodernism don't offer a *description* of the dominant economic and cultural trends so very different from the territory mapped out on these pages as new times, though the analysis differs at a fundamental level. Some versions of postmodernism are patently fatalistic, even potentially fascistic, but the diverse currents and tendencies that theories of the 'post' have sought to bind into and define have *no intrinsic political belonging in themselves*. On the one hand, in those circles where the politics of race and sexuality are taken seriously, critical postmodernism is identified with diversity and difference, a politics of contestation and change. On the other, in Baudrillard's 'obscene' universe, postmodernity is associated with the annihilation of difference in the media age: the end of politics altogether.

For years *Marxism Today* has been arguing for a definition of the political as a 'war of position' in which absolutely nothing is given or guaranteed. Such a 'marxism without guarantees' has already dispensed with Lyotard's 'meta-narratives'. Furthermore, the concentration in the work of people like Stuart Hall on the ways in which language has been used within contemporary British politics to actively construct – to *articulate* – 'imaginary communities' clearly points a way forward beyond the impasse (or the armchair) in which so much of postmodern theory gets stuck. Thatcherism attempts to hegemonise the long-term movements described, though differently inflected, under the rubrics of new times and postmodernism within its project of 'regressive modernisation'. There is nothing natural about the relationship between those forms and forces and that political will, just as there is nothing given or permanent about the 'we' that Thatcherism has called into being.

This much is clear in recent debates over nationhood and national tradition. The struggle over the meaning of modernity, national identity and the past has offered a significant point of tension in Britain throughout the late 1980s — a point of tension which is there to be cracked open in the current controversy around the role of design and architecture in British life. Thatcherite definitions of 'Britishness', national heritage and national pride have sought to align the 'shape of the future' with a selective image of the past so that even the disruptions and upheavals of today's 'communications revolution' are drawn into the charmed circle of national tradition through the analogy with the Industrial Revolution and the Victorian railway boom (the connection is especially pointed in London where the great 19th-century railway termini are being redeveloped as luxury hotel, leisure centre, office and shopping mall complexes).

At the same time, within architecture where the term was first popularised, 'postmodernism' has been used to describe developments as different in conception and appearance as the nostalgic, neo-Georgian repro-kitsch of Quinlan Terry, a planned 19-storey grey, pink and red office block in the City of London and the 'discreet' horizontal 'groundscrapers', huge, lateral, deep-plan dealing rooms located nearby, sometimes concealed behind the original facades of a block of 'historic buildings'. 'Postmodernism' here has functioned largely as a cover for unrestrained development for profit. Some of the attacks on modernism (Terry's) are literally reactionary — *anti* rather than 'post' modern. Some grow out of an allegedly populist challenge to the arrogance and authoritarianism of Modern Movement architecture while others use style and fashion rather than function as a metaphor for the shift out of Fordism into new times. It's significant that whereas the most celebrated examples of Modern Movement buildings tended to be office blocks rather than housing schemes, the examples of *post*modernism most frequently cited in the architectural journals are supermarkets, shopping malls and leisure developments. In fact, the 'postmodern city' may well be the product of what David Harvey calls 'voodoo economics' where finance capital moves in to occupy the hollowed-out centres left by a declining manufacturing sector with the leisure, heritage and retail industries providing architectural light relief. To counter the argument that the culture of postmodernism heralds an entirely new epoch it's worth considering the sober fact that some of the most feted examples of 'modern' *and* 'postmodern' architecture have been banks; from Mies van der Rohe's designs which helped to transform the skyline of Chicago's financial sector in the late 1930s to Richard Rogers' Lloyds building or Terence Farrell's designs for the revamped City of London

What is clear is that in Britain the tower block has become a powerful symbol of a superceded socialist era. In the current debates, the tower block's collapse is used to point up the weaknesses of that other larger edifice – the postwar corporate state, with its mixed economy, its embattled health services, its strained, unlikely social and political consensus forged in the white heat of Harold Wilson's modernising techno-jargon. The acquisition a few years back by Thatcher, of a neo-Georgian Barratt home in an 'executive estate' in Dulwich marks the ideological cut-off point from failed utopia to new realism, from council-house Britain to 'enterprise culture', from stately-home and country-house conservatism to the tougher, 'fairer' contours of the 'property-owning democracy'.

Yet beyond all the ideologising, nobody – not even the architects – would claim that the original 1960s' tower blocks were ever widely popular. There is a vast literature within sociology devoted to the librium addiction and loss of community associated with Britain's 'vertical streets'. The enthusiastic responses to Prince Charles' vision of Britain as first and foremost a landscape to be conserved rather than designed, testified to the strength of popular feeling on the issue. The affirmation within certain types of postmodernism of the particular against the general; the decorative, the 'fantastic' and the 'aspirational' against the 'rational', the 'formal' and the 'academic'; the desirability of maintaining continuity with the past, the reverence for the 'human scale', are all themes that can be articulated to a more imaginative and democratic, more innovative and pluralist version of socialism. In the words of Alexei Sayle: 'No more living 200 feet in the air in a thing that looks like an off-set lathe or a baked bean canner'.

Charles Jencks, the architect who pushed the term 'postmodernism' to the centre of architectural debate, stresses the importance of dialogue with clients, users and tradition/the past in the planning of new buildings. It is this assertion of the legitimacy of other people's desires that links postmodernism to a positive appraisal of new times. In new times the old hierarchical model of the expert standing Moses-like at the apex of a triangle and the masses laid out along the base waiting for deliverance collapses. The favoured metaphors for intellectual activity in modernism were military (the revolutionary 'vanguard', the artistic 'avant garde'), technical ('writers are the engineers of the soul' — Stalin), mechanical ('houses are machines for living' — Le Corbusier) and medical (the critic as 'surgeon'). In postmodernism, ecological and organic metaphors predominate along with the softer model of the expert as facilitator and consultant. Postmodernism here has more value as one key to a pragmatic approach to consumer demands than as a global account of a 'consumer economy' or as an insistence on any particular architectural style.

It's worth saying that within its own terms one of the more blatant paradoxes of Baudrillard's account of postmodernity is that it is itself a totalising 'meta-narrative' — one which makes the media, not the factory or class struggle or science, the 'motivating' force — the literal *end* of history. According to Baudrillard the masses were an invention of the modern period: one of the myths used to legitimate Fordist projects as diverse as 'the dictatorship of the proletariat', parliamentary democracy and selling soap powder. The decline of Fordism exposes the myth of the masses as an active force so completely that we live today — to quote the title of one of Baudrillard's books — literally 'in the *shadow* of the silent majorities', so that all meanings 'implode' into 'the black hole' left by the masses' 'disappearance'. The 'logic' of this position is as circular as it is solipsistic.

Postmodern pessimism of this kind is symptomatic of the crisis of a particular intellectual formation (male, white, European) shaped in the crucible of student politics in 1968. The 'end of history' argument can be safely written off as the product of a bunker mentality spawned among a generation of liberally educated 'critical' theorists by the disappointment that set in after the Road to Damascus radicalisations of 1968. Institutionally located intellectuals are marginalised at the best of times and are likely to feel even more redundant in the face of 1980's 'new realism', new vocationalism, and 'enterprise culture'. But the legacy of 1968 is of course, itself contradictory. The student uprisings highlighted the decline of workerism, productivism and hierarchical, centralised party politics. But they also heralded the growing importance of cultural and identity politics, the politics of gender, race and sexuality, the ecology and autonomy movements. In the light of these new cultural and political forms and the emergent communities of interest attached to them, the pertinent question becomes not *has* history but rather exactly *whose* history is finished? Take, for instance, the relationship between postmodernism and feminism. While some postmodern pundits have tried to co-opt feminism, it's been a highly selective version of feminist theory that's been appropriated rather than the activism, and historic aspirations that from the late 1960s onwards have brought together the various strands that make up the feminist movement. Some feminists have argued that postmodern theory merely involves male intellectuals claiming feminism for (the end of) history where history becomes little more than a long straight line of Great Male Thinkers rather than an uneven process of struggle which is concrete, open-ended and essentially collective. The story of the 'legitimation crisis' begins to lose any overarching explanatory power in the face of that larger historical process. For if the value of particular ideas and accounts of the world is judged against the benchmark of history rather than philosophy then there are what Meaghan Morris calls other more important 'guiding narratives' than the one Lyotard is promoting. Narratives like 'making the world a better place for our children', 'seeking social justice' are from this viewpoint more valuable than the postmodern lament for the end of history precisely because they are more likely to mobilise more people towards some version of ethical or socially responsible action.

What is of course so often forgotten in the hype surrounding postmodernism today is that there is a tradition of cultural socialism closer to home that is rooted in a similar scepticism towards the notion of the 'masses'. The late Raymond Williams always insisted that the 'mass' was a category intellectuals tended to reserve contemptuously for other people, never for themselves. And if, after all is said and done, we still have need of meta-narratives then *The Long Revolution* may ultimately prove more *useful*, more progressive and empowering than the one that frames the theory of postmodernity because it acknowledges the fact that faith and idealism are themselves part of the historical process, vital constituents of the political *will*. It is also possible that something like a sociology of aspiration might grow out of the less totalising approach to 'ordinary people' that Williams recommends.

One of the features of post-Fordist production is the leading role given to market research, packaging and presentation. While it doesn't literally *produce* the social, it's none the less the case that marketing has provided the dominant and most pervasive classifications of 'social types' in the 1980s (the yuppie is the most obvious example). We use these categories as a kind of social shorthand even if we are reluctant to find ourselves reflected in them. We live in a world and in bodies which are deeply scored by the power relations of race and class, sexuality and gender but we also live − whether or not we know it consciously − in a world of style-setters, innovators, sloanes, preppies, empty nesters (working couples with grown up families), dinkies (dual-income-no-kids), casuals, sensibles, the constrained majority, and today's prime targets, the pre-teens and woofies (well-off-older-folk).

These are the types outlined in commercial lifestyling and 'psychographics' − forms of research which don't present descriptions of living, breathing individuals so much as hypothetical 'analogues' of 'aspirational clusters'. In other words the new intensive but speculative forms of market research are designed to offer a social map of desire which can be used to determine where exactly which products should be 'pitched' and 'niched'. All these types could no doubt be translated back into the old language (it would perhaps be relatively easy to return them to the axis of social class) but everything specific would be lost in the translation.

It is clear that such research methods and the marketing initiatives associated with them have been developed precisely to cut across the old social-sexual polarities. The parameters are designed to be transcultural and transnational (the spread of 'psychographics' in the UK is linked to the drive to go pan-European in preparation for 1992). We may find such forms of knowledge immoral, objectionable or sinister − a waste of time and resources which is unforgiveable in a world where people are starving and in a country where people are still sleeping in the streets − but the fact is that they do actively create and sustain one *version* of the social. They depend for their success on the accurate outlining and anticipation (through observation and interviews with 'target' subjects) not just of what (some) people think they want but of *what they'd like to be*. A sociology of aspiration might begin by combining the considerable *critical* and *diagnostic* resources available within existing versions of sociology and cultural studies with the *descriptive* and *predictive* knowledge available within the new intensive market research to get a more adequate picture of what *everybody* says they want and what they want to be in all its radical plurality. The challenge would then be to produce and distribute the required goods and services more efficiently, and equitably than the opposition. Such a mix of traditional academic/social work and commercial/marketing knowledge functions would take the Left beyond the ghetto of 'miserabilism' to which it is regularly consigned by the loony Right. Such a shift would require what certain forms of postmodernism recommend: a scepticism towards imposed general, 'rational' solutions; a relaxation of the old critical and judgmental postures although it emphatically does not necessitate a retreat from first principles and primary objectives: a commitment to social justice, equality of opportunity, and social welfare. The identity and faith on which left politics have traditionally been founded remain in place. But beyond that a new kind of politics − as flexible and responsive to new demands and initiatives as the software that powers post-Fordist production − will have to be envisioned. It may well be true that the two great collective identities through which the masses came together to 'make history' in the last two hundred years − the first associated with nation, the second with class − are breaking down today in the overdeveloped world. But new 'emancipation narratives' are being written round collectives other than the imaginary community of nation or the international brotherhood of socialist *man*. This is true even in popular culture and the 'depthless' field of the media upon which Baudrillard operates:

Within the transfigured 'public realm', established by transnational communications networks, new forms, both of alliance and contestation, are possible. One of the things ignored in the more 'fatal' versions of new times is the binding power of the new transnational media systems: the power they have to move people not just to buy the products of the culture industries but to buy *into* networks that offer forms of community and alliance which can transcend the confines of class, race, gender, regional and national culture. Popular music offers many examples of this kind of bonding. Some of these 'communities of affect' (rather than 'communities of interest') are explicitly utopian. The simultaneously most spectacular yet most participatory examples to date of the kind of bonding made possible across transnational communications systems have been the televised events organised around Band Aid, Sport Aid, Live Aid and the Free Mandela movement. This is where you see the optimistic will in action. Televangelism is another less engaging example of this kind of mobilisation specific to the media age.

Rather than 'psychic autism' (Baudrillard) or 'the waning of affect' (Jameson) such phenomena suggest the possibility of a new kind of politics existing primarily in and through the airwaves and organised around issues of universal moral concern. Such crusades are likely to be extended in the 1990s. Once again the desire to feel and to feel *connected* to a transitory mass of other people, to engage in transitory and *superficial* alliances of this kind is not intrinsically either good or bad. Instead it has to be *articulated*. Jimmy Swaggart managed to articulate the yearning for community and righteousness one way. Jerry Dammers, founder of the Two Tone movement and co-organiser of the Mandela concert, helped to direct the flow of similar desires in a radically different direction.

At the local level, the airwaves are there to be actively occupied (rather than passively tuned in to). In the UK, the use of music and style to articulate new ethnic identities underneath and against the monolithic version of 'Britishness' available within Thatcherism has become one of the most remarkable (and marketable) aspects of cultural politics in the 1980s. Rap, house and funk music, for instance, are merely the latest in a long line of musics that have offered forms of community *across* the international black diaspora. At the same time they have literally plunged the fans back (through rhythms, lyrics and 'quoted' snatches of speech from dead black leaders) into a version of black history and struggle in the New World — from slavery to civil rights to black power and the buppies — which may otherwise have lain silent and forgotten. Through sampling and citation, through rap and talkover, through mixing desks and on turntables, multi-ethnic musical traditions have been transformed and adapted on the ground to give a particular *modernist* voice and shape to a specifically black, British structure of feeling, in a place and at a time when the new Right has been implying that blackness and Britishness are, as Paul Gilroy puts it, mutually exclusive categories. In this way, the new syncretic or synthethic black British styles in the 1980s which rely on musical and sartorial cut-ups – mixes of sounds and images plundered from a range of ostensibly unrelated sources – form part of an ongoing process of active self-definition which is now being consciously extended by a new generation of black British independent film and video makers, writers, intellectuals and record producers.

Now young Britons of Asian origin have adopted similar strategies in the various styles associated with bhangra music which merges traditional Punjabi dancestyles and rhythms with Indi-pop, black US and white GB funk, house and disco rhythms. Through the patterns of belonging and distancing established in these forms of cultural production, new forms of 'British' identity become available which circulate along with the records themselves in the clubs and cassette players and on the pirate radio stations. At a time when the integrity of the national culture is asserted against a common European identity, a genuinely cosmopolitan post-colonial space is opened up within and against 'Englishness' – a set of identities available to all irrespective of their skin colour, 'rooted' in the airwaves. The process is by no means confined to black and Bengali subcultures. The 'break-up' of imaginary Britishness can be heard too in the assertion of the Pogues' republicanism, in The Proclaimers' militant celtic style. It's not just the 'United' in the 'United Kingdom' that is being broken down today. The rise of women singers and musicians like Yazz, Sade and Tanita Tikaram simultaneously challenge the monolithic sexism and heterosexism of 1960s and 1970s 'rock' and racist notions of ethnic 'belonging'.

All these contradictory tendencies and possibilities could be described as part of the landscape of new times – a landscape which has yet to solidify, which is still to be made. They represent real challenges which cannot be written off as part of some linear global 'logic' of postmodernism any more than they can be effectively framed within the old language of the Left. New political agendas and priorities are being forged on the ruins of the old and there seems little likelihood that a new set of universal values or objectives will emerge to bind us all together 'beyond the fragments' into one progressive bloc. Meanwhile we shall have to watch for the significant points of tension in the various contradictory versions of 'identity' offered to us rather than falling back into the positions traditionally reserved for the 'radical' Left – the tension for instance between the new consumerism – the shop until you drop ethos – and the limits on consumption imposed by scarcity and ecological crisis, the tension between the competing demands of 'meaningful' consumption and 'responsible' citizenship. We shall have to go on placing ourselves and being placed in relation to a bewildering set of local/national/European/multi-national and international communities, interests and histories. And meanwhile we shall have to go on negotiating between the various fundamentalist demands for fixed identities and final truths and the modernist realisation that identities are never fixed, that truths are never final. But what's clear is that contrary to what Baudrillard says, there is absolutely nothing 'fatal' or 'finished' about new times. The task for the 1990s has to be how to rise to the challenge, how to abjure certain kinds of authority we might have laid claim to in the past, without losing sight of the longer-term objectives, how to articulate a new kind of socialism, how to make socialism, as Raymond Williams might have said, without the masses.

References

L. Appignanesi and G. Benninton (eds), *Postmodernism:* ICA Documents 4, Institute of Contemporary Arts 1986

J. Baudrillard, *For a Critique of the Political Economy of the Sign*, Telos 1981. *The Mirror of Production*, Telos 1979. *In the Shadow of the Silent Majorities*, Semiotext(e) 1984. *Simulations*, Semiotext(e) 1983. *America*, Verso 1988.

M. Poster (ed), *Jean Baudrillard: Selected Writings*, Polity 1988

M. Berman, *All That is Solid Melts Into Air*, Simon and Schuster 1983

H. Foster (ed), *Postmodern Culture*, Pluto 1985

D. Harvey, *The Condition of Postmodernity*, Blackwell 1989

J.F. Lyotard, *The Postmodern Condition; A Report on Knowledge*, Manchester University Press 1984

M. Morris, *The Pirates Fiancée: Feminism Reading Postmodernism*, Verso 1988

R. Williams, *The Long Revolution*, Penguin 1963

John Urry

The End of Organised Capitalism

Much of the debate about the current crisis of the Left has been focused too narrowly on the effects of Thatcherism *per se*. This is not to suggest that the last ten years in Britain have not been profoundly significant but the concentration on Thatcherism ignores three vital questions. First and most obviously, what would have happened in the absence of Thatcher — would policies have been entirely different with a different Conservative leader or with a government led by a different party? Second, what were the economic, social and political conditions that made Thatcherism likely although not necessary? And third, even if Thatcherism has made a major difference to the 1980s will its 'ending' mean that it will be possible to return to the conditions supposedly existing in the late 1970s?

These are all big questions. In this article I shall suggest that they can only be answered by analysing the much broader set of changes that have been taking place within Western Europe and North America, changes from 'organised' to 'disorganised' capitalism. Thatcherism then in the UK is to be seen as in part produced by these very changes, as crucially important in facilitating their further development, and as having ensured that by the 1990s most of the contours by which we have historically understood British society will have been fundamentally redrawn.

Organised Capitalism

I shall begin here by briefly stating what I mean by 'organised capitalism', a term I use to characterise western societies for the first half to two-thirds of this century.

There were a number of interconnected features of such

organisation: increasing dominance of large national economic, social and political institutions over people's lives; increasing average size of workplaces; rising rate of capital concentration; banks, industry and the state working together; residence and plant locations becoming more and more urbanised; collective bargaining taking place more and more on a national scale; the industrial male working class reaching its greatest size; and politics and culture reflecting the confrontation of nationally organised social classes. Politics, as in Britain, was very much structured by divisions of social class. People largely lived in class homogeneous neighbourhoods; people voted significantly in terms of one class or another; other forms of politics took their patterning from divisions of social class, although classes were not simply homogeneous. The considerable powers of the working class and the labour movement in many countries derived from the leading role of particular groups of workers − of mainly male workers living in certain major cities, largely employed in large plants in manufacturing industry and mining. Relations within the workplace structured social conflict and political life. Furthermore, it seemed that these processes would continue to grow in importance − that is, the plants would get bigger and bigger, that western economies would become increasingly monopolistic, that more and more people would live in large cities, that major manufacturing industries would increasingly dominate whole regions, that male-based trade unions would continue to grow in importance and so on.

Clearly not all of these developments were to be found simultaneously or in the same way in all western countries. It is useful to distinguish between organisation 'at the top' and organisation 'at the bottom'. Organisation at the top here includes the concentration of industry, increasing inter-articulation of banks, industry and the state, and cartel formation; organisation at the bottom includes, for example, the development of national trade-union bodies, working-class political parties, and the welfare state.

The following are three of the factors which determine the timing of, and the extent to which, the capitalism in each country becomes organised. The first is the point in history at which it begins to industrialise; the earlier a country enters its 'take-off', the less organised its capitalism will be. This is because countries which are later industrialisers need to begin at higher levels of concentration and centralisation of capital to compete with those which have already been industrialising for some time. Secondly, there is the extent to which pre-capitalist organisations survive into the capitalist period. On this count, Britain and Germany became more highly organised capitalist societies than France and the USA. This is because the former two nations did not experience a 'bourgeois revolution' and as a result, guilds, corporate local government, and merchant, professional, aristocratic, university and church bodies remained relatively more intact. The third factor is size of country. For the industry of small countries to compete internationally, resources were channelled into relatively few firms and sectors. Co-ordination between the state and industry was then greatly facilitated, if not necessitated. At the same time there would tend to be higher union densities, more 'organisation' of labour, where there were relatively few firms and sectors.

Overall, Germany came closest to approximating the ideal type outlined above of organised capitalism, achieving high levels of organisation very early on both at the top and the bottom.

By contrast, central to the British economy have been the absolute size and international scope of the financial sector, the early export of capital goods, the early shift into production of services, and, especially, a sectoral profile in which concentration was focused not in the characteristically organised-capitalist sectors but in consumer industries such as food and drink. It was the absence of horizontal and vertical integration, of diversification and modern managerial structures in the key organised-capitalist sectors which was the decisive feature of Britain's middleman (or *Makler*) economy. At the same time it was organised at the bottom earlier than it organised at the top and earlier than many other societies.

In the USA, to take a third example, the early and thorough organisation of American capitalism at the top was unmatched by such organisation at the bottom, and the American polity in organised capitalism at the end of the 19th century was characterised by the state acting as very much the instrument of the economically dominant class. Subsequently the 'progressivism' of the New Deal helped American capitalism to organise much later at the bottom and lent relative autonomy to the state for a period in the 1930s and 1940s. The notion of 'progressivism', an ideology and a movement associated with the rising service class and related middle classes from the beginning of the 20th century is key to the understanding of American capitalist organisation and disorganisation. In the 20th century some variety of 'progressivism' has always been the main source of opposition to unregulated capitalist accumulation in the USA. 'American exceptionalism' is due not as much to an ethnically divided and weak working class as to the very early presence, size and access to organisation of the American new middle classes, especially the 'service class' which articulated a progressive ideology.

Causes of Disorganisation

It was, I believe, developments of this sort which provided many on the Left with evidence that the powers of the labour movement would continue to increase and that a variety of 'collectivist' and 'statist' initiatives were both desirable and politically feasible. However, in the last couple of decades many of these processes have gone into reverse in the West, and a process of capitalist disorganisation has been set in motion. This is set out at length in *The End of Organised Capitalism* (Polity, Cambridge 1987, written with Scott Lash), where we show this with regard to France, Germany, Sweden and the USA as well as the UK. There are a number of interdependent processes involved here.

1)There has been a 'globalisation' of economic, social and political relationships which have undermined the coherence, wholeness and unity of individual societies. Such developments include the growth of multinational corporations whose annual turnover dwarfs the national income of many individual nation states; the spectacular development of electronically transmitted information which enables geographically distant units to be organisationally unified; the fragile growth of international state organisations which constrain the autonomy of individual nation states; the growth of means of mass communication which can simultaneously link 20 – 30 per cent of the world's population in a shared cultural experience; the possibility of technological disasters that know no national boundaries; and the awesome realisation that human existence itself is dependent upon the relatively unpredictable decisions of the leaders of two superpowers. There has been a 'globalisation' of economic and social relationships and of a greatly heightened awareness of the 'simultaneity' of events and experiences occurring in geographically distant locations.

2) Mass production of standardised products in manufacturing plants employing thousands of male workers will undoubtedly become a thing of the past. What manufacturing workers there are will increasingly produce more specialised products in plants employing considerably fewer workers with higher levels of capital equipment. There have been a number of interrelated changes in Britain: sizeable increases in the number of self-employed people; the growth in the size of the secondary labour force so that one-third of the labour force now consists of part-time, temporary and home workers; a considerable rise in the rate at which new firms have been formed and hence in the number of small firms in both manufacturing and service industry; a very large increase in the proportion of manufacturing employment found in small enterprises; a sizeable decline in the numbers of people employed in the average manufacturing plant, even in very large multi-plant, multinational enterprises; and a tendency for large firms to be broken up into smaller decentralised units, or to develop new forms of devolved ownership such as franchising or new sub-contracting arrangements which enable much more flexible responses to new products and markets. In 1981 Sir Adrian Cadbury described this as follows:

> We will want, in future, to break these organisations down into their separate business units and to give those units freedom to compete in their particular markets. Large companies will become more like federations of small enterprises − not because 'small is beautiful' but because big is expensive and inflexible ... I would expect tomorrow's companies ... to concentrate on the core activities of their business, relying for everything else on specialised suppliers who would compete for their custom.

3) There have been enormous changes in the spatial organisation of production. Companies are now able to operate on a world scale, to move in and out of countries taking advantage of different wage and strike rates, to subdivide their operations in pursuit of a global strategy, to force workers to compete with each other to gain or keep new production. As the *New York Times* put it, firms had to 'automate, emigrate, or

evaporate'. For example, the components that make up the Apple II E microcomputer are produced in a bewildering array of factories, in California and Texas in the USA, in Cork and in Denmark and West Germany in Europe, and in Japan, Taiwan, Singapore and in various other countries in south-east Asia. The 42 chips that are put together in each Apple microcomputer have travelled in total at least a million miles before being combined together. The development of new forms of electronically transmitted information and of jet transport and travel have permitted extraordinary levels of vertical disintegration and spatial relocation. Even within the UK there has been a marked tendency for whatever new industry there is to be located outside the major cities, and for there to be extremely high rates of depopulation from the major conurbations and for the general growth of employment and population to be away from the industrial heartlands of Britain.

4) At the same time that employers appear to be much more mobile and innovative, the workforce seems to be increasingly reactionary – seeking to preserve or even to return to outmoded patterns of industry, technology and values. Employers increasingly appear as progressive, as being on the side of the new, as being not in favour of the *status quo* but in favour of change, of breaking with tradition, and of modernising for the future. Simultaneously, a number of developments have served to bring about a heightened identification of workers in the private sector with their firms. This has in turn encouraged a commitment to the career chances given by the firm's internal labour market, to becoming employee-shareholders, and to collective bargaining at the level of the individual enterprise.

5) Social life, culture and politics are no longer predominantly organised in terms of social class. This is partly because current inequalities of income, wealth and power do not produce homogeneous social classes which share common experiences of class deprivation, or even vote the same way at elections. It is also because a much wider variety of other social groups are now willing and able to organise. Such social movements struggle around issues of gender, the environment, nuclear weapons, urban inequalities, racial discrimination, social amenities, level of rates, and so on. Such groups are generally organised on a relatively decentralised basis – in the case of urban riots no real

organisation at all — and the focus of their hostility is particularly to the 'state' and sometimes to the labour movement itself. Indeed we may well expect increasing amounts of social conflict simply because there are now more bases of opposition in contemporary Britain. In a paradoxical sense fewer and fewer groups have a strong vested interest in the *status quo*. But that in turn means that the labour movement no longer has a monopoly on principled opposition and struggle. Social conflict has become more pluralistic, structured by a much wider variety of interests, and involving very many different enemies, including the state, bureaucracies, male trade unionists, white workers, and so on.

6) And, finally, culture too has changed. Popular music, styles of dress, new developments in film, TV and theatre have been in part structured by a strong opposition to authority and especially to the authority of 'age'. It was a consequence of the political and cultural changes in the 1960s and 1970s that personal identity and individual self-assertion became highly valued goals of human experience in the west. But this emphasis not only challenges authority structures such as the family, the school, the monarchy, the police and courts and so on; it also questions the basis of joining and participating in collective organisations such as trade unions. As Raphael Samuel says, 'Collectivity ... is seen rather as an instrument of coercion, promoting uniformity rather than diversity, intimidating the individual, and subordinating the minority to the unthinking mass'. There has thus grown up a suspicion of the centralised organisation, whether it is a trade union, a professional association, an educational institution, a political party, or a pressure group. This kind of radical individualism has profoundly contradictory effects. It both leads to challenges to authority in many spheres of social life, *and* makes it harder and harder to sustain oppositional collectivities and collective action. This set of developments has been generated by a number of significant processes: the growth of the electronic mass media, the disruption of class homogeneous neighbourhoods, and the development of a relatively unattached middle class. It has been suggested that what results is a relatively depthless world in which people no longer pursue life-time projects or narratives, and seek short-term advantage in a kind of 'calculating hedonism'. People's lives are not therefore viewed as the pursuit of ideals, or as part of a collective project.

They are much more like those immortalised in the writing of Erving Goffman, of whose vision of human life Clifford Geertz has said, 'life is just a bowl of strategies'.

It is fairly clear how these developments feed into support for the Right and its evident hostility to the 'collective' and especially to the 'state'. I would also argue, though, that in recent years a kind of 'disorganised oppositional/socialist' politics has been developing (in part associated with *Marxism Today*). In this it is accepted that the certainties and optimism associated with 'organised capitalism' are evaporating and this is reflected in three key developments. Firstly, there is a reappraisal of the possibilities of using the state to correct inequities and injustices generated within the economy and society. Indeed it is maintained that there is *and* should be a limit to politics and the state, that there are transformed boundaries. Secondly, it is presumed that the 'class struggle' does not contain a dynamic sufficient *in itself* to transform modern societies in a socialist direction. And in particular, it is held that the working class, whatever its powers once were, certainly now does not possess on its own the powers to force through a socialist transformation of modern Britain. And thirdly, it is believed that there is an important realm of 'small-p' politics, of civil society, which is neither purely private nor purely public, and that many disorganising developments in modern societies are feeding into and generating a much more complex, differentiated, and politically contested set of spheres of social life, of culture, leisure, arts and architecture, consumption, environmentalism, feminism, ethnicity, local democracy, and so on. Many of these spheres have become areas of political conflict as civil society and a cultural fragmentation have developed apace. The structures of contemporary capitalism have thus been transformed by three simultaneous processes: of *globalisation* from above, of *decentralisation* from below, and of *disintegration* from within, with the development of a powerful service class which has been particularly instrumental in the generation of a more diverse, pluralistic and politically contested civil society.

In conclusion, then, it was a characteristic of organised capitalism that the basic parameters of politics were set by social class, particularly by the struggle of labour and capital. Although some of the features of such struggle remain, they are now overlain by a variety of alternative bases of organisation, of new social movements, of an instrumental collectivism, of an internationalised classless culture, of an anti-state neo-liberalism, and of the growth of the institutional and cultural resources of a powerful service class, intermediate between capital and labour. The structures of the 'modern' world are being transformed, and although the social relations between labour and capital structure those developments internationally (where capital is being consistently reorganised), the patterns of social life and social struggle within different advanced *nation* states are becoming decidedly disorganised. Furthermore, it is part of the disorganising of western capitalism that relatively 'classless' cultural forms, of civil society, have become of greater importance in the structuring of contemporary social life. Contemporary culture permits an extraordinarily heightened availability of social situations, events, myths and images which cohere around and 'construct' diverse 'subjects', not merely the class-subject beloved by socialists, or the market-generated subject favoured by neo-liberals. With the sea change in modern society, with the fact that large organisations, workplaces and cities are no longer getting more and more powerful for each individual, the processes of forming, fixing and reproducing 'subjects' are increasingly 'cultural' or 'small-p' political; these processes are formed in diverse ways out of a myriad of myths and images, of consumer products, of available 'lifestyles', of a diverse civil society; they are not at all based on where one lives or who one knows, that is, on those who are immediately present in one's *class* milieu. Thus, to paraphrase the famous phrase from the *Manifesto of the Communist Party*, the fast-frozen relations of organised capitalism which were structured around class, city, region, nation, the party, and even the word − are melting into air.

Göran Therborn

The Two-Thirds, One-Third Society

The 1970s witnessed a new experience in the economic behaviour of advanced capitalism, the simultaneous occurrence of stagnation and rising unemployment, on the one hand, and accelerating inflation on the other. The international vocabulary was enriched by a new word to describe the process. 'Stagflation' broke out of the basic correlations of economic variables, which (most) economic theory had assumed to hold. Thereby, stagflation provided the starting-point for the anti-Keynesian onslaught, singling out inflation as the key target of policy. From a successful control of inflation, growth and employment would follow.

The first spectacular political conversion to this view was that of the British Labour Prime Minister James Callaghan. In a speech to the Labour Party Conference in 1976, Calllaghan told his rather sceptical audience:

> The (Labour) manifesto was right when it said that the first priority of the Labour government must be a determined attack on inflation.[1]

That declaration, and to some extent also a more blunt one by Callaghan's immediate predecessor as Labour leader and premier, Harold Wilson, 'inflation is the father and mother of unemployment', was enthusiastically taken up as a battle cry by the Thatcherites.[2]

By the end of the 1980s, we can see the results of the turn of policy and of economic doctrine, inaugurated in Britain about ten to fifteen years ago and later pursued with much more consistency and ruthlessness than the luckless figures Callaghan and Carter could ever muster. The outcome calls for a new concept, capable of conveying the association of economic growth and unemployment, characteristic of our times. In spite of its jarring sound, but thereby also expressing a terrible experience, the term '*grunemployment*' will be proposed here. Growth and recovery has got linked up with permanent and even rising mass unemployment. Inflation, however, Messrs Callaghan and Wilson notwithstanding, has gone down strongly. The world of the 1970s has disappeared, and its doctors seem to be caught redhanded in inflicting new, and worsening wounds on their patient.

Inflation exhibits a declining trend since 1975, a trend asserting itself as overriding cyclical ups and downs. The mid-1970s turn of political economy has really borne fruit. But overall economic growth is following a downward trend, lower at each subsequent cyclical peak and lower in the second trough than in the first. Unemployment, finally, is rising, over and above cyclical variations. Indeed, unemployment in the business cycle peak of 1984 was higher than in the deep trough of 1982. Recovery of the total economy has ceased to mean a general lowering of unemployment. The paradox of the 1970s was that increasing unemployment went hand in hand with rising inflation. The paradox of the 1980s is that overall economic recovery is accompanied by an average increase of unemployment.

The Callaghan-Wilson thesis has been proved wrong. The bringing down of inflation has not meant a reduction of unemployment, on the contrary. This does not imply, however, a revindication of simple, consumer demand-boosting Keynesianism. The stagflation of the 1970s remains a historical fact, and below we will see that the trade-off between inflation and unemployment is hardly the key to current crisis. Nor are we confronting a new stage of advanced capitalism, to be generally characterised by growth-cum-mass unemployment. More straighforwardly, we are not living through a rapid technological revolution, which inexorably is creating mass unemployment. Instead, what is now becoming clear, is that the same worldwide crisis is having *divergent* effects, above all with regard to unemployment.

There Are Alternatives

The onset of the present crisis led to greater variations of growth and inflation, but since the mid-1970s countries have become more similar with regard to both growth and inflation.

Unemployment, however, was continuously increasingly differentially distributed up until the mid-1980s and still makes a gap between countries. Some peoples are becoming much more unemployed than others.

The enormous and increasing spread of internationally standardised rates of unemployment demonstrates that the current crisis is not an unaffectable fate, and that mass unemployment is not an intrinsic feature of today's developed capitalism. Nor is there a uniform development of employment. Since 1973 employment has grown more than unemployment, in the New World of North America and Oceania, in the Nordic countries of Finland, Norway and Sweden, in Japan, and in Italy. By contrast Spain has had a drastic decline of employment, and very significant decreases of employment with increases of unemployment have occurred in Belgium, Britain, Germany and Ireland.[3] Looking at unemployment only, we may summarise the crisis trajectory and the current situation of the richest OECD countries in table 1.

Table 1. Unemployment Record since 1973 and Current Situation, Standardised Rate of Unemployment in 1988.

Persistent low unemployment (always well below 5%)

Austria	3.5
Japan	2.5
Norway	3.2
Sweden	1.6
Switzerland	0.7

High unemployment (but never above 10%)

Australia	7.2
Finland	4.5
West Germany	6.2
USA	5.4

Very high unemployment (above 10% for shorter or longer periods)

Belgium	10.2
Canada	7.7
Denmark	8.6
France	10.1
Italy	11.8
Netherlands	9.5
UK	8.3

Source: OECD Economic outlook 45, 1989, pp. 188–9.

The 1970s shattered the complacency of simple-minded Keynesianism or, perhaps more aptly put, of naive underconsumptionist crisis theories and policies, repeated with some delay in Mitterandist France in the early 1980s. The 1980s have disproved the Callaghan-Wilson thesis − while inflation has gone down, unemployment has risen. Current history has also disproved the Thatcher thesis: there are actually existing alternatives to deflation and mass unemployment. The successful alternatives − Austria, Japan, Norway, Sweden and Switzerland − have sustained themselves throughout the first decade of the crisis. Their distance from the failures is growing.

Historical Commitments

Analysing the post-World War II history of our sixteen countries, we find that in five of them full employment had been firmly institutionalised in the political and economic system before the onslaught of the current crisis. These were Austria, Japan, Norway, Sweden and Switzerland, in other words the low unemployment countries in the present-day crisis, and nowhere else to the same extent (Finland coming closest thereafter). *Notwithstanding other factors, the existence or not of an institutionalised commitment to full employment is the basic explanation for the differential impact of the current crisis.*

Full employment was institutionalised for two major, quite different reasons. One was an assertion of working-class interests. It owed its success to a politically dominant labour movement, acting against the background of its experiences of the depression of the 1930s, not only of mass unemployment but also of its own capacity to alleviate the latter from government office. That much might be expected from a marxist or Kaleckian[4] perspective. But it fits only Sweden and, with some qualification, Norway, whose labour movements were not only dominant right after World War II but also the only labour movements which emerged both strengthened out of the 1930s − largely because of their anti-unemployment successes, however modest in retrospect − and unscathed by the war.

The second reason for the institutionalisation of full employment is more unexpected. It was a conservative concern with order and stability as of equal importance to capital accumulation. Full employment in Japan and Switzerland has this background. We should be somewhat more precise here. Recent functionalist marxism has not been blind to bourgeois concerns with order and stability, indeed the latter has rather been invoked too easily. The point here is that the postwar Japanese and Swiss bourgeoisies were not at all under any threat from labour (a passing Japanese interlude in 1947 notwithstanding), which was weak, divided, and largely docile. On the other hand, it cannot be concluded in reverse, that because the labour movement was so weak or so subdued, the Japanese and the Swiss bourgeoisies did not have to bother about maintaining an 'industrial reserve army'. Firstly, because the much weaker American labour movement did not lead to any disappearance of high unemployment nor has the most docile of all labour movements, the Dutch, been rewarded by any stable high unemployment. Secondly, the Japanese and the Swiss bourgeois class did not simply stop bothering about maintaining an industrial reserve army: they become committed to an active maintenance of full employment, even at high cost, as became evident particularly in Switzerland in the 1970s.

Austria falls somewhere in between these two poles, and her full employment institutionalisation has a different historical foundation. In policy terms, full institutionalisation came much later, only in the late 1960s, early 1970s, while in the other countries it dates back to the 1940s and early 1950s (Japan).

The postwar institutionalisation of full employment was reproduced and continuously strengthened through its successful re-affirmation. Here the old saying 'nothing breeds success like success' is apt. The primary commitment to achieving and maintaining full employment in the five countries above was neither challenged by other concerns nor by failing performance prior to the major test of the post-1973 crisis. In Britain, by contrast, an institutionalisation of full employment, though never clearly formulated either by Beveridge or by Keynes or by the 1945 Labour government, was underway in the late 1940s and in the 1950s, due both to actual labour market outcomes and to the absorption of Keynesian macro-economics. But clinging to the imperial legacy of the international standing of the pound sterling and the City began to erode this, before becoming solidified, from the late 1950s onwards. By the 1966 – 1970 Labour government under Harold Wilson, full employment was deliberately sacrificed in ultimately vain attempts at rescuing Britain's big financial power status.

Historical economic politics is the main explanation of the historical divide after 1973 between low and high unemployment countries, a divide which unless met by radical reversals of power and policies is most likely to set the stage for the 1990s.

The Policies of Success

With regard to policies, the successful employment countries have all pursued expansive Keynesian-type policies. The important contribution of the latter to Japanese full employment is particularly striking, much more important than the star performance of the Japanese exporters. But Keynesianism is not enough. Firstly successful Keynesianism has to be accompanied by consistent, congenial monetary policy, in particular of low real interest rates. Secondly, in all the low unemployment countries, expansive fiscal and monetary policies have been crucially supplemented by nationally specific direct interventions in the market economy.

In the Swedish case, such direct interventions have mainly taken the form of 'active labour market policy measures', of special public works and public vocational (re)training programmes, at their peak, in 1978 – 79, reducing unemployment by about 4.0 per cent. The extensive vocational training programmes have been rather effective in preparing for jobs on the open market. In 1983, for example, 62 per cent of those who had taken such programmes were employed on the open market six months later. A record effectiveness was reached in 1984, with 70 per cent of the trainees employed after six months.[5] Wages on public works are normally according to going trade-union rates.

The Norwegians have primarily resorted to massive public subsidies of private employment, a tradition built up even before the coming of North Sea oil and gas revenue. In the late 1970s, this was also a measure amply used in Sweden. Soon after the war Norway, moreover, set up a sophisticated apparatus of macro-economic planning geared to the maintenance of full employment. After Sweden, Norway was also a pioneer in establishing a unified administration for labour policies, the Labour Directorate, but training and public works programmes in Norway since the 1960s have had nothing like the same extensiveness of Sweden.

The Japanese have relied on expanding public investment, which provides a much higher proportion of total investment than in most capitalist countries, and on a publicly co-ordinated private labour market policy, organised by the big concerns. Behind the sustained growth and export record of Japan in the crisis lies a massive restructuring of Japanese industry, first from textiles, then from shipbuilding and steel, into car-making, electrical engineering, electronics and services. This has largely taken place without first making people unemployed, typically through intra-concern mobility. Big industrial concerns also opened up service sector activities in order to keep up employment. Maintaining employment of the big concerns has not been bought at the cost of unemployment among the subcontractors and other sectors of small business.

Austro-Keynesianism, as the Austrians proudly call their policy pattern, has mainly focused on keeping up investment, directly by the large slice of public and public enterprise investment, somewhat more indirectly by cheap credit for private investment, channelled through a public banking system and specific investment inducements via taxation changes. The often heard claim, from protagonists as well as from detractors of the Austrian model, about labour hoarding in public industry is not sustained by comparative evidence with respect to the ratio between the development of production and employment in manufacturing. Little heard of but very important, on the other hand, has been a very restrictive immigration policy, significantly reducing the number of foreign workers during the crisis. Immigrant workers in Austria have fewer labour market rights than in almost any other advanced capitalist country, besides Switzerland. A tight incomes policy, the necessity of which has been reinforced by a chosen 'hard currency option', of tying the Austrian schilling to the German mark, has also characterised the Austrian model.

Switzerland met the crisis by a massive repatriation of foreign workers, and by an official policy, propagated by the employers' organisations, of laying off women and of discouraging women from entering the labour market. These harsh policies should not, however, be interpreted as simply a passing on of the costs of full employment for Swiss males to women and Italian immigrants. The Swiss economy had a unique OECD record of zero growth for the period of 1975–1983. The latter has probably also a great deal to do with – among the low unemployment countries – the singularly weak dose of Keynesian-type expansion policies and with the fact that Switzerland is the only low unemployment country which has pursued a monetarist policy, in the technical sense of setting policy targets for the money supply.

The Policy of Failure

Broadly speaking, two policy orientations conducive to high or mass unemployment can be distinguished in the high unemployment countries. One is the consistent 'cut down the public sector, strengthen the market economy' approach. That has been the shortest and fastest route to mass unemployment. The best examples, both of cause and of effect, are Thatcherite Britain and the Netherlands under the right-wing Christian Democrats Van Agt and Lubbers. Belgium since 1981 and in the first years of the crisis has had a rather similar policy orientation.

Secondly, another group of countries has been characterised more by inconsistent and discontinous policies. Though less fast than the previous one, this orientation has also proved a sure road to high unemployment. France under Mitterrand, for example, moved from expansionary policies in its early phase to a restrictionist approach subsequently. While West Germany and Denmark, which also belong to this group, have combined more or less expansionary fiscal policies with tight monetary policies and high interest rates.

Brazilianisation...

Mass unemployment is not a fatality, a necessary effect of 'anonymous evil forces' of contemporary capitalism. It is an inherent potentiality of capitalism. But without the willing or unconscious support or strategic acceptance of right-wing politicians and economic advisers and of faint-hearted or weak-willed social democrats and, sometimes, of starry-eyed trade unionists credulously buying the liberal arguments, high unemployment could have been staved off. And it has been prevented in five of sixteen countries under review.

For the ten countries in which high unemployment is becoming permanent — Finland seems not yet stably set on the course to permanent unemployment — we can indicate two possible future perspectives.

The first one we may call the *Brazilianisation of advanced capitalism*. The basis of this scenario is our historical explanation of current variations in rates of unemployment. Only those countries in which a commitment to full employment had been historically deeply rooted could muster the force to withstand the onslaught of the crisis. Others failed, even if they wanted to resist like, initially, the Dutch Social Democrats in the 1970s or the French Social Democrats in the early 1980s. The failures of the progressive forces in the high unemployment countries have demoralised them and encouraged the Right which, outside Japan and Switzerland, does not care about unemployment, even if it does not actually want it.

Against this background, mass unemployment is likely to become a permanent feature of most advanced capitalist countries, somewhat reduced in years of boom, higher in years of recession, probably with a rising trend. This would produce a society like a richer and somewhat more humane Brazil, with increasing trichotomous socio-economic divisions. At the bottom, the permanently unemployed and the marginally employed, with certain welfare entitlements, almost certain to be reduced over time. Some of these will make a living in the black economy. In a country like the Netherlands, where social assistance and unemployment benefits are still relatively generous, some will initially adapt to a position of supported marginality, a few perhaps drawing some comfort from ideologues (themselves well furnished with employment or writers' fees, or both), that the unemployed are pioneers of a happy exodus from the 'work society'. After a period, however, benefits will be reduced, social controls will be tightened, marginality will become debilitating. Desperation and outcast passivity will both grow, breeding riots, repression, and contempt.

In the middle there will be the stably employed, or with a stable likelihood of re-employment, probably increasingly divided according to enterprise, sector, and hierarchical rung, making a fairly decent living, no more, but being able to congratulate themselves at the widening distance to the unemployed.

The marginalisation of a significant part of the previous and the potential working class has already gone hand in hand, in the 1980s, with the increasing wealth and incomes of capitalists and top business managers. They constitute the third layer of mass unemployment societies. Their distance to the plain folks of employment has already widened in Britain, USA, Netherlands and Belgium. Politically, this ruling class will appeal to the bulk of employees as the guarantors of the latter not falling into the abyss of unemployment.

If the Brazilianising tendencies should stabilise, the only way out to at least a minimally egalitarian division of participation in the economic life and of extra-labour market activities in Western societies would be a social cataclysm similar in range and depth, if not in form, to the solution to the mass unemployment problem of the previous major crisis of capitalism, that of the 1930s. Then there were two effective solutions, the prewar mobilisation of Nazi Germany, and the wartime mobilisation of the other countries.

...or a Labour Comeback

There is also another scenario, which too may be derived from our analysis. The baseline, then, would not be pre-crisis history, but crisis policies in the low unemployment countries. There are actual policies and experiences, which may be learnt from and adapted to different national contexts. There is also an important force, which may be put behind such an effort. In the very early 1980s, the labour movement and other progressive forces in the West were, on the whole, on a historical high plateau of strength and influence.[6] A failure to maintain full employment has significantly weakened the labour movement in many countries since then. But there is a renewed combativity in the post-Wilson-Callaghan Labour Party, and more recently somewhat more unity and perspective, and a fairly impressive new vigour and vision in the post-Schmidt SPD, a returning vitality to Belgian Social Democracy, and the Italian Communist Party remains against all odds intact as the rallying-force of progressive opinion in Italy.

New forces have also come out against the rich man's Brazil

option, most interestingly, many churches and church leaders. Furthermore, not all fractions of capital benefit from mass unemployment. Thus Thatcher has been presented with a series of employment-promoting public investment proposals from the CBI, The Institution of Civil Engineers, and the building-materials producers, the building employers and civil engineering contractors.[7] The Japanese and the Swiss examples may also convince a few enlightened bourgeois that you need not necessarily be a communist or a left-wing socialist to take full employment seriously.

There is then, some reason to envisage a *labour comeback* scenario. What lessons could such a labour comeback draw from the successful and from the failed crisis policies so far?

First of all, national roads to full employment are possible, and given the fragile and mainly rhetorical internationalism of labour parties in office the ones most likely to succeed, although post-1992 the EC will call for a European employment dimension[8]. Secondly, institutional changes are necessary in order to make policies consistent. In particular, this means that progressive control of national bank policies is required and a European monetary union is to be resisted, as long as there is not full employment in all member countries. Reflation has to be geared to investment, direct public investment and incentives to private investment, before boosting consumer demand. Thirdly, active labour market policy measures, of vocational retraining, public works, and special employment in public services, have to be introduced on a massive scale. Productive capital has to be favoured over financial capital and payments of dividends. The supply of part-time jobs, with full social rights and in co-operation with the trade unions, should be massively increased, and in the short run favoured above the much more difficult and risky way of general working-time reduction. Tax structures should shift from payroll taxes and social contributions to taxes on capital assets and/or value added. The labour movement should commit itself to technological change and job flexibility, under conditions of full employment and of non-pollution of the environment, and to nominal wage moderation, under condition of real wages growth.

Those are policy measures, not a programme for political mobilisation. This is not the place, and a single scholar, however politically committed, is not the force to do that. However, a few remarks may be added by a political scientist. In order to become credible, the progressive parties which have a government record of failure to maintain full employment will have to make an open, public self-criticism, pointing out why they went wrong in the past, and elaborating what lessons they have drawn from this. Secondly, the goal of full employment has to be envisaged and designed as a goal of participation, participation in the making of society and of individual opportunities. Thirdly, full employment commitment has to be explicitly related to women's emancipation and geared to providing meaningful, independent, and remunerated jobs for women. While there seems to be little reason to believe the puritannical, near-exhaustion-of-the-resources-of-the-earth austerity prophets, a commitment to full employment and technological development should make clear as an absolute precondition of advance, that pollution of the environment should not increase, but be reduced. Finally, under the conditions above, all ideologies peddled which attack the goal of full employment should be relegated to where they belong, explicitly or by implication, in the arsenal of the Brazilian ruling class, which all progressive people in Brazil are fighting, but which tends to spread to the mainlands of advanced capitalism.

The labour comeback scenario outlined above is not a socialist one, and my socialist comrades may ask where socialism comes into all this, if at all. Being a socialist, and not just a professor of sociology, I do consider that question as legitimate and pertinent. But socialism, seen with the eyes of a realistic historical materialism, is not likely to be a one-blow achievement of the day after tomorrow, but a complex and contradictory epochal transformation, which has already begun and which, if ever, will take a long time to be brought about. And, as long as a large part of the (potential) working class is unemployed and marginalised, no further advances are likely.

Notes

[1] *Report of the 75th Annual Conference of the Labour Party 1976,* p 89
[2] Callaghan and Wilson were both cited as witnesses for the prosecution by the key ideologue of what later acquired the name of Thatcherism, Sir Keith Joseph, in his very important and influential

pamphlet, *Conditions for Fuller Employment,* Centre for Policy Studies 1978, p 3.

[3] OECD, *Labour Force Statistics 1965 – 85*, Paris 1987, tables 4.0 and 5.1, OECD, *Economic Outlook No. 45*, 1989, pp 122, 124.

[4] Cf, M. Kalecki, 'Political aspects of Full Employment', *Political Quarterly* no. 1943.

[5] Evaluation by the Swedish Central Bureau of Statistics for the Labour Market Board, reported in *Svenska Dagbladet,* 16 April 1985, part 3, p 1.

[6] See my 'The Prospects of Labour and the Transformation of Advanced Capitalism', *New Left Review* no. 145, May – June 1984.

[7] *The Economist,* 5 January 1985, p 15.

[8] The international, ambitious and very interesting Out of Crisis project launched and coordinated by Stuart Holland in fact came to nothing. For the plan, see S. Holland (ed), *Out of Crisis*, 1982.

Stuart Hall

The Meaning of New Times

How new are these 'new times'? Are they the dawn of a New Age or only the whisper of an old one? What is 'new' about them? How do we assess their contradictory tendencies – are they progressive or regressive? These are some of the questions which the ambiguous discourse of 'new times' poses. They are worth asking, not because 'new times' represents a definitive set of answers to them or even a clear way of resolving the ambiguities inherent in the idea, but because they stimulate the Left to open a debate about how society is changing and to offer new descriptions and analyses of the social conditions it seeks to transcend and transform. If it succeeds in this, but accomplishes nothing else the metaphor of 'new times' will have done its work.

As the questions suggest, there is considerable ambiguity as to what the phrase 'new times' really means. It seems to be connected with the ascendancy of the New Right in Britain, the USA and some parts of Europe over the past decade. But what precisely is the connection? For example, are 'new times' a product of 'the Thatcher Revolution'? Was Thatcherism really so decisive and fundamental? And, if so, does that mean that the Left has no alternative but to adapt to the changed terrain and agenda of politics, post-Thatcherism, if it is to survive? This is a very negative interpretation of 'new times': and it is easy to see why those who read 'new times' in this way regard the whole thing as a smokescreen for some seismic shift of gravity by the Left towards the Right.

There is, however, a different reading. This suggests that Thatcherism itself was, in part, produced by 'new times'. On this interpretation, 'new times' refers to social, economic, political and cultural changes of a deeper kind now taking place in western capitalist societies. These changes, it is suggested, form the necessary shaping context, the material and cultural conditions of existence, for *any* political strategy, whether of the Right or the Left. From this position, Thatcherism represents, in fact, in its own way, an attempt (only partially successful) to harness and bend to its political project circumstances which were not of its making, which have a much longer history and trajectory, and which do not necessarily have a 'New Right' political agenda inscribed in them. Much turns on which version of 'new times' one subscribes to.

If we take the 'new times' idea apart, we find that it is an attempt to capture, within the confines of a single metaphor, a number of different facets of social change, none of which has any necessary connection with the other. In the current debates, a variety of different terms jostle with one another for pride of place, in the attempt to describe these different dimensions of change. They include 'post-industrial', 'post-Fordist', 'revolution of the subject', 'postmodernism'. None of these is wholly satisfactory. Each expresses a clearer sense of what we are leaving behind ('post' everything?) than of where we are heading. Each, however, signifies something important about the 'new times' debate.

'Post-industrial' writers, like Alain Touraine and André Gorz, start from shifts in the technical organisation of industrial capitalist production, with its 'classic' economies of scale, integrated labour processes, advanced division of labour and industrial class conflicts. They foresee an increasing shift to new productive regimes – with inevitable consequences for social structure and politics. Thus Touraine has written of the replacement of older forms of class struggle by the new social movements; and Gorz's most provocative title is *Farewell To The Working Class*. In these forms, 'new times' touches debates which have already seriously divided the Left. There is certainly an important point about the shifting social and technical landscapes of modern industrial production regimes being made in some of these arguments, though they are open to the criticism that they fall for a sort of technological determinism.

'Post-Fordism' is a broader term, suggesting a whole new epoch distinct from the era of mass production, with its standardised products, concentrations of capital and its 'Taylorist' forms of work organisation and discipline. The debate still rages as to whether 'post-Fordism' actually exists, and if it does, what exactly it is and how extensive it is, either within any single economy or across the advanced industrial economies of the West as a whole. Nevertheless, most commentators would agree that the term covers at least some of the following characteristics of change. A shift is taking place to new 'information technologies' from the chemical and electronic-based technologies which drove the 'second' industrial revolution from the turn of the century onwards − the one which signalled the advance of the American, German and Japanese economies to a leading position, and the relative 'backwardness' and incipient decline of the British economy. Secondly, there is a shift towards a more flexible specialised and decentralised form of labour process and work organisation, and, as a consequence, a decline of the old manufacturing base (and the regions and cultures associated with it) and the growth of the 'sunrise', computer-based, hi-tech industries and their regions. Thirdly, there is the hiving-off or a contracting-out of functions and services hitherto provided 'in house' on a corporate basis. Fourthly, there is a leading role for consumption, reflected in such things as greater emphasis on choice and product differentiation, on marketing, packaging and design, on the 'targeting' of consumers by lifestyle, taste and culture rather than by the Registrar General's categories of social class.

Fifthly, there has been a decline in the proportion of the skilled, male, manual working class and the corresponding rise of the service and white collar classes. In the domain of paid work itself, there is more flexi-time and part-time working, coupled with the 'feminisation' and 'ethnicisation' of the workforce. Seventhly, there is an economy dominated by the multinationals, with their new international division of labour and their greater autonomy of nation state control. Eighthly, there is the 'globalisation' of the new financial markets. Finally, there is the emergence of new patterns of social divisions − especially those between 'public' and 'private' sectors and between the two-thirds who have rising expectations and the 'new poor' and underclasses of the one-third that is left behind on every significant dimension of social opportunity.

It is clear that 'post-Fordism', though having a significant reference to questions of economic organisation and structure, has a much broader social and cultural significance. Thus, for example, it also signals greater social fragmentation and pluralism, the weakening of older collective solidarities and block identities and the emergence of new identities as well as the maximisation of individual choices through personal consumption, as equally significant dimensions of the shift towards 'post-Fordism'.

Some critics have suggested that 'post-Fordism' as a concept marks a return to the old, discredited base-superstructure or economic-determinist model according to which the economy determines everything and all other aspects can be 'read off' as simply reflecting that 'base'. However, the metaphor of 'post-Fordism' does not necessarily carry any such implication. Indeed, it is modelled on Gramsci's earlier use of the term, 'Fordism', at the turn of the century to connote a whole shift in capitalist civilization (which Gramsci certainly did not reduce to a mere phenomenon of the economic base). 'Post-Fordism' should also be read in a much broader way. Indeed, it could just as easily be taken in the opposite way – as signalling the *constitutive* role which social and cultural relations play in relation to any economic system. Post-Fordism as I understand it is not committed to any prior determining position for the economy. But it does insist – as all but the most extreme discourse theorists and culturalists must recognise – that shifts of this order in economic life must be taken seriously in any analysis of our present circumstances.

A recent writer on the subject of contemporary cultural change, Marshall Berman, notes that 'modern environments and experiences cut across all boundaries of geography and ethnicity, of class and nationality, of religion and ideology' – not destroying them entirely, but weakening and subverting them, eroding the lines of continuity which hitherto stabilised our social identities.

The Return of the Subject

One boundary which 'new times' has certainly displaced is that between the 'objective' and subjective dimensions of change. This is the so-called 'revolution of the subject' aspect. The individual subject has become more important, as collective social subjects – like that of class or nation or ethnic group – become more segmented and 'pluralised'. As social theorists have become more concerned with how ideologies actually function, and how political mobilisation really takes place in complex societies, so they have been obliged to take the *'subject'* of these processes more seriously. As Gramsci remarked about ideologies, 'To the extent that ideologies are historically necessary they have a validity which is "psychological"' (*Prison Notebooks* p377). At the same time, our models of 'the subject' have altered. We can no longer conceive of 'the individual' in terms of a whole, centred, stable and completed Ego or autonomous, rational 'self'. The 'self' is conceptualised as more fragmented and incomplete, composed of multiple 'selves' or identities in relation to the different social worlds we inhabit, something with a history, 'produced', in process. The 'subject' is differently placed or *positioned* by different discourses and practices.

This is novel conceptual or theoretical terrain. But these vicissitudes of 'the subject' also have their own histories which are key episodes in the passage to 'new times'. They include the cultural revolution of the 1960s; '1968' itself, with its strong sense of politics as 'theatre' and its talk of 'will' and 'consciousness'; feminism, with its insistence that 'the personal is political'; the renewed interest in psychoanalysis, with its rediscovery of the unconscious roots of subjectivity; the theoretical revolutions of the 1960s and 1970s – semiotics, structuralism, 'post-structuralism' – with their concern for language, discourse and representation.

This 'return of the subjective' aspect suggests that we cannot settle for a language in which to describe 'new times' which respects the old distinction between the objective and subjective dimensions of change. 'New times' are both 'out there', changing our conditions of life, and 'in here', working on us. In part, it is *us* who are being 're-made'. But such a conceptual shift presents particular problems for the Left. The conventional culture and discourses of the Left, with its stress on 'objective contradictions', 'impersonal structures' and processes that work 'behind men's (*sic*) backs', have disabled us from confronting the subjective dimension in politics in any very coherent way.

In part, the difficulty lies in the very words and concepts we use. For a long time, being a socialist was synonymous with the ability to translate everything into the language of 'structures'. But it is not only a question of language. In part, the difficulty lies in the fact that men so often provide the categories within which *everybody* experiences things, even on the Left. Men have always found the spectacle of the 'return' of the subjective dimension deeply unnerving. The problem is also theoretical. Classical marxism depended on an assumed correspondence between 'the economic' and 'the political': one could read off political attitudes and objective social interests and motivations from economic class position. For a long time, these correspondences held the theoretical analyses and perspectives of the Left in place. However, any simple correspondence between 'the political' and 'the economic' is exactly what has now disintegrated – practically and theoretically. This has had the effect of throwing the language of politics more over to the cultural side of the equation.

'Postmodernism' is the preferred term which signals this more *cultural* character of 'new times'. 'Modernism', it argues, which dominated the art and architecture, the cultural imagination, of the early decades of the 20th century, and came to represent the look and experience of 'modernity' itself, is at an end. It has declined into the International Style characteristics of the freeway, the wall-of-glass skyscraper and international airports. Modernism's revolutionary impulse – which could be seen in surrealism, Dada, constructivism, the move to an abstract and non-figurative visual culture – has been tamed and contained by the museum. It has become the preserve of an avant-garde élite, betraying its revolutionary and 'populist' impulses.

'Postmodernism', by contrast, celebrates the penetration of aesthetics into everyday life and the ascendancy of popular culture over the High Arts. Theorists like Fredric Jameson and Jean-François Lyotard agree on many of the characteristics of 'the postmodern condition'. They remark on the dominance of image, appearance, surface-effect over depth (was Ronald Reagan a president or just a B-movie actor, real or cardboard cut-out, alive or Spitting Image?). They point to the blurring of image and reality in our media-saturated world (is the Contra war real or only happening on TV?). They note the preference for parody, nostalgia, kitsch and pastiche – the continual re-working and quotation of past styles – over more positive modes of artistic representation, like realism or naturalism. They note, also, a preference for the popular and the decorative over the brutalist or the functional in architecture and design. 'Postmodernism' also has a more philosophical aspect. Lyotard, Baudrillard and Derrida cite the erasure of a strong sense of history, the slippage of hitherto stable meanings, the proliferation of difference, and the end of what Lyotard calls the 'grand narratives' of progress, development, Enlightenment, Rationality, and Truth which, until recently, were the foundations of Western philosophy and politics.

Jameson, however, argues very persuasively that postmodernism is also 'the new cultural logic of capital' — 'the purest form of capital yet to have emerged, a prodigious expansion into hitherto uncommodified areas' (Jameson p78). His formulations remind us that the changing cultural dynamic we are trying to characterise is clearly connected with the revolutionary energy of modern capital — capital *after* what we used to call its 'highest stages' (Imperialism, Organised or Corporate capitalism), even *later* than 'late capitalism'.

'Post-industrialism', 'post-Fordism', 'Postmodernism' are all different ways of trying to characterise or explain this dramatic, even brutal, resumption of the link between modernity and capitalism. Some theorists argue that, though Marx may have been wrong in his predictions about class as the motor of revolution, he was right — with a vengeance — about capital. Its 'global' expansion continues, with renewed energy in the 1980s, to transform everything in its wake, subordinating every society and social relationship to the law of commodification and exchange value. Others argue that, with the failures of the stalinist and social-democratic alternatives, and the transformations and upheavals now taking place throughout the communist world, capital has acquired a new lease of life.

Some economists argue that we are simply in the early, up-beat half of the new Kondratiev 'long wave' of capitalist expansion (after which the inevitable downturn or recession will follow). The American social critic whom we quoted earlier, Marshall Berman, relates 'new times' to 'the ever-expanding drastically fluctuating capitalist world markets' (Berman p16). Others, with their eye more firmly fixed on the limits and uneven development of capital on a global scale, emphasise more the ceaseless rhythm of the international division of labour, redistributing poverty and wealth, dependency and over-development in new ways across the face of the earth. One casualty of this process is the old idea of some homogeneous 'Third World'. Nowadays, Formosa and Taiwan are integrated into the advanced capitalist economies, as Hong Kong is with the new financial markets. Ethiopia or the Sudan or Bangladesh, on the other hand, belong to a different 'world' altogether. It is the new forms and dynamic of capital as a global force which is marking out these new divisions across the globe.

However, it seems to be the case that, whichever explanation we finally settle for, the really startling fact is that *these* new times clearly belong to a time-zone marked by the march of capital simultaneously across the globe and through the Maginot Lines of our subjectivities.

The title of Berman's book *All That is Solid Melts Into Air* − a quotation from *The Communist Manifesto* − reminds us that Marx was one of the earliest people to grasp the revolutionary connection between capitalism and modernity. In the *Manifesto*, he spoke of the 'constant revolutionising of production, uninterrupted disturbance of all social relations, everlasting uncertainty and agitation' which distinguished 'the bourgeois epoch from all earlier times'. 'All fixed, fast-frozen relationships, with their train of venerable ideas and opinions, are swept away, all new-formed ones become obsolete before they can ossify. All That is Solid Melts Into Air".

Indeed, as Berman points out, Marx considered the revolution of modern industry and production the necessary precondition for that Promethean or Romantic conception of the social individual which towers over his early writings, with its prospect of the many-sided development of human capacities. In this context, it was not the commodities which the bourgeoisie created which impressed Marx, so much as 'the processes, the powers, the expressions of human life and energy; men (*sic*) working, moving, cultivating, communicating, organising and reorganising nature and themselves.' (Berman p93). Of course, Marx also understood the one-sided and distorted character of the modernity and type of modern individual produced by this development − how the forms of bourgeois appropriation destroyed the human possibilities it created. But he did not, on this count, refuse it. What he argued was that *only socialism* could complete the revolution of modernity which capitalism had initiated. As Berman puts it, he hoped 'to heal the wounds of modernity through a fuller and deeper modernity'.

Now here exactly is the rub about 'new times' for the Left. The 'promise' of modernity has become, at the end of the 20th century, considerably more ambiguous, its links with socialism and the Left much more tenuous. We have become more aware of the double-edged and problematic character of modernity: what Theodore Adorno called the 'negative dialectic' of enlightenment. Of course, to be 'modern' has *always* meant 'to live a life of paradox and contradiction ... alive to new possibilities for experience and adventure, frightened by the nihilistic depths to which so many modern adventures lead (eg, the line from Nietzsche and Wagner to the death camps), longing to create and hold onto something real even as everything melts'.

Some theorists argue – the German philosopher, Jurgen Habermas is one – that this is too pessimistic a reading of 'Enlightenment' and that the project of modernity is not yet completed. But it is difficult to deny that, at the end of the 20th century, the paradoxes of modernity seem even more extreme. 'Modernity' has acquired a relentlessly uneven and contradictory character: material abundance here, producing poverty and immiseration there; greater diversity and choice – but often at the cost of commodification, fragmentation and isolation. More opportunities for participation – but only at the expense of subordinating oneself to the laws of the market. Novelty and innovation – but driven by what often appear to be false needs. The rich 'West' – and the famine-stricken South. Forms of 'development' which destroy faster than they create. The city – privileged scenario of the modern experience for Baudelaire or Walter Benjamin – transformed into the anonymous city, the sprawling city, the inner city, the abandoned city...

These stark paradoxes project uncertainty into any secure judgement or assessment of the trends and tendencies of new times especially on the Left. Are new times to be welcomed for the new possibilities they open? Or rejected for the threat of horrendous disasters (the ecological ones are uppermost in our minds just now) and final closures which they bring in their wake? Terry Eagleton has recently posed the dilemma in comparable terms, when discussing the 'true aporia, impasse or undecidability of a transitional epoch, struggling out as it is from beneath an increasingly clapped-out, discreditable, historically superannuated ideology of Autonomous Man, (first cousin to Socialist Man) with no very clear sense as yet of which path out from this pile of ruins is likely to lead us towards an enriched human life and which to the unthinkable terminus of some fashionable new irrationalist barbarism.' (Eagleton p47). We seem, especially on the Left, permanently impaled on the horns of these extreme and irreconcilable alternatives.

It is imperative for the Left to get past this impossible impasse, these irreconcilable either/ors. There are few better (though many more fashionable) places to begin than with Gramsci's 'Americanism and Fordism' essay, which is of seminal importance for this debate, even if it is also a strangely broken and 'unfinished' text. 'Americanism and Fordism' represented a very similar effort, much earlier in the century, to describe and assess the dangers and possibilities for the Left of the birth of that epoch − 'Fordism' − which we are just supposed to be leaving. Gramsci was conducting this exercise in very similar political circumstances for the Left − retreat and retrenchment of the working-class movement, ascendancy of fascism, new surge of capital 'with its intensified economic exploitation and authoritarian cultural expression'.

If we take our bearings from 'Americanism and Fordism' we are obliged to note that Gramsci's 'catalogue of ... most important or interesting problems' relevant to deciding 'whether Americanism can constitute a new historical epoch' begins with 'a new mechanism of accumulation and distribution of finance capital based directly on industrial production'. But his characterisation of 'Fordism' also includes a range of other social and cultural phenomena which are discussed in the essay: the rationalisation of the demographic composition of Europe; the balance between endogamous and exogamous change; the phenomenon of mass consumption and 'high wages'; 'psychoanalysis and its enormous diffusion since the war'; the increased 'moral coercion' exercised by the state; artistic and intellectual movements associated with 'Modernism'; what Gramsci calls the contrast between 'super-city' and 'super-country'; feminism, masculinism and 'the question of sex'. Who, on the Left, now has the confidence to address the problems and promise of new times with a matching comprehensiveness and range? The sad fact is that a list of 'new questions' like that are most likely to engender a response of derision and sectarian back-biting at most meetings of the organised political Left today − coupled with the usual cries of 'sell-out'!

This lack of intellectual boldness on the Left is certainly, in part, attributable to the fact that the contradictory forces associated with new times are just now, and have been for some time, firmly in the keeping and under the tutelage of the Right. The Right has imprinted them with the apparent inevitability of its own political project. However, as we argued earlier, this may have obscured the fact that what is going on is not the unrolling of a singular, unilinear logic in which the ascendancy of capital, the hegemony of the New Right and the march of commodification are indissolubly locked together. These may be *different* processes, with different time-scales, which the dominance of the Right in the 1980s has somehow rendered natural and inevitable.

One of the lessons of new times is that history does not consist of what Benedict Anderson calls 'empty, homogeneous time', but of processes with different time-scales and trajectories. They may be convened in the same conjuncture. But historic conjunctures of this kind remain complex, not simple: not in any simple sense 'determined' but *over-determined* (that is, the result of a fusion or merging of different processes and contradictions which nevertheless retain their own effectivity, 'the specific modalities of their actions' − (Althusser, 'Contradiction and Over-determination'). That is really what a 'new conjuncture' means, as Gramsci clearly showed. The histories and time-scales of Thatcherism and of new times have certainly overlapped. Nevertheless, they may belong to different temporalities. Political time, the time of regimes and elections, is short: 'a week is a long time in politics'. Economic time, sociological time, so to speak, has a longer *durée*. Cultural time is even slower, more glacial. This does not detract from the significance of Thatcherism and the scale of its political intervention, about which we have been writing. There is nothing slow, glacial or 'passive' about the Thatcherite revolution, which seems by contrast brutally abrupt, concise and condensed.

Nevertheless, from the perspective of the longer *durée* of new times, Thatcherism's project can be understood as operating on the ground of longer, deeper, more profound movements of change which *appear* to be going its way, but of which, in reality, it has been only occasionally, and fleetingly, in command over the past decade. We can see Thatcherism as, in fact, an attempt to hegemonise these deeper tendencies within its project of 'regressive modernisation', to appropriate them to a reactionary political agenda and to harness to them the interests and fortunes of specific and limited social interests. Once we have opened up this gap, analytically, between Thatcherism and new times, it *may* become possible to resume or re-stage the broken dialogue between socialism and modernity.

Consider another question with which people on the Left perpetually tease and puzzle one another: what kind of 'transition' are we talking about and how total or how complete is it? This way of posing the question implies an all-or-nothing answer. Either it *is* a New Epoch, or nothing at all has changed. But that is not the only alternative. We are certainly not debating an *epochal* shift, of the order of the famous transition from feudalism to capitalism. But we have had other transitions from one regime of accumulation to another, within capitalism, whose impact has been extraordinarily wide ranging. Think, for example, of the transition which Marx writes about between absolute and relative surplus value; or from machinofacture to 'modern industry'; or the one which preoccupied Lenin and others at the turn of the century and about which Gramsci was writing in 'Americanism and Fordism'. The transition which new times references is of the latter order of things.

As to how complete it is: this stand-and-deliver way of assessing things may itself be the product of an earlier type of totalising logic which is beginning to be superseded. In a permanently Transitional Age we must *expect* unevenness, contradictory outcomes, disjunctures, delays, contingencies, uncompleted projects overlapping emergent ones. We know that Marx's *Capital* stands at the beginning, not the completion, of the expansion of the capitalist 'world market'; and that earlier transitions (such as that from household to factory production) all turned out, on inspection, to be more protracted and incomplete than the theory suggested.

We have to make assessments, not from the completed base, but from the 'leading edge' of change. The food industry, which has just arrived at the point where it can guarantee worldwide the standardisation of the size, shape and composition of every hamburger and every potato (*sic*) chip in a Macdonald's Big Mac from Tokyo to Harare, is clearly just entering its 'Fordist' apogee. However, its labour force and highly mobile, 'flexible' and deskilled work patterns approximate more to some post-Fordist patterns. Motor cars, from which the Age of Fordism derived its name, with its multiple variations on every model and market specialisation (like the fashion and software industries) is, in some areas at least, on the move towards a more post-Fordist form. The question should always be, where is the 'leading edge' and in what direction is it pointing.

The Cultural Dimension

Another major requirement for trying to think through the complexities and ambiguities of new times is simply to open our minds to the deeply *cultural* character of the revolution of our times. If 'post-Fordism' exists, then it is as much a description of cultural as of economic change. Indeed, that distinction is now quite useless. Culture has ceased (if ever it was − which I doubt) to be a decorative addendum to the 'hard world' of production and things, the icing on the cake of the material world. The word is now as 'material' as the world. Through design, technology and styling, 'aesthetics' has already penetrated the world of modern production. Through marketing, layout and style, the 'image' provides the mode of representation and fictional narrativisation of the body on which so much of modern consumption depends. Modern culture is relentlessly material in its practices and modes of production. And the material world of commodities and technologies is profoundly cultural. Young people, black and white, who can't even spell 'postmodernism' but have grown up in the age of computer technology, rock-video and electronic music, already inhabit such a universe in their heads.

Is this merely the culture of commodified consumption? Are these necessarily Trivial Pursuits? (Or, to bring it right home, a trendy 'designer addiction' to the detritus of capitalism which serious Left magazines like *Marxism Today* should renounce − or even better denounce − forever?) Yes, much − perhaps, even most − of the time. But underlying that, have we missed the opening up of the individual to the transforming rhythms and forces of modern *material* life? Have we become bewitched by who, in the short run, reaps the profit from these transactions (there are vast amounts of it being made), and missed the democratisation of culture which is *also* potentially part of their hidden agenda? Can a socialism of the 21st century revive, or even survive, which is wholly cut off from the landscapes of popular pleasures, however contradictory and 'commodified' a terrain they represent? Are we thinking dialectically enough?

One strategy for getting at the more cultural and subjective dimensions of new times would be to start from the objective characteristics of post-Fordism and simply turn them inside out. Take the new technologies. They not only introduce new skills and practices. They also require new ways of thinking. Technology, which used to be 'hard-nosed' is now 'soft'. And it no longer operates along one, singular line or path of development. Modern technology, far from having a fixed path, is open to constant renegotiation and re-articulation. 'Planning', in this new technological environment, has less to do with absolute predictability and everything to do with instituting a 'regime' out of which a plurality of outcomes will emerge. One, so to speak, plans for contingency. This mode of thinking signals the end of a certain kind of deterministic rationality.

Or consider the proliferation of models and styles, the increased product differentiation, which characterises 'post-Fordist' production. We can see mirrored there wider processes of cultural diversity and differentiation, related to the multiplication of social worlds and social 'logics' typical of modern life in the West.

There has been an enormous expansion of 'civil society', related to the diversification of social worlds in which men and women now operate. At present, most people only relate to these worlds through the medium of consumption. But, increasingly we are coming to understand that to maintain these worlds at an advanced level requires forms of collective consumption far beyond the restricted logic of the market. Furthermore, each of these worlds also has its own codes of behaviour, its 'scenes' and 'economies', and (don't knock it) its 'pleasures'. These already allow those individuals who have some access to them some space in which to reassert a measure of choice and control over everyday life, and to 'play' with its more expressive dimensions. This 'pluralisation' of social life expands the positionalities and identities available to ordinary people (at least in the industrialised world) in their everyday working, social, familial and sexual lives. Such opportunities need to be more, not less, widely available across the globe, and in ways not limited by private appropriation.

This shift of time and activity towards 'civil society' has implications for our thinking about the individual's rights and responsibilities, about new forms of citizenship and about ways of ordering and regulating society other than through the all-encompassing state. They imply a 'socialism' committed to, rather than scared of, diversity and difference.

Of course, 'civil society' is no ideal realm of pure freedom. Its micro-worlds include the multiplication of points of power and conflict – and thus exploitation, oppression and marginalisation. More and more of our everyday lives are caught up in these forms of power, and their lines of intersection. Far from there being no resistance to the system, there has been a proliferation of new points of antagonism, new social movements of resistance organised around them – and, consequently, a generalisation of 'politics' to spheres which hitherto the Left assumed to be apolitical: a politics of the family, of health, of food, of sexuality, of the body. What we lack is any overall map of how these power relations connect and of their resistances. Perhaps there isn't, in that sense, one 'power game' at all, more a network of strategies and powers and their articulations – and thus a politics which is always positional...

One of these critical 'new' sites of politics is the arena of social reproduction. On the Left, we know about the reproduction of labour power. But what do we really know – outside of feminism – about ideological, cultural, sexual reproduction? One of the characteristics of this area of 'reproduction' is that it is both material and symbolic, since we are reproducing not only the cells of the body but also the categories of the culture. Even consumption, in some ways the privileged terrain of reproduction, is no less symbolic for being material. We need not go so far as Baudrillard (p62), as to say 'the object is nothing' in order to recognize that, in the modern world, objects are also signs, and we relate to the world of things in both an instrumental and a symbolic mode. In a world tyrannised by scarcity, men and women nevertheless express in their practical lives not only what they need for material existence but some sense of their symbolic place in the world, of who they are, their identities. One should not miss this drive to take part or 'come on' in the theatre of the social – even if, as things stand, the only stage provided is within what the Situationists, in 1968, used to call the 'fetishised spectacle of the commodity'.

Of course, the preoccupation with consumption and style may appear trivial — though more so to men, who tend to have themselves 'reproduced', so to say, at arms length from the grubby processes of shopping and buying and getting and spending and therefore take it less seriously than women, for whom it was destiny, life's 'work'. But the fact is that greater and greater numbers of people (men *and* women) — with however little money — play the game of using things to signify who they are. Everybody, including people in very poor societies whom we in the West frequently speak about as if they inhabit a world *outside* of culture, knows that today's 'goods' double up as social signs and produce meanings as well as energy. There is no clear evidence that, in an alternative socialist economy, our propensity to 'code' things according to systems of meaning, which is an essential feature of our sociality, would *necessarily* cease — or, indeed, should.

A socialism built on any simple notion of a 'return to Nature' is finished. We are all irrevocably in the 'secondary universes' where Culture predominates over Nature. And culture, increasingly, distances us from invoking the simple, transparent ground of 'material interests' as a way of settling any argument. The environmental crisis, which is a result of the profound imbalance between Nature and Culture induced by the relentless drive to subordinate everything to the drive for profitability and capital accumulation cannot be resolved by any simple 'return' to Nature. It can only be resolved by a more human — that is, socially responsible and communally responsive — way of *cultivating* the natural world of finite resources on which we all now depend. The notion that 'the market' can resolve such questions is patently — in the light of present experience — absurd and untenable.

This recognition of the expanded cultural and subjective ground on which any socialism of the 21st century must stand, relates, in a significant way, to feminism, or better still, what we might call 'the feminisation of the social'. We should distinguish this from the simplistic version of 'the future is female', espoused by some tendencies within the women's movement, but recently subject to Lynne Segal's persuasive critique. It arises from the remarkable — and irreversible — transformation in the position of women in modern life as a consequence not only of shifts in conceptions of work and exploitation, the gendered recomposition of the workforce and the greater control over fertility and reproduction, but also the rebirth of modern feminism itself.

Feminism and the social movements around sexual politics have thus had an unsettling effect on everything once thought of as 'settled' in the theoretical universe of the Left. And nowhere more dramatically than in their power to decentre the characteristic conversations of the Left by bringing on to the political agenda the question of sexuality. This is more than simply the question of the Left being 'nice' to women or lesbians or gay men or beginning to address their forms of oppression and exclusion. It has to do with the revolution in thinking which follows in the wake of the recognition that *all* social practices and forms of domination − including the politics of the Left − are always inscribed in and to some extent secured by sexual identity and positioning. If we don't attend to how gendered identities are formed and transformed and how they are deployed politically, we simply do not have a language of sufficient explanatory power at our command with which to understand the institutionalisation of power in our society and the secret sources of our resistances to change. After another of those meetings of the Left where the question of sexuality has cut through like an electric current which nobody knows how to plug into, one is tempted to say *especially* the resistances to change *on the Left*.

Thatcherism was certainly fully aware of this implication of gender and identity in politics. It has powerfully organised itself around particular forms of patriarchy and cultural or national identity. Its defence of 'Englishness', of that way of 'being British' or of the English feeling 'Great again', is a key to some of the unexpected sources of Thatcherism's popularity. Cultural racism has been one of its most powerful, enduring, effective − and least remarked − sources of strength. For that very reason, 'Englishness', as a privileged and restrictive cultural identity, is becoming a site of contestation for those many marginalised ethnic and racial groups in the society who feel excluded by it and who hold to a different form of racial and ethnic identification and insist on cultural diversity as a goal of society in new times.

The Left should not be afraid of this surprising return of

ethnicity. Though ethnicity continues to be, in many places, a surprisingly resilient and powerfully reactionary force, the *new* forms of ethnicity are articulated, politically, in a different direction. By 'ethnicity' we mean the astonishing return to the political agenda of all those points of attachment which give the individual some sense of 'place' and position in the world, whether these be in relation to particular communities, localities, territories, languages, religions or cultures. These days, black writers and film-makers refuse to be restricted to only addressing black subjects. But they insist that others recognise that what they have to say comes out of particular histories and cultures and that everyone speaks from positions within the global distribution of power. Because these positions change and alter, there is always an engagement with politics as a 'war of position'.

This insistence on 'positioning' provides people with co-ordinates, which are specially important in face of the enormous globalization and transnational character of many of the processes which now shape their lives. The new times seem to have gone 'global' and 'local' at the same moment. And the question of ethnicity reminds us that everybody comes from some place − even if it is only an 'imagined community' − and needs some sense of identification and belonging. A politics which neglects that moment of identity and identification − without, of course, thinking of it as something permanent, fixed or essential − is not likely to be able to command the new times.

Could there be new times without new subjects? Could the world be transformed while its subjects stay exactly the same? Have the forces remaking the modern world left the subjects of that process untouched? Is change possible while *we* remain untransformed? It was always unlikely and is certainly an untenable proposition now. This is another one of those many 'fixed and fast-frozen relationships, venerable ideas and opinions' which, as Marx accurately predicted, new times are quietly melting into thin air.

References

Jean Baudrillard, *The Mirror of Production,* Telos 1979.

Marshall Berman, *All That is Solid Melts Into Air*, Simon and Schuster 1983.

Terry Eagleton, 'Identity', ICA 6, 1987.

André Gorz, *Farewell to the Working Class*, Pluto 1982.

Antonio Gramsci, *Selections from the Prison Notebooks*, Lawrence and Wishart 1971.

Fredric Jameson, 'The Cultural Logic of Capital', *New Left Review* 146, July/August 1984.

Jean-François Lyotard, *The Post-Modern Condition: A Report of Knowledge,* Manchester University Press 1984.

II   Identity and the Individual

Charlie Leadbeater

Power to the Person

In much of the postwar era socialist progress was measured by the progressive expansion of the public sector, through nationalisation, public education, and health and welfare spending. If socialism is to be renewed in the next decade it must adopt an entirely different index of progress: the progressive expansion of the sphere of individual rights and responsibilities.

If the Left stands for one thing, it should be this: people taking more responsibility for all aspects of their lives. Whatever issue the Left confronts, its question should be this: 'How can people take more responsibility for shaping this situation, determining its outcome?' It should not be, as it often is: 'What can the state, the council, the expert professionals, do to solve this problem for people?'

Thatcherism's conservative individualism is giving the desire for autonomy, choice, responsibility, freedom from the state, a reactionary form. But there is nothing about these desires which are intrinsically Thatcherite. It did not create those desires: it responded to them and has sought to appropriate them.

The Left offers no alternative. It needs a socialist individualism at the core of its vision of how society should be organised. Socialists should not get trapped in a stale debate, in which they are painted as collectivists seeking to restrain Thatcherite individualists. They should not confine their case to the socially divisive consequences of Thatcherite individualism. They should confront it directly by offering an alternative progressive individualism.

Thatcherism builds up its vision of how society should be organised from a narrow account of the acquisitive, defensive drives which motivate individuals as consumers. The Left should build its vision of how society should be organised from an alternative account of individualism, an appeal to a culture of individual citizenship rather than individual consumerism.

The choice the Left should offer is between Thatcherism's constrained narrow, materialistic individualism, and an expansive individualism which offers people rights to influence decisions in production as well as in consumption; political and civil rights as well as the right to buy; access to a set of universal rights to health care, education and training.

Under Thatcherism the credit card has become the symbol of citizenship, the entrance ticket to consumer society. As an alternative the Left should not offer credit controls. It should offer a wider idea of citizenship based on a much more extensive set of rights and entitlements, which are not purchased through the market, but delivered as part of citizenship.

Expanding the sphere of individual responsibility will require collective action. The aim and expression of socialist policies must be to expand individual rights and responsibilities. But individuals will be unable to achieve this on their own. Many obstacles to individual security and advancement − for instance the inadequacy of investment in housing, education, training and health − will only be overcome by sustained collective action.

The Left has to renew confidence that collective social action is accountable to, and designed to fulfil, individual needs. It has to renegotiate the contract between those who finance collective services, those who provide them, and those who consume them, to ensure they provide value for money, efficiency, flexibility and choice.

The Left's agenda for the 1990s should be formed around these twin themes. Expanding the sphere of individual responsibility, but in tandem renewing a culture of social responsibility and collective provision. It is the lack of a vision of an individually based collectivism which underlies the Left's faltering in the 1980s. For it has been unable to respond to the decay of the old social-democratic order of Fordism.

Fordism was characteristically associated with regulation of the economy and social life by the social-democratic state. The social-democratic project was founded upon the assumption that the state could legitimately act as the representative and guardian of collective social interests.

Full employment and welfare spending were meant to ensure that economic growth had a wider social purpose beyond narrow profit. Tripartite policy-making and public ownership were meant to ensure economic decisions reflected wider social interests. Public spending, state intervention in the economy, were the distillation of social interests: the state was acting on our behalf.

But during the 1970s trust in the state's ability to act on society's behalf withered. Its interventions in the economy seemed an excuse for inefficiency. Its welfare policies ensnared clients in a demeaning web of bureaucracy and delivered poor quality services. It stood as a paternalist landlord over the people it was meant to serve.

This has created a major problem for the Left. Society should be more than an economic jungle of acquisitive consumers. There is no widespread support for society being remade in the image of *Howard's Way*, the BBC soap opera about over-sexed entrepreneurs on the south coast. Collective action will be vital to restore social justice. But most people simply do not trust the large, distant, unaccountable, uncontrollable state to do that job. It is not just that many people think the state cannot act efficiently. They do not believe the Left's claim that it can *represent* social responsibility.

The 'mass' aims of the social-democratic state in providing services and housing were founded upon the 'mass' interests formed by the character of production and work. The Fordist era of mass-production workers and mass consumers confirmed the sense that individual interests could be read off with some confidence from the great social blocs formed by production.

For too long the Left has been addicted to a set of theological guarantees which seemed to allow it to read off individual interests from larger collective interests. There was the historic guarantee that as society developed it would create the conditions for the unity of the working class, a natural constituency for socialism, which would arise from history. It would not arise evenly. It might be impeded by different class cultures. But it was imminent. This was reinforced by some guarantee of linearity: that from the interests formed through work other social interests would emerge. This was matched by a moral guarantee, that not only would the working class see socialism as a necessity but also as a moral vocation. These guarantees amounted to a political insurance policy that the Left could complacently, arrogantly rely upon: that a part of society would always be ours, even if it did not appear to be.

But changes in the character and distribution of work have undermined the unifying tendencies of production and work under Fordism. The economic restructuring of the 1980s has produced deep divisions within the working class. Established occupational, sexual and cultural identities, sources of solidarity and common identification are dissolving. The old demarcation lines between blue- and white-collar workers, the skilled and the unskilled, are being superseded by much more fundamental divisions. The long-term unemployed are separated from the employed; part-time, temporary workers from full-timers; those trained to work with new technology and those left behind; the workers in the South East from the rest of the country. Many of the Left's assumptions about its constituency are forged around the idea of the male, manual, manufacturing, unionised worker: the classic Fordist worker, living in the shadow of the shipyard, the pit or the factory chimney. In the 1990s the largest group in the workforce will be white-collar, non-unionised women working in the service sector.

In addition, in recent years the social theatre of consumption has become more important. Choice in consumption, lifestyle, sexuality is more important as an assertion of identity. The dynamic area of most people's lives is where they can assert their difference from others.

These developments in attitudes towards the state and class have created an enormous problem at the very heart of the Left's sense of its historic purpose. The Left's project depends on a central equation: individuals' security, rights and standards of living, can only be secured in the long run upon a foundation of collective, social action. The Left's case stands on that link between the individual and the collective. The trouble is that for many people that link has been broken. As a result the Left is adrift.

The link has been broken by these three developments: the loss of trust in the state's ability to act as the guardian of collective social interests; the decay of traditional sources of solidarity and common identity forged through work; the growth in the importance of individual choice in consumption, the revolt against centralising sameness, the pursuit of diversity.

This leaves the Left unable to solve a central paradox. Britain has become a savagely divided country under Thatcherism. More than at any time since the second world war, there is a need for collective action, redistributive policies, a culture of social responsibility to overcome the poverty, deprivation, insecurity, and inequality which will be the legacy of the 1980s.

But achieving the sense of allegiance to a common purpose, renewing a sense of social solidarity and responsibility, is perhaps more difficult than at any point since 1945, because the sources of that sense of common purpose have been so weakened. What is most needed − a renewal of the links between individual interests and collective solutions − is most difficult to deliver.

Thatcher's Individualism

The routes through which the Left has traditionally offered some symmetry between the common advance of individual interests and general social interests are closing down. While the Left rested on a complacent belief that the links would remain strong, Thatcherism, on the back of the decline of Fordism, has attempted finally to break them with the promulgation of a narrow, conservative ideology of individualism.

Thatcherism's ideology of individual choice runs far beyond consumerism. To argue that the Left needs an alternative individualism is not a plea for greater attention to consumer choice. It is an argument for putting individual interests at the centre of socialist strategy. For that is how Thatcherism has succeeded, by articulating a vision of how society should be organised which has individual morality at its centre.

Thatcherism's individualism is vital to its economic ideology. It justifies not merely the market economy, but the marketisation of society more generally. For Thatcherism the market is the hegemonic principle to guide the organisation of economic activity. Market choices are not merely a requirement to ensure resources are distributed efficiently. They are vital to the pursuit of higher efficiency. People work harder with the incentive of expanding their opportunities to consume; businesses are made more efficient if entrepreneurs are freed to choose how to organise production. The ideology of choice also fits with structural changes within the economy − the explosion of consumer credit, the marketing and retailing revolution of the 1980s, the stress on product differentiation.

Thatcherite individualism has sanctioned a gorging materialism among the well-off. But it would be wrong to dismiss it simply as hedonism. Conservative individualism is not just about consumer choice, about people buying and selling. It incorporates those everyday acts within a much wider social philosophy. It has asserted the possibility of individuals becoming agents to change their worlds through private initiatives. Aspirations for autonomy, choice, decentralisation, greater responsibility, which were met with mumbling paternalism by the postwar social-democratic state, have been met by Thatcherite encouragement in the 1980s.

Individual choice implies people have the rationality and discipline to interrogate their desires and aspirations, to determine what they really want. Not just what they want in the supermarket, but what they want for their lives, what kind of people they want to be, where they will live, how their children will be educated. The fulfilment of these choices implies that individuals have a measure of power over an external world. In other words it is an ideology which centres not merely on pleasure but on rationality, discipline, responsibility and power. It creates a vision of individuals as autonomous agents, who have the power to remake their worlds.

This offer of remaking the world is dynamic, radical in a way. But it is enveloped by a conservative, but equally powerful, vision of the relationship between individuals and society.

For Thatcherism society is constituted by individuals: it is nothing other than a set of human atoms. One can only determine what society is by going back to its basic, indissoluble constituents – individuals. Individuals are not intrinsically social, their characters, resources, abilities are not formed in a social setting.

For Thatcherism society becomes merely a meeting place for a plethora of individual wills, an arena for individual satisfaction, a set of opportunities for individual achievement, advancement and enjoyment. Society is merely a tool and aid to help people achieve their pre-determined individual ends. People co-operate for purely instrumental reasons, to achieve their chosen ends more efficiently.

Thus all allegiance to collective solutions becomes vulnerable to break-aways. People are not encouraged to feel any sense of belonging or obligation to a wider collective. They are encouraged to examine collective provision entirely instrumentally: 'Am I better off staying with the NHS or going for private health care?' Individualism fosters the myth that people can and should be self-sufficient. They should rely only upon themselves and owe as little as possible to others. It always encourages people to think of opting out of collective provision − for instance in education.

It thus sets up a simple dichotomy between the sovereignty of individual choice and the illegitimacy of attempts by collectives, and particularly the state, to limit those choices. Thatcherite individualism becomes an aggressively defensive view of the individual. The private space, provided for by hard-earned income, is sacred, to be protected against the unwelcome encroachments of the state, with its spurious claims upon individuals' resources.

This protection of the private space for the home-owning consumer incorporates people within a defence of private property in general which strengthens support for private ownership and control in the economy. It also incorporates people within exploitative economic relations. Its message is: if you have an economic asset − savings, skills, willingness to work − exploit it to the full. Thus it justifies the propagation of exploitative behaviour: everyone can have a stake in private property, everyone can make something through exploitation.

Thatcherism's individualism is not merely an economic ideology, but a moral vision of how society should be organised. From a view of individuals as assertive but narrow consumers it generates a much wider vision of how society should be ordered, which justifies the market, private property, the values of tradition and an attack on the public sector. It has become the moral marching song of the rising classes of Thatcherite Britain − the socially mobile, affluent working class, the entrepreneurial classes, the private sector middle classes, the young urban professionals. This narrow individualism is Thatcherism's most fundamental and extensive privatisation: the privatisation of social aspiration, obligation and responsibility. It explains the fundamental nature of its attack on socialism, because it attacks the very sense of the social upon which *socialism* is based.

The Individual and the Collective

How should the Left respond, not only to Thatcherite individualism, but more importantly to the weakening of the traditional Left links between the individual and the collective? While Thatcherism's ideological vision of society is founded upon the building blocks of individual desires and demands, the Left's vision seems to start with social structures and then fit individuals into them.

Socialist analysis is meant to explain a range of macro-social processes – class formation, class alliances, social conflict, the historical trajectory of society's development. But if it is to explain social change it must be clear how these forces systematically affect, and in turn are affected by, individual actions and choices.

Thatcherism's strength is that it has an ideology which makes people feel powerful in a tangible way. The Left's great weakness is that its vision of social organisation seems to leave little room for individuals other than as the passive, powerless bearers of larger social structures.

None of this disables the Left from having a powerful and coherent critique of Thatcherite individualism. Consumer choice does not amount to consumer power. Markets may provide for some choices, but they can deny diversity, and do not accommodate a range of choices which it is unprofitable to service. Thatcherism does not understand the importance of collectives. People do not work in shops, offices and factories as individuals, they work together. They are bound together in some underlying way. It is not socialism which promotes collective cultures and attachments, but the collective conditions of production, work and consumption. It cannot extinguish the collective cultures around the NHS and education.

Moreover it's clear that Thatcherite individualism's command of the moral high ground is essentially contested. It is extremely vulnerable to criticism of the social harshness of its individualism. For it has actually sanctioned an enormous dereliction of social responsibility. Indeed many who have benefited from Thatcherite policies are opposed to the state jettisoning its responsibilities to the poor and the sick.

But the power of this critique in turn raises a troubling

question: if it is so powerful, why has it failed so miserably to *dislodge* Thatcherism from the ideological high ground?

The answer is that by itself this critique is not enough. It is not enough to point to the consequences of Thatcherism, not enough to remind people of the enduring importance of collective cultures. For the Left is caught in a dichotomy which it cannot break out of without a re-orientation of its appeal.

Thatcherism has created a powerful dichotomy between on the one hand state and collective provision, which is associated with uniformity, inefficiency, indignity and lack of choice, and on the other, the market and private provision, which is associated with self-sufficiency, choice, efficiency and rising living standards. Underlying this is a deeper dichotomy, which Thatcherism promotes, between a social life in which free individual choices are sovereign, and another where bureaucratic state control seeks to limit individual choices.

If the debate is conducted in these terms Thatcherism is bound to win, by counterposing freedom of choice against bureaucratic restriction. For socialism's role seems to be to limit individual choice and responsibility. There are two ways to loosen the grip of this vice. The first is to challenge Thatcherism's individualism directly, with an alternative individualism. The Left should counterpose a democratic individualism against Thatcherism's consumer individualism. While Thatcherism distributes individual entitlements according to whether people can afford them, the Left's stress should be on universal individual rights. While Thatcherism confines individual choice within the market, the Left should stress the importance of wider social individuality, diversity and plurality in lifestyles which cannot be delivered by the market.

The second route is to develop a new agenda for collective action. This should involve a decentralisation and democratisation of the state, and the devolution of state power to autonomous collective bodies, independent of the state. It should also involve a much stronger appeal to emerging collective interests, for this generation's environmental responsibilities to future generations.

The Left's agenda should aim to expand individual entitlements, rights and responsibilities. That should be the focus and measure of socialism's progress. What might that mean in practice?

It implies a basic recognition of the importance of choice in consumption. Economic strategy has to deliver clearly that choice. That means the market will play an important role in left economic strategy, simply because it is the best way to co-ordinate lots of decentralised economic decisions. That does not necessarily mean the market should be the dominant force within the economy; it does not mean that competition should not be regulated. But it does mean the Left has to acknowledge the obvious; the market, competition, can be useful economic tools to deliver consumer choice.

But ensuring consumer choice implies much more than that. It means the public sector has to become much more consumer oriented. Providing the standards of the high street in the benefit office will require more resources, but it will also require a managerial and retailing revolution in the public sector. In addition it means that public provision has to become more democratically accountable to allow clients to have more say over how services are designed and provided.

The Left should not allow Thatcherism's view of consumers to go unchallenged. Consumers' rights to standards of service should be considerably strengthened: for instance every British Gas customer should be able to claim a rebate if the gas engineer fails to appear at the appointed hour. A Labour government should stand on the side of the consumer against the price-fixing cartels in the credit card, petrol and other markets. Consumer assertiveness should be politicised to challenge corporate power.

But beyond that the whole idea that consumption is about buying and consuming goods needs to be challenged. The Left should adopt a much wider definition of consumption: time free from the necessity of work. Thus policies to reduce and reorganise working time should not primarily be conceived as workers' demands against employers. They should be seen as the demands of consumers, of parents. A clear instance of what special control of the economy should mean is the re-organisation of working time around the needs of the domestic sphere, as well as the needs of production. The promotion of such policies, to ease difficulties over care for the old, the young and the sick, would be a major public investment in expanding private, domestic spaces.

The dynamic of individualism should be expanded to

production. If people can own their homes, if they can choose where to invest pensions, why should they not have a right to own the machines they work with? Individual rights to consultation and participation at work should be written into contracts of employment. Moves towards social ownership should be based on the idea that individual workers have a right to own a share of the assets of companies they have built up. If, as Thatcherism tells us, individuals are responsible, rational, disciplined, why should these qualities be confined to the high street?

Britain desperately needs a much greater investment in training and education. But the point of such a policy should be conceived and expressed individually, for instance in a right to ten days off-the-job training a year, or to periodic study-leave after the school-leaving age. Both moves would amount to collective action to correct a social problem; but they should be conceived and delivered not as grand programmes, but simply as an investment in a wider package of individual entitlements.

Underlying all these moves must be an attack on poverty and low pay. The greatest denial of choice Thatcherism has delivered is through its promotion of inequality. Britain needs a new incomes policy, not to be drawn up with union leaders, but formed around a publicly declared minimum standard of living. It is unlikely that everyone would reach this threshhold individual minimum income, even after several years of Labour government. But an individual entitlement to a minimum level of income should be the fundamental measure of how civilised a society Britain is.

The best way to provide such an income is through providing reasonably paid work, or training leading to work. Thus there should be an individual right to a guaranteed place on a high quality employment and training programme. Again it should be written into individual contracts of employment that once someone is made redundant they can automatically trigger that entitlement.

This stress on rights in turn implies that people should carry responsibilities. The main responsibility is clear − a responsibility to seek and take up reasonable offers of training and employment, to accept reasonable measures of labour flexibility.

Beyond that the Left's individualism needs to foster individuality, diversity and plurality in civil society. Thus a stronger set of civil rights to freedom of sexual orientation are not a side issue. They are an emblem for the kind of civil society the Left should be aiming to nurture.

When Mrs Thatcher talks about individuals she usually talks about 'individuals and their families' – in other words male heads of households. Thatcherism's individualism is substantially trapped within the social assumptions of Fordism, that wage-earners are men. In the 1990s half the workforce will be women. Thus individual rights to equal pay for work of equal value, rights to childcare provision, would directly address the collective social needs of a majority of the workforce.

The link between these individual entitlements and collective provision is threefold. Firstly, these rights should generally be conceived and argued for as universal rights, for the well-off as well as the least well-off. Only then will these demands bridge and unite different segments of society. Thus there would be something collective written into this individualism: people need and would defend these rights as something they had in common. Thatcherism offers an atomistic individualism, the Left should offer a social individualism. People's interdependence, their mutual obligations, would be written into the rights they share in common. Secondly, securing these rights will require not merely collective action but redistribution. For instance, a universal employment right to childcare provision would benefit both two-earner households and single parents. But it would disproportionately benefit single parents. Thirdly, this should be a democratic individualism as opposed to a consumerist individualism, in the sense that part of the fundamental picture of individuals on offer is that they are rational and reflective, capable of making informed decisions about how society should be organised around them.

This has important consequences for how collective action should be organised. If something is collectively guaranteed and financed, this does not mean that it then has to be provided by the state. These themes should guide the Left's approach to the role of the state and collective, public bodies.

The image of the state's role should be founded on the public park: a publicly-provided, regulated space, in which a range of private activities are possible. Some the state will provide directly (boats on lakes); many others may involve companies (ice-cream vans) or simply individuals doing what they want with the state's help (sunbathing). The state is vital to ensuring a space continues to exist and is developed; but beyond that its direct role depends on whether it is the most efficient provider of services.

In tandem the Left needs to focus on the creation of autonomous collectives, outside the state, which operate much more closely with their clients. So, for instance, childcare provision could be built up from the informal networks which abound among women. An institutionalised, state solution would probably not be flexible enough. So power and responsibility for providing such a service could be contracted to bodies regulated by the state.

In the economy a similar message applies. Local regulatory bodies, for instance, could be set up to oversee the operations of major companies. These could become the democratic focus for collective views about industrial development − for instance environmental concern. Oftel, the body which regulates British Telecom, has managed to change its approach with a sustained attack on its standards of service. Many exasperated telephone subscribers would regard Oftel as their only champion, the only representative of the collective interest over telephone services. The same focus should be provided for gas, electricity, drug, food and other companies.

Thatcherism starts with a view of individuals as consumers and works outwards to a view of how society should be organised. The Left has to offer an alternative view of how society should be organised. But to do so it needs to start with an elaboration of a different view of individuals.

The Left should start with an idea of social citizenship, a democratic individualism, which offers an expansion of the protected individual space of rights, entitlement and responsibility. From that it can establish how society should be organised to fulfil and empower individuals − regulated markets; collectively-financed social guarantees covering health, education, training, childcare, housing; strengthened civil and political rights; decentralisation and devolution of state power; redistribution of resources and economic power.

The Left has to renew the links between individual interests and collective action to shape society. It will not succeed by asserting collectivism ever more fiercely. It will only succeed if it starts asserting an alternative individualism.

Rosalind Brunt

The Politics of Identity

The way to characterise the present situation of Britain entering the 1990s is in terms of a gaping disparity: a tiny minority of various strands of the British left and progressive movement busy rethinking and reviewing its politics while the vast majority of British people continue to anathematise the very idea of being involved in politics of any sort. If the Left's current rethinking is to be at all helpful in actually changing anything or anybody, we might do worse than reflect on this disparity and how we might set about reducing it.

To consider how it is that just a few of us are happy to describe ourselves as 'political' while most wouldn't, consciously, touch politics with a bargepole, I've found the idea of 'the politics of identity' an indispensable one. It seems to me that unless the question of identity is at the heart of any transformatory project, then not only will the political agenda be inadequately 'rethought', but more to the point, our politics aren't going to make much headway beyond the Left's own circles.

I want to try and justify that claim; but first to emphasise that calling identity 'indispensable' is not to make it suddenly the only, or even the main, item on the political agenda, and thereby consign all previous ideas and issues to olden times. I mention this because some left habits die hard and a number of responses to the debate around 'new times' have been couched in the language of betrayal and loss. 'You're abandoning class; you've lost faith in the working people' has so often been the accusation about any attempt to use a politics of identity to render a more rigorous and dynamic concept of class that it can only reflect the attenuated state of British political culture. In a more confident political climate, there might be a clearer willingness to acknowledge that political conviction can never rest on the mere restatement of old verities and that no political views are worth holding that remain off-limits to challenge and question.

A politics of identity offers a way out of this old boxed-in, boxed-off approach of the Left because its stance is including, not exclusive. It is indeed a very welcoming kind of politics because everyone can have a go at defining it in their own terms. 'Identity politics' has been current for some time as contextual shorthand for movements organising around sexuality, gender and ethnicity and working to translate 'the personal is the political' into everyday practice. Learning the lessons of these movements, we can begin applying notions of identity, and identities, to a political agenda for all. A politics whose starting point is about recognising the degree to which political activity and effort involves a continuous process of making and re-making ourselves − and our selves in relation to others − must rightfully be available for anyone to make up as they go along.

What follows then is something I've 'made up'. But I don't mean that in a wholly idiosyncratic sense. Rather, it's an attempt at construing and constructing a fairly new notion out of existing and already familiar sources, some of them quite impeccably marxist. For 'rethinking' is never simply about starting again on a clean sheet; it's more often about recombining and synthesising old elements in the light of the new. My version of 'the lessons of history' is intended to suggest the relevance of a politics of identity to new times for everyone: a confident transformation of the mainstream that offers strategies, theories and styles of organisation which constitute new ways of 'being political'.

For any politics to be successful, it has to match the twin criteria of correctness and effectivity. Does the political analysis that is being offered actually fit the current situation and its potentialities for future movement? And can those who are the organisers and activists of politics win others to this 'correct analysis' in ways which are effectively mobilising?

This may sound an obvious and heavily didactic point. But one of the many blocks on the transformatory process has been the automatic assumption that political activists have never had any other identity: somehow they were always 'that way inclined'. Indeed, it's a common tribute to people who have dedicated their energy and experience to left and labour politics to say, 'The trade union movement is in his blood', 'She was a lifelong

Communist' or 'He is a born socialist'. I respect what these phrases mean in terms of service and struggle, but I deprecate them as politically disabling. They prevent others from joining in, and reflect a damaging type of thinking about how individual lives and politics intermesh. No comrades spring class-conscious from the womb and metaphors that suggest they do indicate how the already-politicised forget the circumstances of their own politicisation and the extent to which these were both product and process of life-choices and contingencies.

It is not after all obvious why anyone, particularly in such an apolitical culture as Britain, should ever choose to define themselves as political. When politics is such a marginalised and minority activity, 'admitting' to being a 'political animal' of any sort, let alone a left one, is distinctly odd. For the common sense opinion of politics is that, like religion, it spells trouble. It is what you do *not* discuss at high points of social togetherness, like family weddings or Christmas, or even just having a drink. 'Come on, you're getting political now' or 'that's all politics', are the warning phrases of the social taboos and lurking distrusts. 'Politics' is what some other people do, in particular, 'the politicians' who 'are all the same really', looking after number one' and managing to mess up most people's lives in the process.

In this climate, it would be useful, then, to reflect on why and how people become political in the first place or indeed, drop out of politics or shift to different positions. Reflecting on politics as a process of social formation and not some given fact of nature, might help us think creatively about overcoming the gulf between those who already count themselves as being 'in' politics and the great majority who don't − yet. In other words, before we ask others to take on a political identity, we need some awareness of what is involved in a politics that opens up questions of identity.

The starting point I'd suggest for any politics of identity is the issue of 'representation': both how our identities are represented in and through the culture and assigned particular categories; and also who or what politically represents us, speaks and acts on our behalf. These two senses of 'representation' alert us to the whole area of culture and ideology as we live it and as it is lived and directly experienced by us. They help us think how we both 'make sense' of the world and get a sense of our 'place' in it − a place of many, and increasing, identities.

The very moment of birth means being assigned a colour, a gender, a class, a nationality and 'belonging' to a family. So how do we make out with this cumbersome set of identities when we never even 'asked' to be born? And how, subsequently, do those two particular dramas of familial possession, being someone's son or daughter and then 'having' a child 'of your own' relate to being somebody 'at work' − or 'nobody' because 'out of work' − and existing through an array of social networks involving colleagues, friends, comrades, lovers, who may, or not, know what you're like 'at home'. And then there is the bedrock sense of 'the real me', the person nobody is supposed to know properly except yourself and who derives from the feeling that, however precarious these other identities, there remains a hidden core, a secret, completely unsocialised and essential self somewhere deep 'inside'. This is a lot of selves to be getting on with. But because we manage and juggle these varying identities of ours and other people routinely everyday, mainly with competence and mostly without much thought, it can seem rather precious and embarrassingly self-conscious to start some reflection about what might be happening here. Indeed, one of the original tenets of left politics is that the very last people who can afford to be bothering with such self-speculation are those engaged with the serious stuff of changing the world. 'We can't be doing with all this fancy navel-gazing comrades: it's a petty bourgeois indulgence', says the steel-hardened revolutionary forged out of an iron discipline, the very metal of self-abnegation.

I'm not myself wholly adverse to the tradition of denial and discipline. But as the best revolutionaries have acknowledged, it cannot be externally imposed, it requires self-motivation. And unless and until we have an adequate recognition of the ways identities work, we are not going to be that effective at world-changing. Antonio Gramsci, the pre-war Italian communist leader, was particularly acute on this point, as on many others, of how to make a politics that was subjectively relevant.

Gramsci placed himself firmly within the rigorous austerity of Bolshevik self-denial and lived and died the consequences of that choice in a fascist jail. But at the same time, and in that prison, he was developing a different revolutionary vocabulary based on what he called 'a critical awareness' that took as its first injunction the ancient Delphic wisdom, 'Know thyself'. Gramsci's point was that if revolutionaries were to develop a clear and coherent conception of the world they wanted to change they should make a start by asking how people experienced the world as it was, how they got by and coped with it on a daily basis. And, 'people' and 'they' included 'me', 'us', the would-be world-changers:

> The starting point of critical elaboration is the consciousness of what one really is, and is 'knowing thyself' as a product of the historical process to date which has deposited in you an infinity of traces without leaving an inventory.[1]

A politics of identity based on 'critical awareness' would start tracking down those 'traces', try making an 'inventory' of personal history, because it recognises that political activists crucially, like everyone else, are determined by circumstances outside their control, but in the process of understanding them can begin to become self-determining. As in Marx's formulation, change is always a process of both agency and determination:

> Men make their own history − but they do not make it just as they please; they do not make it under circumstances chosen by themselves, but under circumstances given and transmitted from the past.[2]

But speaking for my own politicisation, I wasn't going to pay much attention to that until women started remaking history with the women's liberation movement. For the first time then I got a sense of politics actually implicating me. In the early days of 'workshops' and consciousness-raising, we had a practice of always going to talk with other groups in twos because of the 'trouble' we were causing − challenging men's and women's identities and having ours challenged in return: 'But you don't have children/don't you even *like* men?/aren't you all middle class?/where does socialism fit into all this?'

What made these sessions both so hairy and exhilarating was that we could take no refuge in the plight of the people or the condition of the world. For we weren't simply referring to 'the others' as objects of our politics, or turning social constructs into abstract entities − *the* system, *the* state, *the* working class, *the* third world − for prompt remedial action. More painfully and awkwardly we were putting ourselves within the frame of political involvement. This I think is the specific contribution feminism has made to a politics of identity: that it has altered the personal pronouns of politics and contributed a sense of how 'I' and 'you' and 'she' and 'he' could potentially, often with great difficulty and in most hostile circumstances, link up to 'we'. It also provides a way in for considering how those who see politics as enabling and empowering in some way might begin to engage with those for whom 'politics' represents the very opposite: a hostile, alien and coercive force.

One version of socialism has responded to this gap in perception by polarising 'the vanguard' and 'the masses' and saying, 'The vast majority of people are in error; we will teach them better'. When acted upon, this view has had desperately tragic consequences, both for the people and for the development of socialism. Struggling against his own vanguardism, Gramsci began to propose another version of socialism that bears directly on what feminism and other new movements are now saying. In his view, people's common sense understanding of the world was never *simply* wrong or ignorant; it might also contain a rational 'kernel' of 'good sense'. It was not for revolutionaries to rush to judgement about seeing the light: they needed first to listen and account for why so many people rejected politics and could not see themselves as having any sort of political identity.

To take an illustration from the humdrum mainstream. Along with other trade unions recently, my own was involved in balloting under new government legislation over whether or not to preserve what was cunningly described by the Tory government, with maximum alienation effect, as 'the political fund'. In the course of a branch meeting to explain in the nicest depoliticised way what a good thing 'the political' actually was, one member said, 'But I don't see myself as political, somehow', and another commented, 'Well I'm not really a trade union person myself'. To which I instantly replied, tetchily abusing the chair's position, 'Yes you are. You've come to this meeting, haven't you? You're going to vote, aren't you?' And after the meeting I joined in general hack moaning about 'petty bourgeois attitudes, people with cottages in the country who didn't know where their real interests lay, who didn't exactly turn down the pay rises we fought for, who were in for a rude awakening soon, etc.

I won't be too hard on myself and others in hardly new and straightened times, but being analytical about it, that attitude is hardly 'correct'. It is a move up a political blind alley and can't be succumbed to, particularly when the times *are* hard. And talk about history: the first lesson I learned about Communists at school was that they thought they knew better than everyone else and took over trade unions to serve their own ends when they thought no one else was looking. This was particularly *à propos* the ETU ballot-rigging scandal of 1961.

But the attitude that leads to ballot-rigging − the view that it's only 'bourgeois' legality that you're bypassing − and the end always justifying the means, contains within it the notion that it's the people you're supposedly representing who are the real problem, they just haven't got to your advanced stage of thinking yet. So you, the revolutionary agent, do the thinking and the doing for them. But if they still persist in not grasping your revolutionary drift then you may be forced to take action against them. In the tragic history of Communism that is the moment when 'our people' become 'the main enemy'. Stalinism, the killing fields and Tiananmen Square: the desperate end-points of a politics that never listened in the first place, that never engaged with dissenting majorities and asked for what 'good reason', under what real circumstances, the people could not see the official orthodoxies as exactly enabling.

The British road to socialism has had its stalinist and deeply sectarian moments. But it has experienced the extremes of neither tragedy nor triumphant success that mark many other countries' developments. Why the road has been bumpy and uneven, rather than spectacular, can be related to what Marx went on to say in that earlier quotation: 'The tradition of all the dead generations weighs like a nightmare on the brain of the living'. He was actually referring to France, but the remark seems peculiarly apt to describe British identity: the extent to which we, as British subjects, are clobbered by the sheer weight of imperial cultural baggage. A politics of identity, adequately informed by history, needs to unpack and understand all that if it is to grasp how deference and complacency towards British ancestral heritage block the roads to active political agency.

These then are the sort of analytical questions a politics of identity offers to mainstream socialist thinking. But they also need to be linked to some sense of strategy if they are to be any use in helping us move beyond the current political impasse. What is required here is a new approach to the question of power: how it works and what we should do about it in developing new social movements and giving confidence to new, and old, political activists.

In order to work out political strategies that actually match the situations we're in, I think we need a new recognition that power is 'omnipresent'. That is, it operates horizontally as much as vertically, internally as well as externally. It is not simply, as it's previously been thought, a force coming from elsewhere, or above, or from a singly-directed source, and governed by one particular set of people, the ruling class. For even in meeting rooms suffused with socialist goodwill and common purpose, there are constantly shifting 'relations' of power, finding new points of contact, creating different 'networks'. This new approach to power was developed by Michel Foucault in a chapter on 'Method' in his book on, of all things, *The History of Sexuality*. The English title is shocking in itself because it says that so far from sex being a natural, biological given, central to our identity, it is socially and culturally constructed and has a history brimming with power points, and 'regimes' of power, exercised by knowledge-holders like doctors and priests, whose expertise grants authority and legitimates their active hold over those who lack the knowledge.[3]

Foucault throws out entirely the exterior and vertical levels of power, and that is still a bit too drastic for me, but he also suggests that where there is power there is also a 'multiplicity of points of resistance', particularly in the ways that historical identities are constructed. He takes the example of 'the homosexual', a figure first assigned an identity through 19th century medical-sexual categorisation, and relates it to his notion of resistance through 'reverse discourse'. A 'homosexual' subject, so categorised, can start to speak on his/her own behalf, and begin to shift to another, more 'empowering' discourse that describes an identity that transcends the original vocabulary of pathology and illness. Hence the self-defining movements of 'gay' and 'lesbian' politics — a defiant and celebratory 'coming out', though Foucault in his own lifetime felt unable to participate.

But the point that derives from his illustration is that, if power is everywhere, with its reversals and resistances, then the political agenda is radically altered. It makes no sense to talk in any simple way of 'the priorities' or 'the main thing', against which other struggles are subordinated, marginalised, or, as we know, infinitely postponed. It is also no longer possible to think in terms of either/or-ism. We can kiss goodbye to monolithic thinking and restore a sense of 'both-and': a view of politics as fully dialectical.

I suggest this means a return to the principle valued by the old Bolsheviks steeped in dialectical philosophy: unity-in-difference. This actually represents an advance on more recent thinking about 'broad democratic alliances' or 'rainbow coalitions' because it recognises the need for unity around common concerns whilst also understanding that the basis for unity is not homogeneity but a whole variety of heterogenous, possibly antagonistic, maybe magnicently diverse, identities and circumstances. Unity-in-difference opens up the potential, witnessed in all the activities supporting the striking mining communities in 1984 – 85, that people can act in political solidarity in ways that do not subsume or deny real differences, divisions and diversities in the name of some abstract greater good that is predefined as *the* struggle for socialism. The politics of identity recognises that there will be many struggles, and perhaps a few celebrations, and writes into all of them a welcome to contradiction and complexity.

Finally, where does such a politics leave the activists, the ones who have already assigned a political identity to themselves and belong to 'that great movement of ours'? There used to be a vivid metaphor for these comrades: they operated like 'red moles'. Not glamorous figures, but certainly carrying a frisson of excitement and secrecy: they were subversive, dangerous, and above all, *oppositional*. They would keep tunnelling away until, 'Well grubbed, old mole!', courtesy of Shakespeare and Marx, the entire edifice of capitalism collapsed by the combined weight of its internal contradictions and the dirty work of the vanguard.

Facing up to the fact that it hadn't after all happened that way, Gramsci in prison started his own rethinking for a future 'new times'. In the course of which he devised a quite extraordinary metaphor to describe the political activists he saw as 'intellectuals of a new type'. They should become, he said, 'as it were, the whalebone in the corset'. As so often in *The Prison Notebooks*, this figure is offered as a generous hint for other, or later, comrades to elaborate. It is of course suggestive.

What I like about it is that it still preserves some notion of revolutionary stiffening and control whilst also being an intimate, indeed, sensuously materialist figure of speech. Whilst Gramsci himself still kept faith with the notion of a dedicated cadre force of the revolutionary élite, his own metaphor of the activist surpassed his conscious thinking to offer an image which is at once about the discipline that holds you in and also about support and supportiveness. Which relates to another sense of the term, the one Gramsci actually had in mind: he speaks of the activist coming out of 'the masses', but remaining in constant contact with them, literally almost, 'keeping in touch'. So where is the gap now between the actual and potential political subject? In contrast to the oppositionally subversive mole suffering sensory deprivation in isolated conditions, the figure of 'the whalebone in the corset' suggests a quite different way of working: upfront, open and close. Not a bad beginning for a politics about to enter the mainstream.

Notes

[1] A. Gramsci, *Selections from the Prison Notebooks*, Q. Hoare and G. Nowell-Smith (eds), Lawrence and Wishart 1973.

[2] K. Marx, 'The Eighteenth Brumaire of Louis Napoleon' in *Marx-Engels Selected Works*, Lawrence and Wishart 1970.

[3] M. Foucalt, *The History of Sexuality*, Penguin/Allen Lane 1979

Frank Mort

The Politics of Consumption

Take two cultural narratives of consumption.

Spring 1988: the retail boom at its height and the yob and the yuppie are icons of the new materialism. Harry Enfield's bragging London plasterer, Loadsamoney, is working-class affluence personified. A thoroughly modern flash-harry, the tosh with the dosh, Loads is an incarnation of the property-owning democracy. His upmarket soulmate, the yuppie, is hero and heroine of the style manuals and financial markets. A mythical creature of the boom – part agent, part victim – with a lifestyle ruthlessly dedicated to consuming.

Autumn 1989: falling house prices and a sales slump in the shops. The symbolic failure of retailing's Next and advertising's Saatchi and Saatchi. Suddenly, Loads is very much last year's hero: 'I've Lost A Lump In The Slump – Bish, Bosh, I've Spent All Me Dosh.' The rag trade puts it more prosaically: 'Well it had to happen. The bubble had to burst. Like all good things the boom is running out of steam.'[1]

These stories deal not just with material success and failure. Up and downmarket they project profoundly cultural images of economic life. That is why they have stuck in the popular imagination, positively as well as negatively. They condense styles of living, forms of identity which demand attention in any political assessment of contemporary consumption.

The politics of consumption lies at the heart of this essay. Indeed, the twin issues of consumerism and the market lie at the heart of the debate over our vision of the future of socialism. Where you stand on them has become a litmus test for the whole question of renewal and realignment. In the redder than red corner stand those for whom markets are the very apogee of capitalist immorality, denying real freedoms and collective decision-making. The reassertion of this version of socialist morality has of course been prompted by the rethink around the issues of collectivism and individualism taking place within the labour movement and elsewhere. Current thinking, certainly in Labour's policy review, is that public provision and the market can be brought into a new relation. But the point of what follows is not simply to endorse 'market socialism' or a new revisionism. It is to argue that thinking through the politics of consumption must be as much a cultural as an economic project. It needs to be about taking our images of the yob and the yuppie (and what lies behind them) seriously. Despite their profound contradictions, ideologies of affluence have had very real effects on large sections of the population. Some of these have been potentially liberating – consuming as a source of power and pleasure. They will need to find a place within our vision of new times.

Economic Populism

Consumption is now centre stage in the political battle over the economy. Its orchestration by the government was a pivotal part of its vaunted economic successes between 1985 and 1988. This was not just the stuff of money supply ratios and macro Treasury forecasts, central to its command of the economic high ground was the ability to deal in popular ideologies of economics – languages which effectively delivered for people's everyday experience.

This is where Thatcherism, in both its first and second phases, scored so dramatically over its rivals. In its skill in embroidering a patchwork of economic common sense which matched so many of our own notions of managing money. If the first term and a half talked of iron times and the political economy of pain, Mr Lawson gave us quite a different tune. Out went the morality of backs to the wall and the handbag mentality of good housekeeping. Britain was booming again: investment up, inflation and unemployment down. And in this revised version of economic doctrine consumption was cast as a star performer. A retail boom and the bull-market in house prices were flagged up as the most visible signs of recovery. Lawson epitomised it in his own persona – part economic wizard, part *bon viveur*, even a touch sexy. While one-liners from the banks and building societies pushed a brazen regime of consumer pleasure, relaxation and excess. 'Gold Card Service'; 'No Spending Limit';

'Moneycare: Making It, Spending It, Enjoying It', purred Nat West seductively.[2] Here was a slap in the face for both the old maxims of save and prosper and the austere morality of the first term.

There were of course deep-seated contradictions in the consumer boom, rooted in the structural weaknesses of the UK economy, which are now coming home to roost. A high street shopping spree was no guide to prolonged economic recovery, for the growing balance of payments deficit pointed up just how many commodities were import-based. While bank give-aways for cars and Amstrads were a timely reminder of finance capital's disinvestment in Britain's industrial base. And at the back of it all lay the accelerating inflationary wage-price spiral.

Underpinning the retailing expansion and exacerbating many of the sector's current difficulties has been the expansion in credit. The flexibility and innovations in finance capital have set some of the material conditions here. Britons have taken to charge cards and plastic money like no other EEC country. On 1989 figures we owe a cool £28 million on our personal loans.[3] All of the major high street chains − M & S, Dixons, Next − offer their own financial services with annual interest rates at times topping the 40 per cent mark. Boots, conscious perhaps of its philanthropic past, withdrew its own instore card on the grounds that interest charges were excessive. Yet spending on the never-never has never been so acceptable − and for some so necessary. Rising three times faster than annual incomes since 1980, it has thrown up its own growth industries: debt collectors and repossession merchants. We should be cautious, though, in reading this phenomenon over-simply. Some complex patterns are emerging in the *uses* of credit; namely its take-up by sections of the new poor to buy into a vision of prosperity. Students, those in the part-time workforce, as well as the long-term unemployed may be forced to use plastic to purchase essentials, but it seems that they are also taking up the offer to play the system imaginatively − even to their own advantage.

And despite the current economic downturn these ideologies of buying and selling are still very much in place. The partnership between the financial markets and retailing has thrown up some very late-capitalist images of prosperity. The manic compulsion to consume; the hyper-eroticisation of a visit to the shops; economics as a game of chance or wheel of fortune, here today, gone tomorrow — these are now some of the popular representations of material life. Indeed, living with instability is one of the most enduring cultural legacies of the decade. It has replaced the slow but upward gradualism of social democracy (the gold watch for forty years service and merit rewarded) with icons which are much more precarious and fluctuating. Murdoch's popular press in particular has consistently projected economics if not quite as tinsel fairyland, then as something unstable and irrational. After all, like bingo or having a flutter, that's what gives it *frisson* and excitement. And while the rhetoric of the popular press is not a direct mirror of real experience, there are resonances here of some very traditional working-class responses to money and success. Fatalism, economic fortunes like the pools' winners who blow it all in a fortnight, above all a profound sense that economic forces are 'out there' beyond the control of ordinary people. It is through these cultural maps that many council house buyers in Basildon or credit debtors in Billericay must be trying to make sense of the present situation.

The general point to come out of all of this is that consumption is as much about the languages and images of economics as about the nuts and bolts of policy. Thus a successful politics in this area needs to be thought through in a vocabulary which matches people's life-chances and experience. This is where theoretical economics (ever since it defined itself as a science) is left floundering. Thatcherism's orchestration of consumption has been adept at channelling perceptions of growing personal prosperity into its own political discourse equating the ring of tinkling cash registers with political and cultural freedoms. What, of course, the government desperately needs now as the third term draws all too rapidly to a close, is a populist package which can 'sell' the current economic situation as effectively as it sold us recession and then the boom.

Labour and the Politics of Austerity

How to challenge Tory economic populism? What languages to draw on to project an alternative economic future which engages with people's desire for their own as well as collective prosperity? One deep-seated response from the opposition is that government policy is so profligate and the economy's weaknesses now so apparent, that there is little need to engage with any sort of populist rhetoric. But if we accept the argument about the centrality of the images which shape material life, Labour will need to find an imaginative way of translating policy into the popular aspirations, desires, even dreams which cluster around common sense understandings of economics and especially consumption.

Part of the difficulty here lies in the legacy of Keynesianism. For while consumer aggregate demand, along with full employment and public spending, did figure as a cornerstone of postwar consensus politics, it appeared unsung, as an economic abstraction only within Labour's political discourse of those years. There was little attempt to translate Keynesian macroeconomics into a rhetoric which tapped into a burgeoning consumer culture. Again, the Tories had all the best tunes, whether it was Churchill's 'set the people free' slogan to end austerity in 1951, or Macmillan's 'you've never had it so good' slightly later. There were exceptions on Labour's side of course; 'revisionists' (the name says it all) like Crosland and Jenkins did begin to float an expansive scheme for the mixed economy which embraced cultural (albeit tasteful) images of affluence. But Labour never found a way of being easy about prosperity. For the most part when Messrs Wilson and Callaghan did bring economics to the nation we got a lecture about how everything was going wrong − TV graphs of the balance of payments in the red, devaluation and the prices and incomes freeze.

In fact the reasons for that unease, the failure to engage with the politics of affluence, go deeper than failures of policy. They bring us face to face with part of the legacy of socialism's own past − a politics which emerged triumphant in the first half of the 20th century, and which we continue to inherit. Brutally put, the problem is socialism's over-identification with production. This, fused with the input from an older more explicitly moral and evangelicising Labour tradition, is still engraved in tablets of stone on the hearts and minds of many on the British Left. It effectively acts as a barrier to any more imaginative approach to post-Fordist economics and culture.

Here we need to sketch in the other strand of Labour's postwar history. In the 1940s the Labour Party defined itself as the progressive Fordist party, projecting an economic modernism which identified with large-scale production and the workplace aims of those who ran the plants. Culturally it was, as we now know, a highly gendered modernism, which heroised the butch, macho heavy industries and ranked workers in the new service sector as secondary and inferior. But on the forms of mass consumption which accompanied the Fordist revolution, Labour was always ideologically more wary, more suspicious. The dominance of Fabianism, coupled with an austere Methodism, made large sections of the Left uneasy about the cars, fridges and washing machines that were rolling off the production line. Consuming, as opposed to producing, was at best handled as secondary and trivial, confined to the private, feminised sphere of household duties and personal life. At worst consumption was cast as a moral evil, buying off working people with an orgy of goodies − or so the argument often went. Labour's immediate response to the postwar situation was austerity, rationing, coupons *and* the black market. Austerity may have been a hit with top-down economic planners, but it was a dismal failure for consumer democracy. Labour's austerity Chancellor, Stafford Cripps, aimed to purge consuming passions from the national psyche. Cripps wanted the desire for fashionable clothes and jewellery − and their association with feminine pleasures eliminated altogether, for good.[4]

The rationale for rehearsing this history is not to castigate past errors, rather to insist that a simple anti-consumerist politics is debilitating in today's economic context. For Labour, growing government disarray on the economic front presents a major political opportunity and we have had some effective performances from Messrs Smith and Brown as the opposition Treasury team. But their negative gloss on the pitfalls of the consumer economy has been laced with more than a hint of Calvinist sadism and 'I told you so' smugness. Labour should beware of deploying consumption as a purely negative symbol of economic performance. To do so is to ignore all those positive aspirations which have jostled for space around Thatcherism's limited market philosophy.

Lifestyles and Market Segments

Arguing for the politics of consumption inside the Left means enlarging and complexifying our map of economic structures and processes. There is nothing innately Thatcherite about consuming, just as there is nothing intrinsically socialist about the state. A reductionism which collapses the lived experience of consumerism with the official version of Tory popular capitalism, is blind to the fact that what people actually *do* when they go shopping may be quite different from the official script. Commodities and their images are multi-accented, they can be pushed and pulled into the service of resistant demands and dreams. High tech in the hands of young blacks or girls making-up are not simply forms of buying into the system. They can be very effectively hijacked for cultures of resistance, reappearing as street-style cred or assertive femininity.

But we are already jumping ahead. The first move is to take seriously the industries which fix our experience of buying and selling. Getting to grips with advertising and marketing raises the whole question of the Left's strategy for the service sector in the post-Fordist economy: their functions, forms of knowledge and control and, crucially, their cultural and social effects. But advertising and marketing are not only key institutions in the consumer cycle, they command a higher and higher profile within production as well. The role of these industries has grown qualitatively in tandem with shifts away from standardised mass production to more flexible systems and changes in consumer demand in favour of greater choice and diversity. Key decisions in many sectors have migrated away from the plant and factory to these new captains of industry. In clothing and food ratailing, for example, crucial management policy is made largely by marketers and retailers. Marks and Spencers dominate through the backward integration of food processing and production, while Benetton have become famous for their flexible franchising system. Workers in these sectors possess their own reserves of cultural capital − systems of knowledge and training which cannot just be written off as 'Thatcherite'. We are dealing here with fractions of the service class or new petty bourgeoisie whose occupations involve some form representation in handling symbolic goods and services.[5]

Yet for too many on the Left retailing and advertising provokes a rash of socialist moralism. For these are the ones we really love to hate: personifications of yuppiedom, the docklands interlopers, those who deal in slick images pulled into the service of capital. The whole fall-out over so-called 'designer socialism' has produced a knee-jerk response, branding those who raise its profile as middle-class trendies, hypnotised by the glare of Next and Katherine Hamnett. A more serious look at advertising's dialogue with the market puts paid to the cliché that consumption is foisted on gullible populations by hype and the lust for profit. Advertisers and marketers are not simply the slaves of capital. They are the intermediaries who construct a dialogue between the market on thc one hand and consumer culture on the other. Marketers will tell you that this is a two-way process; it doesn't simply come from above. Product design and innovation, pricing and promotion, are shaped by the noises coming from the street. Market research is in the business of collating these noises and shaping them into consumer profiles. The net result is, of course, contradictory. The industry deals in its own social truisms about 'upward mobility' or 'what women want'. But to fail to recognise that marketing taps something of our pleasures and aspirations as consumers is to ignore the how and why of its success.

The late 1980s have witnessed some major rethinks within the industry about the content and direction of campaigns. The retailing revolution on the high street and the shopping malls has gone hand-in-hand with an intellectual change of direction backstage. *Lifestyling* is the end product, a marketing concept which twins designer-led retailing with shifting patterns of consumer demand. Rodney Fitch, of Fitch and Co, the consultants who promoted Next, pinpoints the move quite precisely:

> The consumer is changing. The consumers' ideas, expectations and attitudes towards how they will buy, let alone what they will buy ... are all in a state of flux. High street shopping simply mirrors changes in our society and demonstrates that you are responsive to them ... design has become part of these competitive retail strategies. Design is a visual thing and therefore the end result is visual change.[6]

Two basic concepts are at work here: the move to market segmentation, and the input from design and visual communications. The argument goes like this. Traditional market blocs which were the mainstay of the era of postwar mass production (the working-class family, youth, the housewife, etc, have splintered under the impact of cultural upheavals going on beyond the sales-counter and the supermarket aisle. Consumer profiles have become very sensitive to these social dynamics. They target their audiences with a new precision: Volkswagen for the working woman, Saga Holidays for the young elderly, the pink pound for gay men. In essence it is marketing's bid to come to terms with the cultural agenda of the 1990s. The industry is especially sharp on the new cultures of working-class affluence – in their vocabulary the C1s and C2s in work. *Campaign* deftly rings the changes: traditional Saturday afternoons on the terraces and bingo are out, displaced by saunas, aerobics and eating in with *Liebfraumilch* and *chicken chasseur*.

Greater market segmentation demands different methods of communication. This is where the other factor in lifestyling comes in – the upbeat stress on design and visual awareness. Advertising theory has long since abandoned the hard sell technology which worked with simple notions of social or price competitiveness: the sell 'em cheap, pile 'em high campaigns of the 1960s and early 1970s. In a society where large swathes of the population already possess consumer basics like fridges, TVs and washing machines, advertising must find a different language to promote product awareness. The aim is to suggest atmosphere – a style of life – with a message which is 'emotional' rather than rational or informational. Colour, sound and shape are the things which mark out individuality, nudging consumers to identify with commodities through mood and association. As John Hegarty, the consultant responsible for the famous Levi Jeans account, put it, the thing to crack was atmosphere and quality of the image, quite as much as the brand of product.[7] Recent M & S ads, Next Interiors, or the Debenham's refit on the shopfloor all point to lifestyling in action. Of course late 1980s retailing has not itself invented individualism; appeal to the unique *you* has been the staple diet of so many campaigns over the last four decades. But what is currently happening is a hyping of that process, a proliferation of individualities, of the number of 'yous' on offer.

Our argument is that the service sector industries (not on their own but as part of a broader ensemble of post–Fordist practices) are redefining the economic and cultural horizons of contemporary Britain. We may disagree with advertising's conclusions, but we would be foolish to dismiss the insights thrown up about shifting class relations or the redrawn maps of cultural experience going on inside people's heads. And whisper it not too loud, but aren't there some uncanny resemblances between lifestyle market segmentation and the politics of identity which have been argued for by the new social movements. For the fracturing of solid market blocs read the break-up of postwar class certainties and the eruption of quite different political subjects with alternative agendas: women, gays, the elderly, etc. Both the market and formal politics are being forced to adapt to these sea-changes. Moreover, as in the marketplace so in the political meeting, postmodern structures of identity are less centred around the certainty of a fixed self. We do not often get the reassurance of a coherent subjectivity these days – politically or culturally. We are not in any simple sense 'black' or 'gay' or 'upwardly mobile'. Rather we carry a bewildering range of different, and at times conflicting, identities around with us in our heads at the same time. There is a continual smudging of personas and lifestyles, depending where we are (at work, on the high street) and the spaces we are moving between. It is the speed, the fluidity with which these identities mingle and overlap which makes any notion of fixed subjects seem more and more anachronistic – distinctly early 20th century.

Both politics and consumer culture are registering these structural changes. Yet there is one crucial difference between their two fields of vision – a difference which goes to the heart of our argument about the need to take consumption seriously. It is a difference of style, of language, of presentation, but in the profoundest sense. Political language still speaks a vocabulary of power and authority on the one hand or oppression and struggle on the other. By and large it is also a verbal or written discourse which seeks to appeal through rationality. The new consumerism on the other hand is all about floating visual images, pleasures and impossible dreams. To say that these are false dreams, false promises is to miss the point. Formal politics of all persuasions is rigidly self-policing about this utopian bundle. It defensively ringfences its boundaries and lets only very particular political subjects in through the door. Needs, rights and demands are OK, but lifestyle pleasures and aspirations are still out of bounds. Some of the new politics – and notably feminism – have been about breaking down these watertight distinctions between 'politics' and 'life'. In a no less coherent way, and often targeting the same populations, consumer culture does the same.

The net effect of all this has been to ask some unanswerable questions of the political culture of Fordism. The collapse of old political certainties, the loss of faith in early 20th century forms of organisation and identity − public meetings, canvassing, party literature and the old-style version of citizenship − are not simply the product of apathy under Thatcherism. 'Depoliticisation' registers much more than a pessimism about the political process. It speaks of a growing disengagement of 'life', where people choose to put their energies and invest their hopes, from 'politics'. For more and more people it is *outside* work, *outside* the formal political structures, in the world of holidays, home interiors and superstores, that they have a sense of power and freedom to express themselves, to define their sense of self, to mould the good life. Thatcherism has not created that scenario, but the present political culture has certainly capitalised on it. In the current climate the invitation is to 'buy out of politics', to see it as only to do with restrictive bureaucracy and petty nuisance. Life, it seems, lies elsewhere.[8]

So, to put it polemically, should we just sit back and let the marketeers get on with it ? If we are looking for cultural agendas which energise people and express their sense of self, doesn't consumer capitalism do it better anyway ? Is there really nowhere to go but the shops ?

There is no one political response to the agenda thrown up by consumption; indeed Politics with a big P may itself be part of the problem. Rather, what are needed are inter-related initiatives which confront issues of economic policy, cultural politics and the much-needed modernisation of socialist culture in Britain. Some of these are relatively easy to translate into party policy (if the political will is there), while others have a much longer-term future. At the heart of all of them sits the vexed question of the relation between collectivist and individual value systems in any alternative to Thatcherism.

Given the sea-changes in finance capital as well as marketing, consumption is set to remain high priority on the economic front, despite the recent retail slow − down. More important, it is a key point in the popular imagination where economic policy is judged to succeed or fail − precisely because it touches people where they *feel* active and powerful. Labour's policy needs to take those aspirations and forms of common sense seriously. At one level this has to do with presentation (not a superficial point by any means), of finding languages which engage with economics on those terms. But there are some tough policy issues here as well. Income tax is certainly one of them. Leaving aside the precise details of the policy review, there will need to be some pretty hard talking about the precise balance to be struck between collective and individual demands around taxation. Fixing fair *but reasonable* tax levels is about making choices between goods and services directed through public provision and those determined by the private sector. And if that sounds like revisionism, or selling socialism short, it is precisely because the relation between the market and the public sector remains one of the big open-ended questions of socialist strategy.

But thinking needs to go beyond the purely economic, given that consumerism is the point where material and social life collide. One current response here is to take seriously the impact of consumer individualism, but to work for alternative and expanded definitions of choice. Thus Charter 88 returns to the arena of citizen's rights and freedoms, while the rhetoric of consumer choice has become standard practice in many areas of the public sector. And there is everything positive for the Left in striking a new compact between production and consumption led values. Yet the programme here is ultimately pragmatic, hoping to bind in the new individualisms to existing ideas of policy and politics. What this of course refuses is the bigger issue of whether leisure and consumption haven't already redefined the terrain.

So our conception of politics must again be prised open. Responding to consumption means recasting our thinking: to begin politically from the pressure points where so many of us invest our energies and life chances. Most of the new politics have been saying much the same thing, yet rarely have they put consumer culture centre stage. Consequently the argument is about sites as well as programmes. Today's consumer culture straddles public and private space, creating blurred areas in between. Privatised car culture, with its collective red nose days and stickers for lead-free petrol; shopping as the quintessential expression of consumer choice now carries social anxieties over eco-politics and food pollution. These are the localised points where consuming meshes with social demands and aspirations in new ways. What they underline is that consumption is not ultimately about individualism *versus* collectivism, but about articulating the two in a new relation which can form the basis for a future common sense.

Notes

[1] *Menswear*, 4 May 1989, p2.

[2] National Westminster Bank, *Moneycare*, Spring 1988, front cover

[3] 'The credit boom goes on', *Guardian*, 6 June 1989, p 11.

[4] Sir Stafford Cripps, Budget Speech, 6 April 1949, in Public Record Office, Treasury Papers, T 171/399.

[5] For further analysis of the culture of the new middle-classes see Pierre Bordieu, *Distinction: a Social Critique of the Judgement of Taste*, Routledge and Kegan Paul 1984.

[6] 'Designs on the new consumer,' *Marketing*, 24 October 1985, p 20.

[7] 'How heritage will be used to relaunch a Levis classic *Campaign*, 29 November 1985, pp 39-43.

[8] Zygmunt Bauman, 'Britain's exit from politics', *New Statesman and Society*, 29 July 1988, pp 34-37.

Stuart Hall and David Held

Citizens and Citizenship

Citizenship has been largely absent from political discussion and debate for more than two decades. Only in relation to questions of race and immigration did it carry a deep political charge. Were the boundaries of citizenship to be redrawn with the end of empire? Could there be more than one class of citizenship for people of different ethnic backgrounds? The debate, crowned by the intervention of Enoch Powell in the late 1960s, marked a high point in the political currency of this dimension of citizenship. Elsewhere, the concept seemed rather out-of-date. Suddenly, however, citizenship is once more on the lips of politicians, academics and commentators of all political complexions. Why this renewed concern? What is at stake in this debate about citizenship between Right and Left?

A number of different factors seem to be responsible for the return of citizenship to the political agenda. Some derive from the experience of Thatcherism itself: the dismantling of the welfare state, the growing centralisation of power, the erosion of local democracy, of free speech, trade-union and other civil rights.

Some have a wider, more 'global' context: the growth of regional nationalism in Scotland and elsewhere; the prospects for greater European integration; the weakening of the old East-West frontiers under the Gorbachev offensive; the growing pace of international interdependence and globalisation — all, in one way or another, exposing and eroding the sovereignty of the nation-state, the entity to which, until now, the modern language of citizenship primarily referred.

These changes have been accompanied by shifts in attitude towards the idea of citizenship on both the Right and the Left. It used to be fashionable in some sections of the Left to dismiss the question of 'rights' as, largely, a bourgeois fraud. But the experience of Thatcherism in the West and of stalinism in the East has gradually shifted the Left's thinking on this question. The shift on the Right is more complex and uncertain. Thatcherism's drive towards unrestricted private accumulation, its attack on public expenditure, collectivism and the 'dependency culture' made it the natural enemy of citizenship in its modern, welfare state form. As the prime minister put it: 'There is no such thing as society, only individual men and women and their families.'

However, this unswerving commitment to individualism and the competitive ethic has awakened, in its turn, the spectre of Hobbes' 'war of all against all': the breakdown of a sense of community and interdependence, the weakening of the social fabric and the loosening of the hounds of social violence – so often features of a society dedicated exclusively to competitive self-interest. Thatcherism has therefore rediscovered the need for some concept to help integrate and 'bind' society and has come up with the idea of the 'active citizen', who engages in 'doing good' but in purely private capacity. In this discourse, citizenship is detached from its modern roots in institutional reform, in the welfare state and community struggles, and rearticulated with the more Victorian concepts of charity, philanthropy and self-help. In more recent versions, the 'active citizen' is decked out in the pious homilies of Thatcherism's version of the New Testament.

Clearly, we need a framework for thinking about citizenship and its place in the agenda of the Left which sets it in the context of recent developments. Far from simply returning us to the old language of citizenship, such an exercise requires us to confront new questions and to rethink the concept itself in the light of a new historical situation.

Does 'citizenship' belong naturally and exclusively to the Left? It has been part of what can broadly be identified as a variety of progressive historical movements – from older ideas of just moral order to Paine's *Rights of Man* and Chartism. Nevertheless, it seems to be the case that citizenship belongs exclusively to neither Right nor Left, nor indeed to the centre-ground. Like all the key contested political concepts of our time, it can be appropriated within very different political discourses and articulated to very different political positions – as its recuperation by the New Right clearly shows. The concept can only mean something decisive for the Left if we are prepared to do some theoretical and political work around it, actively integrating it within a whole set of related political ideas.

While there is no '*essence*' to citizenship, it does have a long and rich history with which any new conception must come to terms. From the ancient world to the present day, citizenship has entailed a discussion of, and a struggle over, the meaning and scope of membership of the community in which one lives. Who belongs and what does *belonging* mean in practice? Membership, here, is not conditional: it is a matter of right and entitlement. But it is two-sided, reciprocal: rights in, but also responsibilities towards, the community. These rights have to be defined and specified, because otherwise their loss cannot be challenged, and may even go undetected. But formal definition alone will not suffice. Rights can be mere paper claims unless they can be practically enacted and realised, through actual participation in the community. These then are citizenship's three leading notions: membership; rights and duties in reciprocity; real participation in practice.

The issues around membership — who does and who does not belong — is where the *politics* of citizenship begins. It is impossible to chart the history of the concept very far without coming sharply up against successive attempts to restrict citizenship to certain groups and to exclude others. In different historical periods, different groups have led, and profited from, this 'politics of closure': property-owners, men, white people, the educated, those in particular occupations or with particular skills, adults. However, as the struggles against exclusion have developed and broadened across history, so those stemming from the exclusive enjoyment of the advantages of property, ownership, wealth and privilege — in short, questions of class — have come to dominate the 'politics of citizenship', absorbing a wide variety of different struggles against different forms of exclusion under their rubric.

Certainly, class has constituted, historically, one of the most powerful and ramified of barriers to membership and participation by the majority. But this has also set up a tension within the idea of citizenship itself. For, as the politics of citizenship has been absorbed into class politics, so the citizenship idea has lost something of its specific force.

However, this exclusive reference to class is one of the things which is changing with the renewed interest in citizenship. In reality, attempts to restrict membership and participation take many different forms, involving different practices of exclusion and affecting different groups. This should be enough to convince us that questions of citizenship, though bound to place the issues of class at their centre, cannot simply be absorbed into class politics, or thought of exclusively in class terms, and in relation to capitalist relations of production.

A contemporary 'politics of citizenship' must take into account the role which the social movements have played in *expanding* the claims to rights and entitlements to new areas. It must address not only issues of class and inequality, but also questions of membership posed by feminism, the black and ethnic movements, ecology (including the moral claims of the animal species and of Nature itself) and vulnerable minorities, like children. But it must also come to terms with the problems posed by 'difference' in a deeper sense: for example, the diverse communities to which we belong, the complex interplay of identity and identification in modern society, and the differentiated ways in which people now participate in social life. The diversity of arenas in which citizenship is being claimed and contested today is essential to any modern conception of it because it is inscribed in the very logic of modern society itself.

However, this expansion of the idea of citizenship may run counter to the logic of citizenship, which has tended to absorb 'differences' into one common universal status — the citizen. In the year of the anniversary of the French Revolution, it is worth recalling that its three cardinal principles — liberty, equality and fraternity — formed a matrix within which the citizens of the new Republic claimed *universal* recognition on the basis of a common equality. This language of theoretical universality and *equality* is what distinguished this moment — the moment of the 'Rights of Man' — from earlier phases in the long march of citizenship. But in the light of the expansion and diversity of claims discussed above, the question must be posed as to whether the variety and range of entitlements can be adequately expressed through or represented by a single, universal status like 'citizenship'. Is there now an irreconcilable tension between the thrust to equality and universality entailed in the very idea of the 'citizen', and the variety of particular and specific needs, of diverse sites and practices which constitute the modern political subject?

We will come back to this question of 'difference' later − it is, in some ways, the joker in the citizenship pack. However, what the previous discussion makes clear is that contemporary claims to citizenship are interrelated with a range of other political questions. What we think about this range of political questions will inevitably affect what we think about citizenship itself.

Social or Private Citizenship

What does the language of citizenship rights really mean in contemporary society? And who are the subjects of such rights? Citizenship rights are *entitlements*. Such entitlements are public and social (hence Mrs Thatcher's difficulties with them). They are 'of right' and can only be abrogated by the state under clearly delimited circumstances (for example, in the case of imprisonment, which curtails liberties which all citizens should otherwise enjoy). However, though citizenship is a social status, its rights are entitlements to individuals. Individual citizens enjoy such entitlements on the basis of a fundamental equality of condition − their membership of the community.

Citizenship rights establish a legitimate sphere for *all* individuals to pursue their actions and activites without risk or arbitrary or unjust political interference. Early attempts to achieve citizenship involved a struggle for the autonomy or independence of individuals from the locale in which they were born and from prescribed occupations. Later struggles have involved such things as individual entitlement to freedom of speech, expression, belief, information, as well as the freedom of association on which trade-union rights depend, and freedom of women in relation to marriage and property. Citizenship rights can therefore be thought of as a measure of the autonomy an individual citizen enjoys as a result of his or her status as a 'free and equal' member of a society. The other important feature is that, though they are guaranteed to citizens by the state, they are also, in an important sense, guaranteed *against* the arbitrary exercise of state power. Citizenship in its full sense therefore combines, in rather unusual ways, the public and the social with the individual aspects of political life.

The Left critique of this position is by now quite familiar, and carries considerable weight. It centres on the emphasis, in the language of rights, on *individual* entitlement. There are really three strands to this critique. Firstly, the degree to which individuals really are 'free' in capitalist democracies is open to question. Secondly, everything depends on how freedom is defined. The rights and freedoms which interest the New Right refer to a very narrow arena of social action, and are constructed around a very limited conception of individual needs and desires. Largely, these are restricted to individuals as isolated atoms, acting in their own interests, maximised through exchange in the marketplace. Rights are not considered to have a social dimension or an interdependent character. Thirdly, citizenship rights, particularly in Britain, are largely defined negatively. There are no laws preventing you entering the Ritz or buying property in Docklands or applying for most jobs. Whether in fact you have the means or the capacity to do or achieve any of those things, positively, is a quite different matter. In the famous words of Anatole France: 'The law in its majestic equality gives every man (prince and pauper alike) an equal right to sleep under a bridge or eat at the Ritz.'

This is really another way of restating the Left's critique of classic liberalism in terms of the tension betweeen 'formal' and 'substantive' rights. The citizen may formally enjoy 'equality before the law'. But, important though this unquestionably is, does he or she also have the material and cultural resources to choose between different courses of action in practice? The 'free and equal individual', as one commentator suggests, is a person found more rarely in practice than liberal theory suggests. What liberal theory, in both its classic and contemporary forms, takes for granted has, in fact, to be seriously questioned. Namely, whether the existing relations between men and women, between employers and employees, between the social classes, or blacks, whites and other ethnic groups, allow citizenship to become a reality in practice.

This question lies at the centre of the 'politics of citizenship' today. Any current assessment of citizenship must be made on the basis of liberties and rights which are tangible, capable of being enjoyed, in both the state and civil society. If it is not given concrete and practical content, liberty as an abstract principle can scarcely be said to have any very profound consequences for everyday life. It is difficult to hymn the praises of liberty, when massive numbers of actual individuals are systematically restricted – for want of a complex mix of resources and opportunities – from participating actively in political and civil life. Gross inequalities of class, sex and race substantively hinder the extent to which it can legitimately be claimed that individuals are really 'free and equal' in contemporary society.

There is therefore, much of substance to the Left's critique of the liberal conception of citizenship. On the other hand, this may have led us to go too far in the opposite direction. We must test every 'formal' right we are supposed to enjoy against its substance in practice. But this does not mean that the formal definition of rights – for example, in a constitution or bill of rights – is unimportant, or a matter of 'mere form'. Until rights have been specified, there is no way of monitoring their infringement or of calling to account their practical implementation.

In general, what this discussion suggests is that the 'politics of citizenship' today must come to terms with, and attempt to strike a new balance between, the individual and the social dimensions of citizenship rights. These two aspects are interdependent and cannot be separated. Neither, on its own, will suffice. On the other hand, there is no necessary contradiction between them.

The New Right would argue exactly the opposite, and this is one reason why the relationship between the individual and the social dimensions of rights becomes one of the key issues at stake in exchanges between the New Right and its left critics. The New Right has a very clear and consistent position on the question and the related issues of freedom and equality.

The New Right is committed to the classic liberal doctrine that the collective good can be properly realised in most cases *only* by private individuals acting in competitive isolation, pursuing their interests with minimal state interference. At root, the New Right is concerned with how to advance the cause of 'liberalism' against 'democracy' (or, as they put it, 'freedom' against 'equality') by limiting the possible uses of state power. On this view, the government can only legitimately intervene in society to enforce *general* rules – formal rules which broadly protect, in John Locke's works, the 'life, liberty and estate' of the citizen. Hayek, a leading advocate of these ideas, argues that a free liberal order is incompatible with rules which specify how people should use the means at their disposal. Governments become coercive if they interfere with people's capacity to determine their own objectives. Hence the reliance in Hayek's work on 'law', his critique of the so-called 'totalitarianism' involved in social planning and rejection of the idea that the state can represent the 'public interest.'

Hayek's prime example of coercive government is legislation which attempts to alter the 'material position of particular people or enforce distributive or 'social' justice. Distributive justice, he argues, always imposes on some person or group someone else's conception of merit or desert. It requires the allocation of resources by a central authority acting as if it knew what people should receive for their efforts or how to behave. In his view, there is only one mechanism sufficiently sensitive to determine collective choice on an individual basis without such imposition – the free market. When protected by a constitutional state and a framework of law, it is argued, no system provides a mechanism of collective choice as dynamic, innovative and responsive. The free market is, for the New Right, the key condition of the liberty of citizens. When operating within the framework of a minimal state, it thus becomes constitutive of the nature of citizenship itself.

The Left has always taken issue with this line of argument. The free market, it has argued, produces and reinforces those very forms of exclusion and 'closure' associated with private property and wealth, against which the idea of citizenship was directed. Hence, through the redistributive welfare state, the prerogatives of property and wealth had to be cross-cut, modified or in T H Marshall's famous phrase, 'abated', by the countervailing rights of citizenship. In practice, the only force of sufficiently compelling weight to bring to bear against the powers of property and capital was that of the state. Hence, for the Left, the state was not inimical but essential to the very idea of citizenship.

It is indeed difficult to see how a proper conception of citizenship could be established or effectively secured without the intervention of the state. On the other hand, it is not necessary to accept Hayek's line of reasoning to see that citizenship also entails the protection of the citizen *against* the arbitrary overweening exercise of state power. The weaknesses and limitations of a purely 'statist' conception of citizenship have become much more obvious in the light of recent history.

The Complication of Democracy

There is, then, an inevitable tension in the Left's position on citizenship, since it both requires and can be threatened by the state. One tendency of the Left has been to resolve or bypass this difficulty by, so to speak, dissolving the whole question into that of democracy itself. The extension of popular democracy, it is thought, will resolve all these knotty problems. Hence the Left's advocacy of collective decision-making and democratic participation as a resolution to all the problems of citizenship. Why bother to define and entrench specific rights if, in an expanded democracy, every individual is destined to become 'fully sovereign? Thus, by focusing squarely on the extension of democracy, the Left has tended to leave any further specification of particular citizenship rights, and the complex relations between liberty, social justice and democratic processes, to the ebb and flow of democratic negotiation. From Karl Marx to Lenin to Roy Hattersley (in his recent defence of Labour Party policy against Charter 88) this is a constant and recurring theme. 'The people' are to become sovereign (via, respectively, the Commune, Soviets, Parliament). 'The people' are to become governors of their own affairs — without limit, so the argument runs. Within this broad democratic advance, the specific questions of citizenship and the diffficulty of defining particular rights will take care of themselves.

This 'democratic' solution is in many ways an attractive argument. But it presents certain real difficulties. It is vulnerable to the charge of having failed to address the highly complex relations in modern societies between individual liberty, distributional questions of social justice, and democratic processes. It does not really resolve the question of who 'the people' are whose democratic sovereignty and enfranchisement are supposed to settle at a single stroke so many questions about particular rights. And it poses the extremely awkward issue of whether there are to be any specifiable limits to democracy. In short, is 'democracy' alone, unsupplemented and unmodified by any concept of citizenship, any longer enough?

Should there be any limits on the power of 'the people' to change or alter political circumstances? The experience of ten years of 'elective dictatorship' under Mrs Thatcher may have changed the Left's thinking on this question. For example, should the winning of a majority vote at an election constitute a mandate to destroy parts of the system of local government which has been so important a counterweight to the encroaching powers of a centralising state — especially if achieved under a highly lopsided, first-past-the-post electoral system? Should the nature and scope of the liberty of individuals be left entirely to the 'play' of democratic decision? Don't individuals need to have their rights to freedom of speech, thought and expression protected? Must minorities conform, simply because they are minorities?

By answering questions about the necessary limits to democracy in the affirmative, the New Right at least recognises the possibility of real tensions between individual liberty, collective decision-making and the institutions and processes of democracy. By not systematically addressing these issues, the Left, in contrast, has perhaps too hastily put aside the problems. In making democracy, at all levels, the primary social objective to be achieved, the Left has relied on 'democratic reason' — a wise and good democratic will — for the determination of all just and positive social outcomes. But can 'the people' always be relied upon to be just to minorities or to marginal and so-called 'unpopular' interests? Can one assume that the democratic will will always be wise and good?

This is not a matter of abstract theoretical debate. It is around some of these tensions that the New Right generated so much political capital against the Left. It forced the Left to acknowledge the uncertain outcomes of democratic life: the ambiguous results of the welfare state, for example. It highlighted the fact that distributive justice can also lead to bureaucracy, surveillance and the excessive infringement of individual options (and not only in Eastern Europe). It represented the reallocation of resources by the local state (for example, in the form of 'equal opportunities' and 'anti-racist' programmes) as an imposition of minority interests on the majority! These experiences have not necessarily made people more optimistic about collective democratic decision-making or more ready to fight to defend it.

Take the question of 'popular sovereignty'. Will the fact that we are all members of the great collective democratic subject — 'the people' — provide a guarantee of the rights and the liberties of the individual citizen? Not necessarily. 'The people' is, after all, also a discursive figure, a rhetorical device, a mode of adddress. It is open to constant negotiation, contestation and redefinition. It represents as a 'unity' what are in fact a diversity of different positions and interests. In its populist form − 'giving the people what they want' − it has been exploited by Thatcherism as a form of populist mobilisation against a range of different minorities who are 'not one of us'.

'The people' has also functioned so as to silence or marginalise the conflicts of interest which it claims to represent. Thatcherism has operated within a narrow and exclusive definition of 'the people'. It defines 'the people' as those who identify with or have done well out of the enterprise culture. But since, in reality, only a small number of prosperous people, mainly living in parts of the south east, can be represented in this figure, it is in effect a way of suppressing the rights, marginalising the needs and denying the identities of large numbers of other 'people' − including the Scots, the poor, the unemployed, the homeless, the underclasses, black people, many women, single-parent mothers, gay and lesbian people, and so on. Far from resolving anything, it is a highly-contested and contestable idea, around which a great deal of 'ideological work' is constantly going on.

Then there is the problem of what political entity the citizen is a citizen *of*. Everywhere, the nation state itself − the entity to which the language of political citizenship refers − is eroded and challenged. The processes of economic, political, military and ecological interdependence are beginning to undermine it as a sovereign, self-contained entity from above. The rise of regional and local 'nationalisms' are beginning to erode it from below. In certain respects, this may have negative consequences for citizenship: how to give effects to the 'rights' of the citizens of Bhopal against chemical pollution caused by a multinational company registered in New York and operating worldwide? In other respects, its consequences for citizenship may be positive. The European Court has certainly provided a critical bulwark for the citizen of the UK against the steady erosion of civil liberties under Thatcherism. But whether these processes work to the advantage or disadvantage of citizenship, the question remains: is this the right moment, historically, to be trying to define claims and entitlements made in terms of membership of the nation state?

There are then all kinds of problems which undermine any certainty that greater democracy will, in and of itself, resolve the dilemmas of citizenship. Is there any way through this impasse?

Constitutional Rights

One point which does follow directly from the foregoing discussion can be stated clearly, and provides us with a fresh start. There is a need to think through, and give institutional expression to, the demands of citizenship and democracy as closely related issues: but it is important to keep the questions distinct. Democracy can only really exist on the basis of 'free and equal citizens'. But citizenship requires some specification, and some institutional and political protection, separate from and beyond the extension of democracy. In short, in the relationship between citizenship and democracy is entailed a new balance − a new settlement − between liberty and equality.

Can the parameters of such a 'new settlement' be further specified? It appears that a plausible resolution of some of the dilemmas of contemporary politics can only be provided if enhanced political participation is embedded in a legal and constitutional framework that protects and nurtures individuals and other social categories as 'free and equal citizens'. However, to go down that road has some real political consequences. It requires us, for example, to recognise the importance of a number of fundamental tenets, often dismissed because of their association with liberalism; for example, the centrality, in principle, of an 'impersonal' structure of public power; the need for a constitution to help guarantee and protect rights; a diversity of power centres, both within the state and outside it, in civil society; mechanisms to promote open debate between alternative political platforms; an institutional framework of enforceable and challengeable rights.

In many countries, West and East, the limits of 'government' are explicitly defined in constitutions and bills of rights which are subject to public scrutiny, parliamentary review and judicial process. The Left has sometimes been impatient with this procedural approach − and it is certainly true that no written constitution or judicial review, alone, has been able to guarantee the rights of the citizen against a state which is determined to abolish or reduce them. Nevertheless, the experience of recent history suggests that this idea is fundamental to democracy, conceived as a process which bites deep into the structure of state and society. Constitutional entrenchment, however, is not enough. Any conception of democracy which seeks to elaborate it as a form of 'socialist pluralism' requires the limits on 'public power' to be reassessed in relation to a far broader range of issues than has been hitherto commonly presupposed.

What would be included in such an expanded system of rights? A constitution or bill of rights which enshrined the idea of the 'double focus' of citizenship − equal rights and equal practices − would have to specify rights with respect to the *processes* that determine outcomes. Thus, not only equal rights to cast a vote, but also to enjoy the conditions of political understanding, involvement in collective decision-making and setting of the political agenda which make the vote meaningful. These conditions for real political participation include rights with respect to information, education, the 'right to know', including the defence of the right to make public things which governments prefer to keep under official restriction. There would have to be a bundle of social rights linked to reproduction, childcare and health; and economic rights to ensure adequate economic and financial resources for a citizen's autonomy Without tough social and economic rights, rights with respect to the state could not be enjoyed in practice; and without rights in respect of the state, new forms of inequality of power, wealth and status could systematically disrupt the implementation of social and economic liberties.

For example, a right to reproductive freedom for women entails making public authorities responsible, not only for medical and social facilities to prevent or assist pregnancy, but also for providing the material conditions which help to make the choice to have a child a genuinely free one. A right to the capacity really to choose between courses of action obliges the state to implement ways of distributing wealth and income much more equitably. One way of making such resources available may be a guaranteed minimum income for all adults, irrespective of whether they are engaged in wage or household labour. Strategies of this type have to be treated with caution since their implications for collective or societal wealth creation are complex and not fully clear. However, without a minimum guaranteed resource base, many people will remain highly vulnerable and dependent on the charity or goodwill of others – a condition which, despite Mrs Thatcher's passion for replacing welfare rights with private philanthropy, is in contradiction with the very idea of citizenship.

Such a system of rights must specify certain responsibilities of the state to groups of citizens, which particular governments could not (unless permitted by an explicit process of constitutional amendment) override. The authority of the state – even of a much more democratic one than we enjoy at the moment – would thus, in principle, be clearly circumscribed; its capacity for freedom of action to a certain degree bounded. This challenges some fundamental assumptions still widely held on the Left.

We would go further. The important point about such a constitution or bill of rights would be that it radically enhances the ability of citizens to take action against the state (including a socialist state) to redress unreasonable encroachments on liberties. This would help tip the balance from state to parliament and from parliament to citizens. It would be an *empowering* system, breaking with any assumption that the state can successfully define citizens' wants and needs for them, and become the 'caretaker of existence'. It would redefine the balance between state and civil society, which is at the heart of so much rethinking from Left and Right alike.

Of course, empowerment would not thereby be guaranteed. But rights could be fought for by individuals, groups and movements and could be tested in, among other places, open court. The American system makes it clear that this can lead to interminable wrangles, social change getting delayed and bogged down in 'due process' within the system. On the other hand, the European Convention on Human Rights has been a better defence of civil liberties than Britain's more venerable, customary arrangements. On balance, the gains from going in this direction are preferable to the present situation where it is extremely difficult to bring our archaic state system, operating so much of the time on the basis of undefined 'club' rules, to any open accountability.

Enter Charter 88. Charter 88 is rightly concerned with enshrining the rights and liberties of British subjects in a bill of rights and a constitution – and thereby making them 'citizens' for the first time in their history. The Charter is an immediate and practical intervention in current political discussion of the first importance and, as such, is to be welcomed and endorsed. But, if the argument above is correct, then it is a necessary but not a sufficient means for people to establish themselves in their capacity as citizens. In the context of the long-term struggle for socialism, it can be seen as one, but only one, essential moment in the elaboration of a diverse range of new rights and their conditions of existence.

The question of difference, however, which we discussed earlier, raises much deeper, more troubling issues, which are not easily resolved in the short term. Older European ideas of citizenship assumed a more culturally homogeneous population, within the framework of a strong and unitary national state. It seemed appropriate, therefore, to believe that widening the democratic franchise and participation of all citizens would naturally enlarge the freedoms, rights and liberties of everyone.

But social and cultural identities have become more diversified and 'pluralised' in modern society. The modern nation state is increasingly composed of groups with very different ethnic and cultural identities. Many of these groups belong to other histories, cultures and traditions very different from those of the indigenous people. These cultural differences are crucial to their sense of identity, identification and 'belongingness'. Similar differences are also beginning to show through in the communities and regions which originally constituted the United Kingdom. These differences present new challenges to, and produce new tensions within, what we called earlier the 'universalising' thrust in the idea of citizenship.

Of course, permanent residents in the society, whatever their differences of origin, history and culture, must be able to claim common rights and entitlements, as full members of the political community, without giving up their cultural identities. This is a key entitlement in any modern conception of citizenship – especially in societies whose populations are increasingly culturally and ethnically diverse. But this may not resolve all the problems. Differences of all kinds will continue to create special and particular needs, over and above those which can be addressed within a universalistic conception of citizenship. As the Rushdie affair demonstrates, it is not always possible to keep universal political claims and particularly cultural ones in separate compartments. They keep overlapping and invading each other's territory.

The politics of citizenship, in sum, throws us into the deep end of some very profound, general, theoretical concerns about politics as well as posing a set of complex organisational issues. To think it through − a project only just beginning − we need to attend to both dimensions. The elements of equality and universality associated with the idea of 'the citizen', and the diverse and particular requirements of different groups which have to be met if they are to enjoy 'free and equal' status, demand that the Left clarify, more profoundly than it has so far, both the principles of the politics of citizenship and their institutional requirements. What is at stake is nothing less than reformulating socialism to take better account of 'citizenship' and the conditions and limits this imposes on state action and political strategy.

III Globalisation and Localisation

David Held

The Decline of the Nation State

Mrs Thatcher's recent expression of concern about sovereignty has – in some sense – missed the boat. Britain today is already enmeshed in a tight network of international relations and organisations which infringes upon its sovereignty. The lessons to be drawn from this, however, not only affect Thatcher's Conservatives but also the Left. The Left's traditional anti-European stance is almost as anachronistic as Thatcher's position. Surprisingly perhaps, the Right and Left have a lot in common when it comes to raising the flag and putting – or hoping to put – Britain first. In what follows I shall focus on some of the ways in which the sovereignty of the state has been eroded and on some of the consequences of this.

The concept of 'sovereignty' is usually taken to mean that a nation state has power and control over its own future: that it has, in other words, the ability to take final decisions and to make and enforce the law in a given community or territory. A loss of sovereignty implies a loss of legal and actual control over the determination of the direction of national policy.

Sovereignty must be distinguished from 'autonomy'. The idea of autonomy refers to the capacity of nation states, not to set goals, but to achieve goals and policies once they have been set, because in an interdependent world all instruments of national policy may be less effective. It is a diminution of the capacity to achieve national policies – a loss of national autonomy – which may alone be behind the anxieties about a loss of 'sovereignty'. The question to pose is: has sovereignty remained intact while the autonomy of the state has diminished, or has the modern state actually faced a loss of sovereignty?

In raising questions about sovereignty and autonomy in the modern world, I do not mean to imply that the problems posed by the international order for the individual nation state are entirely new. On the contrary, it seems to be the case that a dense pattern of global interconnections began to emerge with the intitial expansion of the world economy and the rise of the modern state from the late 16th century. Nevertheless, there are many new dimensions to patterns of global interdependence, for example, the growth of international organisations, which have developed especially rapidly since 1945 and which have major consequences for the future of sovereignty.

The analysis below concentrates on a number of dimensions of globalisation which highlight 'disjunctures' or 'gaps' between, on the one hand, the power of the nation state as in principle capable of determining its own future and, on the other, the actual practices and structures of the state and economic system at the global level. In mapping out these disjunctures, I shall draw most of the examples from the processes and relations which impinge most directly on the states of Europe. It is the fate of the states of Europe which will be uppermost, although I will return to some issues facing British socialists in particular at the end.

Disjuncture 1: The World Economy

There is a disjuncture between the formal authority of the state and the actual system of production, distribution and exchange which in many ways serves to limit or undermine the power or scope of national political authorities.

When Marx studied capitalism he concentrated on relations and forces largely internal to society. Change was presumed to occur with mechanisms 'built in' to the very structure of a given society, and governing its transformation. The relevance of such a perspective has been thrown into doubt by the rapid development in the postwar years of global economic relations — relations which operate in a broad international, multinational and transnational context.

The emergence of a complex international divison of labour is one mark of this new age. There has been a steady expansion of industrial capitalism at the so-called 'periphery' of the international economy — South Korea, Taiwan, Singapore and the other newly industrialising countries. If post-Fordism is a growing element of Western economies 'assembly-line production' exploiting cheap labour power is a growing characteristic of many Third World countries. If new systems of flexible production and control are developing in the West, then they are connected directly to a worldwide division of labour which has shifted some of the routine, monotonous and dangerous work to countries in which it can be carried out all too often without political regulation and trade-union challenge.

Two aspects of the new international economic processes are central: the internationalisation of production and the internationalisation of financial transactions, organised in part by fast-growing multinational companies. Multinational corporations plan and execute their production, marketing and distribution with the world economy firmly in mind. Even when multinationals have a clear national base, their interest is above all in global profitability, and their country of origin may count little in their overall corporate strategy: the 'national loyalty' of multinationals is of an instrumental rather than a sentimental kind. Financial organisations such as banks are also progressively more global in orientation. They are able to monitor and respond to developments in London, Tokyo and New York at the touch of a button. New information technology has radically increased the mobility of economic units – currencies, stocks, shares, 'futures' and so on – for financial and commercial organisations of all kinds.

There is considerable evidence to support the claim that technological advances in communication and transportation are eroding the boundaries between hitherto separate markets – boundaries which were a necessary condition for independent national economic policies. Markets and societies are becoming more sensitive to one another even when their distinctive identities are preserved. The October stock-market crash of 1987 is one obvious example of this. The very possibility of a national economic policy is, accordingly, reduced. The monetary and fiscal policies of individual national governments are frequently dominated by movements in the international financial markets. Likewise, the levels of employment, investment and revenue within a country are often subordinated to the decisions of multinationals about where they will locate their production and administrative facilities, among other things.[1]

The loss of control of national economic programmes is, of course, not uniform across economic sectors or societies more generally: some markets and some countries can isolate themselves from transnational economic networks by, among other things, attempts to restore the boundaries or 'separateness' of markets and/or to extend national laws to cover internationally mobile factors and/or to adopt co-operative policies with other countries for the co-ordination of policy. The particular tensions between political and economic structures are likely to be different in different spheres, and between them: West-West, North-South, East-West. It cannot, therefore, simply be said that the very idea of a national economy is superseded: there is still insufficient evidence to support such a view.

However, the internationalisation of production finance and other economic resources is unquestionably eroding the capacity of the state to control its own economic future. At the very least, there appears to be a diminution of state autonomy, and a disjuncture between the idea of a sovereign state determining its own future and the conditions of modern economies, marked as they are by the intersection of national and international economic processes. 1992 − the date set for the establishment of the single European market − will be a further major impetus to these developments.

Disjuncture 2: Hegemonic Powers and Power Blocs

Connected to changes in the world economy, there is a disjuncture between the idea of the state as an autonomous strategic, military actor and the development of the global system of states, characterised by the existence of hegemonic powers and power blocs, which sometimes operate to undercut a state's authority and integrity. The dominance of the USA and USSR as world powers, and the operation of alliances like Nato and the Warsaw Pact, clearly constrains decision-making for many nations. A state's capacity to initiate particular foreign policies, pursue certain strategic concerns, choose between alternative military technologies and control certain weapon systems located on its own territory may be restricted by its place in the international system of power relations.

Within Nato, for example, clear evidence of what might be called the 'internationalisation of security' can be found in its joint and integrated military command structure. When Nato was originally established in the late 1940s, the US sought to limit (if not undercut) the political sovereignty of the European states by the introduction of a clause in the founding treaty which would have allowed Nato forces to intervene in a Nato country in cases of 'indirect aggression', that is, 'an internal *coup d'état* or political change favourable to an aggressor'. The clause was successfully resisted by European states, but ever since then Nato's concern with collective security has trodden a fine line between, on the one hand, maintaining an organisation of sovereign states (which permits, in principle, an individual member state not to act if it judges this appropriate) and, on the other, developing an international organisation which *de facto*, if not *de jure*, operates according to its own logic and decision-making procedures. The existence of an integrated supranational command structure − headed by the supreme allied commander in Europe, who has always been an American general appointed by the US president − ensures that, in a situation of war, Nato's national armies would operate within the the framework of Nato's strategies and decisions.[2] The sovereignty of a national state is decisively qualified once its armed forces are committed to a Nato conflict.

But even without such a commitment, state autonomy as well as sovereignty can be limited and checked; for the routine conduct of Nato affairs involves the integration of national defence bureaucracies into international defence organisations; these, in turn, create transgovernmental decision-making systems which can escape the control of any single member state. Such systems can lead, moreover, to the establishment of informal, but none the less powerful, transgovernmental personnel networks or coalitions which are difficult to monitor by national mechanisms of accountability and control. Having said this, no brief account of Nato would be complete without emphasising also that its members are rivals competing for scarce resources, arms contracts, international prestige and other means of national enhancement. Membership of Nato does not annul sovereignty; rather, it qualifies sovereignty for each state in different ways. Aspects of sovereignty are negotiated and renegotiated through the Nato alliance.

Disjuncture 3: International Organisations

A third major area of disjuncture between the political theory of the sovereign state and the contemporary global system lies in the vast array of international regimes and organisations (of which Nato is only one type) which have been established to manage whole areas of transnational activity (trade, the oceans, space, and so on). The growth in the number of these new forms of political association (see the table below) reflects the general expansion of transnational links.

Date	Intergovernmental Organisations	International non-governmental organisations
1905	37	176
1951	123	832
1972	280	2173
1984	365	4615

The development of international and transnational organisations has led to important changes in the decision-making structure of world politics. New forms of multinational politics have been established and with them new forms of collective decision-making, involving states, intergovernmental organisations and a variety of transnational pressure groups. The International Monetary Fund, for example, pursuing a particular line of economic policy, may insist as a condition of its loan to a government, that the latter cut public expenditure, devalue its currency and cut back on subsidised welfare programmes. In a Third World country, for instance, this may create hunger amongst many people, trigger bread riots and perhaps the fall of a government, or it might contribute directly to the imposition of martial law. It has to be borne in mind that IMF intervention is routinely at the request of governmental authorities or particular political factions within a state and, therefore, cannot straightforwardly be interpreted as a threat to sovereignty. Nonetheless, a striking tension has emerged, between the idea of the sovereign state − centred on national politics and political institutions − and the nature of decison-making at the international level. The latter raises serious questions about the conditions under which a country is able to determine its own policies and directions.

The European Community is an important illustration of these issues. Its significance, however, perhaps reaches further than any other kind of international organisation due to its right to make laws which can be imposed on member states. Within Community institutions, the Council of Ministers has a unique position; for it has at its disposal powerful legal instruments (above all, 'regulations', 'directives' and 'decisions') which allow it to make and enact policy. Of all these instruments, 'regulations' are the most notable because they have the status of law independently of any further negotiation or action on the part of member states. Moreover, the Community's extensive range of activities makes it a form of 'public power' at the intersection of relatively new types of politics. For the Community's command over resources and capacity to adjudicate between conflicting national interests are of intense concern now to, among others, individual governments, transgovernmental coalitions of ministers and officials, and an array of transnational interest groups, from the European steel producers to environmentalists.

The member states of the European Community are no longer the sole centres of power within their own borders.[3] On the other hand, it is important to bear in mind that the Community's powers are limited powers when considered in relation to a typical European state; for the Community does not possess, for instance, coercive powers of its own – an army, a police force and other institutions of direct law enforcement. The Community's powers were gained by the 'willing surrender' of aspects of sovereignty by member states – a 'surrender' which, arguably, has actually helped the survival of the European nation state faced, on the one hand, with the dominance of the USA in the first three decades following the second world war and, on the other, with the rise of the Japanese economic challenge. In certain respects, the European Community has strengthened the national state's ability to act at home and abroad.

In short, the European Community provides opportunities and restraints. The states of the Community retain the final and most general power in most areas of their domestic and foreign affairs – and the Community itself seems to have strengthened their options in some of these domains. However, within the Community sovereignty is now also clearly divided: any conception of sovereignty which assumes that it is an indivisible, illimitable, exclusive and perpetual form of public power –

embodied within an individual state − is defunct.

Disjuncture 4: International Law

There is a fourth significant disjuncture to note − a gap between
the idea of membership of a national political community, ie,
citizenship, which bestows upon individuals both rights and
duties, and the development of international law which subjects
individuals, governments and non-governmental organisations
to new systems of regulation. Rights and duties are recognised in
international law which transcend the claims of nation states and
which, while they may not be backed by institutions with coercive
powers of enforcement, have far-reaching consequences. For
example, the International Tribunal at Nuremburg laid down,
for the first time in history, that when *international rules* that
protect basic humanitarian values are in conflict with *state* laws,
every individual must transgress the state laws (except where
there is no room for 'moral choice').[4] The legal framework of the
Nuremburg Tribunal marked a highly significant change in the
legal direction of the modern state; for the new rules challenged
the principle of military discipline and subverted national
sovereignty at one of its most sensitive points: the hierarchical
relations within the military.

Of all the international declarations of rights which were
made in the postwar years, the European Convention for the
Protection of Human Rights and Fundamental Freedoms (1950)
is especially noteworthy. In marked contrast to the United
Nations' Universal Declaration of Human Rights (1947) and
subsequent UN charters of rights, the European convention was
concerned, as its preamble indicates, 'to take the first steps for
the *collective enforcement* of certain of the Rights of the UN
Declaration' (emphasis added). The European initiative was
committed to a most remarkable and radical legal innovation: an
innovation which in principal would allow individual citizens to
initiate proceedings against their own governments. Nearly all
European countries have now accepted an (optional) clause of
the Convention which permits citizens to petition directly the
European Commission on Human Rights, which can take cases
to the Committee of Ministers of the Council of Europe and
then (given a two-thirds majority on the Council) to the
European Court of Human Rights. While the system is far from

straightforward and is problematic in many respects, it has been
claimed that, alongside legal change introduced by the European
Community, it no longer leaves the state 'free to treat its own
citizens as it thinks fit'. In Britain alone, for example, telephone
tapping laws have been altered after intervention by the
European Commission and findings of the European Court of
Justice have led to changes in British law on issues as
far-reaching as sexual discrimination and equal pay.

Within international law more generally, there are two legal
rules which, since the very beginnings of the international
community, have been taken to uphold national sovereignty:
'immunity from jurisdiction' and 'immunity of state agencies'.
The former prescribes that 'no state can be sued in courts of
another state for acts performed in its sovereign capacity', and
the latter stipulates that 'should an individual break the law of
another state while acting as an agent for his country of origin
and be brought before that state's courts, he is not held 'guilty'
because he did not act as a private individual but as the
representative of the state'.

The underlying purpose of these rules is to protect a
government's autonomy in all matters of foreign policy and to
prevent domestic courts from ruling on the behaviour of foreign
states (on the understanding that all domestic courts everywhere
will be so prevented). And the upshot has traditionally been that
governments have been left free to pursue their interests subject
only to the constraints of the 'art of politics'. It is notable,
however, that these internationally recognised legal mainstays of
sovereignty have been progressively questioned by Western
courts. And while it is the case that national sovereignty has most
often been the victor when put to the test, the tension between
national sovereignty and international law is now marked, and it
is by no means clear how it will be resolved.

Against this background of 'disjunctures', the limits of a
politics that derives its terms of reference exclusively from the
nation state become apparent. This point is reinforced by a
consideration of the principle of 'majority rule'. The application
of this principle is, of course, at the centre of Western
democracy: it is at the root of the claim of political decisions to
be regarded as worthy or legitimate. Problems arise, however,
not only because decisions made by *other* states, or by
quasi-supranational organisations such as the EC, Nato, or the

World Bank, diminish the range of decisions open to a given 'majority' but also because *decisions of a nation do not only affect (or potentially affect) its citizens*.

For example, a decision made against the siting of an international airport near a capital city for fear of upsetting the local rural vote may have disadvantageous consequences for airline passengers throughout the world who are without direct means of representation. Or a decision to build a nuclear plant near the borders of a neighbouring country is likely to be a decison taken without considering whether those in the nearby country (or countries) ought to be among those who are consulted (reflect on the French decision to build large numbers of nuclear reactors in northern France). Or a decision to suspend food aid to a country may stimulate the sudden escalation of food prices in that country and contribute directly to the outbreak of famine among the urban and rural poor (as happened in Bangladesh when the US temporarily suspended aid). Or the decision by a government in West or East to suspend or step up military aid to one side or another in a political struggle in a distant country may decisively influence the outcome of that conflict, or fan it into a further vortex of violence (Central America).

The modern theory of the sovereign state presupposes the idea of a 'national community of fate' − a community which rightly governs itself and determines its own future. This idea is certainly challenged by the nature of the pattern of global interconnections and the issues that have to be confronted by a modern state.[5] National communities by no means exclusively 'programme' the actions, decisions and policies of their governments and the latter by no means simply determine what is right or appropriate for their own citizens.

While a complex pattern of global interconnections has been evident for a long time, there is little doubt that there has recently been a further 'multinationalisation' of domestic activities and an intensification of decision-making in multinational frameworks. The evidence that transnational relations have eroded the powers of the modern sovereign state is certainly strong. From considerations such as these some observers have concluded that sovereignty is fundamentally undermined and that the democratic system of Western states is progressively less viable: a national system of accountability and control risks obsolescence in the face of international forces and relations. The conclusion, however, requires some qualification.

While I have mapped some of the common challenges to the sovereign state in the modern postwar world, it is important to stress that the effect of these challenges is likely to vary under different international and national conditions — for instance, a nation's location in the international division of labour, its place in particular power blocs, its position with respect to the international legal system, its relation to major international organisations. Not all states, for example, are equally integrated into the world economy (compare the USA, Portugal and Bulgaria) and, thus, while national political outcomes will be heavily influenced by global processes in some countries, in others regional or national forces might well remain supreme.

Further states remain unready on the whole to submit their disputes with other states to arbitration by a 'superior authority', be it the United Nations, an international court or any other international body. At the heart of this 'great refusal' is the protection of the right of states to go to war.[6] Despite the fact that states today operate in a world of international political economy, military alliances, international law and so on, it remains that the modern state is still able to determine the most fundamental aspect of people's life chances — the question of life and death. In a complex interdependent world, this element of sovereignty remains a powerful moment.

Moreover, one way in which states continue to exercise their sovereignty is — as indicated by the EC in particular — by participating in the creation of organisations which might better monitor and regulate transnational forces and relations beyond their control. While such organisations frequently create new restraints upon national states, they also create new forms of political participation and intervention. At issue here is the active renewal of the rights of states in and through the international system itself.

It is misleading simply to conclude, then, that sovereignty is wholly undermined in contemporary circumstances. On the other hand, this discussion of the four disjunctures between the sovereign state and the late 20th century economic and political world does reveal a set of forces which combine to restrict the freedom of action of governments and states by blurring the boundaries of domestic politics; transforming the conditions of political decision-making; changing the institutional and organisational context of national politics; altering the legal framework and administrative practices of governments; and obscuring the lines of responsibility and accountability of nation states themselves. From these processes alone one can say that *the operation of states, in an ever more complex international system, both limits their autonomy and infringes ever more upon their sovereignty*. Any conception of sovereignty which interprets it as an illimitable and indivisible form of public power is undermined. Sovereignty itself has to be conceived today as already divided among a number of agencies — national, international and transnational — and limited by the very nature of this plurality.

What are the implications of this for British politics? As the sun set over Britain's empire, and competition among industrial nations intensified throughout the postwar years, politicians of nearly all persuasions placed hopes in general political and economic rejuvenation on strategies geared to the maintenance of Britain's international status either as an independent power or in junior partnership with the United States. These strategies helped sustain the illusion that the decline in Britain's world position could be checked. Symbols of these strategies included the maintenance of a strong pound (the status of which was often regarded as more important than the health of manufacturing industry) and high expenditure on arms and military materials (relative to Britain's industrial competitors). Of course, these strategies have been continued to the present day in one form or other, and have received their most forceful articulation in Thatcherism's dubious mix of patriotism and free market economics.

The aspirations, values and beliefs which formed the culture in support of a great and independent Britain have profoundly affected the Labour Party in and out of office and the Left more generally. It is a culture which contributed to the Left's misunderstanding of the changing pattern of global relations and to its misreading of the political importance of the new institutions and options developing in the postwar world. The 'England right or wrong' mentality led to a naive belief that Britain could either once again lead world politics or, if not, cut itself adrift and live in splendid isolation. The reluctance to participate in the European Community during its formation, and the continuing reluctance to participate fully in its organisations, must be understood in this context. The Left has been as tenacious as the Right, albeit for different reasons, in its anti-Europeanism.

The issue the Left needs to consider more and more is how it should participate in, and seek to shape, the new international order that is emerging. This order cannot be run away from; it cannot be pretended that it doesn't exist. Nor can it be pretended that Britain will again ever enjoy pre-eminence on the world stage. The question is: what is the appropriate form of national and international politics for the Left to develop now? How can democratic and socialist theory accommodate the new reality?

In my view, the Left needs firstly to accept and think through the meaning of Britain's 'second division' status and secondly to examine how it can participate in the development of the international institutions and forces moulding global politics today. High on this agenda must be rethinking the nature of European unity. For Europe presents the Left with a unique opportunity to create a new set of alliances around a concern for greater accountability, extended rights, and a new independence in world politics – concerns which only a *European-wide movement* has any real chance of sustaining in contemporary circumstances.

A European Left could pursue – and perhaps even deliver – three vital things.

Firstly, the extension and deepening of mechanisms of democratic accountability across Europe to cover resources and forces which are already beyond the control of national democratic mechanisms and movements. One issue here is bolstering the role of the European parliament so that it has the capacity to legislate on central transnational issues – then environment, health, new forms of communication and so on.

Secondly, the protection and strengthening of the European human rights programme, and the further development of the role of the European courts system, in order that groups and individuals have an effective means of suing their governments for the enactment and enforcement of key civic, political, economic and social rights.

Thirdly, the establishment of Europe as a major independent voice in world politics. At the centre of this objective must be the pursuit — as a matter of urgency — of a non-aligned European foreign policy and a non-aligned European armed force: a 'Nato' without the USA. Such a development would contribute decisively to breaking up the current division of the world by the two hegemonic powers and would help create the conditions for greater political diversity and choice on the world stage.

If these issues were to be given more priority it would be one step toward creating a politics beyond the sovereign nation state — a new international politics for new times.

Notes
[1] R Smith, 'Political Economy and Britain's External Position', *Britain in the World*, ESRC Compilation 1987.
[2] D Smith, 'States and Military Blocs: Nato', *The State and Society* 6, The Open University Press 1984.
[3] A Whickham, 'States and Political Blocs: the EEC', *The State and Society* 6 The Open Univerity Press 1984.
[4] A Cassesa, *Violence and Law in the Modern Age*, Polity Press 1988.
[5] C Offe, *Disorganised Capitalism*, Polity Press 1985.
[6] F H Hinsley, *Sovereignty*, (2nd edn), Cambridge University Press 1986.

David Marquand

The Irresistible Tide of Europeanisation

Slowly, belatedly and rather grudgingly British political and economic leaders are beginning to realise that something rather important is happening in the European Community, and that the 'something' is connected with 1992. So far, however, few have grasped the full significance of the 1992 project, which has provided the central theme of Community politics since the mid-1980s. Until last summer, the government saw it as an exercise in trade liberalisation and little more. Since Mrs Thatcher's *démarche* at Bruges, some of the wider political implications have entered its calculations as well. But the real nature of the exercise still eludes it. In particular, ministers still seem to think that they can pull out what are, for them, the plums of trade liberalisation and deregulation without sacrificing any of the powers and prerogatives traditionally associated with the sovereign nation state. They do not realise that the transfer of sovereignty which the Bruges speech was designed to prevent lies at the heart of the whole programme.

The fact is that the 1992 project is a response to a complex set of pressures which have called the traditional concept of national sovereignty into question. The first is the growth of international economic interdependence, which has made it increasingly difficult for the medium-sized nation state (and perhaps even for the super-state) to make its will prevail in the economic sphere. Four developments have played crucial parts in this process. Thanks to the extraordinary growth in international trade which has been one of the most marked features of postwar economic history, all developed countries live by taking in each other's washing. This means that the levels of output and employment in country A depend on the level of demand not only in country A itself, but also in countries B, C and D, to whom it sells its exports; and that, by the same token, *their* levels of output and employment depend in large part on the level of demand in country A.

Associated with the growth of international trade, moreover, has been a marked growth in the role of multinational companies, owing allegiance to no national state and, in many cases, disposing of resources so great that they are almost immmune to the sticks and carrots of national policy. The third development is the growth of an increasingly globalised capital market and the deregulation of many national capital markets. Last, but not least, come the effects of accelerating technological change, and the growing ease of technology transfer. The net effect of these changes is to make it more difficult for medium-sized western nation states, with open-market economies, to operate economic policies significantly out of line with those of the rest of the developed world.

The Keynesian revolution of the 1940s was designed to make the nation state master in its own economic house: to give national governments a battery of regulatory mechanisms which would enable them to maintain full employment in the face of the recessionary forces of the sort that baffled the governments of the 1920s and 1930s. In medium-sized nation states, at any rate, the changes just mentioned have undone the Keynesian revolution. Keynes' fundamental insight that the level of employment depended upon the level of demand may still be true in principle, but it is no longer possible for a medium-sized nation state to put that insight to work in the real world, unless it can persuade other medium-sized nation states to do the same.

If it cannot, if it seeks unilaterally to reflate its own economy so as to raise the level of demand and employment within its own frontiers despite continuing recession outside them, it is likely to achieve only higher levels of inflation, a depreciating currency and a deteriorating trade balance. Sooner or later (and in most cases sooner rather than later) these will force it to bring the whole experiment to a halt, probably before a significant improvement in output and employment has taken place. This, of course, was the experience of the Labour government in Britain between 1974 and 1976; and also of the French Socialist government after its victory in 1981. In both these cases, governments committed to high levels of employment, and anxious to use the traditional instruments of Keynesian demand management in order to maintain full employment, were overwhelmed by a worldwide bias towards deflation, reflecting the determination of the 'stronger' economies to give higher priority to the conquest of inflation than to growth or full employment.

These developments have posed hard questions. If the nation state is no longer master in its own economic house, what has become of national sovereignty? If democratically elected governments are no longer sovereign in the economic sphere, how can economic forces be subjected to democratic political control? Is there still any role for public power at all? Or is the currently fashionable neo-liberalism correct in thinking that resources will have to be allocated through the market alone? If there is still a role for public power, how is that role to be played? Plainly, it can no longer be played at the level of the nation state. Can it be played at a supranational or international level instead? If so how? In principle, the answer is straightforward enough. The globalisation of economic forces requires a corresponding globalisation of political institutions to cope with them: since the nation state can no longer exercise sovereignty in many crucial economic spheres, it will have to share some of its power with supranational bodies. In practice, however, the road to such a destination is full of pitfalls. The central question confronting the democratic national states of Western Europe is how to cope with them.

Defence considerations point in the same direction. As a juridical concept, sovereignty has nothing to do with war-waging capacity, but even so the emergence of the sovereign nation state on to the stage of history was closely related to the growth of war-making capacity – notably to the invention of gunpowder and to answering advances in the science of fortification. By and large, states which successfully established their claim to statehood, and thereby to sovereignty, did so, in part, through their ability to wage war more successfully than other would-be states.

In this perspective, the second world war marks as profound a break in European history as did the collapse of the Holy Roman Empire's claims to suzerainty over the rest of Christendom in the early modern period. For the first time, none of the sovereign states of Europe has possessed genuinely independent war-waging capacity. *Vis-à-vis* the super powers, all of them have been in a position of clienthood, reminiscent of Belgium's position *vis-à-vis* the United Kingdom in the 19th century. Hence, of course, the creation of the North Atlantic Treaty and the Warsaw Pact in the immediate postwar period; and hence the effective hegemony of the two superpowers over the alliances formed around themselves at that time − hegemonies underlined in a peculiarly painful way in the crisis year of 1956, when Soviet tanks crushed the Hungarian uprising, and American pressure brought the Anglo-French invasion of Egypt to a halt.

Latterly, however, new trends have called into question the hegemonic relationships which have characterised the two power blocs for most of the postwar period. The United States and the Soviet Union have both begun to suffer the effects of what the historian, Paul Kennedy, has called 'imperial overstretch'. In each case, the economic costs of maintaining superpower status have begun to cut into the industrial base, upon which that status ultimately rests. In each case the effects of overstretch have been magnified by the escalating costs of defence associated with the ever more sophisticated weaponry spawned by the arms race − itself a concomitant of superpower rivalry and hegemony. The result is a paradox. In absolute terms each of the superpowers possesses unimaginable military power. Each can destroy the world several times over; the armouries of each tower above those of their allies. Yet, in the economic sphere, each has suffered acute relative decline *vis-à-vis* those allies; and each is groping for ways to minimise, to share, or in some way to disembarrass itself of, the burdens of superpower status.

That, in turn, has obvious implications for the defence of Western Europe. Since the end of the second world war the nation states of Western Europe have responded to their loss of independent war-waging capacity by alliance with and dependence upon a hegemonic United States. If, as seems increasingly probable, we are now coming to the end of the period of American hegemony, they will have to find some other response. Instead of relying on the United States, they will have to rely on each other. It is hard to see how they can do this without much more surrender of formal sovereignty in the defence field than they have been prepared to make so far.

The evolution of the European Community must be seen against this background. Though it was concerned with economics, the aims of its founding fathers were political. They hoped to transcend national sovereignty within a supranational union; and they assumed that if national economies were knitted together a supranational union would develop of its own accord. Economic integration would lead sooner or later to political integration; by solving the practical problems of 'low politics' in the mundane areas affected by the creation of a customs union, the process of integration would gradually 'spill over' into the glamorous areas of foreign, defence and monetary policy, which were the stuff of 'high politics'. Little by little, an irresistible momentum would be set up, which would sweep away the obstacles to full-scale political union. The Commission would evolve into the executive of this union. The Council of Ministers would become the 'upper house' of its legislature, and the directly-elected European Parliament the 'lower house'.

As everyone knows, events belied these expectations. In the areas of low politics with which it was concerned, the EEC was triumphantly successful. Partly because of this, its attractive power for states on its periphery – revealed in the enlargements which have increased its membership from the original six to twelve – has been formidable. Yet, success in low politics did not spill over into high politics. In the 1960s, France and West Germany – the two major powers of the original six – differed sharply over foreign and defence policy. Though these differences became less acute in the 1970s, Italy and (after its accession to the Community in 1973) the United Kingdom followed sharply different monetary and macro-economic policies from those of West Germany, with shattering results for the relative exchange rates of the major Community currencies.

Meanwhile, the institutional development of the Community had been stultified by the so-called Luxembourg compromise, which President de Gaulle forced on his partners in 1966, and which had the effect of perpetuating national vetoes even in areas which, under the Treaty, should have been covered by majority voting. Worse still, it was beginning to look as though the divergences in economic performance which were both cause and consequence of the differences in economic policy might jeopardise the *acquis communautaire* in the areas of low politics where integration had been comparatively successful in the past. The old notion that the route to high politics lay through low politics had, in short, turned out to be misconceived. If the member states of the Community wished to tackle high politics at all, they would have to tackle them directly. At the same time, the collapse of American hegemony, and also the US dollar, together with the strains which these developments set up within the Western world, forced issues of the highest high politics on to the European agenda.

The response of the member states of the Community was illuminating. Attempts were made to strengthen the 'supranational' elements in the Community's institutional structure. The European Parliament was given certain powers over the Community budget, and after a delay of more than twenty years the treaty commitment to its direct election by the people of the Community was finally honoured. But these developments, however encouraging they might be to those who hoped for an eventual political union, had only a limited impact on Community decision-making.

The most significant developments of the 1970s took place outside the institutional structure set up by the treaties. In the first place, the governments of the Community established a systematic process of 'political co-operation' to co-ordinate their foreign policies. Secondly, and more ambitiously, they established the European Monetary System (EMS) to provide a zone of 'currency stability' in the Community by aligning exchange rates more closely together. Thirdly, they created a more or less formalised 'European Council', consisting of the heads of government of the Community, meeting at periodic intervals.

These developments were all pragmatic adaptations to felt needs. They sprang from no vision of the Community's longer-term future, and corresponded to no explicit doctrine. All of them were essentially intergovernmental in character. They depended for their success on the co-operation of sovereign states, each jealously guarding its formal sovereignty in the policy areas concerned. They enabled the member states of the Community partially to offset the disintegrative tendencies which had started to make themselves felt so acutely when the long boom of the 1950s and 1960s began to peter out, and to tackle potentially divisive issues of high politics which the founding fathers failed to touch. But they did nothing to make Community decision-making more transparent or more accountable, or to push the Community further along the road to a political union.

The Community has developed in a way quite unlike that envisaged when it was set up. Its institutional structure contains federalist elements – notably, the Court of Justice, whose role in the evolution of Community law recalls that of the Supreme Court in the early days of the American union. But, despite some developments of a quasi-federalist character, it is not a federation; indeed, by focusing on low politics, while high politics are left to the member states, it has reversed the normal pattern of a federal system. Nor is there any reason to believe that it is bound to evolve into a federation merely by continuing along its present path. The nation state, not the Community, remains by far the most important focus for the political loyalties of Europeans; Community decisions are taken by a complex process of bargaining and compromise, in which the most important actors are the governments of the sovereign states which make it up.

Yet it is much more than an association of sovereign states co-operating only when they feel inclined – an *Europe des patries* of the sort envisaged by Charles de Gaulle. By virtue of its very existence, the states who compose it are becoming ever more interdependent, and that fact imposes ever more severe constraints upon their freedom of action. Juridically, they are as sovereign as they ever were, but the language of sovereignty is as remote from the realities of the system in which they are enmeshed as is the language of federalism. That system is, moreover, dynamic, not static: a process rather than a structure. And, as it has evolved, the language of sovereignty – whether of the sovereign nation state or the sovereign national parliament – has become less and less apposite to it, while institutions based on the assumption that that language corresponds to economic and political realities have become less and less able to manage it satisfactorily.

Increasing Impetus to Integration

This, then, is the background to the 1985 decision of the member governments to complete the so-called 'internal market' by 1992.

The logic of the decision deserves some discussion. The Commission white paper setting out the steps needed to make it a reality proposed a programme of formidable scope and complexity. It listed 300 actions necessary to create a genuinely single market covering the whole territory of the Community. These were grouped into three categories — those needed, respectively, to demolish 'physical' barriers to free trade and free movement; to demolish 'technical' barriers, and to demolish 'fiscal' barriers. Despite these complexities, however, the underlying logic was simple enough. In essence, what is at issue is a new version of the founding fathers' original project. The objective plainly belongs to the sphere of high politics; the means have to do with low politics. The aim is to strengthen the Community's competitiveness in world markets, particularly in the area of high technology where European companies seemed to be losing ground to their Japanese and American competitors, so as to prevent a relative decline in the economic and ultimately political power and influence of Western Europe *vis-à-vis* Japan and the United States. The assumption is that the chief obstacles to greater competitiveness lie in the barriers to genuinely free competition within Europe, and that the way to reach the goal is to remove these barriers. Free competition internally is assumed to be a necessary (and, in some interpretations, perhaps even a sufficient) condition of competitiveness externally.

On one level, there is nothing particularly new in this. After all, the central objective of the Rome Treaty was to establish a common market, with no barriers to the free movement of goods, services, capital and labour. Looked at in that perspective, the Single European Act is merely a belated decision to carry out the Rome Treaty prospectus — a decision made necessary because, in the intervening thirty years, the prospectus was frustrated by the emergence of a host of non-tariff barriers to free competition, of a kind which the founding fathers did not foresee. On another level, however, there is far more to it than this. What is underway is a massive exercise in national deregulation and Community re-regulation. This exercise applies not just to the movement of goods, services, capital and labour *across* national boundaries, but to the behaviour of governments, subordinate public authorities and private economic actors *within* the member states of the Community as well. For, whereas tariffs operate, by definition, at national frontiers, the non-tariff barriers, which it is the object of the internal-market programme to eliminate, operate behind frontiers and within the national economies bounded by those frontiers. Public procurement, merger policy, company law, health and safety at work, tax rates — all these will be intimately affected and in respect of national as well as cross-national transactions.

This must entail a substantial further transfer of competence and power from national to Community authorities. The object of the exercise is to liberalise markets and demolish barriers to competition. But past experience shows that a free market cannot be created, once and for all, by a single act of will. As Adam Smith well knew, markets do not remain competitive if they are left to their own devices. If they are to stay free, someone has to ensure that market actors do not protect themselves from the pains of freedom by resorting to new protectionist devices of one sort or another. A Community-wide free market therefore implies a Community-wide political authority to police it. In practice, this will have to be done partly by the Commission and partly by the Court of Justice, both supranational rather than intergovernmental institutions. Even on fairly conservative assumptions about the scope of the 1992 programme, in other words, further economic integration, necessarily implies substantial further political and legal integration.

That is only the beginning of the story. If the barriers which have so far impeded free trade and free movement are to come down and stay down, governments must lose much of the freedom of action they now enjoy. If fiscal frontiers are to be abolished, VAT rates will have to be brought much closer together — either as the Commission has proposed, by deliberate decision, or, as the British government prefers, by the pressure of market forces. In either case, governments will have less freedom to manoeuvre in the fiscal field than they had hitherto. The abolition of physical barriers impinges on matters like immigration and counter-terrorism policy, which are currently outside the Community framework. The abolition of technical barriers — particularly, perhaps, in the highly-protected markets for services — will deprive member governments of important regulatory powers, and make necessary the establishment of Community regulations instead of national ones. Opening up public procurement to free competition will weaken the ability of national public authorities to influence the economy.

The longer-term implications go still wider. Economic changes as far-reaching as those foreshadowed by the internal-market programme are bound to have profound distributional consequences. There will be gainers, but there will also be losers. Who will allocate the gains and losses? In a pure market order (not that a pure market order has ever existed in the real world) gains and losses are allocated by the market. In the welfare states of Western Europe, however, it is accepted that public power should intervene to alter market outcomes. So far, this process of redistribution has been left, by and large, to the member states; the Community as such has had little to do with it. By a curious paradox, however, the Thatcher government's long campaign against Britain's 'unfair' budgetary contribution forced distributional issues on to the Community agenda; and the 1992 programme has done the same. The decision taken at the 1987 Brussels summit to double the structural funds dedicated to the Community's weaker regions is a sign that the Community has now accepted at least a partial responsibility for the distributional consequences of its economic policies. Precedents of that sort tend, sooner or later, to be followed. And, if national redistribution is supplemented by Community redistribution, that too will extend the scope of Community decision-making.

Much the same is true of industrial policy, monetary policy and even macro-economic policy and certain aspects of labour-market policy. Few now advocate the kind of industrial policy which France followed, with some success, in the 1950s and 1960s, and which Britain tried, much less successfully, to emulate in the 1960s and 1970s. But it does not follow that there is no need for an industrial policy of any kind. Still less does it follow that the Community should sit back and allow predatory competitors from outside its frontiers to take advantage of the market liberalisation implied by the 1992 programme to kill off Community producers. Yet the 1992 programme will demolish many of the instruments through which member states have implemented industrial policies in the past, and will make national industrial policies virtually impossible. Increasingly, the choice will lie between no policy and a Community policy. Here too the logic points unmistakably to more action on the Community level – and therefore to Community institutions capable of taking action.

The position on monetary policy has been put best in a contribution by Professor Krugman to the influential Padoa-Schioppa report:

> As a simple matter of feasibility, Europe cannot have at the same time (i) stable exchange rates, (ii) integrated capital markets and (iii) independent monetary policies. The experience of the post-1973 period seems to indicate that (i) is not something that can be dispensed with. Given the already close integration of European markets for goods and services, large exchange-rate fluctuations associated with divergent monetary policies seem to be unacceptable. Thus, creation of a unified capital market will also require adoption of a common monetary policy.

The need for exchange-rate stability is now accepted; and it will become greater, not smaller, as and when the 1992 programme becomes a reality. An important part of the point of the programme, moreover, is precisely to eliminate controls on capital movements, and thereby to create the 'unified capital market' of which Professor Krugman spoke.

The conclusion he drew is inescapable. If national authorities follow divergent monetary policies once the capital market has been unified, exchange rates will not remain stable. If they do not, much of the point of the 1992 programme will have been lost. This does not mean, of course, that there has to be a single monetary authority, explicitly designated as such. Nominally independent national authorities could all tacitly agree to follow the monetary policy laid down by the Bundesbank. This is approximately what has happened in the EMS up to now. That, however, makes the Bundesbank the arbiter of the entire Community's monetary fate; and, to put it at its lowest, it is not clear that the other member states will be happy to allow it to play that role for ever. The only alternative is a Community monetary authority of some kind.

On macro-economic policy, the position is less straightforward. Macro-economic policy is, and will remain, a matter for the member states – another crucial difference between the Community and a federal system. Yet it is worth remembering that the Rome Treaty provided for the co-ordination of macro-economic policies. So far that provision has hardly bitten in the real world, but here too the 1992 programme creates new constraints on the ability of member governments to follow policies of their own choosing. Given a common monetary policy, much less divergent VAT rates, and the need to keep rates of direct taxation fairly close together if the free movement of labour is not to produce damaging 'brain drains' from high- to low-tax countries, there will be little scope for variety in macro-economic policies in any case. Quite apart from that, the Commission's calculations suggest that if the Community is to realise all the potential gains from the extra micro-economic efficiency which the 1992 programme is designed to generate, macro-economic policies will have to change – a change which, in practice, would have to be co-ordinated. And even co-ordination requires co-ordinating institutions.

On labour-market policy – in some respects, the most controversial area of all – the issues at stake have to do with Community regulation, not national co-ordination. Other things being equal, the market liberalisation implied by the 1992 programme may give a competitive advantage to countries with weak trade unions, poor standards of health and safety, scanty protection against unfair hiring and firing practices, and poor or non-existent provision for worker consultation. How, then, to prevent a kind of 'social dumping': a race for the bottom. The only possible answer is that the Community will have to step in; that Community-wide market liberalisation will have to be accompanied by Community-wide politics to protect labour from these dangers. That answer is vigorously contested by the present British government, but it has strong support from the Commission, and also from a number of member states. It is too soon to say how the question will be decided. To put it at its lowest, the decisions are bound to impose further constraints on national decision-making and make the language of national sovereignty even less applicable to Community affairs.

The Political Consequences of Integration

All this raises profound questions of political principle. The 1992 programme is almost certainly irreversible. It has captured the imagination of the Community's private sector; and most of the member governments are solidly behind it. Some of it may not become a reality by the due date – though it is worth noting that most qualified observers have been surprised by the speed with which progress has been made. Some of it may never become a reality. But there is little doubt that the great bulk of the programme will be in place quite early in the next decade.

The language of national sovereignty will have even less to do with the real world in which the Community's citizens live and work, and in which its governments seek to promote the interests of those citizens, than it does already. In some fields, those governments will be nominally free to act as they wish, but in practice more tightly constrained than they were before. In many, they will have lost even their nominal freedom. Supranational Community institutions will have acquired formidable new powers of control, supervision and intervention. The Community will not have become a federal state, but its member states will be far more tightly enmeshed with each other and with the Community than they have been hitherto.

The trouble is that the processes of Community decision-making are so opaque, so hard to scrutinise, so difficult to understand and so technocratic in character, that it is extraordinarily difficult to hold the decision-makers to account. The Commission, which plays a critical role in Community politics as policy initiator, manager and honest broker, is elected by nobody. In law, it is responsible to the European Parliament, but in political reality, the relationship between Parliament and Commission is not that of controller to controlled. They are allies, supporting each other against the over-mighty Council of Ministers; and of the two, the Parliament is weaker. The national ministers who make up the Council are, of course, responsible to their national parliaments. But national parliaments find it hard to hold them to account for their actions in the Council, or even to discover what those actions are. Community Europe consists, in practice, of a web of interlocking technocracies – of Commission officials negotiating and arguing with each other; of the officials of organised interest groups negotiating and arguing both with national and with Commission officials. Into that web, parliaments hardly break.

To be sure, the Single European Act has changed the balance of Community decision-making. The Council will decide most of the policies needed to complete the internal market by majority vote, while the so-called 'co-operation procedure' has given the

European Parliament a bigger role than it has had hitherto. In the policy areas covered by the Single European Act, it has acquired some legislative leverage. It is, at last, a player in the legislative games rather than a spectator. It can at least be argued that it has moved part of the way towards co-decision with the Council at some time in the future.

But whatever may be true of the future, it would be wrong to exaggerate the significance of these provisions here and now. If the 1992 policy works, power, and therefore responsibility, will be diffused much more widely than before. Member governments will lose important regulatory powers, and firms will become increasingly transnational in structure. It will no longer be possible to make crucial strategic choices, essentially social in character — for example, the appropriate trade-off between growth and environmental protection or between productivity and employment — on the national level, since the relevant national institutions will not be able to make their wishes effective. Who will make them instead? One possible answer, of course, is that such choices do not have to be made consciously at all: that it is best to allow them to emerge from the interplay of individual choices in a competitive market. That answer, it hardly needs to be said, would be bitterly contested. It is consistent with the reborn classical economic liberalism which has figured so largely in the politics of the Atlantic world in the last decade or so, but it is alien to other political traditions; and it would not be accepted by the social forces which adhere to those traditions. But if that answer is rejected, what other answers are on offer? The truth is that at present, there is a hole at the heart of the internal market programme; and, welcome though they may be, the new powers given to Parliament have not filled it up.

From Intergovernmentalism to Federalism

Is there a way forward? If so, what is it? The key to accountability is transparency. Decision-makers can be held to account only if their identity is known. Community decision-making is insufficiently accountable because it is not transparent: because its processes are hidden from view in a fog of overlapping jurisdictions. The first essential, then, is to clear the fog; and in order to do that, it is necessary to understand how and why it descended in the first place. Contrary to the received wisdom of much of the British political class, it is not the product of power-hungry Eurocrats, unnecessarily extending the frontiers of their Brussels empires. The chief reason why Community jurisdictions overlap is that the member states (and, in particular, the administrations of the member states) have been unwilling to accept the full implications of the interdependence which Community membership has brought with it: that they have insisted on clinging to the habits and assumptions of national sovereignty, while building a system in which those habits and assumptions are out of place. They have walked backwards into successive measures of integration − transferring functions from the national to the Community level, but have refused to transfer authority to match.

The result is that committees of national officials proliferate in the Community system like the tentacles of an octopus, hanging on to every protuberance it comes across. If the Community is to develop transparent and accountable decision-making processes, it must overcome the octopoid tendencies of its national bureaucracies.

The only way to do that is to establish clear lines of demarcation between Community institutions and national institutions, to separate the functions and powers best exercised and held on the Community level from those best exercised and held on the national level. That, of course, is another way of saying that the member states of the Community should move from intergovernmentalism to something much more reminiscent of federalism, or at least pre-federalism.

In Britain, such suggestions are apt to seem both impractical and dangerous − impractical, because they run against the grain of British tradition of gradual evolution; dangerous, because they would lead to excessive centralisation. The first objection draws false conclusions from true premises. The British tradition is indeed one of gradual evolution; and, as we have seen, the Community is most unlikely to evolve gradually into a federation without a decisive act of political will. But it does not follow that a federalist approach should be ruled out. Britain's are not the only traditions in the Community and it is not self-evident that they are the best. Gradual evolution has left this country with fewer safeguards against the abuse of power than any other in Western Europe.

It would be absurd to suggest that the Community should leap from intergovernmentalism into federalism in one bound. But if its member states so wished, they could perfectly well agree to adopt a federalist or pre-federalist model at some stage in the future, and decide to move towards it over a specified period.

The second objection rests on a false premise. Federalism does not mean centralisation, any more than intergovern- mentalism means decentralisation. It is merely a technique for separating powers. A Community decision to reconstruct its institutions on federal or pre-federal lines would not entail giving them the kinds of powers available to the federal governments of the United States, West Germany or the federations of the British Commonwealth. Indeed, it can be argued that because the member states have eschewed first principles, clung to intergovernmentalism and left the Community to evolve higgledy-piggledy in response to the pressure of the moment, it is, at present, *more* centralised than it needs to be. To take one obvious example, it is far from self-evident that a federal or pre-federal Community would need a common agricultural policy. In a well-designed federal Community, functions would be allocated to the lowest possible level of government compatible with the efficient discharge of the function in question.

There is no doubt that that would give important functions to the centre. But most of them would be standard-setting functions. Implementation would be left to the member states. Indeed, on the principle that decisions should be taken on the lowest possible level, implementation might often be left to regional or local authorities; and, if that principle were accepted, the upward transfer of functions from the national to the Community level might well be matched by a downward transfer to the regions.

Only in a comparatively small number of areas would Community institutions themselves have to implement the decisions taken at Community level. The decisions in question, we must remember, will be taken at Community level in any event. That is the logic of the Single European Act. What is needed is a system more centralised than the cumbersome network of technocracies we know today. It would, however, be more open and more democratic. The Council of Ministers would have to conduct its law-making activities in public. The

European Parliament would have to enjoy full powers of co-decision with it. The Commission would have to be made accountable to the people in whose name it acts, either through the direct election of its president or by making it fully responsible to Parliament.

It is easy to see that the technocrats, both European and national, who currently dominate the Community system might oppose a programme of this sort. That is not a reason for the Left to agree with them. For more than a century its central purpose has been to make democratic politics the master, rather than the servant, of market forces. That purpose can no longer be achieved on the national level but only through democratising the Community.

Neal Ascherson

Eastern Europe On the Move

At the beginning of 1989, which already promised to become one of the decisive years of European history, the situation prompted a question and a comment in an article written in *Marxism Today*. The question was about the external dimension of *perestroika*. Did the internal changes in Soviet society imply a similar transformation of the relationship between the USSR and the states of the Warsaw Pact? Nobody in Soviet authority had yet made the crucial distinction between the 'legitimate' security interests of the Soviet Union and the internal political structures of the Pact members. And yet there was a growing hope, a strengthening confidence, that these societies could in fact not only reform but qualitatively alter their political and economic regimes without fearing Soviet military intervention.

The comment was about the changing nature of opposition in Eastern Europe. It was apparent that the old 'dissident' generation — intellectual, internationalist, urban-rooted, sited politically somewhere between social democracy and christian democracy — might now be waning. In the new, far more open conditions obtaining above all in Hungary and Poland, with plans for pluralism of political parties and, more vaguely, for free elections which might eventually remove a ruling Communist Party from government, 'dissident' politics were being challenged by a different force. This force is traditional nationalism, whose predudices are rural and populist and whose ideology may turn out to have more to do with authority than with human rights. A revival of a certain past — that of the old peasant parties at its best, and of *Blut und Boden* nationalism at its worst — seemed to many watchers to be possible.

The unfreezing of the cold war is proceeding at bewildering speed, and highly unevenly. Much has happened since that article was written. The Vienna Review Meeting, in the 35-nation European Security process, finished in January with a closing document committing the signatories to an elaborate list of promises of good behaviour, internationally and internally, and also to accepting the right of other signatories to intervene and protest if one of the 35 failed to carry out the Vienna provisions. Shevardnadze and Gorbachev announced further sweeping arms reduction in Europe, and published the first official figures of force levels. The impetus has been maintained and the new conventional force-level talks at Vienna, following the rapidly resolved Nato crisis over short range nuclear weapons, are moving at uncanny speed.

That January question about Soviet-East European relations received some reply when Oleg Bogomolov, the senior Soviet expert on Eastern Europe, observed that a neutral and bourgeois Hungary on the Austrian or Swedish model would 'present no problem' to the Soviet Union. Shortly before that incredible remark, Eduard Shevardnadze had urged a mainly Western audience at Vienna to tear down what remained of the old iron curtain (although he later evaded the suggestion that he wanted the Berlin wall demolished).

Meanwhile, within a few incredible weeks, Solidarity and the Polish regime held roundtable talks, semi-free elections took place at which the regime was slaughtered and Solidarity candidates won almost every seat they contested, the Rakowski government collapsed and diplomatic relations with the Vatican were established. In Hungary, the leadership of party and state both fell and were replaced: preparations began for plural elections at which — party leaders openly admitted — the Hungarian Socialist Workers' Party might well lose power, while an uninhibited debate about Hungarian neutrality developed and the border fence with Austria was physically cut down.

On the 'populism' front, fierce nationalist confrontation developed again in Kosovo, while in Poland the right-wing KPN (Conference for an Independent Poland) emerged once more on the streets of Krakow during student riots. One result of the Warsaw roundtable talks, incidentally, was to open the way to re-legalisation of Rural Solidarity, suppressed in December 1981. Many events in the short life of Rural Solidarity in 1981 had suggested that it was rapidly becoming a resurrection of the PSL, the huge and radical prewar peasant party. If this project goes through, peasant nationalism will have returned to the political scene of Eastern Europe. And the PSL (if it does emerge from the Rural Solidarity chrysalis) may soon be joined by a revived Agrarian Party in Hungary, at present using the 'Peter Veres Society' as a founding committee.

Beyond these hectic changes and births, the whole continent is altering. If Soviet control is reduced to something like a 'normal' relationship between a superpower and its independent neighbours, if the economic and political reforms keep up their momentum and begin to affect Czechoslovakia and the German Democratic Republic (GDR), if the arms and conventional forces reductions are accelerated still faster by the new talks in the Helsinki process which have just started in Vienna, then we are entering a new Europe. All we know about it is that our children will use the word 'Europe' in senses, with associations, which we of the cold war generation can't yet imagine.

Integration and Disintegration

So much for the *Zukunftsmusik* − the purple passage about the lovely future! There are threatening uncertainties here as well as beautiful ones. Two in particular, both of which hint that this 'new' Europe might simultaneously turn out to be an old Europe − one which its peoples, and the socialist movements in particular, fought for a hundred years to overthrow and to replace. The landscape after the cold war could offer a place to old-fashioned armed conflicts over territory and minorities. It could also divide Europe in a different way, restoring the gulf between the industrialised West and the backward, rural, colonially exploited East and South-East which yawned before 1914, and was not closed between the two world wars.

It is fourteen years since the 'Helsinki Final Act' was signed. It wasn't really final: ever since, the 35 nations of the European Security and Co-operation Conference have continued to extend and to elaborate the Helsinki principles of 1975. But the Final Act did lay down the architects' blueprint for a Europe living at peace, operating a collective security system, applying a minimum of civil rights internally and exchanging goods, information and travellers of every kind without impediment.

But, counting the years of preparatory meetings before 1975, the Helsinki design is now sixteen or seventeen years old. When it was dreamed up in the late 1950s, in the fertile brain of Adam Rapacki, the Polish foreign minister, the Security Conference idea was a way out of the Potsdam idea. At Potsdam, the Big Three − or Four, when the French came in − decided the shape of Europe while the lesser nations waited outside to hear their fate or fortune. Rapacki had the vision of a quite different forum, in which every nation, neutral or Pact member, vast or tiny, would have a single and equal voice. There was much talk of demilitarised or denuclearised zones, and great hopes for direct contact at bilateral level between junior members of the two military alliances. But there was also the underlying assumption that Europe would remain divided into two hegemonies, Soviet and American. The two superpowers would abandon all ambitions to roll back each other's frontier of control; instead, with the consent of the lesser European states, they would recognise the existing frontiers of Europe as inviolable − alterable perhaps by general consent, but not unilaterally or by force. This implied the acceptance of the division of Europe, and of the political prerogatives of Moscow and Washington either side of the line. Certainly, the division was to be rendered harmless and gradually permeable; there would be troop and force reductions, more travel, warmer relations. But the division had to be first recognised, before it could be overcome.

Seventeen years is a long time. The Helsinki design is now out of date, even before it has been complete. Above all, nobody foresaw Gorbachev − an error for which the Europeans can scarcely be blamed. In 1975, the future looked symmetrical: the intensity of superpower presence in the continent would be wound down slowly on both sides at about the same pace. What is happening now, however, is asymmetrical. One superpower is apparently preparing to abandon its positions, without insisting that the rival do the same. The cold war is ending with something like a unilateral Soviet withdrawal from its East European imperium. It's a process which has only just begun, which might halt or go into reverse ... but that is what it looks like.

This would leave two very different Europes looking at one another. The West is closely integrated, for the most part, and will be even more effectively fused after 1992. Its major industries are supranational, its currencies are convertible, and the major territorial disputes between its members have long been settled − with the exception of Northern Ireland. There are few violent struggles for autonomy within Western Europe, apart from the Basque problem; the South Tyrol question is not in eruption currently, and the movements for independence or autonomy in Scotland, Catalonia, Wales and so on pursue their aims mostly through conventional politics.

The East presents a quite different picture. One of the ironies of stalinism was its combination of real but unadmitted Soviet control with the semblance of exaggerated national sovereignty − a version of sovereignty which was as old-fashioned and extreme as it was phoney. Economic integration in the Comecon area is minimal, and the currencies are not freely convertible; trade is conducted slowly and painfully by governmental agreements and often in terms of barter; politically, the component Warsaw Pact nations have had no close relationship save that which runs through Moscow. The mutual ignorance of the populations is amazing, for a system whose official ideology is internationalist. To take an example, the number of Czech or Polish students studying in each other's countries is pathetically small. In these conditions of political and economic autarky, old national prejudices have been preserved in the stalinist and post-stalinist deep freeze. The heavy official emphasis on history and patriotism, even though it was imported from the Soviet Union and even though much of the history was false or incomplete and known to be so, only reinforced this nationalism. Ancient disputes, whose very mention was forbidden, festered merrily in the popular memory.

So central and Eastern Europe slowly warms up, and we cannot be sure that certain wounds won't begin to bleed once more. It is worth listing some of them − leaving purely internal tensions aside. There is the justified Romanian claim to Bessarabia, now part of the Soviet republic of Moldavia, and to the north Bukovina which forms part of the Ukraine. There is the Hungarian-Romanian dispute, which at present is not (thank heaven) about frontiers but about Romania's bullying of the huge Magyar minorities in Transylvania. There is tension, similar but less spectacular, about the Magyar minority in Slovakia, across the Danube. There is the complex but highly explosive tangle of disputes over Macedonia, which involves Yugoslavia, Greece and Bulgaria. There is the Kosovo nightmare, which must in the end involve an Albanian-Yugoslav confrontation if it blazes up uncontrollably. There is still unsettled business between Austria and Yugoslavia about the Slovene minority in Carinthia, who are not happy with the way

Austrian politics are moving. Poland is likely, sooner rather than later, to raise openly with the Soviet Union the treatment and rights of the substantial Polish minority in the Western Ukraine (East Galicia), although the new 1945 frontier would not be challenged. The difficulty of finding smooth and discreet disputes procedures in this part of Europe is illustrated by the fairly petty border dispute between Poland and the GDR over the coastal waters off Swinoujscie, now settled, in which naval guns have been fired. And that leads to the biggest of all the wounds which may re-open: the division of Germany.

The Poles, for good reasons, see this as two wounds: that of the partition of rump-Germany into two in 1948-9, and the earlier wound inflicted when eastern Germany was annexed by Poland and the USSR in 1945 and its population expelled. I cannot believe that, at more than forty years' range, anyone will try to challenge Poland's western frontier on the Oder and Neisse. But the future of the two existing German states is now enigmatic. It can be taken as certain that the West does not want German reunification on any terms: it does not even want the GDR to retain after 1992 its peculiar status as the ghostly extra member of the European Community. But things have changed so much now that one can't exclude a scenario like this: the Socialist Unity Party (SED) regime attempts a radical reform but releases forces it cannot control; authority passes to a quite different political group; the inter-German and Berlin frontiers become permeable; a *de facto* German confederation from the Rhine to the Oder appears and the Soviet Union decides that this is a development it can tolerate. We can only guess whether, in fact, the USSR would tolerate it. But as arms and forces reductions and evacuation of all foreign armies proceed, the two pacts are bound to wither − which is a stated Soviet objective. And the withering of the pacts means that nobody will be able to hinder a German coming-together, short of reunification, if the Germans wish it.

The notion of a united, neutral Germany as main European partner has an ancient appeal to Russian diplomacy. All the same, there will have to be some remarkably good reason to persuade the Soviet Union to abandon the secure position in Central Europe which the existence of the GDR provides. The attitudes of the West Europeans, especially Britain and France, are not entirely different. The division of Germany and of Berlin forms a sort of rug on which stands the top table reserved for 'Victor Powers of the Second World War'. If the division ends, the rug is rudely pulled away from under them, and − sprawling on the common ground − they cease to resemble powers.

To sum up: while Western Europe integrates more closely, the rest of Eastern and Central Europe may develop quarrels, some historic but others − perhaps − new. Is the Helsinki security system strong enough to contain such quarrels? That system was built on the tacit assumption that each superpower would wish to police its own half of the continent. Now it seems that the Soviet Union is removing the pressure which kept those quarrels latent. Does that also mean that the Soviet Union no longer feels that it has any duty to intervene and bang heads together if the quarrels − once released − develop into conflict? If that is so, then the security order designed by the Helsinki process has to be revised: some authority not just for building confidence or measuring force levels but for active peace-keeping has to be constructed.

Uneven Development

The second cluster of uncertainties is economic − or perhaps 'geopolitical'. What will be the economic relationship between this powerful, unified West and that newly-emancipated, reforming but atomised East? The history of that relationship isn't encouraging, and severely qualifies talk of the 'common European house'. Left to itself − or to 'market forces' − the relationship for much of the past century has been semi-colonial. Around the last decades of the 19th century, the German *Mitteleuropa* vision developed and became influential. Roughly, this envisaged an extension of German power to the south-east, into the Balkans, across to Turkey and eventually by rail-links (the *Bagdad-Bahn*) into Mesopotamia and Arabia. The European part of the vision assigned south-eastern Europe to the role of providers of raw materials and food. Capital and what industry was required on the spot would be German, but these territories would essentially be the backyard and kitchen garden of the industrialised West. In the first world war, *Mitteleuropa* became a war aim, enriched by the hope of adding the Ukraine and other spoils to the empire. Hitler's design for a Eurasian land empire whose industrial engine-room lay in the

Germanic West was an extension of all this.

Between the wars, with Central and Eastern Europe the site of new 'successor states' to the old empires, the semi-colonial plight of the region was obvious. (Bohemia always excepted: the Czechs, with their high level of industrialisation and tradition of precision engineering, were really part of the West.) Factories were rare, and most private industry was owned by foreigners. Currencies were convertible against those of Britain, France or the United States, with catastrophic results in hyper-inflation. Agriculture was completely defenceless against price and demand fluctuations, and the Europeans who suffered most from the soaring birth rates, plunging prices for grain and acute unemployment were not the urban working class but the small farmers and peasants. By the end of the 1930s their situation was was desperate.

What was authentic about postwar state socialism in those countries was the attempt to repair that damage and ensure that it could never recur. That was the rationale for collectivisation; for the breakneck industrialisation after 1948 designed to soak up surplus rural population and provide each country with a complete, national industrial economy; for the rupture with the free-trading world outside. We know why that experiment failed – and why some think that it could never have succeeded. What we forget is why it all seemed so necessary in the first place – and whether, in the intervening years, a better answer has been found to Europe's uneven development.

I am not sure that it has. The relations between the United States and the debtor nations of Latin America could find a new parallel in Europe, as 'new model' reforms wash away the remains of socialist protectionism and expose over-staffed, inefficient local industries to market competition with the Brussels super-state. Again, the Helsinki provisions concentrate on economic co-operation and exchanges, which seemed so important fifteen years ago. What is required today is a new European plan, a grand social and economic strategy to prevent a reversion to dependency, to guarantee that Europe east of the Community will not be reborn politically only to grow up into a destiny of providing iron ore, fruit and vegetables, and cheap labour. It would be bitter indeed if the landscape after the cold war consisted only of one vast, advanced economy with a periphery of bantustans.

Gareth Stedman Jones

The Crisis of Communism

In May 1968 when student demonstrations had brought the French government to the verge of collapse, it is reported that General de Gaulle made a secret visit to General Massu to discover whether the army would intervene to restore order if the need arose. In the event, the troops were not called in; conservative sentiment within the civilian population was effectively mobilised and the legitimacy of the government preserved.

It may be presumed that Deng would have followed General de Gaulle's course of action, had the option been open to him. But it seems clear that it was not. Popular sentiment in Beijing was mounting daily, even hourly, against him. Neither the party, the police nor the locally-based military could be relied upon to halt the process of popular mobilisation. Unable to find any accessible source of legitimacy in civil society and incapable of activating its day-to-day apparatus of political authority, the Communist Party abdicated. Its mandate from heaven was irretrievably lost. Political power was surrendered to the military and the result was an act of sickening and mindless terror – a sordid and inhuman end to a great movement whose awesome achievements had once attracted all that was noble and courageous in 20th-century China to its banner.

Thus if May 1989 had begun by resembling May 1968, at the time of writing it is coming to resemble June 1848 when hardened generals like Cavaignac and Windischgrätz led raw and uneducated soldiers, fed on tales of the corruption and decadence of the towns, against the democratic students and workers of Paris and Vienna.

If 1848, rather than the previous history of communism, suggests a better point of comparison, it is because by acting in the way in which it did, the Communist Party leadership turned itself into a form of *ancien régime* and engaged in a form of violence which marks a break with its communist past. Twenty years ago hundreds of thousands of Chinese people perished in the cultural revolution and fifty years ago millions died in the campaigns and purges which followed Soviet collectivisation. From the suppression of the Kronstadt rising in the early days of the Russian revolution through to the quelling of political rebellions in Berlin, Budapest and Prague in the 1950s and 1960s, violence has been an inseparable accompaniment of the history of 20th-century communism.

But this sombre and terrifying sequence of events bears only a superficial resemblance to the violence unleashed in Tiananmen Square. It forms part of a history which is now past; it belongs to an epoch in which a world communist movement considered itself to be engaged in mortal combat with the forces of capitalism, imperalism and reaction. However terrible the initiatives of Stalin and Mao, they can only be understood within this frame. The purges and the cultural revolution were the effects of mass revolutionary processes in which millions were mesmerised and gripped by a radical demonology, a civil war waged between the imaginary social categories conjured up by political rhetoric. They can no more be attributed to the well-oiled machinery of totalitarianism than can the aroused fury of radical Islam unleashed by the Ayatollah in Iran. Similarly, the Soviet interventions in Eastern Europe in the 1950s and 1960s were also presented as the armed defence of an international revolution under threat.

Violence and metaphors of violence dominated communist language from the beginnings of bolshevism. The class war was a war, and the tactics of the vanguard party were conceived as battle engagements. The Communist Party was thus an instrument designed for war; its unique power derived from the recruitment of civilian energy within a quasi-military formation governed by clear lines of command. From the time of Lenin's *What Is To Be Done*, the party's purpose was to concentrate and lead the social forces in the revolutionary struggle, and to divide and disperse state power and its reactionary supports.

The original rationale of Lenin's strategy lay in the special conditions of Tsarist Russia − an autocratic regime − and thus the necessity for the party to work clandestinely. After the success of 1917, this animating idea was extended to all states in which the new Communist Parties were to operate. From the foundation of the Comintern, the international communist movement was to act as one, both in leading the class struggle in particular countries and in defending the first workers' states, threatened on every side by the manoeuvres of world capitalist encirclement.

Out of this emerged the particular communist stance towards democracy: democracy was desirable, but a luxury in a situation in which the international proletarian cause was assailed by counter-revolution and fascism. According to the theory of democratic centralism, decisions within the party were supposed to be arrived at by a democratic process, but once laid down, the line was to be followed by all. It was within this manichean framework held from 1917 through to 1956, that Communists were able to live with and defend even the most stupefying changes of tactic and the most unacceptable uses of coercion.

It is now difficult to understand what looks like the immense credulity of the supporters of communism, unless the foundation of this belief is remembered: that is, that it was capitalism that was in crisis, while communism represented the hope of the future. Such a view seemed to be borne out by the facts of mass unemployment and depressions, of the violence of colonialism and imperialism and of the unreason underpinning fascism and other right-wing movements. But above all, communism seemed to have the solution to the intractable problems and the devastating human waste which capitalism had engendered. The proclaimed success of Soviet collectivisation and the first five year plan forced economists and politicians in the capitalist world to consider the necessity to control capitalism through some form of economic planning. Roosevelt's New Deal, some 'Keynesian planning' for full employment through directed public works and rearmament, were in part influenced by the Soviet example. It is easy to forget that this perception of the communist economy persisted into the 1960s. China had attained greater growth rates than India and Khrushchev could confidently boast, 'we will bury you' when talking of the strategy of 'peaceful coexistence'. Even in Britain, Harold Wilson could still extol the communist economic success when talking of the virtues of the national plan in the early 1960s.

The Collapse of Certainty

It was not until the 1970s that such beliefs both in the communist and in the capitalist sphere were radically transformed. In the thirty years since 1945, mass democracy had become the norm in Western European countries, and the promises of better living standards which apologists for capitalism had been making for a hundred years became a perceived reality for the majority of the population in industrialised countries.

The perceived success of the communist model in underdeveloped countries in the 1950s was also increasingly challenged: the early successes of China and North Korea were now matched by the growth produced by capitalism in such 'underdeveloped' countries as South Korea, Singapore and Taiwan. Conversely, in the communist world, leaders and party officials had been forced to face up to the incompetence and indeed impotence of their economies to provide basic consumer needs and to compete in the field of new technologies, civil and military, which were rapidly developing in the West. Even more galling, it was becoming apparent that such incompetence and failure could no longer be attributed to a legacy of backwardness, but were consequences of this communist command economy itself.

This was a moment of truth of inestimable significance. It put into question the very idea of a communist state-led economy. The choice confronting communist states was either to maintain autarky at the cost of declining standards of living, growing political dissent and increasing technological disadvantage; or else, to open themselves to new forms of economic thinking, attract foreign investment, and to allow for the growth of unregulated market sectors. While smaller socialist countries like Cuba or Vietnam could pursue the first choice, for the communist superpowers themselves, this choice was ultimately impossible. The Soviet Union was already becoming dependent on the American wheat surplus from as early as 1972 and the intensification of the cold war in the early 1980s imposed an intolerable strain on the stagnant domestic economy. In China, the experience of the cultural revolution was a vivid illustration of the consequences of attempting to isolate the communist state from the world.

But if this choice was ultimately inescapable, the political costs were heavy. For economic liberalisation could not but erode the core of beliefs, both dirigiste and egalitarian, which had animated and sustained communism through the first two-thirds of the 20th century. It necessarily meant the abandonment of a manichean world view in which the Communist Party had the leading role to play. The warlike metaphors of leninism no longer possessed purchase in the domestic or the international sphere. The egalitarian priorities of old communist leaderships were now qualified by the language of market efficiency and the necessity of nurturing an entrepreneurial spirit. In the USSR in the Brezhnev era, these contradictions were resisted or ignored. But with the advent of Gorbachev, the need for basic changes, political as well as economic, was confronted.

In China, on the other hand, the policy was more contradictory. Modernisation was declared a priority, foreign investment was welcomed and tens of thousands of students were sent to study abroad. The emergence of a new rich class was openly encouraged and even the army was urged to contribute to its support through involvement in business activities. Yet at the same time, the marxist-leninist organisation of state and party was kept largely unchanged. As the bankers moved in and as friendship with the United States became the cornerstone of foreign policy, the modernisation of China was announced by Deng to rest on 'four cardinal principles': the socialist road, the dictatorship of the proletariat, the leadership of the Communist Party and the fidelity to marxism-leninism and Mao Zedong thought.

Such a combination could not be sustained for long, as hardliners had always warned. Along with the import of commodities and technologies came the import of ideas which inspired new and more worldly ambitions among the young. The rhetoric of revolutionary intransigence was belied by the actions of the government itself. And when students organised sit-ins and hunger strikes and when banners were waved in English as well as Chinese, as the world's press corps looked on, there were neither procedures nor precedents to fall back upon in response. The language of leninism was no longer able to encompass these phenomena. Its once powerful dicta now sounded hollow and formulaic. In previous popular upsurges, rebels had been denounced as 'running dogs', as 'lackeys of American imperialism' or as 'capitalist roaders'. What conviction could this language now possess?

It was perhaps a tacit recognition of the new situation that the government did not in fact employ it. Instead, students and workers were denounced in terms more reminiscent of the sewer metaphors of 1848 — as 'rats' and as 'social dregs'. In China marxism-leninism was at the end of the road, both in word and deed. 'Put politics in command' had been Lenin's first injunction and on the basis of this pronouncement, two of the most powerful armies in the world had remained for fifty years firmly under Communist Party control. Now, bereft of any further ideas, the party abdicated in favour of the army and the People's Republic descended to the level of a Francoist military dictatorship. Deng may dream of returning to normal. But there is no normality to return to. For the great emancipatory movement in China which began on 4 May 1919 has now passed finally out of the Communist Party hands.

Martin Jacques

Britain and Europe

Britain has been a highly internationalised country from some two centuries. Its economy has been very dependent on trade: its imperial history rested on an extraordinary involvement with large parts of what we now describe as the Third World; its language is the most international of all languages. The product of this history is a paradox. Britain possesses to this day a highly internationalised economy and a very developed web of commitments. Yet this is combined with a powerful insularity, a strong sense of xenophobia, much of which is a product of the unequal and dominant relationship which Britain once enjoyed as an imperial power, economically, militarily and culturally.

This sense of insularity and xenophobia has been under pressure throughout the postwar era as a result of Britain's irresistible relative decline. But it now faces a new set of pressures. They are not specific to Britain, but threaten to remake the world of the 1990s, and indeed the 21st century, in very new terms. Not least they will profoundly undermine the postwar international settlement — the special relationship with the USA, the old East-West relationship, the commitment to a notion of Britain as a powerful nation state — which has framed Britain's foreign policy throughout the postwar period.

There are three major forces here that we can distinguish, although they obviously overlap. Firstly, there is the growing trend towards internationalisation and globalisation. This is not new. It has been a persistent tendency since the 1950s, as evidenced by the growth of the international firm. But the capitalist crisis in the 1970s gave it a new meaning and momentum. It accelerated the trend towards global markets; it stimulated the development of leading-edge technologies such as semi-conductors, robotics and microchips, whose production and markets were highly internationalised; it paved the way towards a far more global monetary system. These developments have greatly enhanced the economic interdependence of national economies such that it is no longer possible for the average European nation state to pursue national economic policies in the old way, because of the spill-over effect from other economies.

Although this trend toward globalisation is most obviously economically driven, it cannot be reduced to the economic either in its causes or in its effects. Take, for example, the growth of an increasingly internationalised culture, with the spread of satellite television or the growth of English as an international language.

We live in an era in which Paris, with the opening of the Channel Tunnel, could feel as close to London as Manchester; when events in a far part of the globe can be brought live to your sitting room; when foreign travel including to Third World destinations has become commonplace; when a nuclear meltdown in one country affects a whole continent; when the corruption of oceans can affect the balance of our planet's ecosystem. In short, globalisation is accompanied by a new sense of global intimacy and interdependence.

This tendency towards globalisation has been accompanied by a parallel, often conflicting, tendency towards localisation. As power moves upwards from the nation state towards larger international units, be it the international firms, regional entities like the EC, or transnational organisations such as the IMF and Nato, so there is also a countervailing pressure, whose roots are various, for it to move downwards. Regions and cities have acquired their own economic leverage with international firms, with the decline in the power of the nation state and the rise of more intense global competition for inward investment. There is a new search for identity and difference in the face of impersonal global forces, which is leading to the emergence of new national and ethnic demands. The most striking example of this trend within Britain is the slow erosion of the 'British' identity as it is besieged by the rise of Scottish, and to a lesser extent, Welsh nationalism, though in this instance it is also a revolt against the antiquated British state with its extraordinary degree of centralisation.

The second new pressure we can identify is the break-up of the old bi-polar world which dominated the postwar international scene until it began to lose some of its purchase in the early 1970s. The decline of this bi-polar settlement was postponed by the onset of the second cold war at the end of the 1970s, which resulted from the cold-war mentality of Reaganism and the immobilism and backwardness of Brezhnevism. The emergence of Gorbachev has now transformed that situation.

Gorbachev heralds the break-up of the bi-polar world, the blocs in their old inert form, and the bloc mentality itself. The Soviet Union has abandoned its military/hegemonic ambitions in the Third World and it is now evident that it intends to allow the East European countries to more or less go their own way. Gorbachev heralds a world of interdependence where the old autarchic bloc mentality has no place, where nations and peoples must not just coexist but interact and co-operate, where relations must be informed by universal human values. Of course, we should not forget that the turn by the Soviet Union away from the bloc ideology is also driven by its economic difficulties. The fact is that it can no longer afford to live in the old way, spending enormous sums of money on the armed forces, and intervening outside its own borders when it felt its own hegemonic aspirations were threatened.

But the pressure for change in this context does not come from the Soviet Union alone. The USA can no longer afford to be the kind of hegemonic power it was in earlier decades. Already, by 1975 and its defeat in Vietnam, it was evident that the USA could no longer afford such large-scale military involvement. Reagan attempted to revive US ambitions, but economic reality, notably in the form of the twin deficits, is forcing it to retreat. Over the next decade we will witness a process by which the USA slowly disengages itself from the kind of commitments it has sustained in Western Europe in the postwar period. This is partly because it can no longer afford them. But two other factors are also working here: the growing independence and power of Western Europe itself, and the fact that the locus of international economic power is shifting eastwards to the Pacific Rim, notably Japan and newly-industrialising countries like Taiwan and Singapore, with states like China and India in the background, thereby pushing American sights westwards across the Pacific rather than eastwards over the Atlantic.

Now the breakdown of the bi-polar world is undermining the assumptions of British postwar foreign and defence policy.

These involved Britain being an integral, and in some senses senior, partner in the Nato alliance, directed against the Soviet Union. But the Soviet threat as previously conceived is palpably disappearing before our very eyes. In the 1990s, assuming that present trends are sustained, the cold war will no longer be an adequate basis for the formulation of the main contours of our foreign policy. This will mark a shift of epochal dimensions.

The third pressure which is transforming the shape of the world, and Britain's place within it, is the trend towards Europeanisation. This is of course not new: it started in the 1950s. But it stalled in the 1970s, and has now acquired a new momentum with the move towards a single market in 1992. The process of Europeanisation can be seen in the long run as mainly a response to internationalisation on the one hand, and the decline of the nation state, and specifically the European nation state, on the other. It is the failure to appreciate this long-term historic reality on Left and Right, which has made Britain such a belated and reluctant actor in the European scene. It is now clear that the growth of the European Community is set to transform the very shape of our continent and profoundly weaken the traditional European nation state, which historically defines, in many respects, the very notion of the nation state itself. 1992 will be a key moment in this process. Not least, like the phenomenon of Gorbachev, it is symbolic, helping us to understand the underlying processes and thereby also serving to hasten their development.

The Political Response to New Pressures

Thatcherism's relationship to these three pressures has been fundamentally regressive. Its most positive aspect was the recognition in the 1970s of the new international competitive pressures and the need for Britain to adapt to a new international division of labour. But this was combined with a championing of the old chauvinistic, bulldog little-Englandism. Similarly, while Thatcher has skilfully sought to do business with Gorbachev, she has stubbornly clung to the old cold-war framework and been the foremost advocate of its greatest military symbol, nuclear weapons.

Finally, Thatcherism has always been the reluctant European – for two main reasons. Firstly, at its core Thatcherism is an ideology of little-Englandism. It is the latter which frames its strategy. It always thinks first in terms of nation state. Now that is palpably no longer possible. It is therefore the reluctant European, unable to generate any kind of European strategy of its own. Secondly, Thatcherism knows that when it comes to the EC it is out of step. Only in Britain is neo-liberalism so rampant and unadulterated when it comes to government strategy.

Thatcherism can only be properly understood in the context of the paradox raised earlier: that while Britain is in some respects a highly internationalised society, that inter-nationalisation has been shaped and distorted by narrow national chauvinism and supremacism, an increasingly misplaced notion that Britain is best and knows best. Thatcherism's commitment to internationalisation is basically economic, to the free play of international market forces. In the political and cultural domains, Thatcherism is determinedly nationalistic, racist, patriarchal and parochial. One of the most striking examples of this is Thatcherism's protective attitude towards the apartheid regime in South Africa. Nothing more clearly symbolises Thatcherism's relationship to Britain's imperial past and its racist legacy.

But what informs Thatcherism has also left its mark more generally on our political culture. It could hardly have been very different. After all, we are speaking here of at least 200 years of history. The Left is no exception. It too has been marked by the paradox of a shared imperial past. It remains strikingly insular in its character. The Labour Party, for instance, has always been remarkably ignorant of what is happening in other West European countries, not least in terms of the thinking and experiments of the Left. This insularity has tended to blind it to the process of internationalisation. In the face of Europeanisation, it sought refuge for a long time in the arms of national sovereignty. It misread which way history was moving.

The impact on Britain of the three pressures we have outlined will be profound. Firstly, it will, over the course of the 1990s, force some kind of transformation in Britain's foreign policy. Secondly, and more fundamentally, it will radically alter the meaning of, and distinction between, foreign and domestic, the international and the national.

The starting point here must be this new balance between the national and the international. The trend towards internationalisation means that power is now frequently located outside the realm of the nation state. There is no point in the Left seeking to resist this trend, which has been its instinct in the past. It must go with the grain of internationalisation, which has acquired fresh momentum since the crisis of the 1970s. The outcome of this process can be progressive or reactionary, depending, in the time-honoured phrase, on the balance of political forces.

Let us take a relatively neglected example of the problem: the international firm. It would, in general, be ineffective and positively harmful to nationalise the relevant branch of the international firm operating in this country, and thereby rip apart the fabric of world-wide economic ties and deepening co-operation between national economies. The problem posed by the international firm − which, lest we forget, dominates the internationally competitive sector of our economy − cannot be resolved at a national level. The socialisation of the international firm, whatever this might precisely mean in practice, has to be thought of in regional or even global terms.

As far as Britain is concerned, undoubtedly the key dimension in this new division of labour is Europe. An increasing range of questions which were once dealt with at national level must now be conceived of in terms of the European Community. It makes little sense to think of key environmental problems like acid rain in national terms. For some, like the ozone layer, not even a European response is adequate: only a global approach can hope to match the scale of the problem. For major industries, like telecommunications, there is no longer any such thing as a national solution. A European perspective is essential.

The evolution of this European dimension, however, remains highly problematic. The Thatcherite view conceives of the EC as little more than a giant free market. It wants to restrict the role of the EC institutions, and minimise social intervention and regulation. In this, for a combination of reasons, it is unlikely to succeed.

But equally, the Left is certainly not in the driver's seat. Social Europe is still more of a dream than a reality, lagging well behind the 1992 prospectus of a single market. Moreover, as the EC institutions acquire more power, which they undoubtedly will over the next decade, their unaccountable nature will pose an increasingly important democratic problem. So far, the democratic problem has largely been seen in terms of national sovereignty versus Brussels. But the real question will increasingly be the accountability of the EC institutions. Here there are real dangers. The EC could evolve as a mighty oligarchy with the peoples of the EC countries having precious little control over what they do. Alternatively, a different picture could begin to take shape, with a far more powerful European Parliament and an elected Commission. Of course, EC institutions which enjoy a popular mandate will also enjoy far more authority and therefore further undercut national sovereignty. But that is the choice which the European Left should make.

The point to stress here is that the future of the EC remains open-ended. Its evolution will be a continual process of contestation. Social Europe is one area. The democratic deficit is another. The question of whether or not the EC acquires its own defence capacity, and what that might be, is a further example. Then again there is the future composition of the EC. Will the EC expand to embrace the EFTA countries, Cyprus, Morocco and Turkey, for instance? If it does, it will become a very different organism from what it is now, embracing a very different ethnic and religous conception of Europe. Further, there is the question of the relationship between the EC and Eastern Europe, which has been thrown into the melting pot by Gorbachev's renunciation of the traditional client relationship between these states and the Soviet Union. Will the EC become in effect the engine-room of European growth and cast those states around it into some kind of subordinate and second-class relationship, or will Europe acquire an increasingly cohesive and pluralistic character, that of a common European home?

This list of issues is far from exhaustive. But it serves to indicate how the parameters of the EC's development remain indeterminate. What is clear is that both the Left's traditional defence of national sovereignty and the Thatcherite commitment to the EC as a free market have little purchase on the future of the EC. More generally, the process of Europeanisation undermines the traditional line of division in our political thinking between the international and the national, and must, at a minimum, transform at least the form of the paradox described earlier.

There is one further point worth making here. A key problem

facing the Left if it wishes to be a serious protagonist in the European process is that culturally it remains deeply national in character. Compared with capital, the unions have found it extraordinarily difficult to develop international forms of co-operation, action and organisation. Socialist and communist parties, whatever the internationalist rhetoric, remain deeply national institutions. And while that remains the case it is difficult to see the Left becoming a powerful actor on the EC stage. That concerted forms of action on a European as opposed to national stage are possible is borne out by the peace movement in the early 1980s and the green movement in the last few years. But what a Europeanisation of the culture of labour movements might mean remains a virtually undiscussed question.

Europeanisation does not exhaust the question of Britain's relationship to the internationalisation process. It provides a new frame, a new context. But the EC still remains an institution with limited powers. Moreover, there are many problems which cannot be resolved at a regional level. New global problems, notably the ecological threat, not least in the Third World, require new forms of co-operation which go well beyond what is achievable on a regional basis. The problem of North-South must also be seen in this light. Clearly, the EC can undoubtedly make a contribution to solving this problem, one it has largely avoided making in the past. But it also requires new global agreements, for example a general moratorium on the payment of Third World debt, or a global agreement by the industrialised countries, East and West, to assist the Third World countries in the search for CFC substitutes.

Similarly, new global possibilities, notably in the scientific and technical sphere, space research being an obvious example, necessitate new and different forms of global co-operation. It is unclear what forms such global and multinational co-operation might take, but two things are immediately suggested. Firstly, the role of the United Nations and its agencies could be greatly expanded. Secondly, the process of global co-operation should not be viewed as one confined to intergovernmental channels, but as a conversation between societies.

The third pressure alluded to at the outset was the end of bi-polarism and the emergence of a more multi-polar world. The breakdown of the old East-West division drives a horse and carriage through the postwar international settlement. What will emerge to replace it remains to be seen. One of course cannot rule out some kind of regression, linked to Gorbachev's own position in the Soviet Union. But assuming this does not happen, then the most obvious casualty, in the British context, must be the Right. The whole basis of our foreign and defence policy is now under enormous pressure. What is needed is a new disarmament initiative from the Left which combines unilateral, bilateral and multilateral measures.

The three processes outlined at the beginning – internationalisation, Europeanisation and the breakdown of the old bi-polar world – will transform Britain's relationship with the world outside of itself and therefore its own identity. The political effects are already visible. At the end of the 1970s, and indeed into the early 1980s, Thatcherism succeeded in setting the political agenda in this area, as in so many others. At the end of the 1980s, it no longer looks like that. It is on the defensive in relation to Europe. It is on the defensive in the face of the Gorbachev crusade. It has sought to ride the green tide, but looks distinctly uncomfortable with it.

It is difficult to avoid the observation that the Left is now presented with a historic opportunity. At least two of the forces now underway, namely Europeanisation and the end of the cold war, are serving to weaken Thatcherism. Internationalisation is more ambiguous in its impact. The paradox between on the one hand, Britain's internationalisation and, on the other, its xenophobia could potentially find a new and more progressive resolution. But it is not inevitable. Just as Thatcherism was a reactionary settlement of this contradiction in the context of the internationalisation dynamic of the 1970s, so the Right could transform itself again. The question is whether the Left can come to terms with these momentous new forces and carry through its own intellectual and cultural revolution.

Tom Nairn

Tartan Power

Mr Ridley advocates a total remoulding of Scotland's political culture:

> What is so silly about the Scots is that... He quickly changed tack: I am not sure sitting here in Westminster listening to what the Scottish Labour MPs are going on about, that I have the faintest idea of what the hell it is they are after apart from destruction and criticism. If that is expressing the views of the Scots I am left in total bewilderment as to what they are ...

Nicholas Ridley, interviewed by Chris McLaughlin, *The Scotsman*, 2 May 1988.

A pity about that change of tack. Ridley was clearly itching to put the boot right into Caledonia's political shit (or as our vernacular prefers, shite) while still in the unevacuated state. Regrettably, *raison d'état* prevailed: only three days remained before district elections were due to be held all over Scotland which would furnish the first test of national opinion since June 1987.

Such prudence denied us another great Tory *lapsus* comparable to Thatcher's, who on a recent visit said of Adam Smith, 'Now he was a jolly good Scot': an insight already taken over into folklore. However, little effort is needed to fill in Ridley's blanks since he was pretty unbuttoned in the rest of the interview. His main point was that it is high time the Scots became English:

> The Scots have fastened on their separate identity as a nation to try and establish that somehow all this does not apply to them, whereas the northern English — who are not perhaps so well off even as the Scots — have accepted that they are a part of England and will have to see their way through the remedies that we have made available. I hope the Scots will join them because it will be to the benefit of the Scots. I don't think they can go on having a different political philosophy and at the same time expect to benefit economically like the rest of us. You cannot have it both ways...

Nicholas is the tenth Ridley to hold honourable member status, and by the old family standards this is talk both tough and new. His ancestors took it for granted that the Scots had things both ways: a two-faced lot who remained a nation of sorts yet cashed in on being British. Nor should it be forgotten how useful such ambiguity was to Ridley, England and its appendages in Wales, Ireland and elsewhere: the military, state and imperial machines all relied upon a steady supply of jolly good Scottish cadres — and notably upon the institutional middle class and emigré intelligentsia furnished by a disproportionately large educational system (eight universities for five million people). England may have been chief midwife to the development of modern capital, but it was Adam Smith who invented capitalism.

By the time of the local elections of 6 May 1988 there could be no more doubt: the recalcitrant bastards were more bent than ever on having it both ways. Polling figures higher than usual (and higher than in the corresponding English districts) showed an awareness of the larger issues at stake. Yet, as *The Scotsman* commented, 'Cut them any way you choose, the results of the local elections offer very little comfort to Mr Malcolm Rifkind or his party. But this is a somewhat canny verdict. The overall figures were: Labour Party — 42.67 per cent; SNP — 21.19 per cent; Conservatives — 19.05 per cent; Democrats — 8.33 per cent; Independents and others — 8.76 per cent. Though unevenly expressed in terms of council seats (for the usual reasons), this vote put the Tories back behind the Nationalists for the first time in over a decade. Labour improved its performance slightly but the break-up of Alliance politics in Scotland has produced mainly a shift towards nationalism rather than a Conservative revival, in spite of the huge and well-publicised efforts of that party to reconstruct both its apparatus and its popular image since the Alamo-style humiliation of last year. Owenism has almost vanished. The problem is not one of the little comfort to be got from a stagnant vote: if these trends continue, even gentle evaporation may put Scottish Toryism down among the Lib-Dems and 'others'.

What really exasperates Ridley and his Downing Street evangelists is that all those Scots who by now *ought to be* voting Conservative — council house purchasers, Morningside housewives, electronics operatives — just somehow are not. The economy is 'doing well', at least by comparison with other regions. Yet appropriate gratitude fails to be expressed. As local government minister Michael Howard moaned on election night, the north Britons still will not grasp their advantages of 'joining in the mainstream' of the new British way. Such deplorable obtuseness calls for more Thatcherism to be applied, not less.

Conservative opinion also blamed the poll tax – in Scotland registration was begun during the electoral campaign and everywhere vociferous anti-poll tax groups seem to have been successful in linking the two. On election eve, communal bonfires of community charge leaflets and forms produced the odd effect of Halloween in spring. But that too makes a dubious excuse for Tory failure. There is little chance of this agitation dying down for a long time. Also, the party which came second in the districts has just committed itself to a campaign of outright civil disobedience on the poll tax issue: that is, to non-registration and non-payment on the grounds that the Conservatives 'have no mandate' in Scotland. Whatever success the Nationalists have with this nobody believes the bonfires will die down much before the next general election (and of course, some may by then be started up in the South as well).

Scottish secretary Malcolm Rifkind is a lawyer renowned for his Fred Astaire footwork and glib courtroom punching: 'That man could talk his way out of a Beirut hijack', sighed one friend overcome by a recent Weekend World interview. The programme was entitled 'The Tories' Tartan Gamble' and in it the secretary maintained that his party was really suffering from 'a problem of *identity*' in Scotland. Smarter than the philistines about him, he sought to shift the argument on to the plane of political philosophy: remould Thatcherism a little to suit the 'Scottish identity' better, and its residual problem will be solved.

The Scottish Middle Class

All his approach really shows is how hopeless the situation may already have become. The problem is indeed one of 'identity'. But – as Immanuel Wallerstein pointed out in a history of capitalism – 'One does not construct an identity out of thin air'. Nor can it easily be refashioned by adroit legal rhetoric. The national identity with which Thatcherism has so unwittingly collided is the product of a long material history, and is unlikely to shift much between now and the next set of elections.

What that history generated in Scotland was a predominantly institutional middle class. Organised since 1707 mainly around kirk, law and the education system — the three bastions of Scottish civil society — this service bourgeoisie was also well placed to exploit all the institutions of an expanding British state and empire. Coming from a society with no modern political identity it was politically inept: 'running things' remained a prerogative of the southern ruling caste, while the Scots tended to become an emigrant managerial stratum — the first secretaries, foremen and butlers of imperialism. Unusually, it was only loosely related to the development of Scottish industrial capitalism: administrative rather than entrepreneurial in outlook, it evolved quite separately from the forge and shipyard owners of Glasgow (and has easily outlasted them).

The great moment of this class arrived with the welfare state: public corporatism and patronage had always been its natural element, and in the burgeoning institutions of the postwar consensus it found a suitable replacement for overseas colonialism. These interests led to a profitable switch of political allegiance from Liberalism to Labourism. Indeed the latter soon became in many respects its most authentic quasi-political embodiment: a fourth 'institution' fit to rank with the historical three, and quite similar to them in corporate respectability, influence 'down South', and the substantial if staid career prospects tied to an infinitude of Buggins' Turns. Resting on an orderly working class vote, this has turned into an historical *bloc* complementing national predecessors: through it today's graduates are vehicled into a legalistic Presbyterian 'Socialism' more like the old Moderate Kirk than the colourful secularism so rife beyond Tyneside.

Now, it can be argued that both the deeper historical orientation of the class and its postwar Labourite vestment are severely menaced by Thatcherism's success and that most of what's happening relates to a resultant sense of crisis. The point is that *this* threat was never posed by past cycles of prosperity and retrenchment: the old regime's oscillations within an unaltering framework of gentlemanly governance and administered compromise. It is by smashing the framework itself that Thatcherite radicalism has provoked quite unintended repercussions among the Scots. For the latter have — in that sense which Rifkind didn't quite intend — an historic corporate 'identity' much more invested in public sector institutions than any other part of the United Kingdom. Furthermore, this identification is unlikely to be much affected by all those signs of relative economic success in the Scottish industrial belt to which Tories point with naive pride.

Such advances will encourage the rise of a new capitalist stratum with even fewer links to the core bourgeoisie than the old one: important parts of the new economy are run from Japan and California. And in any case, state initiative (above all via the successful Scottish Development Agency) is known by élite and workers alike to have been crucial in securing most of these plants: most roads in central Scotland are now lined by SDA and EC signs signalling public-sector munificence and help. There is simply less reason there for associating prosperity with 'rolling back the state' and other Thatcher clichés.

The drastic shrinkage in public and institutional employment was bound to undermine the complacent higher-servant *Weltanschauung* of the Scots bourgeoisie. During the 1970s doom was held off to some degree by the bizarre reforms of local government. At a time when emigration was already harder and deflation was under trial, Scotland was endowed with a system of formidable regional councils under Labour control which consolidated public bureaucracy. Only after 1979 did this order begin to crumble, as forced retrenchments everywhere were accompanied by a growing central attack on local spending and administration. The comforts and compensations of the old emigration ceased, as jobs vanished and southern property became impossible to buy. An educated middle class accustomed to a wider welcoming world found itself by the mid-1980s stuck in the homeland, and under assault even there.

It was (for example) suddenly discovered that Scottish higher education is threatened by 'disproportionate' numbers of English students and professors. The universities have become 'colonised' and too many cultural bodies and public boards are run by 'outsiders'. What counts here is of course the alteration of attitudes. I recall an earlier era when such 'domination' was a matter merely for jokes and occasional grumbles. In the 1980s both the statistical facts of takeover and resentment of them are being generated by a real change: the smaller public world where (inevitably) emissaries of the ruling or metropolitan culture enjoy certain advantages and (as individuals) can't help enforcing these upon a less privileged and unprotected environment. 'Protection' here can only mean counter or positive discrimination, to safeguard 'our own' élite. And in Scotland, that means nationalism.

So there are growing reasons for stressing the other and hitherto latent aspect of the Scottish class identity I have outlined: its nationality. The same myopia has made Tories forget what happened when a wave of economic optimism last hit Scotland in the early 1970s. Then, North Sea oil euphoria produced nationalism, not grateful alignment with London. But whereas at that time the middle class was − as later events showed − playing with the idea rather than really addicted to it, circumstances are now very different.

The Growth of Difference in Scotland

The most evident difference is the decline of Labourism. Scotland's institutional investment in that cause depended upon an *entente* as unwritten as the rest of the United Kingdom's constitution. Now and then − at least once per political generation − the Labour majority in the periphery could join up with a significant heartland minority to get state power. By breaking up this minority, Tory radicalism has invalidated the old understanding − and done so, it must be said, ever more consciously and aggressively ('getting rid of socialism for good' etc). The kernel of Great Britain's old regime has in that sense been betrayed at the heart, not in its provincial limbs or by regional separatism.

If the change proves terminal, then the very basis of Scottish Labourism is in doubt. Not surprisingly, there is reluctance to accept this conclusion. The reluctance is commonly expressed in a number of myths. The most painful of these emerged in the wake of the June 1987 general election. Some readers may recall how at that time apparently articulate and sane leaders of Scotland's Labour regiment (not just its rank-and-file mediocrities) could be heard gibbering in public about Ken Livingstone and the 'London Left'. There were even quite serious proposals for sending northern 'missionaries' down to clean up the mess and restore the spirit of Herbert Morrison:

more or less as Edinburgh's mid-17th-century Calvinists once hoped to get rid of Independents, Levellers and other Devil-inspired loonies of the day. Marxism, of course, might lead one to suspect some socio-economic foundation for the whole GLC experience, Thatcher's appeal to ex-Labour voters and the 'North-South' divide. But 'foundation' has a horribly permanent ring to it. The idea that leadership depravity was to blame is by contrast consoling, spiritual in nature, flattering to one's own proven rectitude, and preservative of certain homely and corporate virtues important to the Scottish middle class.

Traditionally, those virtues have been ways of *avoiding* the crude political identity of nationalism. But if the wider system that supported them is breaking down, then they could easily *become* that identity. And in fact, something like this has been occurring − slowly since 1983 and then at a much accelerated pace over the past year. The Scots have been forced to begin seeing themselves as 'different' and under threat. This is not at all the same thing as clinging to vestigial and romantic 'differences' (a baneful feature of Scottish existence since the 18th century). Oddly enough, the situation is a good deal more serious than in the 1970s, when the spectacular first wave of nationalism attracted so much attention. Then a lot of identity was indeed manufactured out of Wallerstein's 'thin air', in a kind of heady prematurity mixed up with old nonsense. But Mrs Thatcher's counter-revolution may be achieving what that impulsive movement did not.

Today's change by contrast is hesitant and slow to find political expression. It clings to the concealment of past forms and vague or frankly preposterous moral notions − the popular myth of a wholesome 'Scottish community' somehow immune from capitalist greed and the profit motive, for example. On the Tory side, Scottish resistance is naturally caricatured as (in Rifkind's terms) 'an anti-enterprise, paternalist, quasi-socialistic culture', over-ripe for dismantling − or more crudely, as a nation of whining spongers curable only by stricter discipline. No one need be surprised by the explosion of such daft ideas, on both sides: they have always accompanied the genesis of real nationalism. What is more surprising is the latter's failure to attain more adequate political manifestation in basically favourable circumstances. Why is this still a creeping, sidelong nationalism rather than one more confident and directly expressed?

The reason is that Scottish politics remains locked in the patterns of fifteen to twenty years ago, with echoes going back much further — locked, that is, in the era of the SNP's breakthrough and Labourism's subsequent embarrassed shuffle towards 'devolution'. Regarded sociologically, political parties are of course generally deeply conservative bodies, slower to change than the social forces they claim to represent. In an inert and traditionally unfocused political environment such conservatism can be chronic: having eschewed separate political identity for so long, the Scottish mentality seems to regard all motion in that area with suspicion bordering on paranoid. The Devil is ever at work, and especially bent on undoing the achievements of Labour's 'purest Kirk under Heaven'.

Thus in the 1980s most Scottish political quarrels disintegrate into the same rancid old row between Labour and 'the Nats', replete with recriminations about the unsaintly and never-to-be forgiven conduct of 1979, 1977 or even 1967: a universe of betrayal and perdition.

The SNP is in fact a party greatly changed and renewed by comparison with the early 1970s. Yet its steady movement to the left has had an unfortunate consequence. This alteration of trajectory has brought it into more direct conflict with labourism, as (inevitably) the working-class electorate of the industrial belt becomes its chosen recruitment area. At the same moment Labour has become much more anxious and vulnerable on the theme of nationality. As the Scottish party (at least electorally) it is in the odd quandry of having both to accept and constantly to disavow national distinctiveness. The result so far is an intensification of mutual abuse and vilification. From the Labourites, trite denunciations of 'narrow nationalism' and Tartan Tories; from the SNP the querulous rhetoric of 'the feeble fifty' and antics like the sending of white feathers to Labour's Westminster MPs.

All movements of national liberation are civil wars of some kind. Scotland's political distinction consists in being unable to escape from a phoney war which prevents the real one starting. That is, the struggle between a majority open to some kind of self-government and a shrinking Unionist minority. Behind that embattled minority there stands the gathering force of a southern state impatient with out-of-date ambiguity and dependence. Determination to have its way and enforce the Thatcherite formulae is turning into the kind of naked assimilationism visible in the opinion of Ridley and many others.

This drive is meeting the unforeseen obstacle of a civil society structurally hostile to many of its implications but − because of its apolitical backwardness and clientilism − slow to mobilise effective democratic resistance. As in all similar cases, what that conflict will demand is some new fusion of the political motifs of class and nationhood. But current events seem to suggest that, where these motifs have been separated and separately repressed for so long by a culture of chosen dependency, any new chemistry of the democratic-popular will remain hard to create.

Gwyn A Williams

The Onward March of a Small Nation

We in Wales live in the aftermath of the Pontypridd by-election, which Labour, with a plausible candidate and a major effort, safely won, though its majority slipped, and in which Plaid Cymru quadrupled its vote and quintupled its percentage, taking a good half of its gains from former Labour voters. We approach the Vale of Glamorgan contest: said to be critical to Labour's recovery. Inevitably, our eyes are fixed on Westminster.

If we go on looking only to Westminster, as we have done for two hundred years, generally with the fixed stare a rabbit directs at a stoat, we can feel ourselves to be some small, freak people clinging to the lip of the Island of Britain in total dependence on this British state.

We are nothing of the kind. We are not alone. We are an European people and we belong to an army of small peoples, numbering many millions, who are becoming the fulcrum of the struggle to create a human Europe of the peoples.

It is necessary to look across the Channel. If we look across that Channel, we can't stop looking until we see Vladivostok. The momentous changes underway in the Soviet Union will prove momentous for the human race. Consider one dramatic decision. In the drive for *perestroika*, the Soviet republics of Estonia, Latvia, Lithuania and Byelorussia, together with the Ural city of Sverdlovsk and the Tatar autonomous region, are to switch to full regional self-financing. They will take control of their own people and resources and the Soviet Union will have to renegotiate its relationships with them. They are to be the vanguard in the struggle to transform society. It is no doubt a measure of the difficulties *perestroika* faces that, at least in the Baltic republics, the implementation of that decision has been postponed.

Those Baltic republics have the bit between their teeth.

Already, with the agreement and in some cases the encouragement of Moscow, they have recovered national flags, national anthems, national days; they are establishing the equality of their own languages and are trying to create their own citizenship. Two of them are talking of the right locally to veto central legislation. There will no doubt be trouble, but there is little doubt either that an effective compromise is in the making.

Despite our very different histories, it is worth taking a closer look at Estonia, smallest of the republics and the pacemaker. They are one and half million people; we are twice that number. Many of them are passionately concerned to maintain and develop their own language and culture in the face of the world language of Russian; many of our people are equally passionate about Welsh. They face a process of immigration and displacement, the threat of historical extinction, as bad as anything which the people of western Wales now face, even as much as urban Wales, which now looks like becoming another Isle of Dogs. 40 per cent of the population of Estonia is non-Estonian; something like 37 per cent of the population of Wales is non-Welsh. But note, at the critical vote in the Estonian Soviet, nearly every one of the representatives of the Russians in Estonia joined with native delegates to call for a genuinely self-governing Estonia, presumably because it was in their interest so to do. This is something we in Wales need to think hard about.

What has driven this Gorbachev generation is not only the renewal of the communist ideal, but brute necessity. They have learned the hard way that they cannot regenerate their society without radical constitutional reform. We are in the same predicament. To talk of 'constitutional tinkering' as a distraction is fundamentally to misread that predicament. There can be no regeneration of our society without a radical restructuring of government on this Island of Britain.

The necessity becomes more urgent as 1992 approaches. Some eighteen months ago, the European Parliament, unreformed and constrained though it now is, passed a major resolution on the minority languages of Europe, which are spoken by some 80 million people. It was a radical demand for serious action in their support. Such a resolution does not today have the force of European law, though after 1992 matters may be different. It has nevertheless gone to the Commission for submission to the states. As far as I know, this resolution passed unreported in the London or even the Welsh press. We learned of it only from our allies in the European Free Alliance within the Rainbow Group in the European Parliament.

Only a few weeks ago, that same European Parliament passed an even more radical resolution. This time, it was at least mentioned in one Welsh newspaper. By a majority of 100, it called for real power to pass to the regions of Europe. It called for elected bodies to run those regions with the cash resources to manage their own affairs. The objective is to reduce the growing gap between richer and poorer regions. It argues that the gradual transfer of powers to the Community must be accompanied by decentralisation and suggests the creation of a second chamber or European senate of the regions.

The fiercest resistance came from a centralist Spaniard and an English Tory MEP. Two features particularly appalled the latter. The European Parliament declared that these powerful elected assemblies of the regions should be able in a number of instances to bypass their state governments, deal directly with the Commission and European agencies and help to shape Community policies on the regions. And it insisted on minimal requirements for the definition of a region, so that it should be a real entity not some public relations exercise. That, for example, would mean that the embryonic Welsh state which exists in the Welsh Office with its cluster of dependent quangos should be controlled by the people of Wales, not by Whitehall.

We are in for great storms as 1992 approaches, frontiers start to dissolve and state sovereignty begins to become redundant. Obviously 1992 poses the threat of yet greater centralisation of corporate power, yet more deprivation for neglected regions like Wales. It is precisely for this reason that the drive for what is called a social Europe, which Jacques Delors has come to personify, is gathering such power and momentum that the true bearers of the Thatcherite faith are becoming alarmed and hostile.

This campaign, which at the hands of those dedicated to a European unity in diversity is becoming something of a crusade, is in part a reaction against the advance of the Europe of the corporations, but in part a product of it. Globalisation and regionalisation are simultaneous processes within the evolution of post-Fordist society which is analysed elsewhere in this book. The newer technology, the newer styles of flexible production directed at consumers of infinite variety and producers of individualised and participatory skills, that whole complex of attitudes and actions which is turning the institutions and practices of both established labour and capital into dinosaurs, certainly can and does cut across states. It concentrates enormous power and decisive control in oligarchies whose decisions can spell death to whole regions and communities.

But the very same process is widely dispersing production with a freedom and flexibility hitherto unknown. It certainly strives, of necessity, to scoop up unorganised and ill-defended pools of available labour, like the legions of underpaid and exploited women, but it also, of necessity, cultivates myriad new skills and new workers who are beginning to assume the independence and the dignity often associated with pre-industrial craft workers and artisans. In an almost classically marxist manner, this capitalism, of necessity, sows the seeds of its own transcendence: much of the social 'libertarian' thrust of Thatcherism opens up all manner of spaces for socialism to move into.

What is urgently needed is direct political intervention of a socialist character. It will need to be a socialism which has understood the society it lives in, which develops the kind of openness, flexibility, initiative and will which have enabled socialists to assume or share power in a dozen countries on the continent. The central focuses of intervention will have to be the local or regional and the European, if possible simultaneously. What will not serve is the state structure of a single country; the old socialist obsession with using the state power of its own 'nation' is patently inadequate.

That is why socialists must commit themselves to the dedicated Europeans' drive for their 'social Europe'. Their objective is to create genuine regional self-government as a necessary complement to increased power at the European centre, to reduce regional differences, to enshrine workers' rights and workers' participation, to establish women's rights, civil rights, the rights of small peoples.

Europe over the next decades is going to resemble Britain in the 17th century when parliament moved to wrest power from the crown. We face endless struggles over the general and the particular. The European Parliament, handicapped by the fifth column within it staffed by MEPs committed to the state power of their own countries, but assisted by its own fifth column within the Commission and the European agencies, will move to wrest power from the Council of Ministers of the states. Jacques Delors is probably correct to say that, by the end of the century, 80 per cent of the decisions which will deeply affect our lives will be taken in Brussels and Strasbourg. What will those decisions be and who will make them? Running through the endless conflicts ahead will be the struggle to transform the Europe of the corporations and the states into what the European Free Alliance calls the 'Europe of the Peoples', which will be a 'Europe of the people'.

That struggle will not be confined to Western Europe. In it, the small peoples, the little, lost nations, will play a critical role, as radical Europeans well know.

The place of the people of Wales, certainly of Welsh socialists, is in that struggle. For there is one glaring exception to a general trend − the separatist and authoritarian British state we live under, which is offering an increasingly determined resistance to a social Europe, a real parliament for Europe, a disarmed Europe.

Nearly every other country in the EC is either an outright federation or grants major autonomy to its regions and minority peoples. The regime which rules us is driving an already over-centralised state into a veritable paroxysm of centralisation. It is relentlessly dismantling local government, eliminating regional democracy, subjecting every quasi-autonomous institution it can get its hands on. The state itself is nakedly invading civil liberties, granting menacing new powers to an already inflated and paranoid world of secret agencies and, in complacent arrogance, erecting a formidably authoritarian system of government − with the precise intention of letting the market loose into every corner of our lives in a process which, in the name of individual freedom, breeds barbarism at the bottom and corruption at the top and destroys all sense of community. Its presiding genius denies that society even exists.

We can see the consequences day by day in Wales, where we face a kind of communal death. There is only one way out. We have to take as much control as is humanly possible over our own society. This means, in the first instance, getting a grip on the

Welsh Office and its associated agencies, which account for 80 per cent of our public expenditure and do not answer to us.

This is entirely feasible. Thatcherite libertarianism is riddled with contradictions into which we can burrow like Marx's Old Mole of Revolution. The most important of them for us is Mr Peter Walker, the prime minister-in-exile. As Dafydd Elis Thomas, president of Plaid Cymru has said, he is acting – no doubt in the service of his ambition to make his Wales what Birmingham was to Joseph Chamberlain – like a Welsh prime minister. His extraordinary performance, which has earned him massive popularity in Wales, has had several unexpected after-effects. His essentially non-Thatcherite styles have operated as something of a shield for the Welsh against the worst effects of his own government's policies. However real or unreal the consequences of his myriad 'initiatives', he has opened sceptical and resigned eyes to the real possibilities of Welsh self-management which exist; he has awoken a sense of self-help among a people bred over generations to dependence upon Westminster.

The creation of an elected Welsh assembly or parliament with real resources, to take over at least the powers of the Welsh Office, is within our capacity. We will need to mobilise a popular front in Wales, focusing in the first instance on a set of minimal objectives around which a majority can unite. We need to work with our friends and allies among the Scots and the many English now restive in their own regions. It will not be easy, but we can do it.

But it will not be enough, because any such victory will prove as transient as the achievements of 1945, anchored as it will be in this grotesque British state structure. Consider what we are up against. The present regime can use and build on an existing state structure which dates in its essence from the revolution called Glorious of 1688, which created that Glorious Constitution, universally hailed and endlessly celebrated as a miracle of human ingenuity which had solved the problems of combining order with progress, liberty with hierarchical authority. That constitution was substantially modified but not in essence transformed by the elimination of the confessional basis of the state over the crisis of 1828-35.

In consequence, we are the only country in Western Europe now where the sovereignty of the people does not exist even in theory. The people in this country are not sovereign. Sovereignty in this country resides in the Crown-in-Parliament, a constitutional fiction (though no fiction in the world of the secret agencies as we have seen!) which both symbolises and entrenches the real power of an endlessly flexible and evolving oligarchy, the governance of the great and the good; this is legitimised by two centuries of carefully cultivated civic and parliamentary practices which are still endlessly celebrated in an odious self-satisfaction fully worthy of that 18th century which initiated it.

The oligarchy has shifted, changed and adapted over two centuries, now opening to admit selected new groups into the élite, now closing up again. We have no written constitution, because that might inhibit the inexhaustible good sense and creative flexibility of the oligarchy and its state government, which needs to be, and increasingly is, more and more removed from control and arbitrary in its action. Contrary to much of our platform rhetoric, we never won the vote in this country. The vote was doled out to us in carefully phased and rationed packages, so that the inner and essentially occult heartland of power survived unscathed. It has been an enormously successful regime, which has skilfully managed consensus through its junior partner of a parliament. A living demonstration of Gramsci's 'hegemony', it has conditioned the people of Britain into the belief that this regime, with its Westminster parliament and its allegedly unparalleled achievement of social peace and cohesion, is the only form of democracy which exists.

It faced two major crises in the 20th century, as social growth accelerated and 'mass society' developed. Both were related to relative decline and war or the threat of it: the upsurge of social Liberalism around 1900 and the breakthrough of Labour after 1945. Both achieved major changes and won major gains, but both were tamed, channelled and contained. As nation states now lurch into their crisis of obsolescence and a reactionary regime here drives ahead in its ruthless counter-offensive, we can see that those gains were, in the long run, precarious. This regime is undoing not only what Labour did and what Lloyd George did; it is even undoing what Victorian social reformers achieved. There is no safe hiding place from this state; at the very minimum we need to build a shelter against it more durable than the Puckish spirit of Mr Peter Walker.

Liberal and Labour achievements proved precarious because both, even at their peak, accepted the essential structure of the British state, indeed, seemed unable even to conceive of an alternative. Their British state is now breaking the Labour Party as it did the Liberals. Unless Labour can cut free from its obsession with that state, it will go stumbling on, hypnotised by paltry and ephemeral opinion polls, with the red cross of historical doom, to quote Marx, stamped on its forehead.

This terrible experience has been a striking demonstration that the original marxist critique of social democracy was correct. We cannot use a state structure created to serve one system to build a radically different one. We have to dismantle this state and reconstruct government on this island so that power passes to its peoples. We can do that only if we make ourselves self-governing European peoples. The struggle to transform the EC offers us the opportunity.

In Wales, we need mentally and spiritually to renounce our allegiance to the British state and make ourselves into a self-governing European nation, eventually to stand alongside our sister-nations on this Island of Britain within a new Europe we have to fight to create.

We need to fight at every level on the terrain of this island alongside as many allies as we can find among the Scots and the English, but in the coming struggle, we must be prepared to act as a European fifth column within it. We must fight for a real presence in Europe. We have allies here in the European Free Alliance, which represents parties from eighteen small peoples, a very mixed bunch, but one which is moving in the direction we need to follow and which works with the German Greens within the Rainbow Group. We will find plenty of allies elsewhere, notably among the German Social Democrats and the Italian Communists. The fact that even this current European Parliament could pass the resolutions on minority languages and regional self-management speaks for itself.

The two struggles are one. They are twin jaws of a nutcracker we must close to crunch on the British state. Those jaws are closing now. This state's powers have begun to drain away to Brussels. In its Northern Ireland province, it has been at war for twenty years. The Scots are going to drive this island into constitutional crisis whether we like it or not. We in Wales have little choice. The alternative is a kind of death.

Geoff Mulgan

The Changing Shape of the City

The Right has never felt at home in the city. The old Right traditionally saw cities as the source of crime and vice, insurrectionary mobs and subversive ideas. For the New Right cities are the places where their narrow individualism and denial of society seem most out of place, irrelevant to the collective problems of transport and health, clean air and water, green spaces and safe streets. It is no coincidence that it is in the cities that the flaws of Thatcherism have been most apparent, as riots simmer and erupt and as transport systems collapse; nor is it any coincidence that despite the prime minister's repeated call for a dynamic new approach to the inner city, no vision has been forthcoming beyond a vague and scarcely inspiring promise of new shopping and leisure centres and orbital ring roads.

The Right's historic unease makes it all the more remarkable that the Left has so clearly failed to sustain a coherent city politics. Although the Left in Britain evolved out of the cities, first implemented its ideas in municipal politics and still controls nearly all the major cities of Britain, it too has no real vision of city life in the 21st century: of how cities can be good places to live, and of how a balance can be struck between collective consumption and diverse identities. In other countries the Left has often used cities as long-term showcases, models of planning, redistribution and civic responsibility. In Britain the Left of the 1980s has often seemed more interested in using control of cities as a quick stepping-stone to national power, a means rather than an end.

There is also a deeper historical problem. Though Britain has long been a very urban society, its experience of large cities is relatively recent by comparison with southern Europe or North Africa. Despite the strong civic traditions of cities like Birmingham, Manchester or Leeds, Britain has none of that subterranean memory of a time before the consolidation of national states that gives a special resonance to the city politics of a Barcelona, Milan or Hamburg. On both Left and Right, particularly in England, there has always been a powerful nostalgic attachment to a rural past of small towns and cottages. For William Morris and Blatchford, Hardie and Macdonald, the city was at best a necessary evil. Come the millenium, the satanic mills would be levelled, the green and pleasant land restored. In the late 19th century many English socialists followed Kropotkin in believing that electricity would remove the need for concentrations of work and housing around sources of energy, returning society to a purer era of rural workshops, a promise that is echoed today in the telecommunications-inspired electronic cottages of writers like Alvin Toffler. There is a long tradition, in other words, of coping with the problems of the city through escape.

But despite this tradition the problems of cities are again at the top of the political agenda, placed there less by politicians than by a widespread public unease about the direction of city life, physical ugliness and physical insecurity, endemic inequality and the decay of infrastructures. Their problems reflect those of the wider society in an accentuated form: the division between a relatively prosperous majority and a pauperised minority (particularly in the South East, the most unequal part of Britain); the decay of civic values and a collective morality, and the familiar coexistence of private affluence and public squalor. In works of fiction there is a remarkable and depressing unanimity about the direction of change in the great cities of the first world. Made manifest in films like *Blade Runner* or *Brazil*, and a thousand derivative advertisements, the cities of the future divide between gleaming skyscrapers housing the core workers in the ministries and transnational corporations, and a brutalised, impoverished, heavily policed periphery, set in the blackened remains of the industrial age. It is the vision of Los Angeles squared, and it is against this, the dark side of post-Fordism, that the Left now needs to present an alternative vision, one that shows how the different communities of the city can share its spaces in relative equality.

The time is ripe. Vast new building works, in Kings Cross and Canary Wharf in London, in the centre of Birmingham and elsewhere, and rapid change in the economy of cities, have coincided with a new interest both in the physical architecture of the city and in its soft architecture, its feel and atmosphere, its social networks and its sense of community and citizenship. Tendencies towards global sameness in product brands, retailing chains and cultural products are being matched by equally powerful tendencies to favour whatever is local and different. Paradoxically, the integration of European countries into the single market of the 1990s is giving regions and cities a higher profile.

In this essay I argue that, alongside new policies for housing, transport and education, the new vision of the city will also emphasise its nature as a means of communication, a place where people meet, talk and share experiences, where they think and drink together. Cities work only if they are places where people engage in a collective process of making meanings and defining their place in the world. I also argue that there is a pressing need to increase the powers of city governments relative to the national state, and that there is no substitute for the role of local government in fostering the culture and communicational ecology of city life. The kinds of policy that can give substance to the city as an independent cultural entity, policies for the creation of industrial districts, for what Manuel Castells has described as the 'milieus' of the post-Fordist economy, for civic videotex systems and town cards, and for evening economies of entertainment and retailing, can succeed only if they are rooted in local institutions. In this sense the problems of communication and culture mirror those of the wider economy. For the footloose and international nature of late 20th-century capitalism has fatally undermined the always somewhat mythic notion of a national economy: cities and regions now have no choice but to define their own needs and their own strategies.

City Economies

This uneven and volatile global economy offers a good starting point for any analysis of cities. It has become a cliché that within this more global economy, national economic boundaries have increasingly lost their significance. Cities and regions negotiate directly with transnational corporations and institutions (whether IBM or the International Olympic Committee), selling themselves within a world market. The economy of a city or region can evolve directly counter to the lines of development of the nation: obvious examples include London's role as an international financial centre, and Silicon Glen's role as a staging post for transnational computer companies entering the European market. Many cities have lost their close relationship with a hinterland of countryside and towns, becoming instead part of a more extensive, less rooted kind of economic life, competing for footloose capital, for manufacturing plants, research laboratories and corporate headquarters. Others evolve as the core of industrial districts, like Munich and parts of Bavaria, the M4 and M11 corridors or Kumamoto on Kyushu, again often with little relationship to the surrounding region.

Communications technologies have played a decisive role. The great power of capital has always been its ability to choose, to decide where to locate and when to withdraw. The satellite, cable and microwave greatly enhance this mobility and the leverage it confers, allowing for much more sophisticated location policies: mental labour can be separated from production, skilled labour from unskilled, service tasks from manufacturing ones. Logical organisation becomes more important than physical proximity. In the financial sector, while head offices tend to remain in the city centres, back office operations are moved to the surburbs and the more routine operations are removed either to peripheral towns or to countries like Barbados, offering cheap labour for routine data processing (the phenomenon of telecolonialism).

A complex economic geography is unfolding. A few cities have emerged as world cities, linked by the transoceanic networks of fibre optic cable. Cities like Los Angeles, London, Tokyo, Hong Kong and Singapore increasingly function as hubs in world financial markets, as concentrations of the 'advanced producer services' of advertising, consultancy and law that service the transnationals, and of the low-wage service and manufacturing sectors that support them. A world city like London can exert an extraordinary pull on the national economy, as evidenced by the close correlation between growth rates of towns and regions and their proximity to London. Nowhere is this concentrating effect more visible than in financial services: at first glance the most footloose of all industries and the most dependent on the telecommunications that allow businesses to disperse, these remain clustered around a handful of streets in London, Tokyo and New York. Banks still cling to the prestige of a central location, and managers fear exclusion from the dense informal networks of the city centre.

In the industrial age, the great cities were defined by their position within systems of material flow. Cities like Liverpool, Newcastle and Glasgow, Pittsburgh and Chicago were located near deep sea ports, on great waterways such as the Great Lakes or the Rhine, near railways and roads, and within easy reach of supplies of energy. Cities could be understood as material switching centres that processed materials into new forms. Production was labour and energy-intensive, and was limited by access to both. Today the economy of the city can be better understood by its position as a centre for switching information and knowledge. Much of the new manufacturing has moved to smaller factories and industrial zones on the city periphery, to greenfield sites and new towns like Stevenage or Telford. In the larger cities, an information economy has arisen alongside older ones based on manufacturing and service. Within this economy the key scarcities are no longer energy and labour but rather knowledge and creativity, and the key exports are knowledge products rather than material ones. In New York, for example, legal services overtook clothing as the city's primary export earner at the end of the 1970s.

The redefinition of the city as a system for producing and switching information is highly visible. Across Britain satellite and microwave dishes proliferate and streets are dug up to lay fibre cables. London's Docklands, the point where materials once came and went, is now centred around the teleport, a cluster of satellite and microwave dishes, receiving and transmitting information. New York has the world's most advanced teleport, built by the City Administration and the Port Authority on Staten Island: through a fibre optic network it links Wall Street to the outside world, completely bypassing the local public network, an 'executive highway' for communications. The changing physical infrastructure of communication is permeating the whole physical fabric of city life. It is estimated that 30 per cent of the cost of new office buildings in central Tokyo is now accounted for by electronics, control systems for heating, lighting, security and communication. The 'smartness' of a house or office has become a decisive selling point.

This new emphasis on smart communications infrastructures has also inspired some of the bolder utopian experiments of the 1970s and 1980s. The American 'wired city' movement that grew out of Lyndon Johnson's social programmes, promised to use technology to build participatory, community-based cities. Utopian dreams fused with the more prosaic interests of telecommunications companies in large-scale experiments like Hi-Ovis in Japan, US projects like QUBE in Columbus and Project Victoria in California, and Biarritz in France, each of which linked homes to an array of interactive services, such as video-on-demand, community information and instant referendums. These 'teletopias' and 'telecommunities' were built not only as testbeds for technology but also out of a faith that technology could be used to recreate communities disrupted by the fragmentation of the traditional city, bringing 'neighbourhood without propinquity'. Despite often confused goals some of the projects hinted at how a communications infrastrusture could sustain new kinds of social relationship: health training and distant education projects on cable television, teleshopping for the old and disabled, on-line access to councils and assemblies (as in the California State Assembly), and videophones for housebound women are all examples. Networks of this kind could also be used by dispersed minorities: one could imagine the Chinese or Gujarati community in Britain using such a network. Unfortunately few sponsors whether private or public have had the will to sustain the experiments: QUBE, Hi-Ovis and Biarritz are all either closed or much reduced in scope. The real 'wired cities' of the late 1980s, such as Aberdeen or Coventry in Britain, are based on relatively old technology (coaxial copper), privately-owned cable systems that do little more than deliver international television channels such as Sky and Lifestyle to a small minority of households.

Yet the long-term promise of the wired cities experiments is undeniable. In France, nearly 200 cities, most run by the Left, now offer a wide range of information on videotex, often providing possibilities for interraction, such as polls on local issues, and systems for finding information about housing opportunities or making a reservation at the local municipal theatre. The better ones have tried to create systems of two-way communication rather than simply dumping propaganda on an inert citizenry. Grenoble has developed probably the most sophisticated set of tools for communicating with its citizens, an approach which has been vindicated by record turnouts for local referendums on such issues as tram policies. Another example of the use of technology as a tool for asserting the identity of the city and its citizens is the town card, using 'smart card' technology similar to those used in credit cards and now being developed for satellite TV subscription. In the 1990s, rather than simply being private tools of consumption and debt, like the Access or Visa, these could be given to everyone as a citizen's right, offering scope for organising access to civic facilities (swimming pools, theatres etc.), for cheap shopping (as retailers give discounts to local people) and for referendums. Already cards like the Thamesdown Gold Card or the Wakefield Passport to Leisure are being used to offer discounts to the unemployed, pensioners or disabled. Wilmslow near Manchester offers a town credit card, used by 5,000 holders and supported by 170 retailers, to encourage spending within the local economy. In the USA there are affinity cards, local credit cards which give a percentage of interest to local charities and regeneration projects. All could be extended and differentiated, offering distinct mixes of services to the different groups of the city, simultaneously fostering collective consumption and diverse identities.

One of the reasons why it is hard to conceive of cities regaining control over their economic destiny is a long history of nationalisation, in effect the concentration of power in London. In Britain cities long ago lost control over their own infrastructures. The privatisation of water and electricity will remove accountability even further. But privatisation and break-up of the old utilities also serve as reminders of the 19th-century municipal traditions of local control of electricity, trams, gas and telephones that preceded their consolidation into monopolies and their nationalisation. In the context of the wired city these traditions again become attractive, offering efficiency and accountability in ways that are impossible for privatised and nationalised utilities. It is surely significant that the most efficient part of the local telephone network in Britain is run by Hull Telephone Company, the last remaining municipal phone company, and a possible model for the future when British Telecom's local networks are placed under local control. In countries like Holland, it has always been assumed that local councils and housing associations should play a leading role in building and running cable networks. In Britain the private cable companies that are now being franchised city by city and borough by borough also unwittingly recreate the scope for local control of the communications infrastructure. Municipal control of the infrastructure could coincide with a much wider access to channels, as in France, where there have been gay, arabic and african radio stations, or the USA with its hispanic, black and neighbourhood television channels.

Soft Infrastructure

If British cities have little direct control over their communications infrastructures, they are at least able to influence their softer infrastructures, their environment of work, shopping and leisure. These soft infrastructures are turning out to be as crucial to the post-Fordist economy as fibre optic cables and just-in-time networks. As cities compete for capital and skilled labour, they are also emerging as tools of local industrial policy. Education is particularly important, involving both the provision of a skilled and flexible workforce, and open academic institutions with which business can collaborate. Education has arguably come to play the role once attributed to the 'manufacturing base': ultimately the prosperity of any city or region depends on the value of the labour of those who work within it, which depends in turn on its level of skill and education. The new economic geography of the knowledge economy has brought clusters of new industry around cities like Cambridge and the leading scientific universities. Cambridge now has 250-300 high-technology companies employing around 12,000 people. MITI's great science city, Tyushu, 30 miles from Tokyo, is probably the classic example. By 1985 there were 47 science parks in Europe, 13 in the UK, supporting 180 companies and research institutes, all attempts to create living communities around research and its application (and all dependent on public support).

The success of the post-Fordist industrial districts such as Silicon Valley has also focused attention on the economic role of milieu, the social atmosphere of an area and profession within which people develop new ideas. These milieus allow academic and commercial institutions to cross-fertilise. Significantly, transnational companies are unable to create environments of this kind on their own. In the USA the dynamic districts of high technology emerged not in New York and New Jersey where IBM and AT&T concentrated thousands of PhDs, but rather in the more convivial and open environments of Palo Alto and Boston.

As important as education is the overall physical environment of a city. Even the most powerful transnationals depend on their ability to attract the most skilled workers, who are even more mobile than capital, and who now increasingly demand an attractive physical location, a congenial and convivial setting within which to work and live. The advertisements for the new towns (Telford, Milton Keynes) and old ones like Swindon offer semi-rural paradises: small cities promote themselves by pretending not to be cities at all. Throughout the world cities now compete in terms of league tables of 'liveability'.

These lessons have not been lost on declining cities desperately seeking the means to attract new, high value-added industries. Art spending has come to be seen as one of the easiest ways to change the feel of the city and to give it the appearance of conviviality and prosperity. Spending on theatre groups, visual artists and concert halls could also be justified as a cheap way of creating jobs and masking the physical manifestations of decline. Murals on the walls of deserted factories somehow seemed to make economic collapse more acceptable. More recently, however, it has become clear that arts and cultural policies can do much more than that, that they too can be understood as part of a soft infrastructure supporting new industries. In its recent study of the arts economy, the Policy Studies Institute estimated that each of the 14,735 arts jobs in Glasgow gave rise to a further 2.7 jobs because of spending by arts customers and organisations, with a similar figure applying in Merseyside. There was also a less quantifiable multiplier effect as the level of cultural provision brought in first restaurants and shops, and later higher value-added activities. The changed image of a city like Glasgow, designated as European City of Culture in 1990, makes it easier for firms like BP to persuade their staff to relocate there. Conversely, Birmingham's rather dismal cultural image was held to have seriously undermined its Olympic bid. Pittsburgh in Pennsylvania is often cited as the classic success story, a terminally run-down industrial city that used arts as part of a broader strategy of regeneration that resulted in it being voted the most liveable city in the whole USA.

In Britain the use of art and culture as tools to reverse urban economic decline has been primarily associated with some of the larger Labour councils, notably Glasgow, Liverpool and Bradford. National government and the Arts Council have been both irrelevant and ineffective despite attempts to co-opt the 'urban renaissance'. Starting from gallery projects (like the Tate of the North), garden festivals and museums (Bradford being the most successful example), councils have learnt that rather than simply supporting a thin layer of subsidised activity and letting in the developers they can also mobilise the economic potential of the arts more directly, to create thriving cultural industries producing design, films, television programmes, comics and records. One of the ironies of the modern, global cultural industries is the cultural and economic success of the records, books and films most rooted in the decayed cities of the industrial age, Detroit and the Bronx, Liverpool and Sheffield. Relative decline can be turned to advantage. In the past, however, this advantage has rarely benefited the cities themselves. With many of their creative workers inadvertently funded by the DSS and its counterparts, and lacking a local infrastructure of support, the profits of cultural success for a Human League or Frankie Goes to Hollywood generally went elsewhere, to London and New York, rather than back into the urban economy.

Councils in Liverpool, Sheffield and elsewhere are now trying to develop the means to retain local control and reinvest profits in the local economy. Equally important, they are supporting the kind of environment within which the creation of ideas, images and design can take place. Even more than fields like computing, the cultural industries depend on critical masses of activity, an organic and convivial milieu in which people emulate and argue, and eat and drink with each other. Examples include Sheffield, with Red Tape studios and other projects in the music industry, Birmingham in the film and broadcasting industry with plans to create an 'audio-visual district', and Cardiff which seeks to promote itself as a media city, reflecting the fact that 4,500 people are now employed in broadcasting, compared to 11,000 in the whole of the South Wales coalfield. Liverpool has built on the successes of *Brookside*, *Letter to Brezhnev* and dozens of successful rock groups to present itself as a uniquely cultural city (appointing Britain's first film location officer). Other examples include Glasgow in the visual arts, Oxford in book publishing, and more recent arrivals such as the cluster of galleries and visual artists in East London.

It has to be said that in some cases the use of art is suspect: there is a tendency to favour high arts, and to orient cultural provision to an executive and professional audience in a sterile wine bar culture (witness the bitterness many feel towards Glasgow's claimed rejuvenation). The arts can also serve as a wedge to drive out the original inhabitants as property prices rise. This has been well-documented in New York where relatively impecunious artists have moved into an area, thereby gradually increasing its cultural cachet, and also its property prices. Developers have come to understand the dynamics of the 'loft living' phenomenon, and now seek to emulate it synthetically, using the artists and small galleries as unwitting tools. Similar phenomena are already apparent around the centres of some British cities. Properly conceived, however, cultural regeneration strategies can marry economic goals with the political one of giving expression to the marginal communities, to those living on the run-down estates, and to the young and old of the ethnic minority communities which remain largely cut off from the mainstream of urban cultural life.

City Centres

Nearly all the attempts to create cultural milieus and industrial districts have focused on the centre of cities. Despite occasional exceptions (like the recent, essentially suburban movements of Acid House and Balearic), it is towards the city centre that cultural life has always tended to gravitate. Traditionally the centre of the city also acted as a magnet for shops, cinemas, pubs and restaurants. Areas like the West End of London would sustain a vibrant evening economy where people could congregate, perform, hang around and feel themselves plugged into the life of a city. In most towns and cities the same few streets would collect both retailing and entertainment, together with the public buildings, the town hall, libraries, advice bureaux and churches.

New forms of retailing bust apart the ecology of the city

centre. In 1987 it was estimated that an unprecedented 500 shopping centre applications were being processed in Britain. Many aimed to move retailing out of the city centre, to malls and superstores on the city periphery, to carefully controlled environments, self-contained shopping capsules. Retailing becomes cut off from the rest of city life in more ways than one. New centres like the Metro in Newcastle tie the local retailing economy yet more closely into that of national and international chains, the Nexts, Boots and Crabtree and Evelyns. Rather than being rooted in the history and buildings of the old city, the valid spectacle that shopping becomes is removed from the generality of city life, from public buildings, parks, theatres and pubs. Those deemed unproductive as consumers, particularly the young and the homeless, are often physically excluded from the new shopping centres. This retailing-led restructuring of city life can prove extremely destabilising for the rest of the city. As retailing moves away from the city centre, like manufacturing before it, economically bereft wastelands are left behind. Physically and psychologically the centre decays, and as fewer people use it for shopping or entertainment its streets tend to become less safe, setting in motion a vicious spiral of decline. This trend is as damaging for the suburbs as for the city centre itself.

Some cities, particularly in North America, have tried to reverse the trend, with co-ordinated policies to rebuild the evening economy and emphasise their nature as social and convivial centres. Planning powers can be used to concentrate restaurants, entertainments and independent shops (as in Covent Garden or Faneuil Hall in Boston). Policing policies, efficient late night transport and good lighting can be harmonised to make it easier and safer to come into the city centre. Transport in the city centre can be free as in Denver. Busy streets can be shown to be safe streets, and to favour spending in the local economy, setting in motion a virtuous circle of improvement. Busy streets also make the city an easier place to live in, particularly for women who have become increasingly incarcerated in their own homes.[1] Alternatively, people can also be brought into the city by spectacular events. Alongside the idea of shopping as spectacle, cities can themselves be turned into spectacles, as in the vast pyrotechnic displays of Philip Alain-Huppert in Berlin, Algiers and Paris, Jean-Michel Jarre in the Docklands and Houston, the festivals of Rome and the GLC in the mid-1980s, or the modern counterparts of the ancient traditions of carnival that turn the city into a theatre and a world turned upside down.

Unfortunately, in Britain at least, there is a wide gulf between what is possible and what is likely. Few cities retain either the resources, the planning powers or the political will to move in these directions. In the immediate future, a more likely trend may be the recreation of the council as private corporation, as in Bradford, which in the past provided a model of how to use culture, with its tongue in cheek publication of the Bradford-English dictionary for tourists, and the building of the hugely successful Museum of Film, TV and Photography. The current Conservative-run council in Bradford is now trying to project an idea of the city as a corporation, providing a defined set of services to its 'consumers' and dividends to its shareholders, a pale shadow of the kinds of bold and long-term visions of the successful cities of the past, visions that understood the city to be much more than an economic entity.

But though we can denounce the trend to civic privatisation it has at least revealed just how emaciated the alternative civic and public traditions have become. The weakness of these traditions has also shone out clearly from the debates about architecture sparked off by Prince Charles, Rod Hackney, Richard Rogers and others. For though it is not hard to understand how the piazzas and boulevards of the past asserted an idea of public life, it is much harder to apply their lessons to cities riven by roads and studded with shopping precincts.

It is worth recalling just how much of the 19th-century civic tradition was carried through its physical forms. The town halls and concert halls of the northern cities and, perhaps grandest of all, the town hall in Walthamstow in London (modelled on Versailles), the public architecture of phone boxes, parks, clock towers and museums, all asserted an idea of the city as a shared and public space. Public provision was not philanthropic (that is to say provided by the rich for the poor) but could be for all, a means of creating social solidarity across classes through the shared use of transport, health and educational facilities. The vision of the city was one of active congregation and communication. These various traditions of public and civic architecture stood in stark contrast to the very different traditions of the temple, the arch and the palace, traditions which are sustained today in the monumental buildings of AT&T in New York, of NatWest and Lloyd's in London, and of Citicorp in many of the cities of Latin America, buildings which boldly assert their power and wealth.

Reviving Public Life

It is an indication of the weakness of socialism in the 1980s that it is almost impossible to conceive of the physical manifestation of socialism that could match Morrison's armies of red buses, the LCC's housing and schools or indeed stalinist gothic. The standardised public goods of the past certainly seem less appropriate in the 1980s. Uncertainties about how to crystallise a vision of the city echo those of socialist politics more generally, the problems of achieving diversity without inequality, balance without excessive central planning. But it is also hard to visualise convincingly the physical forms of public life in the 21st century for another, possibly deeper reason. This concerns the vulnerability of the very idea of public life to an era of electronic communication and what Raymond Williams described as mobile·privatisation. Any plans for the creation of convivial, communicating cities inevitably find themselves struggling with a long erosion of the traditional political structures of the city within which people think, argue and organise.

Most of our conceptions of politics derive from the theories and practices in city life. The Greek *polis*, from which the word politics derives, was the city. The city was defined as a political entity, human in scale and shaped by the active interaction of its citizens. The city also was clearly understood to be shaped by its means of communication. Plato limited the size of the ideal city to the number of citizens who could be addressed by a single voice. Historically, democracy is closely associated with the rhythms of dense city life, from Athens and Ghent to Paris and Glasgow, instant and egalitarian in nature, and based on the streets, outside the factory gates and in the great squares of the city. The popular imagination of the Left is filled with images of public city life, with speakers on street corners, assertive crowds, soap boxes and barricades.

Yet it is precisely this kind of public life that now seems to be withering as public spaces are privatised for retailing

developments and as other activities relocate to the home. Marx
argued that capitalism was creating the seeds of its own downfall
by concentrating people into factories and neighbourhoods
where they would learn to organise and co-operate. Now, as late
capitalism disperses people to new towns, smaller workshops
and offices, and to the private pleasures of the living room, these
cultural roots of democratic, public life are under threat. The
same communications technologies that permit the dispersal of
production are also part of a broader privatisation of life: the
relocation of leisure, work and democracy in the home. Some of
the underlying pressures are economic: atomised, electronic
communications are potentially much cheaper than socialised,
face-to-face ones. Electronic, push button democracy could be
much cheaper than the ballot paper. The television costs 2p each
hour compared to £2 at the cinema or more at a theatre: the
off-licence drink and the takeaway food are also cheap
alternatives that have rapidly shifted the locus of social life. This
trend need not be entirely anti-social. Many people have
discovered that the VCR can be a more social tool than the
cinema: but what is changed is the nature of the social or public
experience. The public is no longer general, but rather comes to
be composed of a myriad of small groups and of the spaces,
described by Sharon Zukin as 'liminal', that lie between the
public and the private, spaces like the apparently public piazza of
a private office development, the street of a private housing
development, the club that replaces the pub. It is the world of the
Dagmar rather than the Vic, a world of separate tables and
hushed voices rather than a communal bar.

There is a sense in which this trend away from a 'mass public'
is irreversible. And it is in the city more than anywhere that
people need privacy and the means of excluding others. But it is
also here that the economic pressures towards providing a
liveable city run the risk of generating divisive social
consequences. The economic value of a convivial milieu for
creative and scientific work provides an obvious incentive for
developers and public authorities to support it. But conviviality
for others, particularly for the underclass, the homeless and the
unemployed, is if anything seen as threatening, to be cordoned
off, monitored and policed (as in Coventry's new system of video
cameras to monitor the city's shopping centre). The old
stereotype of a convivial working class counterposed to a

domesticated suburban middle class, cosseted behind the lace curtains of detached houses, is turned on its head. Instead conviviality is offered to those for whom it has an economic value, those involved in the many forms of knowledge work, while those in less skilled work live an increasingly privatised existence, away from the city centres, and dependent on homebased entertainments. Marx's comment threatens to be turned on its head: perhaps in the 21st century it will be the dominant classes that learn the experience of co-operation and organisation in the wine bars of the City while the working class sits at home behind steel doors watching re-runs of those innumerable films that have portrayed the city either as a prison (*Escape from New York*, etc), as a jungle for the survivalists (*Omega Man*, etc) or as an arena for vigilantes (*Death Wish* 1 – 45).

The dangers posed by such a rift in public life hardly need to be spelt out. There is a real sense in which the achievement of a new vision of the city, and practical policies to realise it, are essential if much of the political life of the larger cities is not to reduce to the confines of the sound bite and the opinion poll. Yet the new vision of city life remains only half-formed. Though some of its themes are clear – new forms of collective consumption, the emphasis on liveability and conviviality, the idea of an interdependent ecology of city life, of the city as a means of communication, and of the city as a potential defence against the volatilities of an overconnected world – these still need to be fleshed out, experimented with and articulated.

Their ultimate promise is that out of the ashes of recession and de-industrialisation a new, greener, and more social city can arise. Tony Lane offers one of the best accounts of why a vision of this kind could become compelling. Lane foresees the 'Garden of Kent turned into a huge car park and railway siding for cross-Channel traffic and the rest of the Home Counties made impossible by the density of people crushing in to look for the jobs squeezed out of the North ...' Early in the 21st century, he writes, 'horrified northern viewers will be seeing videotapes in which the metropolis and the South-East are portrayed as a ratmaze of a modern urban hell. Life in Liverpool meanwhile, but also in Newcastle and Sheffield, Leeds and Bradford ... will be extraordinarily civilised. Relieved of overdensely populated acres, these will be spacious, open cities of tree-lined streets, coppiced corners and wooded hollows, teeming with wildlife where tenements and tower blocks once stood...'.[2]

Notes

[1] See, for example, the excellent CLES pamphlet: *City Centres, City Cultures*, 1988.

[2] Lane, *Liverpool: Gateway of Empire*, Lawrence and Wishart 1987.

Beatrix Campbell

New Times Towns

The tenth anniversary of Thatcherism has occasioned a mighty inspection of its meaning, its sweep, and its reordering of political society in Britain.

But Thatcherism is not a sufficient word for the story of change today. Debates about the weakening of social class as the key determinant of political behaviour are important, but they tell only part of the tale. Our landscape, our workplaces, our cities, cultures, classes and ourselves — they are all changing as we look. We need a bigger picture. This article is an attempt to draw in some of its features.

According to the new times theory, the institutions and infrastructure of the postwar settlement were already breaking up long before Thatcherism arrived to bury consensus. Thatcherism was not the start of the new industrial and cultural revolution contained in the concept of new times. Rather it represented one of many possible responses to it. According to Robin Murray, the modern transition is fundamental. 'The focus of employment shifted first from farm to factory,' he says, 'and now from factory to office and shop.' For a country with a political tradition which for a century cradled the notion that the factory was the crucible of consciousness, and that the new model army of baby bolsheviks would be forged in its heat, all this is a helluva shock.

The reason it hurts is that the advocates of new times are suggesting that more than a temporary halt in the forward march of labour is at stake. They argue that the very forms of industry and work which have dominated our century, capitalist and socialist, are disintegrating. This form of industry was symbolised by the Ford Motor Company and gave its name to the influential 'Fordist' theory of the structure of markets, industrial relations and the welfare state. The Fordist world was derived from theories of scientific management which defined corporate culture: the objective was to steal from workers the one thing they possessed, skill. An intensive subdivision of labour structured the manufacturing process in the great hangers of the modern motor industry. Tasks were stripped to their bare uniform essentials. Mental and manual skills were separated, thus dissolving workers' opportunity to think and to manage their own work. Standardised products on a vast scale emerged from standardised components put together by workers performing standardised tasks and were launched into standardised markets.

Big Macs, Mars Bars, tower blocks, Coca Cola, Barratts' Homes, Model Ts and TVs. These are the apogees of Fordism. Its culture impregnated the whole of society, from the management of the market itself, to the 'mass-produced administration' of public services and the political process.

But, says the new times theory, there has now been a popular revolt against Fordism. There's a revolt in the cities, challenging their subordination to the Faustian imperative. There's a revolt against the privatisation of public space and the privatisation of public service, against horizons hijacked by windy slabs, against streets transformed into subways, forest into deserts, oceans into sewers.

The politics of new times challenges tradition. It moves away from a stark politics formed by dominant protagonists — capital, the state and labour — to a view of the world which is made up of multiple points of personal and public power. It is about people in all their dimensions and identities — as sexes, races, workers, consumers, playmates, parents, pensioners.

Robin Murray reckons that the industrial emphasis has shifted from manufacturers' economies of scale to the retailers' economies of scope. John Urry calls the new phase the 'disorganisation of capitalism'. Companies are becoming vertically decentralised and spatially relocated. Within Britain's shores, new industry is settling outside the fastnesses of the urban industrial revolution. The implications of all this for class culture are enormous. Nobody can any longer assume that practical proletarian politics will arise spontaneously from the factory cauldron. This Great Labour Movement of Ours — a movement built in the image of manufacturing man — is now the movement of a minority of members of manufacturing man's own class.

So, what comes next? Some commentators have watched the break-up of old solidarities as if all solidarities were, like the dodo, dead. But are they? Might not the fragmentation of the old order also imply the construction of new collectives? Perhaps it is in what Antonio Gramsci called civil society — the informal networks of our towns and cities — that we can best map the new times.

That is the purpose of this series of accounts. I have tried to find out whether the new times really exist and what they are like by travelling to diverse parts of Britain — to Livingston, a new town growing old, to Sheffield, a city of lost labourism, to Swindon, a boom town and a Labour town then and now, and finally to Basingstoke, a Thatchergrad for today. They're very different places and yet they're each emblematic of some of the ways that British cities and classes are changing.

Livingston

In Livingston, key works are being purged from the industrial vocabulary. 'Did you say discipline?' asks Graham Steven, a young man with an iron grip and the confidence of a corporation. 'Well, wash your mouth out with carbolic soap !' He was smiling, but he meant it. He's Apollo's personnel director here in Scotland's Silicon Glen. Apollo is the work station computer manufacturer based in Massachusetts, Dukakis country, with a European base in Scotland. In less than five years it has just bounced off the leading edge and merged with one of the major mainstream computer companies.

Graham Steven has a few more un-words. Like class, for example. They belong to the dustbin of history which his company is burying as it makes its mark on Scotland's new industrial belt.

Apollo is one of the 34 American computer companies which have settled here. Livingston, a 1960s new town, which became a 1970s depression town, is now a 1980s hi-tech boom town.

Together with the Japanese companies which have brought chip production to the town, the incomers' dominant presence in the local economy, housed in the pretty sheds painted in primary colours and svelte grey, is transforming the old industrial landscape and its economic and political culture. 'This is culture shock for the people who were used to the old trade-unionised environment, like British Leyland at Bathgate', says Graham Steven.

As it has turned out, first generation Livingstonians hardly had the chance to recover from the shock − the biggest group of the unemployed is over 35, and they're concentrated in some of the first estates to be built in Livingston, like Deans and Cragshill.

Livingston's new economic order is unencumbered by the class consciousness created in the 'old' industries which infused Scottish politics. The seemingly seamless strands between the production of ships, cars and coal and party politics are unravelling. Livingston's political ecology is going through an epochal transition. The town's new employers have achieved not only a strategic assult on the old economic order, they have also organised a kind of economic euthanasia.

Ann McGuinness is a cleaner in her 40s who has become a voluntary welfare rights adviser in her long sabbatical from waged work. 'There was a Mitsubishi job, I thought it would suit me part-time. But you had to be 20. I thought, 'I can't even lead them on that I'm 30 never mind 20.' Every job I've been after is for 18 to 25s. I went into the unemployment office today and it was all for people up to 30.' The future? 'There isn't one.'

Livingston development corporation's chief executive James Pollock has been extraordinarily successful in attracting inward investment. But he's cautious about the exile of McGuinness's generation from the town's new industrial base. 'I wouldn't like to say they're unemployable, but it is difficult...' Employers simply by-pass the last generation with a collective memory, a history and a notion of them-and-us. 'There's a memory gap', mused a West Lothian economist, 'trade unions are like gas masks, rationing and Suez.' That suspicion was confirmed by conversation with class 4J1 at Inveralmond Community School. Had they heard of unions? Another silence until one recalled, 'I think we heard about trade unions in modern studies.' None of them want to work in the electronic factories. 'They mainly look for young people, so they can pay them less', one pupil reckoned. Some of their mothers work there and say 'Never!' Livingston's new employers, particularly the Americans, offer an attractive ambience, a range of rewards, and a company culture which deftly pre-empts trade unions' *raison d'être*.

Graham Steven explains, 'Every three months we close the factory down and we all go to a meeting and present "the financials". From a unionised environment, to be presented with the financials ..! It's the openness that differentiates us. Honesty is always the best policy with staff. There are also weekly production bulletins and instant reports about staff turnover, an impressive 6 per cent. A departure is instantly posted, everyone knows when somebody is leaving and why.

'We leave nothing to the grapevine', says Steven. Which means nothing is left to gossip but, more than that, it means the suppression of alternative networks. The company controls everything that is knowable. It controls pretty much everything else − the staff have no spatial or political autonomy.

The offices and production area are calm and pleasant, with ubiquitous, bland furnishings. But there's no sign of the bric-a-brac, the photographs, postcards, plants and affectionate graffiti by which people own space and make their boundaries. The only evidence of individuality is the cups stacked by the tea machines − folks bring in their own.

Is this then post-Fordism incarnate? Certainly the company breaks with the coercive culture of Fordist 'scientific management'. Companies like Apollo don't operate in markets defined by mass volume production, standardisation of commodities and intense price competition. Apollo makes 80 systems daily, which are grouped in five product families with 200 variables in each. And they cost around £26,000.

They field their highly specialised commodities in targeted, segmented markets, with sophisticated sales teams. And instead of policing the proletariat by heavy-duty layers of management and rigid enforcement of the separation of conception and execution, they cultivate their workers' commitment to their commodities.

The company also unifies the workforce by designating everyone staff, sponsoring higher education, offering the same holidays (25 days) to everyone, providing free cancer screening, a smart gym on site and private health insurance. It has compressed the management structure, and assembly staff travel along the line with the computer they are making. A faulty product goes back to its producer. That generates its own discipline. 'We're all quality managers', says Steven.

Livingston's Japanese companies operate differently.

Mitsubishi has two factories in Livingston, part of a larger web of European factories, and is increasing its production of over 380,000 video recorders for Europe and Scandinavia by 100,000 next year. Mitsubishi instils stiff discipline, guaranteed by regular quality· audits, quality campaigns which monitor workers' time-keeping, records of faults — and housekeeping: workers clean up their own work-stations. Unlike Apollo, workers don't travel with a commodity — the product travels along a traditional assembly line. But, like Apollo, employees are not allowed to make their mark on their environment — politically or physically.

And like Apollo, Mitsubishi prides itself on the flexibility of its workforce, and the way it takes care of its employees. 'It's like being members of a family and we want to let them know what is happening in the family', claims personnel officer Bill Barker. By which they mean, presumably, an old fashioned patriarchal family, in which wives, children and servants know their place.

Livingston has been targeted for trade-union recruitment by the Scottish TUC. Some factory gates have been leafleted. 'We went to Mitsubishi when the workers were going in', said one activist, 'But the management — they were very polite — told us to leave the carpark because we might get run over'.

And Paul White, who works at Bathgate's Legal Resource Centre (in an old cinema) reports that people bring their grievances to the centre. 'There's a lot of gut anger, but it's not taking shape. I don't mean to sound despondent, but the firms are way ahead'.

These companies exemplify the modernisation of central Scotland's economy. Work is no longer the crucible of class consciousness. Trade unionism, insofar as it exists, belongs to the public sector, not on the leading edge of industrial innovation.

A comparison between the town's spacious landscaped industrial 'campuses' and its housing estates tells you who and what is important in Livingston. The housing is dense, standardised, monotone, modest. Its boundaries are green fields and a seemingly endless circuit of roads. Ask anyone the directions to anywhere and they always say 'start from the dual carriageway'. That, not a clock tower or a cinema or a bank or a department store or a town hall, is the town's central landmark. Livingston embodies the typical postmodern topography of a town without a municipality — it has no local government, only an unelected development corporation. It is a quintessentially Thatcherite town relieved of civic proprieties, like local democracy, tradition or memory.

It has no public realm in which to sit up or sup, no civic identity, not to mention a city culture. When the town's youth are not gazing in Edinburgh's Next windows or following heavy metal bands in Bathgate, and when they're not in a new wave of gangs, with style, and labels − Pananari − and gelled hair, then they're doing what teenagers have been doing for decades. 'We hang around chip shops', explain Inveralmond's class 4J1.

Livingston is still a poor old place. In the shopping centre there's eight television shops sporting satellite discs and plenty of propaganda about rentals for the unemployed. 'But there's nowhere to buy a pair of pyjamas', complained Margaret McPherson. The local economy can't support a Marks & Spencer.

'When I bring the Americans over here I bring them straight to the campus − I make sure they don't see that place', says a consultant who recruits companies to Livingston. His clients need never see it. They don't live in Livingston − they pick up cottages in the lovely villages around, which are becoming commuter territory. This gives a poignant inflection to the notion of core and peripheral workers which is the common currency of students of industrial relations − the new 'core' lives at the periphery. 'Even on the better estates, there's nothing to do, no shops, nobody but a neighbour. They don't go out. You wonder how many women up there are hitting the bottle or going round the twist', says Margaret McPherson. 'I came here in 1973 and went off my head. I just kept bursting into tears'. Alcoholism and tranquiliser abuse among mature women is Livingston's biggest drugs problem − 93 out of 151 people admitted to the local hospital in 1986 for overdosing were married women.

But the place is anything but passive. It may have no labour movement, it may have a declining Labour Party, despite the best efforts of its diligent MP Robin Cook. But in the informal space marked civil society, the place where people actually live, Livingston is heaving with activity. Voluntary organisations? 'There's hundreds of them', says community worker Carolyn Stenhouse. A glance at Livingston's community centres reveals a plethora of participants in zillions of women's and children's groups, dance and sports and health clubs, and neighbourhood

forums in particular – Livingstonians are good at being good
neighbours. When Union Carbide, of Bhopal infamy, tried to
relocate here, a fierce and popular crusade resisted it.

That's another new times thing about Livingston. It seems
fragmented. The old pillars of politics have crumbled. Yet the
place is full of activists. Their activism is local and practical, and
it seems mostly organised by women. But, the traditional party
militants complain, they're not political.

Sheffield

In the old days, Sheffield's labour movement was its civic fifth
estate – it was a proletarian city, with an amicable division of
labour between the Labour Party, the Communist Party and the
trade unions. Labourism has defined this city's political
ambience, securely and seamlessly, for decades – a monument
to clean, decent, legal municipal tradition. Or, to put it another
way, to municipal traditionalism.

It was never paradise.

Sheffield was a landscape for labour – mass housing on steep
hills wrapped around the epic red brick hangers where men
(mainly) made machines and special steels. It had fewer cars
than the rest of the nation, though like the rest of the nation's
cities, it was still carved up for cars. But it had a better bus
service than anywhere else – that is until deregulation
amputated routes.

Before that children could travel anywhere for 2p. Today, says
the council's economic development chairperson Helen Jackson,
'The youngsters feel trapped on estates – I used to listen to a
gaggle of ten-year-olds round my house deciding where to go.
'Shall we go for a swim or shall we go to Rotherham?' That was
real choice!' Old Sheffield was a man's place. Few women found
their way into its labour market or its labour movement –
although there were the famous buffers – women doing rough,
tough work in the cutlery trade, with a reputation for bawdy,
boisterous independence.

It was symbolic in more ways than one when the National
Union of Mineworkers shifted its headquarters up from London
after Arthur Scargill took over as president in 1982.

The refurbished miners' headquarters is only a short stroll
away from the great Victorian town hall. It looks lovely. Like a

mausoleum. I'd hoped to wander in and look around the foyer for the promised plaque to the women who sustained the miners during their marathon strike. But there didn't seem to be a way in. The building could have belonged to United Biscuits or Securicor for all we knew.

I tried round the back with a Yorkshire union official with a similar problem, and still we couldn't find a way in – until we discovered a young man inserting a plastic card into a security device. 'How do we get in?' asked the official. 'You'll have to phone first', said the young man.

In the era of Thatcherism 44,000 people were thrown out of work in Sheffield. The great battalions of the labour movement were decapitated. The trades council was no longer dominated by the men of steel and engineering. Now the NUM has lost half its members too. It is the end of an era.

Sheffield still sees itself as radical, though. Shoppers were actually queuing up to sign petitions opposing the NHS legislation. And they're voting in more Labour councillors than ever.

But that doesn't describe Sheffield's newness. The town was never known for its modernism. Now the icons of modernity are to be found in the crucible of decline – around the old haunts of the cutlery industry's 'little mesters' there's the city's science park, directed by a woman. And nearby there's the cultural industries quarter, a unique web of open-access recording studios called Red Tape, next-door to Untitled, a photographic gallery and darkrooms, and an independent film studio – all sponsored by the council, with more than a little help from the city's biggest band, the Human League.

Helen Jackson thinks 'it's the most fabulous place'. So does Jane Kitson, who used to listen to Radio Sheffield's youth access programme, ROTT, then worked on it until the BBC axed it. Now she's a sound engineer working at Red Tape, where she also helps put out another youth access show.

She is 22, watches *Brookside*, *Blind Date* and *The Right to Reply* on TV, she's got many hundreds of records, all catalogued, she's got every issue of *Smash Hits*, reads *Sky* magazine and used to read Mills and Boon 'until the 250th when I cottoned on they were all the same'. Apart from her passion for pop she can sing along with the Andrews Sisters 'and Ella Fitzgerald is the one woman I'd run away with'.

Is she working class? 'Yeah, I can't imagine being anything else.' Is she a feminist? 'Yeah, definitely.' Does she worry about Aids? 'Yeah.' Does she worry about the future? 'Yeah. We'll end up with identity tabs, or behind bars. And God forbid if you're not educated. That's why I'm applying for the poly, I'm doing it now. Next year I won't be able to afford it.' She's a modern woman.

The council is also sponsoring the rescue of the old Lyceum Theatre which will supplement the city's flourishing arts. The Crucible Theatre, run by the iconoclastic Clare Venables, plays to average 80 per cent capacity. What was once only a city of work is now also a place of pleasure and culture.

The signs of modernisation are also expressed in the city's euphemistic idylls – Orchard Square, Crystal Peaks and Meadowhall. Shops, shops, shops. But it is shopping with a difference, and these sites express the contradictory new times in which the city lives. Orchard Square is a subtle and successful shopping enclave with space to congregate and communicate, secured by a landlord's resistance to the bulldozer and the council's insistence on a user-friendly space. Crystal Peaks is an out-of-town shopping and leisure centre where, just to show who counts, there's a creche for the shoppers but not for the staff. And there's Meadowhall, a £2.25 billion shopping and leisure complex being laid across the Don Valley. Where once there was only dirty work, there now will be play and work (since someone's play is someone else's work). It wasn't what the council wanted there, but in the absence of the powers to resist the redevelopment it sought instead to influence it.

There are constant complaints that there's no real work coming to Sheffield. Real work, for real men, that is. There won't be an army of boiler-suited boys, extras from Fritz Lang's *Metropolis*, inheriting a craft and a culture in that peculiar relation of intimate authoritarianism known as apprenticeship. Instead, women pop in to Crystal Peaks to shop or to work, no tea breaks if they're working rather than buying, often no rights because their hours aren't long enough, no union because nobody ever told them they've got rights worth defending anyway.

So Sheffield staggers towards the end of the 20th century lumbered with a 19th-century division of labour. But it is being challenged – the women trade unionists at the Midland Bank's

Sheffield headquarters have pioneered what will be the first of Midland's 300 workplace nurseries. Not that all the city's employers are as enlightened in self-interest, but it is evidence that what the postwar welfare state failed to deliver — collective care for children — will be generated by employers confronted by a skill shortage.

The great debate in Sheffield these days is about the World Student Games in 1991. Without doubt it will renew the city's sports and leisure infrastructure — but there will be a price to pay. But epic city centre pools, like the one now being built for the Games, don't come free.

Sheffield council is a major mover in the modernisation of its economy. Helen Jackson was one of the new councillors elected at the beginning of the decade. In 1986, when she was the chair of economic development, the council commissioned a report on regeneration which called for massive capital investment. She hoped that by collaborating with the private sector a consensus for renewal could be taken to the government, which was by then punishing high-spending authorities with rate-capping.

Chamber of Commerce chief executive, John Hambridge, reckons that 'In the Sheffield context, some of the government's constraints are less than helpful. Sheffield's survival has been built on partnership. The local government legislation is placing very severe restraints on local authorities, it is making the job almost impossible.'

The chamber emerged from the first half of the 1980s as a fierce critic of the council, but then 'stopped the public squabbles, we agreed to go into purdah almost'. Together they commissioned a consultants' report on regeneration, and armed with their consensus took it to the government, which agreed to throw £50 million into the pot, but only on condition that regeneration was under the aegis of an Urban Development Corporation — unelected.

At the swimming pool site the trade-union convener makes it his business to monitor recruitment, together with a council equal opportunities worker. Mowlem manage the contractors and when one of them, Gleesons, were hunting for joiners, the convener scoured the job applications. 'There was one from a woman and an Asian man, fully qualified and with site experience. They weren't given a second glance, the site agent didn't want to know.'

The tenants of blocks of flats like the horrendous Hyde Park, which are being decanted for refurbishing as part of the games, are wondering how come repairs happen for visitors but not for residents. The council's answer is that the games is a device — there's no way it could afford — or would be allowed — to renew the city otherwise.

The games debate begs another question: has the council sold out to capital? Council leader Clive Betts says they haven't. 'We have to get involved in the economy, because nobody else represents the whole community', he says. But he's clear that, for Sheffield, there's no turning back. 'We aren't going to reinstate what was there before Thatcher.'

Swindon

Swindon matters. It is being seen as an icon of postmodernism, as an urban sphinx, as an emblem of new times.

It was always thus. First there was Isambard Kingdom Brunel, a man of majestic invention, then there was his railway, and later there was clever municipalism.

Post-industrial Swindon is also an epic story, although its built environment can hardly match the elegance of that earlier era, not even the new Brunel Centre, a mighty, canopied precinct which echoes grand Victorian arches.

The town has been almost a company town. Its concentration on railway engineering defined its class and its culture. It was a moderately respectable, moderately right-wing social democracy. The kind of proud, self-sufficient, self-respecting class consciousness that never produced a revolution but did produce a superior kind of survival. A clean town. A Labour town.

The railway workshops have been decanted and largely, though not entirely, thank goodness, destroyed, and a great site of industrial archaeology will be preserved.

So postmodernism captures Brunel and — some would say — mocks him: what was once a place of work becomes a place of consumption; the punters will be piling in there by the 1990s, consuming history-as-heritage and cakes and cuppas.

It will add to the town's exemplary public facilities (underwritten by free mobility for the wageless, courtesy of plastic card) provided by its stalwart Labour council.

But it lacks a public realm — the streetscape has become the shopping precinct.

Asian citizens feel it acutely — there are not any large public meeting places where they can gather for their bonding communal ceremonies. The death of the street, more a feature of modernism, is visible in Allied Dunbar's new, low-rise blocks, blank, bland walls. It's cheap, of course, 'but it is an insult to the passer-by', says Patrick Hannay, of the *Architectural Journal*.

Allied Dunbar, the financial services company with 4,500 sales staff, is one of the town's dominant private employers and as the occupant of eight, soon to be nine, of the town's office blocks, it is transforming the landscape. The company, which moved up from London for the cheaper land and labour, flags the decentralisation of financial institutions away from the City. It has also transformed the economic atmosphere. Employing around 2,000 workers in the town itself, and still growing, it prides itself on being a liberal company. 'When we came to Swindon we felt a responsibility to put something into the community', says company chairperson Joel Joffe, an émigré white South African.

It is one of the country's largest charitable donors, and established a fund in Swindon which offers start-up grants to every new voluntary organisation. Its management philosophy is typically new times: paternalistic while aiming for massive self-motivation. 'We demand high professional standards, but we are very caring and we create an environment in which individuals can flourish without authoritarian influence', Joffe says. According to Bob Reynolds' book, *The 100 Best Companies to Work For*, the company ethic ruptures the reticent etiquette of the insurance industry. 'It is aggressive, tightly controlled, not easy but pays well, offers plenty of promotion and lavish benefits. For the dedicated, a rewarding environment.' And there's no trade union. 'If you manage well, people don't need it', says personnel manager Peter Stemp.

There's an equal opportunities policy, but that doesn't mean positive action, says Stemp. Allied Dunbar, for all its modernism, still shies away from anti-discrimination employment practices that would be commonplace in some of its US counterparts. Swindon's Community Relations officer Jigind Bassi says that although the company funded one of the CRE's training officers, 'you don't see black faces coming out of Allied Dunbar offices'.

Will modernisation of its economy replicate the old sex and race divisions?

This was once a union town. Now the demise of the old, white, male, manual industries has extinguished trade unionism in Swindon — it now has fewer union members than the national average, 14,000 in a working population of over 50,000. 'I can remember when the engineering union alone had 10,000 members here', says former engineer Clive Norris, now a white collar worker.

The impact on politics is hard to gauge. People are still voting Labour in local elections, but Labour lost to the Tories in the last two general elections. Swindon seems to be certainly out of sync with much of the rest of the south: Labour recently surprised itself by winning two seats it fully expected to lose in the new boom territories of the town.

Jon Akass of the *Daily Express* hails the new town as Thatchergrad. But its economic renaissance has been sponsored and secured by the council. Indeed Swindon has been heavily punished for its foresight — it has been rate-capped by central government since 1985. The reason? Since the 1950s Swindon's local authority has been bankrolling a new infrastructure.

The council's latest project is to refurbish the city centre shopping facilities. It brought together all the major developers involved to discuss the council's terms. 'They came up with a scheme', says council leader Tony Huzzey, a redundant railway electrician whose hobby — rural photography — brightens his bland council office, 'but it would have involved closing the shopping area for twelve hours a day for security reasons.'

Surveillance and security increasingly define the urban landscape. 'We don't agree with that. So we came up with a compromise — 11pm-7am closure. And while it is open there will be toilets, disabled access, baby-changing facilities and we'll be asking the developers to provide public spaces.'

His deputy Jim D'Avilia, a convener at the town's Austin Rover factory, said they'd scoured some of the latest shopping developments, like Newcastle's Metrocentre, 'and we weren't very taken. We want something pleasing and practical, and we want it to contain facilities for women that shopping centres usually don't'.

Neither of them lament the demise of the old industries which were the spine of Swindon. 'People don't want to go to work to get their hands dirty', says D'Avilia. 'And anyway it was all completely male dominated', says Huzzey.

Swindon's workforce is being feminised − though without any commensurate commitment to resourcing child-care. It's a measure of the alienation produced by decrepit or coercive old industrial processes that Allied Dunbar can now boast that having first taken on daughters, they are taking on their middle-aged fathers.

'I've done my stint of the manly jobs', says John Perkins, who used to work at Austin Rover's car plant. 'I wanted to change my life, I didn't want another twenty years working in a filthy environment. Fortunately I had two daughters working at Allied Dunbar.' Perkins had been a shop steward in Austin Rover. He is no longer in a union.

Sid Mills began his working life as a coppersmith and ended, after many years as an active union man, as chairperson of the Vickers works committee. He quit in his late 40s. 'I was climbing up 144 foot ladders to put rigs in, and I thought: 'Why am I doing this for £123 when I would earn more at Allied Dunbar?' I just wanted to get away from the horrible filth and environment of a factory'. He now works in the company's warehouse.

Mills is no longer a skilled man, nor union man either, but not without a little regret. 'Some bits I don't like. Middle management are hard to get through to, they've got their ways and they're stubborn.' So what can he do about it? 'Nothing. You are fighting as an individual. All right, you get good rewards. You have meetings. At one they said we're going to tell you, but we don't want any questions. People say they are frightened to have their say because it will affect their money.' Sid Mills's and John Perkin's changes of life exemplify the death of institutionalised class consciousness sustained, for men at least, in the trade-union tradition. But there is, in its wake, a new tradition. 'There's been a huge expansion of self-help activity, a lot related to health and women's issues', says Brian Whittaker, director of Swindon's Council for Voluntary Service. 'Many are controlled by the users, many aren't huge, they aren't bureaucratic, they come and go as needs change.'

A paragon of this tradition is Pinehurst People's Centre, a school on one of Swindon's oldest council estates with 47 per cent unemployment. The community resisted the school's closure and fought, successfully, to turn it into a community resource. Dot Castle turned up at the centre looking for something to do, and ended up canvassing every household to discover the needs of the estate's 1,200 elderly people. With other volunteers she collects pensions for them, shops, organises outings, offers advice on benefits and rents. The centre is managed by Sue Beasley, a former nurse. 'It was after I was in the throes of divorce that I got involved in my own community − it was part of my transition from being a stranger in my own community.' Martin King used to be a shop steward. 'I was out of a job, on my own with two babies to look after. The kids went to a playgroup, so I started helping there. Then I started a Saturday morning cinema club for kids.' He was also involved in the unemployed movement and launched a massively popular rock-school at the centre several nights a week for the young unemployed men and women. 'There was terrible opposition from some councillors − 'rock on the rates' − but nobody came up with a good reason why we shouldn't.'

Chris Sharp runs the independent Pinehurst Training Initiative open to anyone, able-bodied or disabled, who is unwaged. A mobile woman on wheels, Sharp also advises local business on facilities for the disabled. Half its students find paid work. Another 10 per cent use their new skills in the voluntary sector. Others come to rebuild their confidence − one of its older students is learning to use a computer so that she can do the accounts of the Allotment Association in case anything were to happen to her husband.

Pinehurst's working class no longer expresses itself predominantly through the filter of the labour movement but in another tradition − it's local, shaped by its users, it is feminised, it has nothing in common with Samuel Smiles, but it represents a new class consciousness expressed in militant self-help.

Basingstoke

Where will we find an urban monument to Thatcherism, pure, unpolluted by municipal modernism, or socialism by stealth, the Thatchergrad that tells us what British society is becoming?

How about Basingstoke? Don't laugh. For here we have a flourishing economy unimpeded by planning, by civic pride, or by community politics. It's a monument to the Thatcherite version of new times.

It seems to be a society that strives to express Mrs Thatcher's mantra: there's no such thing as society.

A pocket Faust seems to have been at work, a developer with no fear and no flair has bulldozed the ancient and organic heart of this market town, inhabited by 14,000 souls in the 1930s, to build a downtown Dallas for more than 100,000.

If you are prehistoric and still use public transport you arrive at the prettiest building in the place, a glorious red brick railway station nicely refurbished by British Rail in partnership with Provident Life.

Before you is an eccentric landscape: a moat (actually it's a motorway) surrounds what looks like a modern castle, with sulking walls and secret tunnels.

It would make Prince Charles weep.

It's the shopping precinct, built in the genre of brutalism, and sternly policed by the developer, the Prudential. Social congress is reduced to one simple act: consumption. Citizenship has none of the multiple identities implied by the broader vision of the new times theory. Here the citizen is only a consumer.

The place dies at night − one evening I counted precisely fourteen people in the town centre − six were at cashpoints, the rest were on their way to somewhere else.

Legend has it that the Pru's security people have rid the place of undesirables. 'Watch out if you've got pink hair down there,' lamented a young police officer, who thought it a bit much that punks had to be purged from public space. 'They make people move on from their own town centre', complained a local doctor.

Another legend confirms the relentless privatisation of this public space: the WRVS in one story, and the WI in another, was thrown out of the marketplace for selling cakes − unfair competition with Marks & Spencer. Whither the free market?

Basingstoke is now the apotheosis of all our British municipal traditions. It is rich and yet repudiates those other Victorian values enshrined in what Asa Briggs calls the 'civic gospel'.

There is no discernible planning. In the 1960s it became a London overspill new town − typically, dual carriageways encircling homesteads with rustic euphemisms scattered around the periphery.

Now, its suburban modesty is blown in the big, butch buildings which overshadow the townscape. They're mainly speculative office developments, post-brutalist if not postmodernist glass towers.

Council leader Stephen Reid, a young data processor, reckons he is a Prince Charles man. Asked what cities have influenced his thoughts on the urban environment, he says, 'I don't know that I've taken any models. I've taken my own feelings. I'd proudly call myself a reactionary. My wife and I live in a traditional, three-bedroom house with brick on the outside, a pointed roof and a proper front door.'

Did he extend this ideology to industrial and commercial architecture? 'Yes, I think I do. Some of the monstrosities ..!' How could he justify demolition of the old town centre? It was necessary to keep shopping central.

Basingstoke is one of the pioneer privatisers in local government. Now it is supporting a private leisure complex. 'It is being built by a private developer on council land. We'll not take rent, that will be our contribution – forgoing income. And as a result we'll get a cinema', says Reid.

For a boomtown hungry for leisure facilities, isn't that rather giving it away? 'It won't cost the ratepayers a penny', he insisted. But it won't earn them a penny either. 'That was the way we were going to get the deal.' According to Ken Worpole, 'The Tory towns in the South are washing their hands of any civic responsibility. They don't believe in civic culture.'

Culture, in the sense of social life, seems thoroughly privatised. Civil servant Ann Horrocks says, 'At weekends everybody cleans their cars or gets into DIY. Half the people came here for jobs and then they'll move.'

Rita Smith, a policewoman, says 'I cried for three days when I got posted here. People come for a good job, a good marriage and a good divorce. The men want a company car and a wife who'll warm the slippers between her thighs.'

Secretary Jane Moore summarises an evening's entertainment in Basingstoke: 'a wine box and a video'.

The vacancy marks Basingstoke out from the other cities and towns I visited. It is mirrored in the poverty of its voluntary sector. The drugs centre receives no grant from the borough council. The local rape crisis line receives small grants from some local businesses, from the county council, and the police authority, but despite three visits and six formal applications, it receives no money from Basingstoke council.

Class and party find little correlation in Basingstoke, where the new employers, hi-tech manufacturers and financial services, have pre-empted the trade unions, and their inner life provides clues to the labour process implications of economic restructuring.

Basingstoke council's minority Labour group leader Jack Evans works in an American-owned engineering company where, he says, 'There's been a couple of attempts to unionise, but nothing came of it. There's not the reason we used to have in dirty old workshops: the wages, the bonuses, health and safety. The workers have got the majority of what we used to want.' At IBM, for example, whose world-wide anti-union strategy and secrecy are well documented, the role of secretarial staff is being eroded or eliminated by the impact of computerisation. It no longer seems to be a sign of status to have a secretary. Highly qualified technical or accounting staff talk to each other via their keyboards and screens, asset-stripping the secretary.

'Each job is very narrowed down, very repetitive and very boring', says an IBM secretary. 'It's so robotic, they seem to be trying to make the secretaries redundant. I'd have my toast in the morning and doughnut in the afternoon just to relieve the boredom. If there was a very long document to do, middle management would call on the secretary. But, typing-wise the men – there were very few women – would do routine communications themselves. They organise themselves and their own diaries. So you'd think, 'Why does anyone need a secretary?'

IBM is well-known for its internal company culture, 'Everybody who works here thinks it's brilliant. But everything is about money, shares and houses – that's the conversation. It's the kind of place where you hide the *Guardian*. When I admitted that my boyfriend was a teacher that didn't go down well, because it was obvious we weren't into money.'

A more subtle refinement of clerical functions is taking place at Sun Life of Canada housed in a prestigious glass block built around an airy atrium. Hitherto, clerks would have worked in a Fordist assembly line process. According to personnel manager Frank Gregory: 'They'd simply respond to enquiries from policy-holders. It's a system relying on paper – well, people and paper.' They might have to make enquiries among other colleagues. 'That's wasteful and not very satisfying. With our new system all that would be in the computer. Contact with humans will be reduced.'

And so, instead of working on one aspect of a client's policy, the clerk would be expected to gain more job satisfaction from handling the whole client, though, of course, dependence on the networks of knowledge shared between humans would be replaced by dependence on the machine. 'Obviously we'd reconsider if staff felt they were chained to their screens seven hours a day', says Frank Gregory.

But that risk of isolation and computer dependence is compounded by the absence of alternative comforts and collectivity to those generously provided by the company. Trade unions, almost inevitably, seem irrelevant in such a place.

Instead, there is an almost authoritarian blurring of hierarchies. You see it in the canteen available to all, in the system of individualised salary assessment, and in the provision of free lunches and insurance benefits − death and disablement schemes and group life cover. There is tyrant equality too in out-of-work leisure and the working environment, in the standardised furniture and fittings found everywhere, including the stark black and white prints on the office walls. It is a relentless, ubiquitous identity. 'We're not allowed to put anything of our own on the walls', said a technician in a large computer company. There's a lot of jockeying and backstabbing and a perceptible consultant attitude − they wear the confidence of their commodity − knowledge is what they sell.

Politics? Pro-Thatcher, although a colleague standing as a Green councillor was acceptable. Labour would not have been. 'They're desperate to retain staff and ensure that they're happy. I'm sure my manager recognises I've got a skill he doesn't have and that it would be very difficult to replace me. That leads to loose management − they have to ensure that we are happy.

When I came here my university friends said they'd use me as a tool not a human being. That's true but they're interested in servicing the human aspect to ensure that the tool is effective. So, I'm used but not managed.'

Companies like Sun Life of Canada participate in a committee studying women and work. Some employers are considering collaborating to provide a creche, though they'd prefer to extend office hours and flexibility. A group of professional and businesswomen has surveyed women's needs in the town and discovered that 70 per cent of non-employed women would work if they could find child care. Among employed women, child care was cited as their biggest problem, followed by transport. The market doth not provide, however – only the public sector (the local hospital) provides a workplace nursery.

IV Response of the Critics

Michael Rustin

The Trouble with 'New Times'

Several years after the first discussions of arguments about post-Fordism in *New Left Review,* they have become central to political debate in Britain, through series of interventions by *Marxism Today*. And, such is the thinness of the Labour Party's political culture that *Marxism Today* has, since the virtual demise of *New Socialist*, become more or less the theoretical organ of Labour revisionism too, sometimes lining up the Left of both parties in opposition to its new realist positions.

The 'post-Fordist' hypothesis on which these new positions are based is the nearest thing we have to a paradigm which can link widespread changes in forms of production to changes in class relations, state forms and individual identities. It thus pursues the far-reaching scope of explanation and connection between disparate phenomena that has previously been expected of marxist political economy. As Geoff Mulgan has pointed out, it is marxist in its basic *form* of analysis (notably in the causal priority it assigns to the new information-based technologies of production and distribution), even though it is highly subversive of left-wing orthodoxy in what it infers for the position of the working class, the appropriate forms of state and welfare institutions, and the roles of communist or socialist parties.[1] It is valuable to have had this new paradigm placed so firmly in the centre of debate, and none of the criticisms made in this article should be taken to diminish appreciation of that.

As is so often the case, the sense of an ending of an era has illuminated its general shape. What have been unmistakably clarified are the social relations of Fordism: the link between the systems of mass production and mass consumption, the role of Keynesianism and the welfare state in underwriting long-term growth and profitability, and the integration of trade unions, on an industrial and later national-corporatist basis, in the management of the postwar Fordist economy. The counterposed model of post-Fordism also has the power to explain the shape and direction of the emerging economic system, at least in part. Modern technical systems do depend increasingly on the rapid and powerful processing of information, more than on their sheer mechanical power. The speed of knowledge-production, and of technical innovation, has vastly accelerated. Product ranges are modified more quickly, and are more internally diversified, than in classic forms of production for mass consumer markets. Modern information systems allow both finer tuning of product flows and mixes in relation to changing and segmented markets, and greater producer influence over consumer demand. The social relations of these new systems of production and distribution are different from those of 'mass production', as was pointed out long ago by sociologists of organisation. Where there is rapid change and uncertainty, flatter hierarchies and greater lateral communication between members are more functional for organisational goals than bureaucratic command models, in which all communication must pass up and down hierarchies or lines of command. Markets capable of rapid innovation and flexible specialisation may encourage the diversification of demand rather than tending to homogenise it in the interests of economies of scale. Hence the phenomena of market-niching, life-stylism, etc.

The value of this model is that it attempts an historical materialist explanation of the changes associated in Britain with Thatcherism, at the level of changes in the means of production and their consequences for class structures and ideological forms. Without such a model, we are liable to be left with explanations set in basically neo-classical terms: either a view of the market as the norm, from which state intervention, trade unionism, 'political overload', etc, are deviations; or else an argument against markets that is made in mainly normative language, in terms of distribution, externalities, public goods, etc. We finish up with a largely prescriptive antithesis of state versus market, the claims of equality versus those of freedom, whilst the sphere of factual definition and explanation – the description of how things are – is left to the liberal Right. The post-Fordist model, in which production remains at least one dominant category, has the great merit of being an attempt to theorise structures and their effects. It thus becomes possible, in principle, to derive explanations, predictions and strategic choices based on assessments of possibility. By contrast, liberal and social-democratic models tend to confine us to historical and normative choices, and a politics based on the ethics of redistribution.

This model appears to have considerable cogency and explanatory power, and its theoretical ambitions are admirable. There are, however, serious problems in determining its scope of application. It is far from clear how much of the emerging economic system fits this new pattern of technology and organisation, and how much still operates either in old 'mass production' modes, or by still more technologically-backward methods dependent on unskilled labour such as those found in most of the (expanding) hotel and catering trades. Even the state-of-the-information-arts example of television raises this question in acute forms. Just when the 'Channel 4' model has been established to the general acclaim of the post-Fordist intellectual public, the system as a whole is threatened with regression under pressure of market forces to the worst forms of mass formula-programming on a global scale. What seems to be emerging is not one 'progressive' mode of information-based production, but a plethora of co-existing and competing systems, whose ultimate relative weight in the system is impossible to predict. Since socio-technical systems do not develop completely autonomously, but only in response to cultural definition, conflicts of social forces, and political decision, it is dubious in principle and possibly misleading in fact to make linear extrapolations from what might seem to be 'leading instances', or current trends, to the shape of a whole system.

There is even greater uncertainty with regard to the social and political relations of the post-Fordist means of production. It is possible to see a clear logic in the coexistence of mass production and consumption and the Keynesian welfare state after the war, though the implicitly somewhat 'functionalist' approach of 'post-Fordists' understates the importance of political and class factors − the effects of social conflicts − in achieving this temporary settlement. Similar extrapolations are now being attempted for the post-Fordist mode of production, as if flexible forms of welfare, politics and administration could be 'read off' from these new forms of production. Decentralisation of government, greater consumer choice in the welfare sector, a larger informal or voluntary welfare sector, and more spontaneous or 'networked' forms of political organisation are all supposed to follow in some ways from the new technical and economic order. Thus, the kind of Fordist 'fit' between the mass production of goods and a similarly 'massified' provision of public services is taken as the model of the relation we should be looking for between 'flexible' consumer-led systems of production, and equally flexible, consumer-driven systems of welfare. Mass production was to mass welfare as flexible specialisation should be to consumerised welfare; the content of the terms varies, their relation remains constant. For exponents of the new paradigm, socialists must be persuaded that to defend 'mass', Fordist patterns of welfare, politics and resistance is to remain locked into obsolete and discredited structures. Forms of resistance that were appropriate in the old system are deemed to be mainly an obstacle to progress and fresh thinking in the new.

Production, Welfare and Politics

But it is not at all clear what the causal connections are supposed to be between the spheres of production and those of welfare or politics in this new post-Fordist era. One implicit hypothesis is that consumers who are led to expect variety and choice in consumer markets will or should settle for nothing less in the welfare sector. There is some validity to this, though there are great dangers in turning commodity markets into a normative model for other social relations. For good reasons, socialists have historically subordinated rights and powers of individual choice in the sphere of health, welfare and education to the claims of relative and absolute need. The contractual relations between buyers and sellers in the market have been contrasted with the claims of human obligation and relationship in the public sector. The ethos and goals of consumer choice cannot be pushed very far in these spheres (for example, health care) before they conflict severely with the over-riding values of human needs.

Another possible level of connection between production and welfare lies in technological innovation itself, though the welfare sector so far has been backward in this area of development compared with industry, retailing or financial services. (This relative technical stasis is one aspect of the pressure to 'marketise' the welfare system. A situation where productivity gains are confined to the private industrial sector, but where an increasing public welfare budget has to be funded from them, is seen as unstable and unsustainable for capital, and in reality presents a real problem for any economic system.)

One can see the potential of information technology in public spheres − for example, more individual and flexible access to medical information and educational provision, or more flexible and decentralised management of public services such as education. Some aspects of present Tory reforms of welfare services − requiring audit of medical performance in the NHS, or establishing measures of comparative success in the school system − are positive in principle, if not in their political intention. Similarly, better technical resources may make it possible to operate an income maintenance or combined tax/benefit system that is more flexibly, transparently and speedily adjusted to meet differentiated needs − for example, those of single-parents or the low paid. The customisation of personal insurance and pensions by the private financial sector is an example of what new technologies might have made possible for the public sector in this sphere. One could similarly imagine a public housing system in which allocation, transfer and choice would be made much more competitive with private ownership, through the use of appropriate information systems. One can also conceive of new interactive technologies being used in support of public access to information, and to make involvement in the political process more direct and easy. Participation in neighbourhood council, school governors, or even internal party elections could be made much less onerous if votes were cast through computer terminals linked into urban or national fibre optic cable networks. Technological developments favouring 'customisation', and the culture which emerges from their diffusion in the market sector, undoubtedly change both the environment of provision and choice and people's expectations of services. There are good reasons for thinking about how the provisions of the public domain could be improved by such technical means.

However, it is clear that the shape of this environment is not and will not be determined by new technologies alone. The interests of competing collectivities, above all of social classes, are paramount. It depends on both specific technical conditions and local balances of social forces whether one socio-technical system or another is adopted or preferred. It is for this reason that capital may in the same period introduce quite different systems of technology and organisation in different social contexts. For example, small-scale, network-based, differentiated, flexible systems of television production (the Channel 4 model) are used at the same time as mass-market, formula-produced, highly capitalised television series to be beamed by satellite for international consumption. Or post-Fordism in the West, where highly educated and skilled populations render one set of producer and consumer forms possible, coexists with 'primitive Taylorism', 'peripheral Fordism', and ultimately Fordism in Third World economies. The unifying explanation of these differences is to be sought in the strategies of capital, in the context of the resistance presented to its activities, not in technological imperatives *per se*.

What is argued here, in other words, is the primacy of the actions and strategies of classes in the explanation of changes in the political economy of capitalism. Post-Fordism is better seen as one ideal-typical model or strategy of production and regulation, co-present with others in a complex historical ensemble, than as a valid totalising description of an emerging social formation here and now. The partial and localised breakdown of the Fordist system of mass production and regulation is to be understood in part as an innovative, profit seeking response by capital to the potential of the new technologies. But it has also, in large measure, been a response by political interests representing capital to the adverse balance of social forces produced in the latter years of the Fordist system. This had increased the bargaining strength and political weight of trade unions, social-democratic parties and the constituencies they represented, and of the decommodified public sector, to the point where it seriously threatened the viability of some capitalist economies. Where severe economic or political crises occurred, notably in Britain and the United States, radical forces of the Right won control over formerly consensus-oriented conservative parties, and effected a deliberate and sustained 'roll-back' of the countervailing powers of the Fordist era. The panic of the dominant classes at the social gains of the subordinate classes and their institutions (which could be locally oppressive in their own ways) was the primary energising and integrating force behind 'Thatcherism' and its parallels elsewhere.

New technologies provided the resources for an alternative strategy (of 'restructuring') for capital in some sectors, though in others − for example, the motor industry − the transfer of Fordist systems to parts of the world where labour was less able to contest them than in the metropolitan countries was more important than any general shift away from the economics of mass production. A consumerist culture generated expectations which could be successfully played by the Right against the limitations of mass welfare provision of the postwar decades.

But the underlying purpose of this was to remove collectivist threats to capital accumulation and authority, and to give private capital access to potential markets (in health, insurance, pensions, education and training, transport, energy, prison building and management) from which it had previously been excluded. Capital as a whole sought to gain by recommodifying sectors recently excluded from the market, and by the disorganisation of resistance to capital which followed from the restoration of market disciplines. Particular sectors (for example, finance, private health, telecommunications) gained new commercial opportunities. The freeing of British capital markets to international competition and take-over has had the effect of subordinating the whole economy to universal and standard measures of profit and loss, as we see in the exposure of companies to take-over, of whole industrial sectors to rationalisation and sometimes extinction, and in the current pressures for the massification of the publishing and television industries. The humanised environments for 'leisure shopping' in rehabilitated city centres are designed to sell often-standardised kinds of commodities and lifestyles in apparently more sociable and identity-rich settings.

For those sectors of capital which have to operate in different environments, there is no contradiction between the centralisation of many powers of state, sometimes using modern technologies to assure more uniform control, and the decentralisation of certain aspects of production and consumption. It makes sense, from this point of view, to standardise educational provision at the lower levels of the system (allowing local decision only within a rigid framework of curriculum and financial allocation), while at the same time encouraging its customisation and marketisation at the top. This is also the intention of Thatcherite policy in the sphere of health, where public provision has been subjected to disciplines intended to reduce it to low-grade 'mass production', at a moment when a rhetoric of consumer choice and diversity is encouraged at the higher levels of the system. Flexible specialisation makes economic and strategic sense in some sectors and locations, whereas other systems of regulation are being deliberately re-invigorated in others.

There are larger continuities in the operation of the Fordist and Thatcherite states than is usually recognised. No less than in the Keynesian period, state power is being used by the Right to construct and maintain class allegiances. Whilst the rhetoric may be individualist – the state as the strong guarantor of competition and market discipline – the reality is the calculated deployment of material resources and regulatory power to construct new class alliances favourable to capital. While the redistributive powers of the local state are restricted, the tax policies of the national state have massively reallocated income from poor to rich. The aim is nothing less than the restratification of British society, in which a minority (because of the electoral system, majorities are not presently needed for this strategy) entrenches itself in power by the use of the distributive and disciplinary powers of the state. The Thatcherite strategy is in its own ways as collectivist as Fordism. It seems an odd time to be debating the obsolescence of class, or the irrelevance of central state power to class interests.

One needs to see Fordism and post-Fordism as specific, willed resolutions of conflicts at the level of social relations, not as the automatic outcomes of the technological imperatives of 'mass production' or its information-based successor. The key to understanding these forms are the relations between the strategies of capital and labour, and the material conditions in which they are conducted. These are, above all, relations of power. It is paradoxical that at the point when the fit between the class interest and the political strategy of the New Right has become so close (more transparently so than in periods dominated by class compromise), theorists of the Left have become so critical of class-based approaches to political strategy on their own side. The political identity crisis proclaimed by *Marxism Today* (the attack on class theory, the idea of a 'socialism without guarantees', etc) seems to have no counterpart on the Right, where the scope of application of market theories is even bolder (what can't plausibly be privatised?), and where ontological self-doubt seems non-existent.

The focus of *Marxism Today*'s 'New Times' positions on the implications of the information economy for production, consumption, organisation and identity is thus both illuminating and partial. It makes new links between hitherto unconnected phenomena, as all theoretically informed political analysis should do. It manages to sound up-beat and almost optimistic in a period of almost unrelieved defeat. Let us ask an old-fashioned question about this emerging perspective. To whose particular world-view and social situation does it primarily give expression? Who are these relative optimists able to see bad times as 'New Times'?

The Roots of the New Times Thinkers

'Designer socialism', as its critics sometimes call it, really is the socialism of designers. That is to say, the world of flexible specialisation is the world as seen from the point of view of some of its beneficiaries — themselves 'flexible specialists' such as researchers, communicators, information professionals and designers, whose specific capabilities involve the handling and processing of information. In the 1960s, John Kenneth Galbraith developed an early version of the concept of the 'new service class', now re-identified in the 'New Times' symposia as the key movers of post-Fordism. This perspective is most evident in the high programmatic priority given to education, training and research as functional for 'progressive modernisation', but also, of course, as central to the life-world of the man or woman for whom the capacity to acquire, apply and transmit knowledge is *the* market resource. Arguments for the decentralisation of decision-making, for the informal welfare sector, for neighbourhood control, parent power and co-operative housing, also reflect the central position that this new and enlarged intelligentsia is likely to occupy in more pluralised and devolved systems, as the strata who have the cultural capacities to make use of such spaces to find fulfilling and influential roles. Even the liberated view that consumption and shopping are now really 'all right' cannot but reflect the fact that the bearers and primary intended recipients of this message are not the poor but the active enfranchised participants in consumer and cultural markets. Indeed, they are among their prime customers. Likewise there is a connection between the theme of identity (and the 'New Times' writers' surprising open-mindedness towards the positive aspects of individualism) and the social formation of these products of education, modern communications, and mental labour.

It is the nature of things that radicals (and others) scripting scenarios for new societies write themselves some of the best speaking parts. Ideology broadly amounts to the universalising of sectional interests, though there can be debate about what is and what is not universal in a given period. The Fabian conception of socialism privileged the high-minded, socially responsible roles of a fraction of the professional and administrative middle class. Leninism in its classic and more recent forms gives prominence to the vanguard role of the party militant. The socialist utopias of skilled artisans in the 19th century were similarly modelled on their own life-experiences, and on the values, roles and distinctive vision of the good society to which they gave rise. It is therefore nothing unexpected, or to be criticised *per se*, that we find now a socialism of this intelligentsia. But we should keep in mind that it is precisely that, and remember that there remain other groups in society for whom it does not easily speak.

Of course, the leading role assigned to the information industries, the intelligentsia and mental labour in this theoretical system is not only a consequence of special pleading. It seems certain that in this late phase of capitalism information has become a greater productive force than ever before, as the resources devoted to technical discovery increase, and the lead-time between the development of new knowledge and its industrial application shrinks. The enhanced role of the cultural sphere has been a dominant theme of postwar marxism (the influence of Gramsci and Althusser, for example). Political struggles − notably the events of 1968, which no doubt formed the politics of the French regulation school − have themselves sometimes seemed to take a mainly cultural form. The new concern with style and fashion, as matters of political interest, resonates with actual pre-occupations of consumer culture, though whether the Left should follow or resist these is another question.

These developments perhaps call for significant revision of the classical marxist models of the labour process. The importance of technical innovation and development was insufficiently understood by Marx, who mostly saw the process of production as a zero-sum conflict between labour and capital, not as a positive-sum process in which all might sometimes gain. It is this development which is implicitly acknowledged in the distinction between extensive (pre-Fordist) and intensive (Fordist) regimes of accumulation. In so far as mental labour does become more central to the production process, it is not surprising that those who live by it gain in social power, just as the depopulation of the countryside earlier had its consequences for class relations. It is understandable that in this environment, the new intelligentsia should develop an optimistic view of its leading role.

Various constraints and distortions have been imposed by political purposes on the development of the post-Fordist model. The pressure of Thatcherism and the wish to see its defeat have led the 'New Times' project, as well as the Labour Party, to adapt itself unduly to certain powerful Thatcherite assumptions. The priority given to the problem of contesting Thatcherism electorally, with its implicit model of the political process as the marketplace in which this competition has to be won, leads some 'New Times' contributors to make unfortunate concessions to values that are proably better simply regarded as those of the other side. The positive emphases given to modernisation, consumption and individualism are instances of this tacit accommodation to the values of resurgent capitalism, in order (they hope) the better to fight it. The idea of a 'progressive restructuring of society', or 'socialist modernisation', gives centrality to vapid notions of 'modernity' which in this form should have no place in socialist programme-making. It should be a question of modernisation or restructuring for what or whom. Charlie Leadbeater's idea of 'socialist individualism' involves an even worse confusion of language, evading as it does the choice that socialists make, more or less by definition of their position, for altruistic and social forms of life against competitive and individualistic ones.[2] It is not that the choice can be a simple or absolute one – rather that it is our role to give substance and vision to the relational half of this antithesis, leaving egoism and the blessings of the hidden hand to others.

The criteria socialists might use to evaluate the quality of life of a society should have to do not only with per capita income, consumption or individual choice, but with people's enjoyment of and fulfilment in their work, participation in public life, roles of responsibility as active citizens, and contribution to a shared culture through arts, sports or other kinds of expression. We need to recover the idea of a more dense and participatory culture, not merely endorse the goals of greater individual freedom to choose between commodities or services. (One index of the quality of life of an institution, such as a school, neighbourhood or work-group, might be whether or not it is able to generate live performances – whether cabaret, dramatic, or musical – which reflect and celebrate its common life and concerns.) One thing which the marxist tradition has been right about all along is its emphasis on creative work (whether paid or unpaid) as the central form of human fulfilment, and the work-group as one of the most potentially creative forms of relationship. Consumption is no moral substitute for the values and experience of production: for socialists there has to be more to life than shopping, enjoyable as this on occasion may be. Whilst Charlie Leadbeater tries to give his 'socialist individualism' a co-operative and universalist shape, by means of ideas of extended social rights, it is difficult to draw telling distinctions between individualisms of one hue and those of another. The problem lies in the limitations of the language and concept of the individual. The project of redefining the socialist project in individualist terms for tactical or rhetorical reasons seems doomed to concede more to the ethos of the Thatcherite age than it can ever hope to win back from it.

Too Much Too Soon

The new revisionist position claims too much, too soon, for the post-Fordist paradigm over more orthodox socialist and social-democratic definitions of the situation. The ideal-typical model of post-Fordism, abstracted from the larger field of strategies pursued by capital, is used to generate a particular set of programmes, social agents and residual negatives, to the disregard of older theoretical descriptions which continue to have explanatory power. For example, priority is given to emergent social strata in constructing an oppositional force, as if conflicts of an earlier phase between industrial labour and capital were about to disappear for ever.

Equally, critiques of the state, which may be apt in the sophisticated context of post-Fordist aspiration, may also fail to take adequate note of the continuing roles of democratic institutions in defending working-class interests against those of capital and the market. In the case of the National Health Service, overwhelming priority continues to be due to the defence of an institution whose overall performance and ethos have been good. Whilst improvements with regard to efficiency, accountability and consumer choice are of course desirable, as new levels of aspiration grow, it is simply mistaken to suggest in the case of this institution that its defects are responsible for the crisis in which it has been placed. Rather, the crisis has been imposed by deliberate strategy of a government committed to markets (which is to say, to opportunities, both global and local, for capital). Public reaction to attacks on the service has shown how successful, by absolute and comparative standards, its overall performance has been. This is a prime example of the non-obsolescence of the main traditional conceptions and ideals of social democracy.

Even in other, less popular sectors of provision, such as housing and education, it has taken heavy discriminatory social engineering by the Thatcherites to undermine support for public provision. Council house sales have succeeded not primarily as a result of the innate defects of public housing management (real, and needing remedy as these are), but through adjustment of tax, rents and sale-discounts, to ensure massive redistributive advantages to a particular segment of the upper working class who can afford to opt for home ownership. Whilst, of course, some high-rise housing designs have failed, and systems of repair have been unsatisfactory, the worst problems of housing estates are probably due more to poverty and unemployment among their tenants (naturally concentrated in the least desirable housing) than to the quality of housing provision itself.

Disorganised communities are much more liable than badly managed or designed buildings to generate vandalism, loneliness and disrepair. Meanwhile difficult conditions on public estates, where they occur, are used as evidence against council housing *per se*.

The various spheres of contest over public provision show the continuing relevance of several superimposed frames of political argument. On the one hand, the resources of elected government still need to be deployed to defend the powerless against the forces of the market. On the other hand, they reveal the relevance of the new agenda of individual choice and difference, exploited by the Right to expose the limitations of state provision. The intellectuals insisting on 'New Times' see themselves as the improvers, decentralisers and customisers of welfare, in contrast to old-style bureaucratic providers and political bosses. But unless they can meet the basic interests of majorities in providing these services, and maintain their belief in them, mass public services will not survive to be managed.

The current restructuring of welfare-state systems poses difficult problems for the Left. For the time being, health and education remain overwhelmingly dependent on public funding, and the challenge is to make the newly imposed forms of decentralisation, consumer control and mandatory competition work ultimately to strengthen public provision. Even though the government intention is probably to achieve a stratification of these systems, and the privatisation of their top segments, the fact that they remain public at this point means that the battles are not yet lost. Faced with the imposition of market forces, socialists have to demonstrate the superiority of public participation and the advantages of planning over competition in meeting universal human needs. They have to show that measures of quality can count for as much as the measures of money. There do need to be new values for public services though 'differentiated collectivism' describes them better than any kind of individualism. They won't emerge through the denunciation of earlier social-democratic achievements. Some basic loyalty to and respect for what was made in the past is the prerequisite of any further advance.

The central dynamic force of capitalism remains, of course, as strategies for the accumulation of capital, on a global scale. How to modify this force so that its destructive effects are contained, how to build countervailing powers which support values of need, community, equality and social relationship, and how to advance the claims of democratic, participatory institutions against the unequal powers of private property, must remain the broad agenda of socialism. Issues of strategic power − for example, to constrain the operations of a globally integrated financial system where they cause intolerable damage to living standards and ways of life − are no less vital than they ever were to socialist strategy.

There is an evident shift in both *Marxism Today* and the Labour Party's thinking from these central but intractable problems of how to control the systems and circuits of capital, to more immediate and apparently manageable issues of electoral recovery and progamme construction. The problematic of ideological hegemony (how to win it back for the Left) subtly displaces the deeper issue of how to achieve and exercise economic and political power over structures. A disposition to methodological idealism − a preference for the level of culture over that of structure − has always been latent in neo-Gramscian thinking, the obverse of its great power to illuminate the ideological sphere. The rejection of *a priori* economic and class determinism seems sometimes to carry with it an implicit voluntarism, and the intractable problems of how to effect lasting changes are pushed into the background. Yet the history of Labour governments since at least the 1960s shows that the problems of how to achieve and exercise power over this system are as essential to solve as the problems of how ever to win back a foothold in government.

Our strategic conclusions will clearly depend on whether we conceptualise post-Fordism as only one ideal-typical option of capital in a field in which others remain important, or whether we read the whole political map in post-Fordist terms. Particular social strata are constituted by new forms of production. The possessors of 'cultural capital', especially in the new forms generated by the information industries and an expanded education process, are social strata which it is vital for the Left to win. Certain issues and political priorities follow from this new development, and since these new strata are a rising social force, their world-view can be expected to have especial weight in contemporary political strategy.

But capital uses its technological resources, and the human

inputs which it has to combine with them, in various ways, and each of these defines different potential fields of social conflict. Specialisation and diversification establish local concentrations of skill and knowledge, but since monopolies of skill potentially impose high supply costs on capital, strategies are also adopted to negate the benefits they might confer on sections of the workforce. Routinisation and mechanisation may be pushed to their limit at one end of the production process, whilst a self-motivated and interactive style of work-group is deemed functional at the other. Exposure of the labour market to the widest national and international competition — through attacks on all 'restrictive practices', the weakening of trade-union powers and the freeing of the international movement of labour — is another strategy for reducing labour's bargaining resources. Such measures, however, together with failures in the education and training systems, have helped to produce a large underclass of long-term unemployed, whose needs and hopes need also to be addressed in the formulation of political programmes.

The Unification of Resistance

The models of Fordism and post-Fordism, each with some partial explanatory force, suggest a methodology for more temperate and systematic thinking about programme and strategy. These models identify a variety of potential agents and sites of resistance, which will need to be unified in opposition to the Right. For example, in seeking to protect the life-chances of the least skilled in the labour market, one conscious strategy could be to enrich the content and requirements of work, by upgrading its specifications of skill. An example of this may be taken from the field of welfare. Menial custodial functions will be humanly less satisfying, and materially less rewarded, than forms of care which involve a higher 'value' of human relationship and understanding. To supply skills through education and training, and to encourage more sophisticated demands for them by raising expectations of the quality of goods and services, are therefore ways of defending the interests of workers as well as benefiting consumers and citizens. Enhancement of the 'mental' (and emotion-rich) content of labour may thus be a feasible goal as well as a secular trend of the modern process of production. Advanced economies can benefit from the addition of skills and 'value-added' work to the production of human services as well as material goods.

In the sphere of economic planning, positive opportunities follow from decentralisation and technological sophistication. The local state has a potential role in economic development where small firms require a network of supporting and interdependent services to succeed in competition. But on a national and continental scale too infrastructures of telecommunications, research and transport remain necessary for economic success. Regulation of unfair competition, damage to environments and defence of consumers also imply large economic roles for the state. Both the old and new agendas of social-democratic regulation and intervention are relevant in these conditions.

Thatcherism may be understood as a strategy of post-Fordism initiated from the perspective of the Right. That is to say, a determined attempt to use the advantages of new technology, mobility of capital and labour, the centrality of consumption, and more decentralised forms of organisation, to strengthen capital and to attack the corporate structures of labour. It is important not to celebrate these new formations, but to ask if these new conditions of production can also give rise to counter-strategies for the Left. The issues identified above suggest that they can be − but only if one recognises the over-riding centrality of the contest of capital and labour, and the ways in which these different superimposed forms of production remain essential resources for each party to the conflict.

The essence of this argument is that the variety of strategies of capital − post-Fordist and others − which will continue to coexist with one another each generate specific sites of potential resistance and conflict. Whilst there is a tendency to see issues of consumption as taking precedence, these remain connected to, and dependent on, the material resources provided through capital and labour markets. People cannot for the most part consume unless they earn, or own. The old socialist emphasis on how people earn, and what they own, does not lose its primacy because they earn or own more, or earn or own differently from before. At the level of social agency, it seems obvious that socialists have to find ways of linking the claims of 'old' and 'new' constituencies. It would be premature and self-destructive to write off the old social divisions as irrelevant, and to construct a radical politics wholly on the interests of the middling strata. But more interesting than the issue of agency is the argument at the level of analytic models. The need here is to relate post-Fordism to the full range of strategies of capital, and to consider strategic political issues in terms of the social relations of the whole contemporary mode of production, not simply of one advanced segment of it.

Perhaps what is necessary at this point is to define the space, both within and beyond the Left, in which a new paradigm might be developed and a holding strategy put in place. It is not possible to know the relative weight of pre-Fordist, Fordist or post-Fordist components in the emerging political economy, and potentially fatal to neglect the existence and problems of any of them. The new post-Fordist analysis needs space and time for its elaboration, without being foreclosed by the demands of strategists or programme-makers for instant political pay-offs. It is not only different social groupings and identities but also different political forces within the Left, and within the socialist movement, that have to learn to live together in constructive dialogue. Otherwise, the Right will continue to win all the crucial battles.

Notes

[1] Geoff Mulgan, 'The Power of the Weak', *Marxism Today*, October 1988 and in this book.

[2] Charlie Leadbeater, 'Power to the Person', *Marxism Today*, October 1988 and in this book.

Paul Hirst

After Henry

According to *Marxism Today* and the Communist Party we are now living in 'New Times' – in a post-Fordist era. The concepts of post-Fordism and postmodernism are used to suggest that the 1980s mark a decisive break with the economic and social patterns of this century. It is true that there have been major changes in the international economy and in manufacturing strategies since the early 1970s but the questions are whether post-Fordism is the best way to explain these changes, and whether Britain has shared fully in the changes in manufacturing organisation that have taken place in other parts of the advanced industrial world.

The post-Fordist idea is widespread, and it is not a *Marxism Today* exclusive. It is an amalgam of various intellectual sources, both marxist and non-marxist, and uses the ideas of Antonio Gramsci and the French 'Regulation School' in particular. Some of the most sophisticated users of post-Fordism, like Robin Murray, avoid its worst defects and incorporate some of the alternative views I shall advocate here. Post-Fordism starts from a characterisation of the preceding form of economic organisation. Henry Ford's name is used to sum up the great innovations in manufacturing introduced in the first two decades of this century: mass production seeking fully to exploit economies of scale and based upon assembly line methods, factories making standardised goods for homogeneous mass markets by means of specialised machinery and unskilled or semi-skilled labour. It was only when coupled with suitable macro-economic policies on the part of national governments that the Fordist system could exploit its full potential, and that the mass purchasing power to sustain mass production was assured. Fordism and Keynesianism together were responsible for the great postwar boom from 1945 to the oil price crises of

1973. Fordism led to a concentrated and relatively homogeneous male and full-time manual working class. The assembly line and a full-employment economy gave the manual industrial worker a central place in the labour force and also great political influence.

The collapse of the boom undermined the foundations of the Fordist era. The international economy after 1973 became both more interdependent and more volatile. Keynesian strategies were undermined both by inflation and the greater interpenetration of national economies. Unemployment rose, weakening the position of labour. Markets for industrial goods fragmented and differentiated. Manufacturers sought to respond to uncertainty by introducing flexibility in both working methods and labour markets, breaking with Fordism and segmenting the labour force into a permanent core and an unskilled, often female, part-time or casual periphery. Both market and social differentiation are the hallmarks of the new era, and with them go an orientation away from production toward consumption and the service sector, from collectivism toward individualism, and from substance toward style. A traditional socialist politics based on a homogeneous and mass working class is therefore irrelevant.

What is wrong with post-Fordism? To begin with it invokes a traditional marxist explanatory prejudice: that the features of the production system can be used to characterise the wider society. This has now slipped from rigid causal determinism into casual metaphor. Technological determinism is passé to modern marxists, but its consequences persist in seeing broad processes of social change in terms of a metaphor taken from industrial production like post-Fordism. This has consequences for the interpretation of change in manufacturing itself. The switch from Fordism to post-Fordism is seen as market-led, capitalist entrepreneurs of the classic type responding with new strategies to changed market conditions. In this account Fordism is the more coherent concept, whereas post-Fordism is less an idea of a coherent manufacturing system than a way of registering a bundle of reactive social and economic changes. Fordism is supposed to have prevailed throughout the industrial world — the USA serving as a model for others. Post-Fordism is likewise a phenomenon of the whole industrial world. It is identified as present in Britain less through the specific analysis of manufacturing than through its supposed wider economic and social effects, market and labour force differentiation. But what if British manufacturing methods and strategies have changed little? The problem is that the over-generalised metaphor, post-Fordism, while taken from the world of industrial organisation, is an inadequate means of *actually* analysing changes in manufacturing.

Fortunately a more rigorous and less generalised concept is available, one that applies directly to manufacturing strategy and one that is precise enough to approach the issue of whether Britain has succeeded in introducing the methods of her more successful industrial competitors. The concept in question is 'flexible specialisation', developed by Michael Piore and Charles Sabel to account for the new forms of manufacturing responding to the crisis of mass production.[1] Flexible specialisation is best defined as a technological paradigm or model of industrial efficiency: the manufacture of a range of specialised goods for particular and changing markets using flexible general-purpose machinery and predominantly skilled labour. The production units utilising this strategy can vary from multinational corporations to artisan workshops. Flexible specialisation is developed in contrast to another paradigm 'mass production' or the use of specialised machinery to produce standardised goods using predominantly unskilled labour. This concept is more specific than the concept of Fordism used by *Marxism Today*. It is restricted to an ideal type of a manufacturing process, and no attempt is made to directly derive or deduce wider social and political consequences from a particular type of production technique.

The use of the term 'paradigm' here is important and not just a fashionable affectation; it implies that changes in industrial organisation are a matter of *policy* and that they are not simply dictated by changing market conditions. Manufacturing organisation is not invariant and the immediate result of economic necessity, rather economic pressures are filtered through a process of choice, with complex conditions, that can best be thought of as *political*. Choices involve not just market conditions or financial calculation, not just the prevailing models of industrial organisation, but wider considerations made possible by the existence of certain institutions, by a social and regional context. Economic decisions are embedded in a context of institutions and it is the network of social relations surrounding the firm that is so often crucial to its performance.

Flexible specialisation can be developed in many social contexts. It is possible to demonstrate the social embeddedness of the flexible specialisation strategies of large firms, and Japan offers good examples but it is too complicated to cover here. A more apt illustration of the influence of social context on flexible specialisation strategy is the *industrial district*. Such districts are well-developed in those countries that have adapted successfully to the new conditions of international competition since 1973. The most quoted examples are Baden-Württenberg in West Germany and Emilia-Romagna in Italy.[2]

Industrial districts are organised in different ways but their most general characteristic is institutions which link firms into networks that combine both competition and co-operation. Firms develop ongoing relations with sub-contractors. Firms share work with one another. Firms co-operate in institutions linking public bodies and private enterprise in a common 'public sphere'. This provides valuable resources for the industry or region in question – collective services like research bureaux, common publicity or institutions for training labour. The important point is that the district provides firms with mutual support, and with resources that it is difficult for the individual firm to purchase directly in the market and which enhance its flexibility. There is no typical district nor is there one pattern of social organisation appropriate for flexible specialisation strategies on a regional scale. Sakaki in Japan is essentially an overgrown mountain village. It has evolved from a traditional peasant and artisan basis to a network of 300 units producing a range of advanced products by means of numerically controlled machine tools. In Bologna the Communist municipality co-operates directly and unashamedly with go-getting entrepreneurs. In Massachusetts the computer industry (non-unionised and fiercely competitive) created networks between firms through their executives' connections with the region's universities.

Post-Fordism pictures industrial change as market dictated, controlled by big capital and as leading to the dissolution of security for labour. Flexibility in this context means greater uncertainty and further loss of control for the majority of workers. Flexible specialisation, on the contrary, pictures change as less dictated by markets than directed by policy, involving a variety of economic agencies, and as by no means invariably bad for labour. Firms *anticipate* as well as respond to market changes and create new markets by developing new products. Flexible specialisation builds on regional institutions and legacies of labour skill that were not swamped by standardised mass production. Those regions that develop or preserve institutions of economic collaboration between industry and public bodies, and patterns of co-operation between firms, are often the most innovative in technology and work organisation. Firms can make rapid internal changes because they have a social environment that compensates for and cushions the negative effects of change and offers a measure of insurance against risk. Labour is by no means subordinated in a flexible specialisation strategy. Indeed, its position may be enhanced because the skilled utilisation of general purpose machinery demands both greater autonomy for the worker and greater trust between workers and management.

Marxism Today sees the post-Fordist society as highly fluid and rapidly changing, as more individualistic and more concerned with style than the supposedly highly organised, collectivistic and rigid social structures of Fordist industrialism. However, many of the industrial districts and regions that have adopted the new flexible specialisation forms of manufacturing organisation are anything but models of postmodernist social and cultural fluidity. Economic dynamism is often in fact linked with a deep social conservatism. Japan is the classic example. The Japanese re-invented their traditions on the ruins of 1945. They made the family and the firm the core institutions of the new social structure. The firm is considered a collectivity in which management and core workers share common membership and common goals. Japan is the last home of the Protestant Ethic and of a suffocatingly traditional 'bourgeois' family. But Japan is not an exception. Small town virtues, old-style familialism and deeply conservative social attitudes are also prevalent in the most successful regions of Italy and Germany. Change in manufacturing, far from causing change in the wider society, is often most effectively promoted in a context of relatively stable and supportive institutions.

To return more specifically to manufacturing organisation, the irony is that if we use the concept of flexible specialisation rather than post-Fordism, we find that Britain has not participated fully or very successfully in the new patterns of industrial organisation. Britain used to have industrial districts which still flourished in the 19th century – like Sheffield or south-east Lancashire.[3] Their remnants have been steadily broken up by take-overs, mergers and de-industrialisation. Not only are regional economies weakly differentiated in Britain, local political institutions and forms of local economic co-operation are weak too. The Conservative's assault on local government has not helped, but British local government has been ill-adapted to perform the role of the orchestrator of an industrial 'public sphere' in which firms, labour interests and the local state could collaborate to further business development. To many Labour local politicians the very idea would be anathema – working to enrich private firms? Fortunately the massive scale of local industrial decline has promoted a new pragmatism in certain areas, like the West Midlands. But, at that very moment, Conservative policy has struck at both local authority finance and local autonomy.

When one turns from districts to the industrial firms themselves, there is considerable evidence that British managements can neither fully exploit nor fully understand flexible specialisation strategies. Flexible manufacturing systems, automated processes capable of greatly enhancing both the virtuosity of labour and the variety of products, are run as if they were mass production dedicated machinery. British firms are still failing to develop on a wide scale interactive and ongoing relationships with sub-contractors based on trust and information sharing. Britain's shortages of skilled labour stemming from its inadequate and obsolete system of industrial training, and the persistence of hierarchical and authoritarian practices of managing workers, both contribute to undercutting the possibility of giving skilled workers greater antonomy, trusting them and engaging in dialogue with them, which is what the most advanced flexible specialisation strategies require.[4]

Macro-economic phenomena show up this micro-economic failure of British firms to match the strategies of their more successful foreign competitors. Since 1983 the balance of trade in manufactured goods has been negative – with a £10 billion deficit in 1987 and accelerating thereafter to perhaps £18 – 20 billion in 1989. The high propensity of Britain to import foreign consumer durables and the failure to hold a positive balance of trade in manufactures, that has existed since statistics began to be collected, shows that British industry has been able to respond neither quickly enough by expanding capacity, nor effectively enough by enhancing product quality to a booming home market. British exports remain highly sensitive to the value of the pound, which again shows that Britain cannot compete well enough in foreign markets on non-price terms.

The continuities of British manufacturing are as striking and revealing as the radical changes in the international economy and the change in the composition of the domestic labour force. The concept of post-Fordism finds it difficult to register these continuities, given its propensity to analyse Britain in terms of one world-wide and common process of change more or less directly enforced by changing market conditions. Flexible specialisation offers a more interesting account of the successful manufacturing adaptations to a changed international economy after 1973 but it also points sharply to the failure of Britain to adopt such strategies. The main reason for such failure lies in the social and institutional context.

Britain's relative failure in manufacturing is not due to some anti-industrial spirit. For ten years the government has energetically advocated an 'enterprise culture' and has sought to liberalise markets. But as the above analysis shows, successful manufacturing strategies do not directly stem from free market pressures. Flexible specialisation strategies depend on a context of institutions and non-market resources that are not amenable to a quick-fix solution at the level of the individual company. In pursuit of a free market strategy the Conservatives have weakened rather than strengthened the possibilities of co-operation between firms, unions and public bodies. They have not reformed industrial training to ensure an adequate supply of skilled labour. They have not promoted research and development. They have not encouraged collective services for industry, in particular for small and medium-sized firms. This neglect of the social fabric of an advanced industrial economy in the pursuit of an enterprise culture has made life, if anything, more difficult for the manufacturing sector and in particular it has done nothing to improve its access to low-cost finance for industrial investment. The wave of take-overs and mergers has further enhanced the domination of industrial firms by the financial sector. Talking in terms of 'New Times', accepting even in part the Conservatives' myth that they have engineered an economic miracle, is the last thing the Left should be doing.

In criticising manufacturing failure, the Left has a strong card against the free market philosophy of the government. Liberalising markets does not do the main thing claimed for it, promoting technical change and industrial investment. It reinforces the trend for economic actors to concentrate on those markets where short-term market and financial information is adequate for successful participation – markets in national currencies, commodities, equities and property. If the Left can begin to understand the social embeddedness of successful manufacturing strategies – the need for co-operation as well as competition and the need to build partnerships between companies and public bodies to enhance manufacturing performance – then it will begin to be able not only to criticise Conservative economic policy but to offer an alternative to it. That alternative is quite different from both economic liberalism and state socialism. We do need to rethink our political approaches to the changing economy but *Marxism Today*'s advocacy of 'New Times' and the use of the idea of post-Fordism will not help us. *Marxism Today* is good at challenging dogmatic and old-style socialism, but in coming close to celebrating Conservative economic success it offers the Left few weapons to challenge economic liberalism. The alternative offered by the concept of flexible specialisation does offer tools both for criticism and the development of new policies.

Notes

[1] M Piore and C Sabel, *The Second Industrial Divide*, Basic Books, New York 1984.

[2] For Japan see D Friedman, *The Misunderstood Miracle*, Cornell University Press 1988. Charles Sabel offers a broad survey of industrial districts in his contribution to P Hirst and J Zeitlin (eds), *Reversing Industrial Decline?*, Berg 1988.

[3] See J Zeitlin and C Sabel, 'Historical Alternatives to Mass Production', *Past and Present*, No. 108, 1985.

[4] These points are made in the contributions of B Jones, E Lorenz, A Campbell, W Currie and M Warner in P Hirst and J Zeitlin (eds), *Reversing Industrial Decline?* Berg 1988. We have further discussed the failure of the British manufacturing sector in Hirst and Zeitlin, 'Crisis, What Crisis?', *New Statesman*, 18 March 1988 and 'Flexible Specialisation and the Competitive Failure of UK Manufacturing', *The Political Quarterly*, Vol. 60, No. 2 1989.

V Political Culture

Sarah Benton

The Decline of the Party

The political party as we have known it is an anachronism. Out of all the tasks it is set there are only two it can carry out with any adequacy: it can contest elections and it can produce a caste of professional politicians to take part in the ritual of public affairs. People have expected so much more. But the party can rarely enforce democracy in government or civil life; where 'the private' advances, so the party's control of the state recedes. It does not usually emancipate its individual members; it is not a means through which people can exercise more choice in their lives or more control over their lives. It is not an 'authentic' voice of the people: the most common view of party politicians is that they lie. Far from standing for democracy for most people, the political party represents ritual tedium for the masses who, at worst, fear they are subjected to the professional exclusivity, fanaticism and manipulation of the few.

It is not surprising that political parties of the old sort are in decline all over Europe and North America. Only those that have changed their ways face the future with anticipation. In the countries of the communist bloc, the ossification of economic and cultural life has come to be synonymous with the rigidity of a monolithic party. As they experiment with power-sharing (Poland), *glasnost* (the USSR), or looser central control (Hungary), the only question is whether there is enough time for reform from the inside before the the demand for change will destroy the old party in a welter of new ethnic and regional citizenries.

The 'old parties' are those that were established by the 1920s. They differed from each other in ideology and social composition but they were all a response to two phenomena: the advent of the mass vote and the emergence of the all-powerful nation state. Each of these − the state and the mass vote −

shaped the development of the other through the medium of the party. The pacemakers were the mass parties with a formal ideology of socialism – including the fascists of Italy and the Nazis of Germany, both of which began, at least, with a rhetoric of power to the masses via the state, as of course did the communist parties. Unlike the upper class, with its access to many forms of power through the army (Prussia in particular), church (Italy), land (most of Eastern Europe), and business (Britain, Germany, USA), both the professional middle class and the then huge working class had access to power only through the state. Unlike the upper class, their only access to the state was through the party. The contemporary development of systems of mass production, especially in the USA, Germany and Britain, also shaped the mass vote and produced the potent imagery of the working class as a single, dynamic whole.

Even those who were dismayed by the dawn of the party age noted the exciting power of mass politics.

> All is hurry and agitation; night is used for travel, day for business, even 'holiday trips' have become a strain on the nervous system. Important political, industrial and financial crises carry excitement into far wider circles of people than they used to do; political life is engaged in quite generally; political, religious and social struggles, party politics, electioneering, and the enormous spread of trade-unionism inflame tempers, place an ever greater strain on the mind, and encroach upon the hours for recreation, sleep and rest.

(This is Freud in 1893 quoting a contemporary in *'Civilised' Sexual Morality*. Both are trying to explain the mass outbreak of nervous illness. Freud demurs on just one point in this account of modern life: it omits the injurious influences on sexuality.)

The catastrophic failure of capitalism after the first world war ensured that the mass parties represented the best claim to manage the future. With the dereliction of mass unemployment, only a greatly enlarged role for the state could produce balance, stability and social equity. To socialists of all sorts this was so obvious it was just common sense. Where social democrats diverged from communists and fascists was in their pursuit of a state that would be invulnerable to demagogues and the mob.

It was their parties that took the lead in shaping modern politics. In the name of delivering power to the people, socialist parties from the 1930s, and particularly after the second world war, treated politics as a profession and reforming society as a matter of good management. The crunch came in the 1950s; those governments which had ceded fewest political rights in civil society, for workers or consumers for instance, found themselves the most stultified. They produced a form of government which cannot regenerate its own political drive, whether it was the Soviet Union's 'era of stagnation' or Britain's Labour Party. Labour's first postwar government survived just six years, defeated less by a newly triumphant conservatism than by its own internal exhaustion. In this inability to regenerate itself, postwar British socialism has been different from most West European countries. It has had fewer roots in essentially heterogeneous communities, which in turn have had less political autonomy from the state. It is no accident that the British Left, especially the Labour Party, has responded by a bitter turning inwards.

While the Left pursued professionalism, the Right, especially in Britain, still offered up amateurs. (Indeed *the form* of British political government is still a sham anachronism of monarchy in collaboration with amateurs. Its members of parliament in both Commons and Lords are notionally, and, in the case of many Tories, actually, part-time.) Through much of Europe after the war, the Right resisted socialism's claims in the name of small 'c' conservatism, and a long-drawn out nostalgia for the images of empire and supposed social harmony of the pre-party era. It was the inability of conservatism in the 1960s to face the modern world, as much as Labour's claims that it was the modern world, which brought in Wilson's government − and obviated the need for a radical rethink about the party.

For Wilson had brilliantly mastered the images of an anachronistic, anti-democratic Conservativism in contrast with 'scientific', productive socialism. His denunciation of the Tories for choosing a peer, Lord Home, as their leader in 1963, said it all: instead of the democratic party, he jeered, the Tories had used an 'aristocratic cabal'. 'After half a century of democratic advance, of social revolution, of rising expectations, the whole process has ground to a halt with a fourteenth earl. How can this 'scion of an effete establishment', he demanded, 'lead the scientific revolution and mobilisation of the skill and talents of all our people in the struggle to restore Britain's position in the world?' If that accurately represented the Tories' deferral of tomorrow's world, it also disguised how the deferral allowed

Labour to speak for a winning alliance without any serious rethinking. Only the emergence in the 1970s of a New Right which claimed to represent the future scuttled conservative nostalgia, replacing it with a contempt for the immediate past and a curious silence about the heyday of the mass party. It was as though their party had no history.

Images of the Party

Today's Right is quite right to recognise that an era was ending in the 1960s. Before 1950 it was still possible to conceive of the political party as the 'modern prince' − modern because the collective agency of party had superseded the mediaeval individual leader, but a prince nonetheless, an heroic entity. This romantic conception of party endured until the 1960s; it nestled even in the most prosaic bosom of British Labour. For instance, Francis Williams, a true Labour loyalist, friend of Clem Attlee and former editor of the *Daily Herald* describes the birth of the Labour Party (*Fifty Years March, The Rise of the Labour Party*) in this way:

> And now, on that February morning in 1900, the curtain was rising on a new act in this tremendous drama ...The Party born on that grey February day in a drab commercial street off Fleet Street was to ... mobilise behind it and become the chief instrument of a political uprising of the working-classes of Britain that was to change the social and economic face of the country out of all recognition ...

This hero would go on to carry through 'a programme which would have seemed the wildest and most revolutionary utopianism to those passing along Farringdon Street about their ordinary business on that February day in the first year of the new century'.

Romantic? Undoubtedly. Francis Williams was writing in 1950. A dip into any account of politics between 1890 and 1920 will come up with even more stirring stuff. Thus (and quite randomly), a Mr Pickles urging political unity at the Co-operative Movement in 1917:

> I am attending meetings one night as a Socialist, another as a trade unionist, and another as a member of a co-operative board, but I am working for democracy in sections ... Let us put all our cards on the table, stand together, and go forward for democracy − (applause) − triumphant democracy.

His rallying cry was for party unity – but he spoke too for the unity of the masses who made the party. The hero of modernist imagery in the 1920s and 1930s was, if not the mass itself, an anonymous worker, individual in statuesque form but not in character.

Like a prince of old, the party demanded loyalty, inspired love and devotion, promised delivery from evil, fought battles on behalf of the needy, brought nobility into the grey, drab lives of the many. Because it was a collective, it also exacted discipline and demanded sacrifice. It would not have been heroic had it not. (The forms and imagery of the military were never very far away either.) And if the party was an heroic warrior, so too were the people. The party was the people, they and it were a single whole.

Nobody today regards the party in this way. Lingering romantics see it as having been 'corrupted' by power or betrayed by weak, susceptible men, while the working class retains its character as a martyred unity. A recent study of modern democracy pays fulsome tribute to democratic party systems as 'an early modern invention of bold and pathbreaking dimensions' but acknowledges that 'the reality of the compromise party falls dismally short of the ideal of democratic party competition' (John Keane, *Democracy and Civil Society*). For others, the loss of illusion is just part of the modern condition. The loss of faith is in the party, in the state, in politics itself – and in the masses. To read today the futurists quoted by Marshall Berman (*All That is Solid*) – 'We will sing of great crowds excited by work, by pleasure and by riot; we will sing of the multicolored, polyphonic tides of revolution in the modern capitals.' – is to know we live in a different era.

Today we do not believe that the mass can be made into a single, heroic whole by a political party. As Marshall Berman notes, a distinctive feature of today's modernity is the sense of fragmentation, accompanied by a generalised loss of meaning. The 'New Times', argued Stuart Hall in *Marxism Today* (October 1988, see *The Meaning of New Times*, in this book) are characterised thus: 'greater fragmentation and pluralism, the weakening of older collective solidarities and block identities and the emergence of new identities associated with greater work flexibility, the maximisation of individual choices through personal consumption.' Not only is the whole fragmented, so is the 'self' too. The Co-op's Mr Pickles in 1917 perhaps felt the same; unlike us, with our kaleidoscopic selves, he felt all could be made whole by the party. He felt his individual, sensate self should be lost in the party surge to democracy.

Our conceptions of party, and of democracy, have not been brought into line with this new reality of multiple selves who can no longer be marshalled into one mass party with a single aim: to win control of an all-embracing state. The attempts by party leaders to reshape their parties as both professional élites and purveyors of popular political culture are jagged with these contradictions. In January 1989 the Labour Party launched a campaign to double its membership. Neil Kinnock insisted that they faced no political obstacles, only administrative blocks. Yet the Tribune Group pamphlet, *A Mass Party*, homes in on the need to create a new political culture, in the party and society at large. Paddy Ashdown, leader of the SLD, measures his party's claim to replace Labour in membership figures. Yet his new party, under tremendous pressure to produce its first professional élite able to move with the media times, is disconsolate as the hold-true Liberals turn their back on professionalism to haunt the old/new community politics.

Only the Conservatives appeared to have no qualms. Peter Brooke, the then Conservative Party chairman, launched their recruitment campaign in June 1988; but they were quite clear about their aims; more members meant more money and the next generation of a professional élite (see Sarah Benton, *New Statesman and Society*, September 1988). Their political culture, of garden parties for the women and clubs for businessmen, seemed quite sufficient for their needs. Yet this, so resilient a political culture when protected by its cocoon of Englishness, is finding its limits in its very Little Englandism. When Tory discontent focuses on its chairman rather than its leader, this is not just a displacement of its real anxiety; it also marks an awareness that the form of the party may not be up to conquering the foreign terrain of Wales and Scotland. Yet alone Brussels and Strasbourg.

Amongst the traditional parties, the crisis of purpose runs deep. What are all these members for? If party members are the cadres of a political mission, what exactly is that mission? For the old form of party is an anachronism not only because it's the wrong shape, not only because we no longer come in just two or three classes, but because so much power has been shifted out of the state machinery which the party was shaped to control.

Parties and Power

The desultory connections of people, party, parliament and state are common to many countries. They are testament to the disappearance of power; like the Scarlet Pimpernel, political power no longer has a fixed, visible locus. It is not found firmly in the British state and certainly not the British parliament; it is not tucked in the pockets of MI5 pursuing its paranoid fantasies through our keyholes nor is it filed in the cabinets of Luxembourg or Brussels. It is not floating in a silicon valley or sitting snugly in the IMF, Group of 7, the headquarters of Coca Cola, amongst Italian freemasons circling the Vatican or in the safe of a mighty arms manufacturer.

It's in all those places and none, here, there and nowhere. There is no single citadel to be captured, no commanding height which, once scaled, gives a political party power over the civic universe. As the fragments of power whirl frustratingly in and out of vision, conspiracy theories multiply. Many of them are correct; there are indeed conspiracies hatched and carried out by private companies, shady networks of military and commercial interests, the state's secret underworld. Some do considerable damage; all are anti-democratic. Never dismiss a good conspiracy when one is hauled into the daylight. But do not either attribute to it a Boys' Own capacity to rule the world through its secretly acquired powers. The world's not like that. If political power cannot be delivered by simple control over the nation state, then the form and function of parties, designed to win such control, have to change if they are to survive.

It is for this reason, as much as the changing sociology of class relations, that the Conservatives were the dominant power in the 1980s. Their rhetoric of rolling back the frontiers of the state acknowledged the limits of the state. This is not because the Thatcherites were immensely more percipient than socialists; rather it was because Conservatives have never been as dependent on state powers to get what they want. They thus had a freedom of manoeuvre denied to parties of the Left. The fact that much of what constitutes 'Thatcherism' has been, as in earlier Conservative eras, an ad hoc response to circumstances is clear. In *Popular Capitalism* (1988), John Redwood, a tipped-for-the-top MP who once worked in Thatcher's policy unit as well as Rothschild's privatisation unit, describes how accidentally they arrived at privatisation. The strategy that became the driving force of Thatcherism was not planned but stumbled upon. And Thatcherites were confident that this was destined to become the hegemonic force throughout the capitalist world.

But Thatcherism assailed the state *in the name of the nation*; for fifteen years Mrs Thatcher's story has been that the 'spirit of Britain' will become great again by destroying the shackles of the state. This contradiction which she set up is now threatening to fracture the Conservative Party, a body of people whom she dubbed the embodiment of the spirit of Britain. Thatcherism, and the British spirit, must be the leading force, the dominant ideology, or it is nothing. It becomes empty if it is merely one country amongst equals. Capitalism can flourish in a European polity of compromise and corporatism and state regulation. Right-wing parties which accept this strategy in a European parliament can survive. Thatcherism, as an ideology of superior nationhood, cannot. Thatcherism was the adaptation of Conservatism to a specific British opportunity, of exercising political power without having to check private capital. It has been blocked less by a renewal of Labour as the party of the nation state, than by Thatcherism's own imprisonment within a nation state when the forces it is trying to control have broken those bounds.

In contrast, Labour saw the national interest as being a compromise of the classes managed by the state. The party's task was to capture the machinery of the state where, it was convinced, national political power resided. This was the common pattern of social democracy throughout Europe. Though the diminution of national political power has been a cause of social-democratic decline throughout Europe, it has been particularly acute in Britain. Only here has the Labour Party proposed such an extensive, and formal, role for trade unions in operating the machinery of state. Whereas in Italy or Scandinavia the party spoke for the class in the institutions of state, in Britain the trade unions spoke for themselves, leaving the party to validate their actions. In no other country have union, party and state been tied together so intractably in what became a deadening mission to create a bureaucratic corporate state.

Labour's Reforms

Given the recent history of the Labour Party, it seems absurd to suggest it has not changed its form, or that it has failed to look self-critically at how it works. The political crisis of the 1970s, which split virtually every party on the Left, produced the most protracted drive to change Labour's structure in the party's history. Its successes came from an energetic drive for democracy and against domination by the old labourist officials; its weaknesses from the conversion of demands for democracy into a punitive war against betrayal conducted in an increasingly suffocating political vacuum.

The immediate results are well known. Led for the most part by the Campaign for Labour Party Democracy, with allies in the Labour Co-ordinating Committee and most of the left-wing groups, the party introduced the right of constituency parties to re-select their MPs and, in a desperate juggling manoeuvre, to keep its by now fractious parts together, an electoral college for the party leader and deputy. The focus on internal party change continued through the 1980s. For the first half of the decade it was dominated by two demands which were tactically linked, though had little connection in principle. The first was for leaders' accountability, the second for representation of modern communities.

The drive to reform provoked the most long-drawn out turbulence in party form and allegiances in modern Britain. The Social Democratic Party broke away not, contrary to its later mythology, because of policy differences, but because of the form of the party which, they thought, took power away from the professionals in parliament. It constituted itself under the proud banner of creating a new form of politics; its watchwords were modernity and breaking the mould. The efforts to create a centre-left 'of a new type' failed because no political form could be devised which delivered both professionalism and community populism. Nor could the merged Liberals and Social Democrats deliver both the new and the historic continuity which gave party members their sense of political identity. The difficulty of finding a political form came not least from the inability of these parties to define where they thought political power lay. Electors felt the SLD was adequate for the little political powers of neighbourhood and county; but not for national or international powers.

The failure to remake the centre of British politics allowed the Right and soft Left of the Labour Party to unite in a programme of renewal that isolated the Left. It was helped by the Left's own presentation of itself in the decade as a victim of a witchhunt. The tradition of distrust of all leaders surged to the top to dominate its political culture. But this bitterness came also from the barely articulated recognition that political power was escaping from the party. Only by tightening the screws might some hold be kept on it. This left the Left claiming for itself the distinction of defending the past against betrayers. It was not a basis from which a campaign to renew the Labour Party could be launched.

The demand for representation by the new political identities of race and sex acknowledged the shift of social and political power; class was no longer the single embodiment of oppressors and oppressed. Just as the power of the state lost its central locus, so power in society had fractured. The one-time unity of the working class had been a unity imposed by the dominance of the skilled, white male worker. His authority at work, in the union, at home was under threat from all sides.

The new, informal constituencies of women and blacks could bring fresh life when the old bureaucracies of union and party officials could not. But the desperation to secure political representation divorced from any political programmes on race or sex was a mark of the wholly formal, empty quality of the politics.

And it is precisely here that we see the fateful inadaptability of party forms to modern life. The activist, preoccupied with council affairs or resolutions to party committees, became increasingly remote from life outside the party. And the further away real power seemed from the Labour Party, the more ferocious became the demands that its symbolic form be redistributed round the members. As the state receded as a focus for political demands, the party expanded to fill the space.

Movements

Labour is not alone. No party in Europe based on domestic working-class movements alone is expanding. All social democratic parties have been profoundly influenced by the movement politics of the 1960s and 1970s, but none has been the direct inheritor of these ideas and people. What is frightening the Right even more than the old Left is that a multiplicity of new political identities is moving into the space left by the shrinkage of two-party politics. From the tiny party of Lombardian shopkeepers to the mass West German Greens, via a welter of progressive and reactionary groupings, the ability of any political party to get a grip on political power seems in doubt.

Does this matter? Is this not, after all, the flowering of the movements which seemed to be Western Europe's only hope of political renewal in the 1970s? Unlike the party, harnessed to the needs of the state, the movement was truly 'modern'. It rejected class as a determinant of individual political choice. It sought to eliminate the gap between personal feeling and public action. The liberation of the political actors was as important as, if not more important than, the conquest of opponents. The movement rejected institutions for itself, as these would tend to freeze political positions and embed conflicts to win control. It upheld direct action both as a form of self-expression and as more effective than formal political procedures. The movement was oriented towards action, but changing culture and attitudes were goals as legitimate as law reform. Here its modernism lay in its rejection of the idea that there is a single oppressed people or a single source of authority to be undermined or of power to be captured.

Most of these ideas were common to the black movement, the women's movement, the gay movement and later the green and peace movements and, to a limited extent, those disabled by injury, illness or addiction. They have in common the fact that their potential membership is circumscribed, and their goals are not universal. In this, they differ from parties.

Nationalist movements, now so powerful as the agency against Communist Party *ancien régimes*, as well as the British party *ancien régime*, differ again. Though they share the emphasis on culture and speak the language of liberation and radical change, they have powerful roots in old traditions of masculinity, land and family honour, all of which bind together dominant racial communities. They look backwards to an old brotherhood as well as forward to a new democracy. For every nationalist movement which, like Plaid Cymru, has allied itself with an egalitarian and liberating ideology, there are two which speak a rhetoric of hostility to outsiders, of blood and fatherland. In Eastern Europe some nationalist movements, like the Latvians, have spoken the language of the French revolution. Others have asserted blood brotherhoods, as in Serbia, Uzbekistan and Azerbaijan, their rise accompanied by reports of mass violence and rape.

Green parties in all countries have attempted to be 'parties of a new type' and to a considerable extent they have succeeded. Their structures are much looser and, in particular, they acknowledge the 'person' in politics. From its inception as a po-faced very English Ecology Party in the 1970s, the British Green Party has borrowed most from movements and from abroad; its conference now falls over itself to help members feel themselves, so to speak. Like movements, green parties expect individual members to embody political principles in their personal life. In West Germany in particular. Die Grunen were the inheritors of the anti-party, 'alternative' movement of the 1960s and 1970s.

These trends are a direct result of the movement ethos, which sought to dissolve the barrier between public and private principles. There is the same stress on authenticity; only that which comes direct from the self, the author, has validity. The SDP, in its early days when feminism was a strong influence, demonstrated its modernity by establishing 'networks' to encourage women's participation. But, in opposition to the Liberals especially, it also raged against 'old-fashioned' sloppiness. New practices were designed as much to create a professional élite as to dissolve the gulf between professional and amateur in politics. The requirements of power and the exigencies of size both count against new forms. The larger and more established the West German Greens have become, the harder it has been for them to maintain their ethos of an open democracy. The more urgently the times seek out the British Greens to be their vanguard, the more stress and strain will be placed on their movement-style party. As CND found, the price of success is the creation of a professional élite.

We should not be romantic about movements. While Geoff Mulgan (see 'The Power of the Weak', in this book) is right to commend the openness and resilience of movement networks, he slides over the actual political weakness of 'weak' structures, in particular, their inability to change the state. Many of those we still refer to as the 'new movements', as representing the spirit of a new age, have lost their élan and cohesion. Their values survive, networks have proved resilient and most of the participants still hold strongly to the tenets of the movement. But the mood is of consolidation and solace, rather than advance.

There have been successes. All the 'new' movements achieved lasting changes in awareness. They have been truly liberating. They have changed the lives of the direct participants and of those around them. They have given a political voice to those who would otherwise be silent. They have all challenged the conventions of politics. Movements have been the main agents in exposing the anachronistic structures of party politics.

New Forms

Parties are not, of course, going to wither away. How then can the party be changed so that is a positive agent for freedom and democracy? How can parties aim both to win state power and to act independently of the state, as voices of the people? How can national parties play a representative role in the remote forum of Strasbourg?

The re-formation of parties is going to accompany the re-formation of national, regional and ethnic identities. The nation state is seen to be both too oppressive of 'marginal' communities, and too puny to take on international capitalism and environmental destruction. Different political forms for different layers of political power will emerge. The person who votes for the same party at every election, perceiving political power as homogeneous, will become rarer. Local campaigns, racial and ethnic oppressions and backlashes, regional demands, national governments, international concerns, are likely to produce a multifarious voting habit. This will be no more than an accurate political perception that the nation state does not embody total political power.

In what form then can the national political party survive? How can it expand to take on new responsibilities and identities as a transnational party and at the same time cut itself up to represent various new local and regional demands? The short answer is that it can't; that the reshaping of politics for new times is just beginning, rather than having come to an end with the decline of the British centre parties. This is because we are only just entering the new era in which the nation state is being superseded by the new political institutions of Europe, and of regions and nations within the nation state. We are not talking about how the Labour Party can recapture its old form. We are talking about whether Labour can gain a new authority by its ability to transcend the confines of the nation state.

If it does, will this increase its remoteness from those trapped inside the narrow confines of street and estate, for whom Strasbourg might as well be on the moon? If the activists flock to European politics, 'Britain' will be claimed by the ugliest, most xenophobic voices of street and football ground.

The dangers of that are very real. The hope for the survival of democratic political culture in Britain depends on a pincer movement. Political and economic rights have to be enforced nationally. Political and social identities have to be spoken for locally. The party can only play a role in both these movements if new political forums are established. There are some signs in Labour's policy review that it recognises this need. It has committed itself to constitutional reform and decentralisation, to consumer power and user groups. Whether it has the leadership to begin to effect this transfer of power is in doubt. It should not doubt the urgency of the need to champion new forms of democracy. Neither it, nor a progressive popular culture, can survive without them.

Geoff Mulgan

The Power of the Weak

Soft and weak overcome hard and strong
Tao Te Ching, 36

Engineering theory describes two types of control: strong power and weak power controls. Strong power controls use large quantities of energy relative to the processes they control, while weak power controls use very little. Most manual labour and most mechanical machines depend on strong power forms of control. The human brain by contrast is an example of a weak power control, using much less energy than the body it controls. Unlike the machinery of the Fordist production line, most of the machinery of post-Fordism uses weak power controls: the central processing unit of an automated factory, the chips that run a washing machine and the networks that control invoicing, warehouses or flows of accounting data all use much less energy, both physical and human, than the systems they replace. The weak power controls of post-Fordism also share one other characteristic with the human brain, their flexibility and adaptability: control can be quickly and easily reprogrammed through software. In this they reflect the essential properties of the computer, designed as the universal machine that could copy any other.

   This article argues that the replacement of strong power by weak power controls in the physical machinery of post-Fordism is being matched by a parallel transformation of social organisation and control, a transformation that is also one from strong to weak types of control. Like any deep structural change this one presents both threats and opportunities. Being able to use it as an opportunity depends on an understanding of its character. The argument developed here seeks to do this by analysing the changing nature of control in the advanced sectors of the economy, in political movements and in the state; the aim is to show not only that weak power structures usually work better than strong power ones but also that they are in many ways closer to the spirit of socialism and democracy. Though a discussion about structures, the argument is also about the escape from structure, and from the tendency to give too much weight to the formal lines of power, democracy and accountability.

Fordism was in many ways the apotheosis of faith in structure and strong power control. Within its organisations authority derives from position rather than from knowledge or ability. Formal rules determine how decisions are to be made and responsibility allocated. Structured as a pyramid, the organisation depends on vertical lines of authority and accountability. Control absorbs a lot of time and energy. Most communication is vertical, between superiors and subordinates, rather than horizontal. It is built around the bureaucracy, which developed in its modern form in the 19th century and was modelled on the armies' strong power command-and-control structure. As anyone who has worked in a large bureaucracy knows, most of its energy is used simply reproducing itself. The same is true of the classic modern corporation, dictatorial, hierarchical and bound by a rigid division of labour. Both aim to bring predictability and order to a chaotic world. As a result neither leaves much scope for initiative, imagination or autonomy.

The weak power structures of the new times are very different. They tend to be decentralised, without a single point of leadership; communication is horizontal; structures are cellular rather than pyramid-like, a shifting mosaic rather than the kind of structure that can be drawn as a diagram. The units and cells tend to regulate themselves, rather than being governed by rules and commands that flow downwards. Accountability can flow in more than one direction at once. Where the strong power structure is concerned with predictability, the best weak power structures thrive on fluidity, change and the creative use of chaos. Above all energies are directed outwards rather than inwards to sustaining and reproducing a fixed structure.

The distinction between the strong power systems of Fordism and weak power structures of the new times has obvious implications for the socialist project at the end of the 20th century. Like most of the really compelling utopian visions, Marx's communism was a vision of great autonomy, in which the individual's creative control over his or her own life is reconciled with the common needs of the community. In theory the state was to wither away, to be concerned only with the 'administration of things', a light layer of co-ordination over an organic, self-regulating society. In practice, however, socialism has been associated with strong power structures − with the bureaucratic public institution, the central plan, the hierarchical trade union and party, organised as layer upon layer of committees and officials − structures that leave almost as little scope for autonomous control as the Fordist corporation. Democracy in socialist traditions has also usually been conceived in terms of pyramid-like, vertically layered structures. Moreover what we are brought up to see as the highest form of politics, the face to face meeting, the direct democratic control of the athenian agora or the branch meeting is also a strong power structure, using prodigious amounts of time and energy relative to the things that are the subjects of its decisions. This is why periods of intense politicisation tend to be short, why pure democracies often degenerate into control by self-appointed cliques, and why Oscar Wilde said that socialism would never come because there are not enough evenings in the week.

Though weak power structures have a long history in socialist thought, in co-operatives, mutual aid organisations and guilds, and more recently in the traditions of 1968 and the new movements, it is on the leading edges of capitalism that they are now developing most quickly. During the recession of the late 1970s and early 1980s, many transnational corporations found themselves too unwieldy and inflexible for the environment in which they had to work. The failings of Ford's global car strategy, an attempt to create worldwide strong power structures around common designs, are well-known. The economic pressures of intensified competition, of a more internationalised and volatile economy, protected by fewer regulations and barriers, engendered a forced march of organisational experiment in search of the elusive key to sustainable competitiveness. The intellectual labour of a small army of management consultants, business schools, think-tanks, theorists and corporate strategists, was mobilised to answer the question of how structures could be re-ordered to improve productivity and efficiency.

The result has been a widespread conversion to the virtues of more flexible, weak power structures. Central to this view is a sense of the growing importance of creativity and knowledge in advanced economies: in new sectors such as biotechnology or artificial intelligence, knowledge, creativity and imagination become as important to economic success as narrowly conceived efficiency. The organisational problem is to mobilise people's commitment and mental powers rather than to exploit them more intensively. Though pyramidal bureaucracies are very good at implementing a given set of rules, they are strikingly ill-suited to creation and innovation, discouraging the kinds of risk and radical thought that produce the most lucrative values in a knowledge-based economy.

Traditions of cultural production offer more suitable models: artists are left to themselves because they produce better art that way. The same is true of the inventor or designer. Their managers and paymasters can only have a limited understanding of what they do and must leave to them the job of organising their own work. Rather than issuing a stream of commands like the army general or the manager of a traditional factory, managers become more like the conductor of an orchestra, or the publishing editor, a co-ordinator of groups with specialised skills. A degree of control is ceded so as to improve the quality of what is produced. Looser structures of this kind work better at encouraging risk and innovation and at spreading knowledge. The pre-eminent centres of high technology production such as Silicon Valley and Route 128 around Boston operate like networks, linking groups of inventors, entrepreneurs, academics and investors, in a form of industrial district that is quite distinct from the Detroit of General Motors or Ford, or the classic corporations that produced steel, chemicals or ships. Even IBM, the dominant corporation in the information industry and a famously 'tight' organisation, has experimented by creating weak power, network structures within itself, with quasi-independent units in fields such as medical instruments and robotics: the aim is to to emulate something of the hot-house looseness of Silicon Valley while maintaining tight central oversight.

Though weak power structures are most apparent in leading-edge sectors, they are also spreading throughout the economy as all firms take on some of the characteristics of knowledge producers. Around half the value of a car or aeroplane is accounted for by electronics and computers. The design of a product, even a piece of furniture or clothing, is an informational task, and the quality of this design has come to be seen as a more important source of competitive advantage than low costs of production. This emphasis on the informational content of products is reflected in organisational structures. Many large firms, both in the advanced sectors and more generally, are taking on the character of networks of independent units, often organised as profit centres, able to choose whether to co-operate with other units of the same firm and able to take their own initiatives. There is also more collaboration across company boundaries whether in the form of the joint venture, the licensing agreement or the intercorporate network linking suppliers and distributors. Small firms are moving in a similar direction, organising loose federations, marketing and research co-operatives, or joint training projects, often in collaboration with local government and academic institutions. Communication in all directions is both more intensive and extensive, a sometimes confusing mix of competition and co-operation.

The strong power structures of Fordism were held together by discipline and the contract. In the faustian compacts of Ford and Taylor the worker traded autonomy for the wage packet; in the factory every task was specified in detail, every deviation punished. The same was true of relationships with other firms, where contracts sought to cover any possible outcome and where price competition acted as a ruthless discipline. Within weak power structures there are very different kinds of bond. Within the firm, ethos, self-esteem and peer pressure are emphasised. Corporate ideology takes on a new significance, demanding loyalty and devotion from the worker, so that discipline is internalised within the worker's own conscience. It is no coincidence that investment in corporate television has in recent years come to match investment in the communications networks used to oversee flows of goods and money. Soft control has become as important as hard control.

Within networks of firms the experience of working together and the accumulation of trust come to replace explicit controls. Long-term relationships become more important than short-term profit. This is the essence of the successful joint venture or industrial district: companies learn to co-operate, to share ideas and contracts. Designers, researchers and inventors meet and argue in cafes, pubs and restaurants, creating a milieu of social creativity from which all benefit. Universities, source of the raw materials of the knowledge industries, become 'like the corner cafe where artisans solve one another's problems and share − or steal − one another's ideas'. Sociability has taken on an economic value in the era of post-Fordism, something recognised by the many governments trying to create synthetically sociable environments to foster science and innovation in such diverse places as Phoenix Arizona, Sophia Antipolis in Southern France, Novo-Sibirsk in the USSR and Kyushu in Japan. Japan's ambitious Technopolis project, aimed at creating nineteen futuristic knowledge cities under the aegis of academia, industry and local government, is probably the purest example of this.

A similar pattern can be seen in the plethora of new, semi-public bodies springing up around computing, once thought of as the most chronically entrepreneurial and competitive of all industries: Sematech, MCC and COS in the US, Esprit, Alvey and JESSI in Europe, are all semi-public programmes and institutions within which companies learn to co-operate and compete at the same time.

These practices are reflected in theory. The dominant business theories of the late 1980s, popularised in the writings of John Naisbitt, Waters and Peterman, Rosabeth Moss Kantor and Shoshana Zuboff, are awash with ideas that seem like pale echoes of 1968 (and indeed the 1840s), stressing the virtues of relative equality, of network forms, of creativity, the abolition of hierarchy, and the definition of work as play. It is easy to be cynical about capitalism's ability to co-opt the counter-culture, and it is certainly true that these ideas often play the role of ideology in its pure sense, systematic distortions that mask the real play of power. But it would be quite wrong to ignore the basic insights they offer. Most important perhaps is the sense that the authoritarian, vertical, corporation is beginning to outlive its usefulness: dictatorial organisation may still work in assembly plants and supermarkets, but it is inefficient in research and development or in the production of such things as semiconductors and cars. If people are treated like things they will behave like things, unwilling to care about what they produce, or to use their intelligence to solve the problems that inevitably arise. This is one of the striking features of the experience of automation. Automation seemed to offer the ultimate form of Fordism, an electronic guarantee of total control from the top. Instead it has turned out to depend on highly motivated, highly skilled workers able to continually reprogramme machines; computer aided design, manufacture and engineering (CAD/CAM/CAE) cannot be imposed from on top but rather depend on the permanent collaboration of teams working on design, production engineering and production itself.

These experiences of automation point to the second factor underlying the move towards weak power structures: the properties of new communications technologies. These properties are not as straightforward as they at first seem. In principle any communication technology can be used to tighten centralised control. The telephone strengthened the central office, while the computer network allows it instantly to monitor sales in shops or the output of factories. The Polish economist Oskar Lange believed that the computer could solve all the problems of socialist central planning, monitoring every detail of economic activity at the centre so as to perfectly match supply and demand. In practice however, technology runs up against the context in which information is produced. Within pyramidal structures those lower down usually have good reason to distort the information they give to their superiors, an experience common to East European central planning and Western multinationals. Manipulating information to magnify successes, hide failures or bid for resources, is about the only means available for negotiating control with superiors.

Communications technologies have a paradoxical effect in this respect: their potential cannot be realised unless people have an incentive to provide good information (on the GIGO, garbage in, garbage out, principle). As a result, even when brought in to centralise control they often turn out to bring a devolution of power and responsibility in their wake. This points to a more general feature of the post-Fordist economy: each investment in communications technology brings a reappraisal of how control is organised. The inherent flexibility of computerised systems means that the revolution in the means of production described by Marx has been joined by a permanent revolution in techniques of control. Change and flux come to be accepted as normal rather than being seen as destabilising threats, while structures come to be seen as inherently malleable.

Communications technologies can also be used to undermine strong power pyramids more directly. Within a few years of its invention it was recognised that the telephone could subvert hierarchies, making it possible for the chief executive to speak directly to the foreman and vice-versa. As networks carry more information, not just conversations but also data about accounts, patents and market research findings, pyramid structures dissolve from within. The traditional role of middle management was that of a relayer of commands and information. Commands were relayed downwards, while information about what was happening on the shop floor or in the office was relayed upwards in the form of written reports. With advanced networks, the LANs (local area networks) and private ISDNs (integrated services digital networks), these functions become redundant: specialised units can communicate horizontally, overseen by much slimmer top managements which themselves have instant access to data from the shop-floor. Decisions can be decentralised precisely because central oversight is easier; once decentralised their quality often improves because they are made by people familiar with the complexities of the situation. Again, good control depends on knowing when it needs to be loosened. This is not a new insight. In the 18th century the Empress Maria Theresa even awarded a special medal to officers who turned the tide in battle by disobeying orders, an unusual example of an autocrat encouraging insubordination.

Weak and Strong Power in Politics

The combined effect of new technologies and new attitudes has yet to have anything like the same impact on other areas of social life: political parties and voluntary organisations are only just beginning to think about how the networking of computers allows them to rethink their organisational structures. But the more general move to weak power structures is already apparent. Awareness of the economic inefficiency of strong power structures is matched by a growing awareness of their inefficiency in politics. Where the economic organisation is concerned with productivity and profit, the effective political organisation is the one that can respond to its constituency, successfully articulating alternatives and mobilising energies for campaigns. It is the inability of political parties, unions and single issue movements to be efficient in this sense that has prompted a new interest in more flexible weak power structures. Many of these echo older models: the corresponding societies of 18th-century Britain, radical religious movements, co-operative and mutual aid organisations were often organised as what we would now call networks, polycephalous or many-headed, without fixed rules, bound together horizontally and by common beliefs. Weak power structures have also often co-existed with strong power ones, albeit uneasily: the shop stewards movement with the trade-union bureaucracy, the guerrilla cells with the party in exile. Over the last fifty years however it has been the strong power structures that have generally predominated: Fordism in the economy was precisely replicated by the most successful social-democratic and communist parties.

The era of strong power political institutions may now be coming to an end, at least in the advanced industrialised countries. Their weaknesses have long been apparent. Like the Fordist corporation, the 'Fordist' parties have proved ill-equipped to exploit the opportunities offered by crisis and chaos. On both Left and Right the parties have become the rather sluggish mediums for change and new ideas rather than their instigators. In the 1980s, more than ever, it is the weak power structures that seem most in tune with the times, the most creative and the most effective at mobilising new energies. Obvious examples include the women's and peace movements which have usually been organised as horizontal networks, without the need for a single programme, a single leadership, a hierarchy of officials and committees. Instead communication is horizontal, a continually negotiated relationship between autonomous groups bound together by shared ideas and values rather than a single structure. The same is true of the New Right: the ideas and programmes of Thatcherism and Reaganism were generated not within political parties but by a loose web of think-tanks, writers, executives and politicians, a weak power network, often in considerable tension with the formal structures of party and civil service.

In some countries technology is beginning to assist in the move to weak power structures. On a videotex network like

Minitel in France or Compuserve in the US, activists can very quickly link together on a campaign, sharing ideas, research and best practices without the need to meet together or establish a formal institution with committees, standing orders and officials: the 'virtual' campaign comes to stand alongside the 'virtual' classroom and the 'virtual' laboratory, existing in electronic space rather than the formal, physical space of meetings and conferences, its structures instantly formed or dissolved.

The one area where weak power structures have yet to make a major impact is in the organisation of the state. Governments remain quintessentially strong power structures, devising policies and programmes at the top and passing them down through a hierarchical bureaucracy to people at the bottom. Governments' inefficiencies as control systems have been recognised for a long time: their basic failing, probably most effectively described by Friedrich Hayek, is their inefficiency as information systems. The minister or permanent secretary is meant both to represent the public and to control a vast bureaucracy. Both are inherently impossible tasks. No-one can realistically represent the interests of 55 million different people. Equally, no one can really know what is happening in each section of a nationalised industry, each DSS office or hospital ward. The solution governments adopt is to simplify in order to control: the form, the account and the statistic are all ways of coping with an over-complicated world, and are of course the very lifeblood of a bureaucracy. To borrow a term from computing, the state preprocesses: it simplifies the information it gathers in order to make it easier to process.

This characteristic of government colours any attempt at public or democratic control. The public control that is exercised through the Morrisonian corporation and the stalinist bureaucracy is channelled through the summit of a pyramid (the minister), and is then passed downwards through the apparatus of the state. The public's interests and aspirations are passed all the way up the pyramid and then all the way down. Like the strong power corporation this approach worked fairly well at providing standardised solutions, such as standard housing, large-scale industrial manufacture, or standardised benefits. But as societies become more differentiated, with very different needs and interests, an interdependent web of specialist groups, the flaws of the strong power state become more apparent. Like the strong power corporation it is better at treating people like things, in one dimension: it deals with quantifiable indicators so that in the case of housing, for example, it uses a points system rather than qualitative indicators such as a preference for a high or low position, a style or type of neighbourhood. Faced by complexity the state responds with simplicity.

This critique of the state long predates the age of post-Fordism. However it takes on much greater weight now because it is essentially an argument about complexity. The more complex a structure is the harder it is to exercise top down control, and complexity is at the heart of the new times of post-Fordism, of less standardised products, a more complicated division of labour, more differentiated cultures and identities. In a more complicated, interdependent system, the traditional socialist programme for radically simplifying society and replacing the convoluted structures of entrenched powers with a unified programme, becomes less effective. The solution, parodied by Brecht, as that of 'dissolving the people and electing another', becomes too costly as the state is unable singlehandedly to replicate the complex social ecologies of advanced systems of health, education or agriculture.

The failings of the strong power, standardising state have become one of the Right's trump cards. The Right's informational critique of the state, given at its most coherent form by Hayek in the 1940s, argued for the virtues of the market as an information system. The ideal market could be seen as a decentralised processing system, a weak power structure instantly responding to the changing needs of consumers, by contrast with the simplifying, standardising, and remote state. The market could even be seen as more democratic than the formal institutions of democracy: in the market everyone at least exerts influence, whereas in the democracy the choices of up to two-thirds of the population may be completely ignored. The democratic election offers at best a handful of choices, while the market, at least in theory, offers an almost infinite array of choices for those with the money to exercise it.

At a time when the market was mainly producing very standardised products using highly centralised decision-making structures, Hayek's argument was only partially convincing. Forty years later, when capitalism has learnt much more quickly than the state the virtues of flexible specialisation, differentiation and of more subtle, multi-dimensional market research techniques, the critique becomes devastating. In contrast to the strong power structures of public control, the private control of the sovereign consumer can be portrayed as real, visible and tangible.

Forms of Control

This promise of control is central to the Right's success in setting the political agendas of the 1980s: control is promised not only at the individual level, through owning your own house or determining your children's education, but also in terms of influence over larger institutions. As a customer or shareholder of British Telecom or British Gas, control can be portrayed as real ('we answer to you'), where the control exercised through parliament and ministers was abstract and remote. But though the Right has articulated a clear vision of control that is human in scale and accessible to the majority, it is a vision that is only partially formed. The Right has found it hard to develop a coherent position on control over one's own body (through food, health or reproductive choice), or on control over one's own work; moreover control is seen as something that can be exercised only by the individual, rather than by the small group or the community.

Faced by the Right's assault on the strong power state, the Left has generally answered with a call for more democracy. Democracy is seen as the way to give people control over their own lives, the solution to the remoteness and unresponsiveness of public services. Real democratic structures, however, can be as unsatisfactory as strong power states and one-dimensional markets. Some of their flaws have already been touched on: the dictatorship of the majority, the tendency for the demands of the structure to override a concern for the quality and contents of decisions. An equally important flaw derives from the nature of control. Real control is never costless but requires investment of time and resources. The control of the consumer depends on finding out what alternatives are available, about the real qualities of what is being bought. The control of the voter, or of someone who sits on committees, is equally dependent on time invested in finding out about alternatives, about how to implement them, about what representatives and officials are really doing. An understanding of the connection between knowledge and real political control was of course central to the 19th-century workers' libraries and educational movements: the connection between time and participation has also formed part of the feminist critique of the labour movement's cult of meeting-going machismo.

The simple fact is that our ability to exercise control is strictly limited by time. Most people intuitively understand this, and happily leave jobs to others. One of the virtues of complex societies is that we don't actually need to understand how a VCR works or how municipal rubbish collection is organised. We do not control every aspect of life because if we did there would be no time for work, love and play. The fully democratised society in which we had to take part in all decisions is for many a vision of hell, an endless branch or committee meeting writ horribly large. Because most people limit the time they devote to participating in democratic structures, control always threatens to fall onto self-appointed cliques who effectively disenfranchise those unable or unwilling to participate. As a result democratic structures that demand intensive participation often prove unstable. This has also been the experience of many collectives and co-operatives, where the principled commitment to full participation in decisions results in ever more time being spent in meetings, and, in the worst cases, a sense that people are interfering in each other's work.

It should be stressed that these are not arguments against democracy, but rather arguments against the idea that democracy is any more a universal panacea than the market. Both give the individual some control, but both also limit the scope of this control, and tend to become distorted. Any convincing vision of a future society must recognise the need for multiple structures of control: the coexistence of representative and direct democracy, rights of removal or veto, market-type controls and the control that is exercised through ethos and moral suasion. A convincing view of change also needs to reflect such a pluralism of structure.

The manifestos and programmes of the Left have usually asked how control can be exercised over society; they search for the commanding heights, the alternative sources of power that need to be neutralised. In societies more dependent on weak power structures this approach loses its purchase: rather than being concentrated in clearly identifiable centres, power becomes systemic in nature, less respectful of boundaries whether geographical or sectoral. Where there are fewer pyramids, control can no longer be exercised through appointing a few new chief executives. Change can no longer be conceived of as something that can be imposed by a government seen as outside society, nor as something that can be achieved through imposing a structure, whether democratic or technocratic, onto society; instead lasting change must be seen as organic and endogenous, harder to achieve but, equally, harder to reverse.

Escaping from what could be called the vertical view of change is essential to understanding the promise of weak power structures. The promise is of a very different kind of state that does not seek to control society directly but rather sets the parameters within which society controls itself, such as rights and obligations, rules on buildings or pollution emissions. Such a state, acting as an enabler and a catalyst, engaged in permanent dialogue with specialist groups, trade unions, banks and community organisations, would begin to take on some of the character of weak power systems. This is not to say that it would be enfeebled, but rather that it would be aware of the limits of effective control. The outlines of such an approach are already visible. One example is in the regulation of industry. Deregulation of industries was meant to bring the removal of state controls and their replacement by the market. Instead, in industries like air, telecommunications and trucking, regulations have often had to become stricter as competition has been introduced and protections eroded, so as to prevent tendencies towards monopoly. What has changed has been the nature of control. Where in the past governments could lay down operational guidelines, could seek to run an airline or telephone company, today their rules concern the parameters of operation, the rules for access and interconnection of networks, the setting of technical standards or maximum prices that can be charged. In a more complex environment top-down control becomes ineffective: instead the state becomes an overseer, a regulator of independent and competing organisations. This does not mean that control becomes less effective. In the case of telephones, for example, it may be easier to lay down targets and penalties to encourage British Telecom and its competitors to provide cheap services for those on low incomes than it is to initiate and implement such a programme downwards through the public bureaucracy.

This example shows how public controls can interweave with the discipline of markets. It also illuminates the limits of the Right's thinking. For the Right the problems of restructuring the state are relatively simple. Across the board the market must be allowed to penetrate and replace administrative structures. Regulations must be swept away. On the demand side the individual consumer must be allowed to exercise choice, while in supply, subcontracting and privatisation use the discipline of the market to achieve efficiency. This fetishisation of the market reveals the Right's only partial understanding of weak power structures. In the Right's vision of the reconstructed state, control is exercised only through price and profit: though they have been pioneered in the leading sectors of capitalism, none of the soft controls and loose structures of post-Fordism have yet to make an impact on the Right's theory of how the world works.

Real markets combine many types of control and communication. Price works alongside trust, flows of inside information and shared knowledge, authority and ethos. The same would be true of the weak power post-Fordist state. Wherever possible small groups would become responsible for their own day-to-day decisions, as is already happening in education, health and social services. These would be able to form networks, to share resources and collaborate. Accountability would be restructured so that it flows in several directions at once, simultaneously to funding bodies, to workers and users.

There are concrete examples of this happening already: housing associations co-operating on public housing projects, accountable simultaneously to their members, to the state and to prospective customer/members; another example is the Bologna law that requires developers to gain the support of local people as well as planning authorities (as in Bologna), so that they are disciplined simultaneously by the market and by two parallel democratic structures. Other possible examples might include publicly-funded old people's homes where managements are also accountable to those they look after; independent networks of midwives or acupuncture specialists providing services to NHS patients and regulating their own training and standards; credit unions (independent community organisations offering cheap loans) evolving out of estates to co-operate with municipal town card credit schemes of the kind beginning to emerge around the country; competing publicly funded development or training agencies, each with a distinct identity and ethos, and each developing its own networks and constituency amongst firms and workers; and finally, closer to British politics in 1989, the simultaneous use of parent/pupil election of school governors with voucher systems to allow for choice between schools. Each example recognises the need for multiple structures of accountability that allow the citizen to exercise control simultaneously as a voter, a customer and as a participant.

Many local councils are beginning to learn these lessons, using subcontracting not as a discipline on labour but as a means of enriching the democratic process. The GLC in particular was a pioneer in forging loose networks of activists, experts and voluntary bodies and in using independent organisations to carry out its policies. Though sometimes a victim of the rhetoric of direct democracy, behaving as if a single meeting could be in some sense representative of all the gays or Bengalis of London, it recognised in its practice that informal structures often work much better than formal ones and, above all perhaps, it recognised the need for experiment. For the essence of weak power structures is their variety and flexibility. In organisation as in technology there are far more options than under Fordism.

Weak power structures can never wholly replace ones based on strong power. We need, and will continue to need, strong, relatively centralised bodies to protect the environment, to negotiate with multinationals and to reduce social and regional inequalities. Strong and weak must coexist, as indeed they always have: even in the most hierarchical organisations informal networks have always shadowed formal structures. But what is happening now is a shift in the balance between the two. This shift from strong to weak power forms of control, though still fragmented and uncertain, still resisted by those in all areas who cling to more heavy-handed forms of control, is an epochal shift. It is a necessary and unavoidable response to more complex societies that are increasingly dependent on knowledge, creativity and communication for their economic survival. It is a shift that socialist and radical movements and parties ignore at their peril.

In principle the virtues of weak power structures should be immediately evident to socialists; they resonate with the best traditions of self-definition and activity, the radical response to the impositions of capitalism and governments. But tradition dies hard, as does the attachment to formal, vertical structures. As time passes, the costs of this attachment will grow, manifested as political failure, frustration and disillusion; as is the nature of strong power structures, energies will be absorbed internally rather than directed outwards. Against the odds capitalism will have successfully defined a radical set of ideas to its own ends.

If, however, the Left does learn to experiment with weak power structures, with the organisational forms that are most in tune with the times, it will become clear that the crisis of socialism is more a crisis of structures than one of values. Moreover it will be harder to doubt that just as the moral and philosophical roots of socialism, the belief in co-operation, compassion and responsibility, in values that transcend the narrowly material, all far predate the historical forms of socialism, so will they also outlast them.

Paths to Renewal

The Left will only be renewed as a modernising, progressive political force in society if it can encompass the changes in the realm of politics. At the heart of that renewal must be a new division of labour between social movements and political parties, in mobilising people, expressing aspirations, challenging power and enacting change.

The rise of social movements, such as feminism and the green movement, has partially dislodged the political party as the unifier of political demands. But the social movements have been weakened by the failure of the opposition parties. The party remains critical for two reasons. Parties form governments, which can exercise an important measure of control over the state and enable change in civil society. Parties also play a vital role as a focal point to cohere social coalitions.

The social movements are extremely diverse in form, objective and duration: some are relatively issue-based, others are essentially about social and personal identity. But they share some central characteristics which mean they occupy an increasingly important place in the division of labour in progressive politics. They challenge capitalism's separation of production from its consequences and the sphere of reproduction (by which is meant the reproduction of daily life, of the conditions of production itself, and of the environment). The challenge to this separation − which has been mirrored in much of the culture of the labour movement − is what is new and is what connects movements as diverse as feminism and green politics.

They deploy flexible forms of organisation, which allow people greater choice about how to become involved in politics. They do not constrain politics to a single area or a single sense of identity. Thus feminism creates the conditions for women to become not merely the authors of parts of their lives, but their lives as an integrated whole. It is about the production and reproduction of life itself, rather than just the production and distribution of commodities. Most combine a social philosophy with a personal politics. Feminism and the green movement aim to transform society gradually, in part through transforming people who become involved in their politics.

As well as carrying visions of a transformed society they are all deeply practical. All involve people in direct challenges to power in the state, and in civil society. They are realistic about the process of political change. Feminism for instance has revealed the social power which oppresses women, stretching from paid employment through to the culture of advertising and the social norms of familial, heterosexual life, as much more diverse and complex than much of the socialist Left had appreciated. Feminism's idea of emancipation is both more complete, more practical and more gradual than many of the established ideas of social transformation embedded in the traditional Left.

The social movements are thoroughly modern movements. They are a response to new aspirations and problems. They mobilise new constituencies in struggle. They deploy modern forms of communication and organisation. They are relatively non-hierarchical, relying on horizontal, flexible, networking forms of organisation. They are in touch with society because they live and breathe within society, rather than pacing the musty corridors of narrow institutional power.

The unions stand between the social movements and the Labour Party. They have one foot in the issues which confront people in their everyday lives and the other in formal politics. Like the social movements, the union movement has to respond directly to the issues of the new times. A daily confrontation with restructuring at work, and the changing aspirations and make-up of the workforce are forcing the unions to modernise. Yet, unlike the social movements, the unions have very formal, hierarchical structures which link them to the Labour Party. At the heart of the unions' modernisation must be a new combination of their industrial, social and political roles.

The passage to new times is not just disrupting the old bases for union organisation within the economy. The dismantling of the tripartite state means that unions need to find a new political role within society. During much of the postwar settlement the unions stood not just for their members, but for wider social progress through expanding employment and welfare. In the 1970s, however, they became increasingly distrusted as unrepresentative, sectional interests, acting for their members against the interests of society as a whole. The unions need to find a new way for renewing that link between their interests and the interests of society as a whole.

The unions should become a vital bridge between the social movements, the voluntary sector, pressure groups and the Labour Party. In taking up women's demands over childcare provision, discrimination and flexible working time, the demands of the green movement over sustainable production, and the interests of all workers in the rights that might come with Europeanisation, the unions should establish themselves amid a network of social movements and pressure groups. The unions would be working for society at large as well as their members. They would also transmit this social politics to the Labour Party. The future of the unions' political role does not lie in breaking their links with Labour. It lies in recasting them. The unions remain a vital link between the party and the outside world.

But in addition the unions need to take on a wider political role, independently initiating debate. Thus, for instance, the health workers' revolt has become part of a communal defence of the NHS. In electricity and water privatisation unions should seek to represent the interests of consumers concerned about quality of services, price rises and the protection of the countryside. The industrial modernisation of the unions, opening them out to the changing labour market of post-Fordism, must go hand in hand with a political modernisation, which opens the unions out to society.

Finally, a new division of labour is emerging within progressive politics. The old division of labour was based on demarcation lines between the personal and the political, the state and civil society, parliamentary politics and extra-parliamentary activity, with the Labour Party as the apex of left politics. But the fragmentation of the centre-left parties, the rise of the social movements and the changing character of the state means a new division of labour has to be created. Like the production systems of the new times, it has to be more flexible and less hierarchical. It must work in civil society as much as the state, the national and the international, the personal and the social, the production of commodities and the sustenance of life.

Whether such a multi-skilled politics emerges will depend on the renewal of the Labour Party. Like a Fordist factory it has long chains of command, and a strict division of labour. Discipline, bureaucracy and hierarchy predominate over initiative, flexibility and manoeuvrability. It is introverted where the social movements are extrovert. It offers people only a limited role in politics, through the branch vote on a resolution. The branch, like the production worker in Fordist factory, has specific, limited tasks, within a pyramid of political managements. Branches exist primarily within the Labour Party's internal divison of labour rather than as political agents in society. Branch life is not about people changing themselves or society around them. It is about winning votes, passing resolutions, internalising rather than projecting politics.

Labour constrains people's political consciousness, when the social movements transform consciousness. It militates against imagination, produces intellectual ossification, and rewards ideological caution.

These are the components of realignment: the social movements, the unions and the Labour Party. The new division of labour produced by realignment should create a broad, progressive politics capable of moving through all spheres of society to enable it to develop in a more humane and democratic way in the new times. The process of realignment will have two linked stages. The defeat of Thatcherism through a political and electoral agreement between the opposition parties. But this must open the way to a second, deeper, longer-term realignment which would fundamentally alter the meaning, purpose and organisation of progressive politics.

Defeating Thatcherism

The Labour Party will be the central force in defeating Thatcherism, but its persistent go-it-alone approach, including its opposition to proportional representation, has acted as a barrier to building the unity of the anti-Thatcherite forces.

As things stand it is extremely unlikely that the Labour Party will win the next election on its own. The importance of preventing another Tory victory is so great that it should in the next few years determine the approach of all political parties who want Britain to develop differently. Arguing that it is unlikely Labour will win on its own is not defeatism, it is realism. But there are some forms of political-electoral agreement which will not work. If it were an agreement designed to rehash old policies and share out parliamentary seats based on the lowest common denominator, a pact would almost certainly fail.

A political and electoral agreement has to stand for something more than the defeat of Thatcherism. It needs to be based on an agreement about why it should be done. An electoral agreement needs to have political foundations. It needs to open the way to a political future beyond the defeat of Thatcherism.

The political foundations must be laid now. An electoral agreement will only succeed if there is a groundswell of popular pressure for a joint approach to the next election. A wide range of groups opposed to Thatcherism – the unions, green campaigners, the peace movement, nationalists, the church – need to be drawn into the debate over a joint programme of government. A politics of alliances needs to be forged through political campaigns over the future of the NHS, the poll tax, local government and devolution.

There is already some measure of agreement on policy declarations between Labour, the Democrats, Greens and nationalist parties on:

measures to promote civil liberties and local democracy

electoral reform and devolution

adequate funding for the NHS and the state education system

scrapping the poll tax

greater investment in economic modernisation, through improved training and education, research and development

measures to protect the environment

active opposition to apartheid, and the promotion of international co-operation to achieve nuclear disarmament

a critical engagement with the European integration programme to promote a 'social dimension' of rights for workers and consumers, and greater European democracy.

An agreement on policies will only emerge from a wider political agreement on the priorities for change. It is vital that the opposition parties meet their responsibilities to society by settling differences and agreeing those priorities.

Renewal

It is impossible to say in detail what the longer-run renewal and realignment of the Left might entail. But the history of other major realignments gives some clues.

It will almost certainly involve not just ideas, but an intellectual revolution, to map out a new vision of progress, new social values and new ideas about how they should be implemented. Developing these ideas will require political pluralism. The Left has to listen and learn from ideas produced outside it. The ideas of the Liberals – Keynes and Beveridge – were vital to the labour movement's agenda after the second world war. Their ideas on economic and welfare policy had historic stature. They also produced very practical plans for changing institutions.

Thatcherism's intellectual revolution proceeded through a plethora of think tanks and informal groups. Much of Thatcherism's agenda is still gleaned from businessmen, and part-time politicians on the fringes of formal politics. It has created a new political-intellectual culture on the Right. A culture where people can take risks, think the unthinkable, where imagination is rewarded. The Left needs to develop a similar culture. It needs to move from a defensive intellectual culture of criticism, towards a creative, risk-taking intellectual culture, which is dynamic, open, energised. But Thatcherism's revolution also rehabilitated a radical Toryism which had been marginalised by the one-nation, Butskellite Tories in the postwar years. In similar vein, socialists need to recuperate past traditions of non-statist, humanist socialism – of the co-operative movement, for instance – which were pushed aside as the labour movement burrowed into the bunkers of the state.

The new flexible division of labour between social movements and political parties needs to be given greater form. The corporatist, tripartite state was vital to the postwar settlement. It was the machinery of decision-making which formalised the postwar consensus. We need an analagous revolution in political decision-making for the new times to involve a wide diversity of social movements. New forms of democracy, at a local and national level, which would give social movements, the voluntary sector and pressure groups a direct involvement in decision-making, will be vital.

The internationalisation of politics means that the labour movement has to internationalise itself. This is already happening within the union movement. The TUC is playing a leading role over the European single market, and individual unions are starting to open up European agendas on collective bargaining. International links will be vital to the Left in the 1990s, to co-ordinate common left perspectives on European issues, and also to fertilise ideas.

Finally it is almost certain that this sort of realignment will require significant changes in the contours of party political opposition. That could in principle mean the creation of an entirely new progressive socialist party for the new times, incorporating a range of existing parties. The reality is that it will probably involve some form of federation or strategic alliance between the opposition parties: Labour, the SLD, the nationalists and the Greens. If such an historic realignment is required no opposition party will be able to escape its responsibilities and consequences.

David Marquand

Beyond Left and Right: The Need for a New Politics

In normal times, the combination of myth, tradition and self-deception which prevents the opposition parties from making common cause would pose no threat to the values for which they stand. They would be at leisure to regroup and rethink: and they could safely leave it to the slow processes of cultural and social change to determine how and when a new left-of-centre majority might emerge.

But, of course, the times are dangerously abnormal. In ten years, the Thatcherite crusaders have redrawn the social and political map of Britain far more thoroughly than most anti-Thatcherites thought possible in 1979. The postwar mixed economy has been largely dismantled. The postwar welfare state barely survives. The principles they embodied have been systematically rubbished — to such effect that, in his last budget, Nigel Lawson felt able to abandon the basic commitment to progressive taxation, now nearly a century old. Most ominously of all, most of the intermediate institutions which stand between the state and the citizen, and which embody and transmit alternative values have either been rendered ineffectual, like the local authorities, or ruthlessly harried and intimidated, like the trade unions, the universities and the BBC.

This does not mean that the crusaders will achieve all their purposes. Their market-liberal faith rests on a twisted conception of human nature and human possibilities. As some of Mrs Thatcher's ministers have recently begun to recall, men and women are not Benthamite calculating machines, responsive only to the sticks and carrots of the market or the commands and prohibitions of the state. An ideology which assumes that they are must, sooner or later, go adrift. Britain will not, in the end, be remade in the image of the thrusting yuppies of the foreign exchange market, any more that Russia was remade in the image of the Heroes of Socialist Labour.

But the fact that the Thatcherites cannot attain their squalid Holy Land will not prevent them from dragging the rest of us a long way towards it. They have already pushed the authoritarian potentialities, immanent in the doctrine of absolute parliamentary sovereignty, further and harder than any previous peacetime government has done. By the next election, they will have pushed them further; and if they win then, they will push them further still. The last ten years have shown how easily a government of zealots, suffused with the arrogance of office, can neuter opposition. How much opposition will be left when that government has enjoyed sixteen years of uninterrupted power? The forms of democracy will survive. But what will happen to the flow of criticism and dissent without which the substance atrophies?

Analysis of the Centre's complex and paradoxical position in British politics should begin at this point. After all, the opposition parties together easily outnumber the Conservatives. If the votes which went to the Alliance in the general election could be added to the votes which went to Labour the nightmare of another Thatcherite government would be averted. And the rise of the Green vote adds a further possibility for alliances. Yet no one has so far managed to construct an electoral coalition of that sort and no one seems likely to do so in the near future. One of the chief reasons is that part of the Centre, at any rate, is no longer conventionally centrist in assumption or aspiration, while part of the Left is not, in most of the familiar senses of the phrase, genuinely on the Left; and, because of this, the familiar language of Right, Left and Centre now confuses at least as much as it illuminates.

The language dates, of course, from the French Revolution. It is also impregnated, however, with assumptions ultimately deriving from the Industrial Revolution. One of the legacies of the first is that the Left is supposed to be the party of the Revolution and the Right of Reaction; that the Left stands for movement and the future, and the Right for order and the past. Thanks to the second, the Left is also supposed to be the party of the exploited − by definition, the proletariat − and the Right of the exploiters, by definition the bourgeoisie.

Implicit in the whole terminology of Right, Centre and Left, are three crucial assumptions. The first is that the 'Left' is in favour of change and the 'Right' against it. The second is that change − radical and far-reaching change − is inherently 'progressive', emancipatory and anti-exploitative, to be welcomed by the dispossessed, and feared by their dispossessors. And, although this is less obvious, a further implication is that the 'Centre' is, in some sense, uncertain, pusillanimous or two-faced − in favour of trivial changes, perhaps, but not of fundamental ones; sympathetic towards the exploited, but unwilling to wage war on the exploiters.

All these assumptions have now broken down. Since the middle 1970s, Britain has been caught in the back-wash of two overlapping crises. The first is a worldwide 'Kondratiev' crisis of rapid technological change and lagging societal adaptation. Its origins lie in the inability of institutions and practices shaped by the imperatives of old-style Fordist mass production to cope, on the one hand, with the growth of flexible specialisation, small-batch production and knowledge-intensive processes and, on the other, with globalised markets and global companies. The second is a peculiarly British crisis of legitimacy and governability. Behind this lies the inability of the traditional institutions of the British state to halt a century of relative economic decline, while at the same time operating a mixed economy, dependent on public intervention and therefore on an ethic of public purpose.

This double crisis has shattered the old political categories and the assumptions embedded in them. It no longer makes sense to assume that the Left is for change, the Right against it and the Centre undecided. By a terrible irony, the most radical, change-welcoming and change-promoting tendency is Thatcherism. It is a moot point whether the most conservative, change-fearing and change-opposing is the hard Left, what remains of the old-fashioned, blue-collar Labour Right or the equally demoralised remnants of traditional, *noblesse-oblige* Tory paternalism.

What is true of ideas is equally true of interests. The unionised, heavy-industry, manual working class, locked into the old technologies and the mind-set they engendered, can only lose from the disappearance of the Fordist order of the past. Alongside it on the conservative side of the barricades is the growing underclass of the handicapped and unskilled − the late 20th-century equivalent of the undeserving poor who haunted the imaginations of respectable Victorians. Equally, if less blatantly, conservative in that interest is the old-established, upper-middle-class, public-sector professional salariat, which used to manage the now diminished institutions of the postwar settlement. Ranged against all of these, on the radical side of the divide, is a motley army of, among others, small builders, millionaire stockbrokers, health-insurance sales-people, garage mechanics, whole food restauranteurs, software designers, desk-top publishers, property dealers, council-house purchasers, electricians, makers of garden furniture and members of workers' co-operatives.

If we are to pick our way through the confusion, and make sense of the way in which the double crisis of the 1970s and 1980s has impacted on our politics, we must, as a first step, supplement the categories of 'Right', 'Centre' and 'Left' with the categories 'conservative' and 'radical'. Thatcherism then emerges as a radical right response to the crisis, combining a strange kind of British Gaullism with a most un-Gaullist neo-liberal economic ideology, an almost Jacobin willingness to engage in top-down cultural engineering and a populist contempt for old élites.

The opposition to Thatcherism is, however, divided against itself − obviously by party and ideology, but much more importantly by mood, assumption, instinct and approach. Parts of what is conventionally classified as the Centre offer radical left responses − notably, though not exclusively, the community politics wing of the pre-merger Liberal Party, in many ways the closest equivalent to the Greens, and therefore the most threatened by their rising vote. Sections of the Labour 'soft Left', most of the Greens themselves, parts of the feminist movement, sections of the Scottish and Welsh nationalist parties and some of the socialist groupings outside the Labour Party also belong in the radical column. David Owen's social market is a sort of sub-Thatcherite sub-radicalism. On the other hand, 'wet' Toryism, Croslandite revisionism, clause-four state socialism and, most obviously of all, traditional, mainstream labourism are quintessentially conservative.

Against that background, the confusions and uncertainties of the anti-Thatcher oppositions begin to fall into place. There is no truth in the notion that Thatcherism is, by definition, unstoppable − the wave of the future, which we must all ride or drown. It is, at most, a wave of one possible future. But although it can, in principle, be beaten, it will not be beaten simply by adding together all the votes of all its opponents, and trying to procure some quick fix through which they will all be delivered to the same camp on election day.

A successful anti-Thatcher coalition would have to include conservative interests and tendencies as well as radical ones − British equivalents of Walter Mondale's constituency as well as that of Dukakis, of the PCF as well as of the Rocardian French Socialists. But, as those parallels imply, it would have to be radical-led and inspired. With all their faults, the bleak, demeaning doctrines of the New Right do at least address the issues of the 1980s and 1990s. Its solution to Britain's double crisis may be riddled with contradictions, but it can propose a solution. The conservatives in the anti-Thatcher camp − whether of the conventional Left or of the conventional Right − cannot. And, if the last fifteen years of British history have any single lesson, it is that even bad solutions will prevail against an intellectual vacuum.

The question that really matters, then, is not how to assemble an anti-Thatcher coalition capable of offering a convincing radical alternative to the radicalism of the Right, while at the same time appealing to non-radical interests and opinions. Seventy years of British history suggest that no opposition party can do this all by itself. The Conservatives have been the normal party of government since 1918. They have been so because the Liberal-dominated progressive coalition, which seemed to be on the verge of winning hegemony before the first world war, fell apart thereafter; and because the Labour Party never managed to construct a Labour-dominated equivalent. Of course, history may suddenly take a new turning. Kinnock may succeed where MacDonald, Attlee, Gaitskell and Wilson all failed; Ashdown may, even now, be carrying Asquith's baton in his knapsack. But it would be foolish to bet much money on it. Both the established oppositions are prisoners of their pasts, and neither knows how to escape.

Labour's prison is almost palpable. In ideology and interest it is the child of Fordist mass production, shot through and through with the assumptions, myths and values of the industrial order which is breaking up before our eyes. Almost as damagingly, it is also the foster-child of the British state, stamped indelibly by the experience of seeking and holding power in an increasingly bankrupt system. The evils of this parentage go much deeper than is generally realised. *Pace* most current media comment, Labour's problem is not that it is a socialist party in a post-socialist era. The socialist tradition is enormously variegated, and some of the strands in it are remarkably well-adapted to the needs of a post-industrial society in the late 20th century.

The real problem is twofold. Ever since Labour became a potential governing party, most Labour socialists − like most Labour social democrats − have taken it for granted that they could achieve their purposes only by taking control of the central British state, and using it to engineer change from the top down. Ever since the foundation of the Labour Representative Committee, moreover, mainstream Labour socialism − again like Labour social democracy − has been mediated through the institutions, values and collective memory of British labourism. It is this fatal combination of centralism and labourism which shackles the Labour Party to the past, and prevents it from addressing the crises to which Thatcherism is a response. So long as that combination lasts, it has no hope of building a new, and appropriately radical, equivalent to the progressive coalition of 1910-1914.

Herein lies the true meaning (and irony) of the current policy review. With enormous perseverance and not a little courage, Kinnock, Hattersley, Gould and the rest are refighting the battle which Hugh Gaitskell lost nearly thirty years ago. They are trying to prove to the world that Labour has jettisoned clause-four socialism, and embraced revisionist social democracy. If they succeed, they will have given the Labour Party of the 1990s an image and stance ideally suited to the 1960s. Indeed, the irony goes even deeper than that. Kinnock and his colleagues can win only by mobilising the block votes of the great unions − in other words, by manipulating the institutions and culture of labourism to repudiate socialism. Yet, in spite of the contrary trumpetings of the media, it is labourism, not socialism, which most alienates the actual or potential anti-Thatcher voters who do not belong to Labour's inward-looking culture, and to whom the party most needs to appeal.

At this point, re-enter the Democrats, the miscalled Centre.

In the long term, in spite of recent problems, they are better placed than Labour to spring the trap in which anti-Thatcherite Britain is caught. Their structures are suppler and more open to new currents of thought and feeling. They have no institutional or sentimental ties to the disappearing Fordist order – no sacred rites of proletarian solidarity or misleading memories of the martyred dead – and, apart from a handful of unreconstructed Croslandite revisionists, most of them also have a much smaller ideological stake in it. Indeed, by a strange irony of cultural mutation, their largely pre-Fordist ideological inheritance – an amalgam of 19th-century popular radicalism and early 20th-century social liberalism – speaks more convincingly to the post-Fordist late 20th century than does Labour's top-down fabianism.

Much the same is true of their approach to the crisis of ebbing political legitimacy. Though Democrat parliamentarians succumb as easily as Labour ones to the narcissistic *mores* of the Palace of Westminster, the party as a whole is instinctively suspicious of the central state and, as such, willing to be convinced that its institutions are at once corrupt and hollow. It is, after all, the only mainstream United Kingdom party committed to constitutional reform; and although its support for PR is partially dictated by self-interest, PR is nevertheless an indispensable first step towards a citizen democracy. Growing support for the Greens may be cutting into SLD support, but there is no doubt that the Democrats still represent an important strand of modern radicalism. It is not clear at the moment what the long-term effects of the green vote will be, but, despite Labour boasts to the contrary, the Democrats have not been 'seen off'. They have, however, suffered serious setbacks. Far more important than the details of electoral problems are the forces which produced them.

The Democrats' partial downfall in the 1987 general election was due, above all, to the resilience of the Labour vote. One reason, no doubt, was that David Owen went out of his way to demonstrate his antipathy to the Labour Party and his preference for the Conservatives. But it would be a mistake to give much emphasis to that. The real reason was that, except in a handful of inner-city constituencies politicians had managed to build a local base, the Alliance's themes struck no chords with traditional Labour voters. And the reason for that is that

Labour's core constituency, though far too small to elect a Labour government, is far too deeply embedded in the Labour culture to vote for a party which seems alien to it: that in the archaic and collapsing world of 'us' versus 'them', only the archaic politics of 'us' and 'them' have resonance. That, of course, is another way of saying that the very factors which confine Labour to its shrinking base also tie its base to it.

So what is to be done? For the time being, at any rate, electoral politicians are trapped in the routines of a majoritarian electoral and party system. Whatever they may think privately, no member of parliament in either major opposition party is willing to talk publicly of electoral co-operation. A common agenda, however, is another matter. Oddly enough, there is not much doubt about its outlines. What is needed is a British version of what the American political scientists, Charles Sabel and Michael Piore, have called 'yeoman democracy': a marriage between the communitarian, decentralist, participatory radicalism to which the Democrats, and perhaps the Greens, are heirs, and the communitarian, decentralist, participatory strands in the socialist inheritance: a marriage, if you like, between Thomas Paine and William Morris. On that, the radicals in the miscalled Centre and the radicals in the miscalled Left could honourably converge.

Geoff Mulgan

Uncertainty, Reversibility and Variety

Once we lived in a world of certainty. We knew which way things were moving, and it was our way. Now the world is characterised by uncertainty, imbalance and danger. Geoff Mulgan argues that our thinking should be brought into line with reality.

The new times are characterised by uncertainty, danger and fear. The spirit of the age is reflected everywhere, in the cultural theories of postmodernism which call into question the very idea of a single truth and a single reading of the world, in the physical sciences' new interest in theories of catastrophe and chaos, concerned with how small causes can have large and unpredictable effects, and in a climate of doubt about the great stories of enlightenment, progress and liberation that defined the politics of an earlier age.

Uncertainty is a product of perpetual change. In the past, and especially in the marxist tradition, change was associated with predictability, certainty and progress. The transformation of the world, the means and the ends, could be known and understood. After the experiences of the 20th century it is no longer easy to be certain which particular means will lead to what ends, or that today's solutions will not turn out to be tomorrow's problems. Change no longer seems to move in a straight line: it zigzags, and goes back and forth in discontinuous leaps. With unpredictable change comes endemic uncertainty, about everything from culture and truth to the climate, the air we breathe and the skills we learn. Above all, perhaps, there is the fear that the environment, both natural and human, is changing more rapidly than our means of adapting to it.

Uncertainty makes for a different kind of politics. Some become more cautious, more fearful of the effects of grand designs. Some turn away from politics altogether, towards the everyday and the personal, while for others uncertainty feeds an ever more intense search for the simplest and starkest faiths and certainties. In this essay I suggest a different response. I argue that the Left needs to use uncertainty as a strength and not a weakness. By recognising the limits of our knowledge, and by gaining a more sophisticated understanding of change we can draw practical lessons about how policies should be formulated and about how the world can be changed.

The argument is also about how best to respond to dangers and to the fact that so many processes, economic, ecological or social, are beyond any possibility of direct control. The more cautious and defensive view of politics that follows from this argument loses something of the inspirational power of the brave new worlds of 1789, 1848, 1917 or 1968. But it does have the virtue of being more congruent with what the Left actually is. For nowadays the Left is in many ways most effective when it plays a defensive role, carefully constructing the space for freedom and real life, and protecting people from the dangers of this world rather than promising them a new one.

The Heritage of Certainty

One hundred years ago history was generally seen as a smooth progress. Whether through evolution or revolution it was a cumulative progress of human capabilities and reason, and a movement away from uncertainties, superstitions and falsehoods into truth and certainty. The Left was very much a part of this tradition. It was shaped by that familiar mix of scientific hope and millenarianism, the belief that the world could be built anew, and that people are basically plastic and perfectable.

As refined into the programmes of social-democratic and marxist-leninist parties, the belief was that power could simply be used as a tool. Once the working class took over state power, the world could be moulded into an ideal form. Influenced by the optimism of science, there was a widespread belief that all problems could be rationally solved. The social world could be as plastic as the natural world, as susceptible to control.

This perspective had profound implications. One was that under socialism there would be no more dangers. There would be no need for protection from other people or from the state: the state's powers didn't need to be balanced by citizen's rights.

Often there would be no need even for an army. Utopia is, literally, no place, that is to say a society without boundaries and therefore without the need for forces to balance those of the enemy. As in the dream of international socialism, the problems of danger disappear because there are no longer boundaries and enemies. Another implication of faith in rational control was that humanity could break free from its limits. Socialism shared with much of capitalist ideology the expectation that we were moving towards a world without scarcities, a world of abundant material goods that would solve the problems of distribution and struggle.

This idea of breaking free from limits is the common heritage of capitalism and socialism, of Lenin, Brunel and Robert Moses. It permeates all the dominant political philosophies. It sustains faith in growth, in science and technology, in grand projects to build tunnels under the sea, to divert rivers and to send rockets into space. It is a faith that is bound up with reason. The world can be changed because it can be clearly understood, mapped, and, in the age of the computer, simulated and modelled.

Uncertainty and Imbalance

Today history is as likely to be seen as a cumulative disaster as a steady progress. On the Left the turnaround was marked by Walter Benjamin's famous vision of progress as a terrible storm that drives history hurtling backwards, a vast heap of debris accumulating at its feet.[1] It is this sense of imbalance, a sense of things out of kilter, that separates us from the blithe confidence of the 19th century. Today the imbalance may be economic and social, an imbalance of material provision and life opportunity, an imbalance between short-term greed and long-term survival, and it may be psychic or spiritual, an imbalance between inner needs and what is offered by the prevailing culture and mores. Rather than being steady and cumulative, change has come to be seen as destabilising.

The shift is reflected in disillusion with the dominant political philosophies, and in the various green and new age movements where there is a heavy emphasis on notions of balance, and on the whole rather than the parts. New catch-phrases, such as sustainability and the steady-state economy, reflect the concern. The influence of Taoism, Buddhism and Hinduism, and of the deep ecology movement, has also brought a new equation between the wider imbalances of society and personal, psychic imbalances.

Traditional ideas of balance and harmony long ago lost their currency in the world view of the West. They survive only partially in such pre-industrial creations as the US constitution, devised as a mechanically equilibrating system, balancing executive, legislature and judiciary, or in the economists' bizarrely inappropriate vision of the capitalist economy as a system of general equilibrium.

By contrast revolutionary capitalism and revolutionary socialism alike have always sought to foster dynamic imbalances, to drive social change or accumulation through difference. For both it is the vanguard groups, those who are marginally ahead, those with an edge, who drive the system, pulling the mass, the average and the ordinary along in their wake. This is the very essence of industrial societies: permanent, cumulative change, and the sweeping away of constraints. In the face of this force, the storm of progress, ideas of equilibrium came to look reactionary and conservative, barriers to the application of reason and progress.

As forces associated with reason and rationality, neither socialism nor capitalism ever suffered from too much doubt about their historical inevitability, a sense that there was no alternative. But in the century of the concentration camp and gulag, the nuclear bomb (built for freedom or for socialism), of eugenics and the artificial intelligence guided missile, their certainties have brought a heavy cost. Reason itself has turned out to be a tricky servant, just as power turned out to be a corrupting tool, demanding constant vigilance, care and criticism. During the course of the 20th century almost every movement and ideology, without exception, has been touched by unforeseen disaster. The good intentions turned out to be a road to hell. Ecological disaster, mass starvation and chronic financial instability are amongst the costs of 1980s global free market capitalism.

Genocide turned out to be the destiny of stalinist communism, of nazism and of the extreme anti-industrial, green ideology of Pol Pot. In each case the revolutionary belief in a single set of universal principles, in the need for a *tabula rasa* to create the world anew, turned out to be profoundly dangerous.

In each case, too, ideas were given such weight that there could be no compromise.

These experiences have given us a much stronger sense that limits are an inherent part of the world. The desire to escape from limits seems to bring pathological results, psychic and material costs that show up in unexpected places. We also have a better understanding of the difficult nature of the world and of the problems involved in changing it. And, if there is one unarguable conclusion to be drawn from the experiences of the 20th century it is that all systems are imperfect, not just coincidentally but fundamentally. From today's perspective we can see that for all their subtleties and complexities the dominant political philosophies of both Left and Right remain fundamentally one-dimensional and fundamentally unbalanced. They draw on a set of principles or assumptions about human psychology, selfishness or sociability, to deduce universal principles of living and for organising societies. All, whether capitalist, socialist, communal or religious, impose simple structures onto a complex reality. And though all might work well if run by angels, all in practice work with human egos, jealousies and prejudices.

The Tradition of Defence

The Left has paid a particularly heavy price for hopes betrayed, and for its excessive faith in the world's malleability. But it also has another tradition which has been less vulnerable to uncertainties and imbalances. This is the tradition of politics as a defence against danger.

Danger and insecurity are a natural part of the human condition, and much of social life, language itself, rituals and altruisms, can be understood as collective responses to threat. The presence of danger also explains why co-operative, food-sharing creatures have often been favoured over selfish ones in the history of evolution. Danger has also always shaped political discourse, providing justifications for strong leaders, for laws to sustain civil peace, and for rights to defend against the overweening power of states. Many socialist organisations were built more as organs of defence than as vehicles to attack and replace the old order. Trade unions and mutual aid societies offered collective protection against a hostile, unpredictable world, food co-operatives defence against hunger, militias defence against professional armies and mercenaries. This idea of defence is also one of the sources of egalitarianism, which arises not from envy or a simple desire for equality, but rather from the experience of subordination and the wish to defend against it.

Nowadays there are new dangers. The thin envelope of biosphere within which human life takes place suddenly seems extraordinarily vulnerable (though James Lovelock and the proponents of Gaia might disagree). Nuclear weapons threaten not only human life, but all life through the nuclear winter. Danger is no longer only material and personal, but also macroscopic, a threat to the very idea of living, loving, thinking beings. Other dangers flow from multinational corporations and unstable and uncontrollable global financial markets. One of the difficulties with politics in the late 20th century is that these new dangers are of a different order than our means of redressing and containing them.

In the past it was the belief in a revolutionary transformation that provided much of the inspiration and vision of socialist and radical movements. In recent years, however, this belief has made the socialist project less relevant to an interconnected world of more porous boundaries, a world of very real limits. It has made it inarticulate in the face of acid rain or aids. As a result there is a striking gap between the power of the Left as a radical, oppositional force and its power as a utopian alternative. As an opposition the Left plays the role of look-out, warning about dangers, about wars and petty violences, pointing out the costs and limits that lie behind the glossy facade of late 20th-century capitalism. As a utopian alternative, by contrast it now seems merely fanciful, wishing away the real problems of the world. Where a century ago the utopias of Morris and Wells were bestsellers, the new left utopias of people like André Gorz have little resonance beyond small circles of intellectuals. Instead it is the sense of limits and trade-off, of dangers that capitalism ignores, that has become more potent and that makes people listen.

The Left's influence as a warning system feeds on widespread distrust. Where in the past the radicals fed on popular distrust of churches, priests, kings and bosses, today it is the multinational corporation, the government and the bureaucracy that are likely to be distrusted. The widespread predictions made a few decades ago that increasingly sophisticated media and propaganda techniques would produce a passive, credulous and malleable population have been proved wrong. The techniques of information and misinformation, 'swamping', spin control and the calculated leak have all simply engendered greater scepticism about whether anyone can be believed. This has had its impact on the political process, where trust and distrust play an important role. Parties seem to win elections because they are less distrusted than the other side. Within institutions there is a greater stress on structures of accountability to remove leaders for incompetence, betrayal or corruption (on the grounds that power corrupts and absolute power corrupts absolutely).

A similar effect is visible in relation to political systems and ideologies. Nowadays people are much more likely to ask whether they can trust a system to deliver what it promises, and whether they can trust it to relinquish power if it fails. The problem is more acute for some political philosophies than for others. The world's communist movements are particularly tainted by their history; having won power, irreversible structures were created so that they could not be removed. This experience of trust betrayed now has its effects in the often very naive faith of East Europeans and Chinese in the virtues of liberal markets.

But the problem of trust is not confined to communism. Parallel questions can be asked of neo-liberalism and the global market, and for that matter, of Europe's 1992. We have to ask whether they can be trusted to deliver the various rewards they promise. And, if they fail, and trust turns out to be misplaced, we have to ask how we will be able to reverse them.

This question is particularly important in Thatcherite Britain where market mechanisms are being used to replace political ones. This process is often very hard to reverse. Property rights turn out to be difficult to remove, and individuals defined solely as consumers can no longer collectively organise around issues. Irreversibility has become an important goal for the New Right. In the writings of Hayek and others, laws are used to force the replacement of the state by the market: their ideal is to use irreversible constitutional means to minimise the realm of political decision-making and take power away from what they view as irresponsible democratic assemblies.

The Right's new interest in irreversibility mirrors the Left's traditional concern with blocking reaction through similarly irreversible shifts. Both now look illegitimate. Today's uncertainties and distrusts suggest that a structure or decision that can be reversed, that leaves us able to change our minds, is inherently better than an irreversible one. A development that leaves an old community and old architecture intact is better than one that does not; a general skill is better than a specific one that may soon become obsolete; and a political restructuring (perhaps to pass powers to the European Parliament) is better if there's scope for democratically reversing it at a later date.

The idea of reversibility isn't new. It is one of the virtues of democratic structures, and the powerful argument against dictatorships and one-party states, unaccountable managers and trade-union general secretaries elected for life, who cannot be removed however appalling their rule. But it takes on a new significance when, as now, a lot of energy is being spent rectifying old mistakes. We need reversible decisions precisely because we are uncertain about outcomes. For the same reason we need agencies to warn us, to monitor actions, to act as watchdogs, and we need constitutional rights (for workers, consumers and citizens) to balance and limit those in power.

There is also a second implication, equally relevant when policies and programmes are being decided. If we can't be certain that a system is trustworthy, that our principles are universally applicable, or that our chosen means will deliver the desired ends, then it follows that we should always favour the coexistence or more than one system over just one, however perfect and appealing it may seem. The coexistence of more than one system reduces the scope for damage when things go wrong; it makes a society better able to adjust to unforeseen circumstances; it creates competition between systems, a competition that can be philosophical as much as economic, forcing each to live up to its ideals, or to adapt: and it gives the individual or group a degree of philosophical choice about the right way to live and work.

Competition in this sense can be read either at a superficial level, as in the social-democratic mixed economy which was mixed as to ownership rather than ethos, or at a deeper level as competition between different ways of life. Examples from the past might include the coexistence of different monastic orders within a church, offering a range of choice to different characters. Present-day examples might include the coexistence of very different approaches to education (traditional and modern, authoritarian and libertarian, religious and secular), of alternative energy sources or transport systems (public, private and community-based). Within the economy competing systems might include private enterprises and socialised ones, worker and consumer co-operatives and individual traders, each with a differently structured relationship to capital markets and consumers, and different ideas of participation in work. Alternatively they might include competing approaches to health (orthodox or homeopathic) or housing (private, communal, condominiums or public).

These ideas suggest a different approach to the role of the state. Rather than applying uniform rational principles its task becomes one of overseeing the balance between systems, redistributing resources, and creating the conditions for a variety of groups and institutions to organise themselves. Rather than engaging in social engineering (the old mechanistic metaphor), the state's legitimate task becomes one of creating the space for social experiment.

The idea of competing systems also has another implication. Where the traditional socialist model of change assumed that the levers of power could be won, and used to achieve a blueprint or vision of society, the alternative approach starts from the assumption of weakness rather than strength, defence rather than attack. The aim is not to create society anew but to create balancing forces. Rather than seeking to overthrow hostile forces (the traditional aim of revolutionary movements), the aim is to build up countervailing powers, so as to create a balance of systems, a protection against the danger of any one set of powers or interests becoming too strong. Transformation comes from shifting balances rather than demolition and reconstruction.

Rather than trying to eliminate them, the socialist state would try to create countervailing powers to multinational capital, to the military-industrial complex, or to well organised professional groups. Similarly it would balance police rights by those of the citizens, those of doctors by those of patients and so on. Rather than trying to resolve inherent conflicts of interest it would instead try to create a new balance between them.

This approach demands a break with old habits of thought. In socialist thought there is a long tradition, with antecedents in millenarian ideas, that sought a final resolution of the world's problems. The individual and the social were to be resolved in a higher synthesis; conflicting class interests were to disappear in a common interest. Today, we're more likely to see conflicts of interest as inevitable in any society: they can be reduced and contained but not eliminated. Recognising the dangers of resolution is also important at a philosophical level. The point was perhaps best put by Schumacher when he wrote that societies need

> stability and change, tradition and innovation, public interest and private interest, planning and laissez-faire, order and freedom, growth and decay. Everywhere society's health depends on the simultaneous pursuit of mutually opposed activities or aims. The adoption of a final solution means a kind of death sentence for man's humanity and spells either cruelty or dissolution, generally both ...[2]

The ideas of reversibility and of competing systems pose problems for the marxist and socialist traditions, though neither is in any way contrary to their spirit. Both principles are primarily concerned with means rather than ends, a recognition of uncertainty as to which means will achieve which ends, and a recognition that any conscious, participatory society will often change its mind: that under socialism the plan will be a continuous process rather than a blueprint that is then put into practice. Marx was correctly suspicious of socialist blueprints. The future would be forged out of struggle and experience and could not be foreseen. His scepticism of an over-reliance on fixed means and ends suggests why it is that a socialist movement more than any other should understand the need for competition and experiment between systems. Starting from a world structured by the consciousness of capitalistic, patriarchal societies it is inherently impossible to determine the right path, the universal principles, in advance except in the most general way. It should be the very hallmark of a genuinely radical movement that it is prepared to distrust even its own predispositions.

Variety and Change

The need for plural solutions is corroborated by evidence from systems theory and biology. A famous law in cybernetic theory states that any controlling mechanism requires as much variety as the system its seeks to control. According to W R Ashby's 'law of requisite variety', it is impossible to control a complex system without an equally complex set of tools. It is, for example, impossible for a government to guide a complex economy simply by using a single measure, such as the money supply or interest rates. Since governments are rarely able to match the complexity of the societies they govern, the implication is that control must be devolved and spread.

Variety also has another value that takes us back to the problems of uncertainty: it allows systems and societies to cope with unforeseen changes. In biology it is well-known that species benefit by maintaining a variety of different forms or mutations so that they are better placed to survive when the environment changes in unpredictable ways. Grasses with the same genetic codes will tend to take a variety of forms, some small, some large, the better to ensure survival in the event of being eaten by animals or starved by drought. In the same way it is because we don't know which institutions or societies will best respond to a dramatic shift in the climate, to supercomputers the size of a grain of sand, or to new, virulent diseases, that we need variety in all the forms of social life.

This is one of the reasons why the diversity and variety associated with post-Fordism has to mean much more than a choice between ten different brands of jeans or baked bean. The more profound philosophical sense of variety, that recognises different kinds of value and different kinds of meaning, may turn out to be necessary for survival.

The failure to understand this, the deep meaning of variety, is one of the weaknesses of Thatcherism and neo-liberalism. They have only one organising principle for society: the demands of the market, of competitiveness and of a world turned into commodities. The effect is to standardise even amidst a rhetoric of diversity. All kinds of institution must be run according to similar principles of management. All must be run 'by the numbers', through accountability to monetary values. And all parts of the world and all spheres of life must be made commensurate within a single system of exchange and value.

The Left by contrast has begun to understand the meaning of diversity and variety as it comes to terms with the fact that it is constituted by many currents and experiences (to such an extent that it has begun to doubt whether it has any coherence at all). Where it is weaker is in its understanding of the nature and problems of change. This is one of the reasons why the debate about new times is always hard: the Left has been brought up always to search for a new steady-state (after the revolution, the election of Labour government, etc), rather than seeing change and adaptation as natural. In this sense the Left shares some of the weaknesses of the modern green movement with its search for a new, static harmony. Neither fully accepts the idea that change might be continuous and unavoidable, whether it be towards a more ecologically based economy, towards greater material equality or towards a greater realisation of human potentials.

There is also another weakness in the Left's view of change. It remains strongly influenced by the 18th- and 19th-century views of societies as machines or buildings. In these metaphors changes came from a new driver or a new architect. Change was associated with the certainties of the map and the plan.

We now recognise that change is deeply uncertain and unpredictable. This new view of change suggests that the most appropriate metaphors are to be found not in physics and mechanics (though physics has had its own encounter with uncertainty), but in the various life sciences, within which change is conceived as a process of searching, and of trial and error. In the past biological theories of evolution were resisted on the Left because of their association with reactionary apologists who used them to legitimate inequalities and hierarchies. 'Organic' views of society denied the reality of conflicting interests. Evolutionary theories were also resisted for another reason, namely that they seemed to give undue weight to natural processes that are the opposite of the realm of the political, of active choice and determination. This tradition of hostility is unfortunate, since a grasp of basic evolutionary processes is helpful for understanding almost any process involving people or living things.

Modern evolutionary theories view societies as open systems in exchange with their environment, continually adapting and creating new forms of complexity. Theories of this kind are beginning to have an impact on economic theory,[3] challenging the static, ahistorical approaches of neo-classical orthodoxy. In political theory they remain very much on the margins, but in this area too their less mechanistic metaphors offer useful lessons about the nature of change and political transformation. One is the familiar idea that a changing environment requires continual adaptation: a socialism appropriate for the year 2000 will almost certainly be inappropriate in the year 2100. What marks humans off from other species is the extent to which evolution has to be conscious, however little we understand the environment for which we're trying to evolve: however deep the uncertainties, we have no choice but to plan and to attempt to impose order.

Precisely because of these uncertainties, evolution depends on risk, experiment and chance: without random genetic mutation there can be no change (one reason why sexually reproducing creatures, which multiply the scope for mixing and mutation, dominate the world). Similarly without experiment in the forms of economic life, in family life, in morality and political institutions, without allowing for failure as well as success, societies stop evolving and slip into stagnation.

A further lesson follows from the fact that evolution is not synonymous with change. Instead successful evolution is always both conservative and radical. It must be compatible with what goes before it, and if it is too radical the very thing that is being changed falls apart. In the case of political institutions too much change tends to lead to a crisis of faith and legitimacy. The problems of change arise, both in biology and in political life, because a new environment will tend to throw up more apparent possibilities than are compatible with what has gone before. In the case of a society, there will always be many new ways of doing things that seem to fit the new times but which are too destabilising to traditions and habits, too threatening to the society's coherence and solidarity. The same is true of political parties, trade unions and voluntary organisations.

Attemping to find this balance is never easy. Different parts move at different speeds, some too fast, too willing to grasp the latest modern thing, some too slow even to see that the world has changed. Obsolescence, a difference in rates of change, is endemic not only for the old but also for the failed avant-gardes and futurisms. One implication of this argument is that those societies which can encourage a culture of experiment while also minimising the costs of changing too fast or too slow will tend to be the ones best able to adapt without losing their basic solidarity and coherence. A society that doesn't penalise people too heavily for being in a declining region or industry, or for being too far ahead of their time, will tend to be happier than one that does.

These various reflections on uncertainty, balance and change have a common theme. It is that too much certainty, and too much rigidity is dangerous. In the world of politics and social life every problem has more than one valid solution. Socialism needs to learn from the lessons of evolution, where the end point of planning is unknown, and where the process is more important than the plan itself. There is also another implication for an age beset by uncertainties and dangers, one that goes to the heart of what politics is about. It concerns what we mean by freedom. In a dangerous world of continuous change freedom must mean more than the absence of restraints, a freedom for dynamic enterprise or personal hedonism. Instead it must mean something different: a protected sphere for autonomy and real life, protected from an array of threatening forces, from concern about air or water, from the need to sell oneself on the labour market, from prejudices and oppressions. In a highly interconnected and interdependent world, freedom in this sense, freedom for real life, has to be carefully constructed and carefully guarded, both from physical threats and from other people's excessive certainties. It is this idea of freedom, of freedom within limits and balances, that suggests how socialism can at last distance itself from its complicity in the storm of progress, and from the massive costs that progress has brought.

Notes

[1] W Benjamin, *Illuminations, Theses on the Philosophy of History*, Fontana 1970.

[2] E F Schumacher, *A Guide for the Perplexed*, 1978 p 127.

[3] An impressive recent attempt to apply these metaphors to economics can be found in Dosi *et al*, *Technical Change and Economic Theory*, Pinter 1988.

VI   The Shape of Things to Come

Charlie Leadbeater

Thatcherism and Progress

Vital to the assessment of Thatcherism is the answer to this central question: has it marked or enabled a new stage of progress in British society? It could be that Thatcherism marks a new stage in a journey which British society embarked upon long ago. The distance travelled in the last ten years could easily be compared with the distance travelled during past decades.

But it could equally well be a new stage of progress in a different sense: that Thatcherism and the decade of the 1980s marks the demise of an old social ideal of progress and the rise of a new ideal. Thatcherism is just the first, radical right-wing version of that ideal. But in future years there will be others drawn from different parts of the political spectrum.

Which it is − a new stage in a familiar journey or the start of a new journey − is very important, not just to the assessment of Thatcherism but to the future of the Left.

If it is just a new stage in a journey embarked upon long ago − a journey of capital accumulation and industrialisation, of struggle between capital and labour, Right and Left, a journey marked by relative ups and downs in living standards and economic strength − the consequences for the Left are far-reaching but not fundamental. The Left will have to develop new ideas and policies, but the journey would remain the same: the Left's ideas of what progress amounts to could remain largely intact. It would simply be a question of winning people back by offering new ways of achieving progress.

If Thatcherism and the decade of the 1980s marks the arrival of an entirely different idea of progress, the consequences are fundamental. We have only just begun to discern what they might be, not just for ideas of how progress is achieved, but of what it consists of. The Left would need not merely to adopt new practices and policies. It would also need to reformulate the very idea of social progress.

Socialism has always claimed to speak for the future. But in the last fifteen years its authority to do so has been thrown into doubt. The historic exhaustion of the Left is rooted in the exhaustion of its idea of progress. This exhaustion is evident in the lack of vision of socialist governments in France, Spain, Greece and Australia, and the rethinking underway in Eastern Europe. The task of rethinking and renewal for the Left is to establish the links between socialism, progress and the future. It is to renew the ability of the Left to galvanise and release social energy to remake society. The question of how that should be done has been posed for the British Left most pointedly by the decade of Thatcherism.

One way of addressing the way Thatcherism has refashioned the links between politics and progress, is to draw up a balance sheet of poverty and prosperity, winners and losers, economic decline and resurgence. It shows that Thatcherism has at best carried out a stunted, conservative, regressive modernisation which has created an abundance of poverty, the exclusion of at least one-third of society in acute and deepening deprivation. British industry has become better at withstanding international competition. But in some areas, such as small-screen televisions and machine tools, international competition is no longer a worry because British industry has completely disappeared.

Home ownership has grown to new levels, as have standards of living for two-earner couples – more televisions, videos, compact discs, freezers and cars. This has been accompanied by a massive growth in the dependency culture of American Express and Access. It has also been accompanied by an enormous growth in homelessness and deteriorating living conditions for many council tenants. Britain remains a perilously under-educated, under-trained, under-skilled nation. Despite making education a priority more than five years ago, Thatcherism has done little to improve the situation.

This kind of assessment could go on and on, marking those things which Thatcherism has done which might be good, those which might be irreversible, and those which are both bad and reversible. It would yield some ideas for what a modernising Left should offer as an alternative. But it does not provide the basis for developing a credible, comprehensive alternative.

A simple balance sheet of progress and regress is not enough because the accounting conventions to draw up the balance sheet are changing. They are changing with the shift to new times and post-Fordism. But Thatcherism is ensuring that they are shifted to the Right as they are brought up to date. For what the decade of Thatcherism has marked is the demise of an old ideal of progress; an entire, embracing conception of how society moves forwards and what it is moving towards.

The focal point for politics in the period lasting from the 1930s to the 1970s was an ideal of progress which was to some extent shared by Left and Right, business and unions. The politics of the time was the struggle between competing versions of this ideal.

It was as if society was on a great collective train journey into the future. There were struggles over how much space there should be in the first- and second-class compartments, whether seats should be allocated through the market or by the state, what sort of access people should have to the buffet car and so on. But the idea that everyone was on a common train journey was shared.

Progress was modernism, an unquestionable line from the past into the future. This commitment to progress as modernism stands out in the tower block, in the ambitious awfulness of buildings such as Alexander Fleming House at London's Elephant and Castle, in Corbusier's visions of truly modern environments for truly modern people, which would wrench them at one fell swoop from the past into the future.

Progress was also industrialisation: it was very physical and instrumental. It was the transformation of the natural world around us, the extraction from it of resources to provide products. The measure of economic strength and success was the output of steel and coal, the transformation of materials dug from the ground. This was the vision implicit in Ford's River Rouge Plant in Detroit, the first fully-integrated car plant in the world. Every raw material needed to produce cars, from rubber for the tyres to iron ore for the body panels, would arrive up the River Rouge. Model T Fords appeared at the other end. That was progress: to take natural resources, combine them with modern production methods and armies of disciplined workers, and transform them into something tangible.

Progress was measurable, tangible, physical, it was the mastery implicit in size and scale, quantity and volume.

Industrialism was progress and mastery over the physical world. Modernism was progress and mastery over our social and built environment.

The trajectory of progress was set by a clear, linear rational path to the future, from the start of the production line to the finished item, from the basement to the 20th floor of the office block. The instrumentalism of industrialism and modernism, the power to act upon an external, manipulable world to change it, was rooted in a commitment to the power and authority of 'science' to master the natural and social world.

Thus progress was very quantitative. It was about the power of volume: a waterfall of products flowing from big production lines. That was achieved through imposing order upon an unruly world. Not just the unruly world of nature, which has to be brought to heel to serve human ends, but the unruly social world. There is little room for emotion in the disciplined, ordered, rational world of Ford's flowline, Corbusier's housing estates or Stalin's Communist Party. Progress was imposing order upon the world.

This combination of order, rationality, linearity, science and instrumentalism meant that select groups had a special role in carrying progress. They were the bearers of the social energy to remake the world. Planners, technocrats, scientists, were the producers and guardians of progress, whether in the multinational company or the socialist state. For socialism, progress was ultimately carried by the ranks of the organised, disciplined working class, the big battalions of the labour movement bred by the conditions of work, housing and social life within the great factories and conurbations of Fordism. They were also disciplined by their political task within the institutions of the labour movement, marching forward, rank after rank, on its great linear march from the past to the future.

Progress was expressed through collective achievements and institutions, from the great mass housing estates and factories, to the welfare state and ideas of collectivisation within socialist countries. This notion of collective advance underpinned the mass affluence of the 1950s in Britain, the spread of mass welfare services such as housing, the 'keeping-up with the Joneses' ethos of the postwar era and the spread of the mass market for consumer durables.

This in turn underpinned a fairly simple idea of social justice as a measure for collective advance, in the commitment to full employment and the provision of minimum standards of welfare. The material, quantifiable costs and benefits, needs and wants, of distinct but relatively homogeneous social groups, could be easily compared and traded off one against the other.

The state and the nation had a crucial role in this vision of progress. State programmes, public ownership, big housing estates, were the expression of collective progress. The state was the central guardian of social justice. The state was vital to planning, promoting and delivering social progress. It could do so in large part because the arena for the planning and execution of progress was the nation, as a discrete, controllable, economic and social arena.

This notion of progress was a tremendously powerful idea. It underlay Ford's decision to build the mighty Dagenham plant at Essex in 1931 as the largest integrated car plant outside the United States. It was implicit in the spread of mass welfare housing after the war. It was in socialist ideas of mass sacrifice on the altar of modernisation in the vast and now-ailing tower blocks, and the car and tractor plants of the Soviet Union. It is in the Bulgarian industrial complexes which churn poisons into the Danube. It was implicit in the great projects to dam and divert rivers to extract energy in Africa and Europe. Those notions of the power of progress as order, mastery, domination, also underlay the cold-war division of Europe into its blocs.

Progress in Basingstoke

It was also in the foundations of Basingstoke, the town that I grew up in. In 1966 as a seven-year old, I used to wander through old Basingstoke, as Victorian buildings were demolished, churches torn down and streets which had followed the same course since medieval times were uprooted.

I loved it. I was not sure what was going on, but it was something big. It was a brave time, a time of expansion and achievement. In time a brutal shopping centre appeared, like a fortress, with turrets, gates and entrance ramps. On the edge of town imposing warrens of mass housing estates appeared: Oakridge, with not an oak in sight, Popley 1 to Popley 8. For years Basingstoke, which once had the most roundabouts per head in any town in Europe, was littered with roads leading nowhere. They were leading to housing and industrial estates not yet built. But nobody knew that: neither the old inhabitants of the market town, nor the 'overspill' from London, being soaked up by the planners' sponge.

The only people who did know were a small team of planners working in 'the development office', a set of pre-fabs in the grounds of an old maternity hospital. They were Basingstoke's midwives. They were planners, producers and experts of rational, scientific, instrumental, unrelenting, ordered and disciplined progress – the collective nightmare which Basingstoke became.

As a sixteen-year old in the mid-1970s, I used to work every Saturday in the town's vast, pre-set concrete multi-storey car park – the largest multi-storey car park in Europe. From its parapets I used to watch thousands of people swarm around the town centre, seeking relief from the awful town which had been built in their name, the plan they were living under, as if it was a great weight upon them.

They shopped and shopped. The only collective space the planners had allowed people was for individual consumption, buying and selling. There were no parks, nature, theatre or cinema to speak of. There was no sense of community, solidarity or obligation, and very little hope. Is it any surprise that the people who suffered that ideal of progress turned on its defenders to create a symbol for acquisitive Thatcherism in the 1980s? The seeds for that shift were laid within the failure of the modernisation of the 1960s.

Redefining Progress

In the 1980s a successor to that old vision of progress is taking shape. It sets new parameters and conditions on how progress can be achieved and what it means. It is a new sense of how and why society can move forward. The contours of that new idea can be seen in the politics of Left and Right, in Thatcherism but also the green movement, feminism, and modern nationalism. It is evident in the way companies are restructuring work, production methods and innovating new products, as well as in new social aspirations for social change. This shift in society's centre of gravity from an old ideal of progress to a new one is not confined to Britain and it is certainly not confined to the politics of the

Right. There is something much more geological going on, which is affecting all the central components of the old idea of progress – modernism, industrialism, rational planning, the role of the nation and also the state.

It is vital to an idea of progress that there should be some core commitment to modernisation and efficiency. One of the foundations for the old ideal of progress was the industrial modernisation set in train in the 1930s, as industry shifted from the old 19th-century technologies of coal and steam to new technologies based on oil and electricity. They spawned both new production methods like the flowline, and new products like cars and consumer durables.

In the 1980s we are in the midst of another profound technological shift towards micro-electronics and information technology. All ideas of progress in the 1980s will have to offer to ride with this, to make the best possible use of the potential it has, for high productivity, and also new products, services and jobs.

New technology – computer screens sprouting in offices and shops – is one of the most obvious and clichéd images of a new stage of modernisation and progress. But the association of modernism with progress, a fairly straight line out of the past into the future, is under sustained attack. It is no longer tenable as a guide to progress.

For the 1980s have also been marked by a search for a sense of continuity with the past, a sense of identity and stability, to secure us as we plunge into the future. Thatcherism's modernisation has been a memorial to the past, to Victorian values. It is these traditional British values which are meant to provide us with our ballast as we lurch uncertainly into the future.

Resurgent nationalism in Scotland is seeking a characteristically modern form of independence, within a refashioned European Community. But it does so by reaching back into the nation's history, to rekindle a sense of national identity. It is reaching back into the past to find a sense of identity it can project into the future.

The green movement is, perhaps more than any political movement, about the future – our responsibility to bequeath a decent environment to future generations. But to elaborate this vision of the future it too reaches back into the past to pre-modern, pre-industrial notions of nature.

The old ideal of progress was like a steamroller sweeping all in its path as it moved so certainly away from the past into a better future. The new ideal of progress is about incorporating an attachment to the past within a vision of the future, to provide a sense of continuity, stability and identity.

Industrialisation is becoming increasingly exhausted as a measure of economic progress. A set of structural shifts in the economy means that its standards of physicality, scale, size, volume and quantity are no longer adequate ways of conceiving of the economy. This is in part due to de-industrialisation, which Thatcherism hastened in the early 1980s through its economic policies. Thatcherism has also been committed to promoting service-sector employment, especially in financial services and in personal services such as retailing and tourism.

But beneath this apparently familiar long-run shift from manufacturing to services something much more fundamental is going on. The ideal of economic power as the capacity to transform things is increasingly in doubt. Instead new ideas of economic power are emerging, focused more on the ability to handle information, or to work with people, rather than acting upon things. The archetypal worker within the old idea of progress was the assembly-line manufacturing worker, acting on raw materials to transform them into a tangible product. The archetypal worker within the new ideal will be the service-sector worker, acting with other people to provide a service.

The old ideal had within it a very tangible, physical idea of productivity which could be easily measured. Measuring the productivity of a tourist guide is much trickier − what is the product, where does it exist? Financial services are often no more than a transitory flicker across a computer screen. Even within manufacturing, notions of productivity are changing, to encompass quality and innovation, as well as sheer quantitative output. Many manufacturing workers do not work on things, they work on computers, which control robots which work on the products.

Thus there is a profound shift going on in our notions of economic power. The capacity of a worker, a company or an economy to become economic subjects, was founded on their ability to manipulate and act upon completely discrete objects, like raw materials. The power in the service and information-technology economy is much more difficult to pin down, when the products cannot be touched, when the raw materials are packets of information rather than mounds of steel.

But industrialisation is equally powerfully coming under attack from another direction, from the rise of the international green movement. This seeks to measure production in terms of environmental despoliation and renewal − what might be financially efficient may not be environmentally efficient. Economic and technological developments and the green movement are heading in the same direction. They are heading away from the old manufacturing economy, towards a new kind of economy, in which measures of productivity, efficiency and thus progress will be less physical, tangible, quantitative and instrumental. The old idea of progress as industrial mastery over nature, a world of external physical objects, is withering.

Nor can progress be conceived of in purely national terms. In many areas, progress has to be conceived of as an interdependent international process. Neither financial markets which allow currencies to be switched from country to country at will, nor clouds of pollution, respect national boundaries. The growth of the international aid campaigns, spreading a new international humanism in the 1980s, also suggests there is strong public support for an idea of progress which takes into account the international effects of economic and development policies. It is not just that ideas of progress *have* to be internationalised, they *should* be.

Thatcherism has always been partially open to international forces. More than any other political force it has stressed that Britain's economy cannot be separated from the international economy. It has repeatedly emphasised that we cannot have a parochial attitude towards economic decisions when decisions made in Bonn, Tokyo or Detroit have such a bearing on investments and jobs.

But the new ideal of progress will not involve a simple commitment to international interdependence, to replace a previous belief in the power of the nation state. It will require a new division of labour between national and international politics. This is not just a matter of finding the right balance between, for instance, national and international economic policy initiatives. Internationalisation raises troubling threats to people's sense of identity, security and power.

The internationalisation of economic decision-making means it is far more difficult to plan what happens within a national economy. Under the old idea of progress it was possible to plan for the future with some degree of predictability and stability. It was a matter of extrapolating from the past and continuing the line out into the future. But the uncertainty created by the intensification of international competition and the easier international movement both of production sites and financial capital means that sort of stability and certainty has vanished.

Take ICL, the British computer manufacturer. The market for its main product can change dramatically within months, depending on what competitors from the USA and Japan bring out. Panasonic, the electronics manufacturer, reckons its products have a shelf life of about three to four months before they are overtaken. The pace of technological and competitive change means the stability for predictable planning has gone.

Companies cope with this rise in uncertainty by acting strategically to minimise their vulnerability to sudden shifts, and becoming more flexible so they can respond more effectively. For individuals it is slightly different. The uncertainty of life within the global market, the way it reduces everything into price and cost comparisons, has provoked a search for an escape. The escape is into a sense of particularism − a sense of having a particular identity which cannot be crushed by the market or be rendered uncertain. Thus Thatcherism has always appealed to a recidivist British bulldog nationalism while welcoming Japanese inward investment. The prime minister strides out into the international arena − to fight our corner in trade talks in Kuwait, or in budget arguments in Brussels.

Thatcherism has promoted the private home as an escape from the ravages of the market world outside. It is within the home that people can find the real, private, particular meaning in their lives, a meaning which endures despite the ups and downs of what goes on outside. Thus Thatcherism is open and closed. It forces people out into the market, but as a compensation offers them a retreat into a secure, private world. It has forced a recognition of Britain's interdependence with the international market, but it also stresses the particularity of distinctive British values.

Again this search for particular identities which cannot be

reduced to the calculus of the market is not confined to the Right. Throughout our culture, there is a search for particular, lasting attachments which can withstand the vicissitudes of the uncertain market. Thus different forms of religious belief seem to be undergoing a resurgence. Much of the British Left is concerned with the assertion of diverse, particular identities which cannot be subsumed within a homogenising economic collective.

Thus new ideals of progress seem likely to be poised between the international and the national, between a recognition of interdependence and a search for independence, between a tendency towards globalisation and localisation.

This ambiguous recognition of the power of the international market economy also raises questions about the links between rationality and progress. Thatcherism has strongly reasserted the importance of market rationality, calculations of value for money, profit and loss. The inescapable logic and discipline of the imperatives of the market have been central to the power of its drive to restructure the economy.

At the same time it has drawn tremendous strength from the irrational. It has more openly and effectively played upon emotions, fears, prejudices, instincts and feelings than any other political movement. It is superb at parcelling people up as outsiders, malcontents or moral undeservers – 'on your bike', 'moaning minnies', 'scroungers'. The intensification of the power of market rationality to dominate people's lives is compensated for with an escape into the emotional.

This interplay of the rational and the irrational within the politics of Thatcherism masks something much more fundamental: a mounting doubt that progress is rationality's conquest of the irrational. Thus feminism has always been concerned with the links between prevailing notions of sexuality, emotionality and rationality. The green movement appeals to something deep inside people about their intimate interdependence with the earth they inhabit. At times such a link seems obviously rational. At other times it seems such a fundamental thought that it is almost biological, in 'our nature', pre-rational.

The idea that progress is the liquidation of unruliness, through the imposition of a rational order on people or things, is weakening. This has contributed to the demise of planners and experts as special guardians of progress.

The old progress gave the élite technocrats a special authoritative place. Future ideals of progress − especially where they involve publicly-provided services − will be more populist and anti-élitist. They will revolve around new relationships between experts and users, professionals and consumers.

Responding to Changing Times

Thatcherism has articulated this populist backlash to the Right, in an authoritarian, inegalitarian way, especially through its proposals for opting-out. Its attack on the status of 'planners' is one aspect of a search for new social groups to generate progress. Thatcherism has been significantly more successful in this search than the Left.

It has not merely sought to align itself with rising social groups, but to create them, by offering people new cultural identities to live within; as home-owners, share-holders, credit-card holders. This appeal has been particularly important among the affluent, multi-skilled, working-class technicians. This group, often bridging the manual/non-manual divide, occupying an important position within computerised production processes as the maintainers of robots, the programmers of computers, is becoming strategically important, both economically and politically. Thatcherism has fashioned an appeal to them which the Left has yet to match.

Thatcherism has also turned to rising entrepreneurial and international capital to renovate British companies. These groups are at the heart of its attempt at a creative destruction of the sclerotic élites of the old corporatism, whether in the failed manufacturing combines of the 1960s, the universities, the media or the arts. These are the new social bearers of progress − the social leading edge, as much as new technology is at the leading edge of production.

The Left is similarly engaged in a search to realign itself socially. The old manual working class is in permanent decline. It is being superseded by both a new unskilled service-sector working class, and the new technician class of multi-skilled workers in both services and manufacturing. Fashioning a political appeal which stretches across the new divides within the working class will be central to the renewal of the Left. In addition there is the Left's relationship with new social movements and groups. Throughout Europe there are debates about the relationship between the green movement and socialist parties, the links between a broad 'progressive' politics and a socialist politics.

But this is not simply a question of coming to terms with the rising energy of new political movements like the greens. Beneath that, new collective identities are emerging. Thus the green movement appeals to and is attempting to build a sense of global collective identity, over the greenhouse effect, as well as local collective interests, over industrial development in the green belt. In different ways nationalism, feminism and black politics attempt to appeal to and create distinctive collective identities.

Thus the Left's search for new sources of energy is much more than a political or electoral numbers game. At its heart must be something more fundamental, an understanding of how notions of belonging and shared interests are changing, how they are generated and woven together.

Running in tandem with this is the issue of individualism. For both Left and Right, individualism and individuality will be much more important to future notions of progress than they used to be.

Thatcherism's narrow individualism has been vital to unleashing a social energy for people to attempt to remake their lives as they want them. That offer to people – to be able to make choices and enact them – has been central to Thatcherism's dynamism. But so too on the Left, for feminism and green politics have spread partly though their impact on individuals as much as through a great collective appeal. Both women's politics and ecological politics involve people changing themselves and their sense of themselves through their politics. Both green politics and feminism are vitally about how people produce themselves through what they consume. Thatcherism, feminism and green politics are all in their different ways concerned with people as political agents, as potential authors of their lives. The old ideal of progress was wrapped up with a vague but nevertheless powerful notion of collective, all-embracing progress. New ideas of progress will be more complex. They will have to win the support of rising social groups. They will have to appeal to and create new senses of belonging and collective interest, as well as new notions of individuality and individualism.

This in turn means that old ideas of social justice have to be revised. Social identities and needs are becoming more diverse. A welfare state designed for a world of full, male employment is having to cope with persistent mass unemployment, the growth of women's paid employment, the rise of one-parent families, the ageing of the population and a move by some sections of the affluent into more privatised forms of provision. A notion of social justice which was built around simple transfers from one relatively discrete group to another will not do. We need more a complex and variegated idea of social justice — complex equality, which recognises people's different needs, rather than simple equality, which reduced them to the same common denominator.

Thatcherism's marketised individualism does indeed promote a more diverse idea of social justice — fragmented, unequal and polarised. But as yet there is no effective counterpart, no new idea on the Left which combines a commitment to social justice and redistribution with a recognition of the new role of diversity and difference.

Finally, the role of the state as an agent of progress has undergone tremendous change. The old idea of progress was founded upon the belief that the state had a special power to promote and cohere change. The modern state faces a bewildering range of pressures and demands which are forcing it to be recomposed. One thing is certain — the state in future will be less unitary and more diverse than the Keynesian welfare state. It will in part have to be internationalised, ceding sovereignty to international bodies such as the UN and the EC.

Economic modernisation will require a concerted investment in science, research and development, new technology and skills. That will require the state to play a strategic role. But at the same time there is a widespread desire for a more open, enabling, responsive state, which does not tower over its consumers and clients. The politics of the state has also been circumscribed by the growth of politics in civil society, the growth of a politics which is not about what a party would do when it gets state power.

Thatcherism has been very effective in adjusting to these changes in the demands and limits upon the power of the state. It has used the state to restructure the old industries which threatened the dawn of the enterprise economy – coal, steel, shipbuilding and cars. It has also strategically set the agenda in areas like education.

And yet it has used the state in an enabling way, to promote change within society, through private-sector task forces, or privatisation. It also well understands the importance of acting as a political force within society to promote a wider cultural change, through enterprise culture and popular capitalism. Thatcherism is much closer to having a modern conception of how the state's different roles might fit together than the Left.

When I conjure images of the old ideal of progress I see a fleet of combine harvesters sweeping relentlessly, blindly, through a field of corn. When I imagine the new ideal of progress I see an agitated metronome clicking erratically backwards and forwards. For the new ideal of progress is not about linear, straight, predictable lines. It is about a series of dualities and tensions. Tensions between modernisation and history, uncertainty and security, strategy and flexibility, open and closed, national and international, experts and users and so on. The metronome is constantly moving between these poles, it is never still. Indeed sometimes it appears to move in both directions at once.

That is why it is so difficult to work out where we are: what is a step forward, what a step back. Moving with such an ideal which has within it such insecurity, uncertainty and unpredictability requires much more confidence than the old, linear, plannable ideal of progress. But it also explains the potential in the new ideal. Its unpredictability means that it opens up new avenues for progress. Thatcherism has begun the ride with it. But it does not own it. The Left's task is to move with it more effectively into the new times of the 1990s and beyond.

The collapse of the old ideal of progress amounts to more than the demise of large manufacturing plants or the revolt against the mass housing estate. It attacks something deeper in our society, our conceptions of politics and social change. It means our notions of how authority is won, discipline maintained, power exercised, energy released, have to be rethought. At root, the association of progress with the movement of history rather than individual and social choices must be challenged. And with that challenge some comfortable, objective, dehumanising yardsticks of progress disappear.

It is in this domain, the realm of ideas, that the insights of post-Fordism and postmodernism most fruitfully meet. True they also meet in the architecture of the new, city centre office block, built for transnational service-sector companies, or in approaches to design, lifestyle and advertising. But underlying this there seems to be a deeper affinity. Both post-Fordism and postmodernism challenge our inherited ideas of rationality, order, power, authority, hierarchy and justice. Both attack that 'one-big-narrative', whether it be scientific rationality or Ford's flowline which attempts to explain and order everything.

Giving up that old ideal of progress does not imply pessimism. The oppposite is true. Relinquishing it is the precondition for renewed optimism. It means embracing a far wider diversity of ambitions and aspirations, grievances and complaints. It means working without the guarantees that progress, history, the class and the party would march inexorably hand-in-hand — those guarantees which have contributed to the complacency, arrogance and at times violence of the socialist project.

Within this embrace is one of the central dilemmas of contemporary left politics. For another guide to our ideas of progress has been moral, the idea that progress could be measured by the gradual improvement in people's standard of living and the gradual equalisation of the distribution of resources. Even if we accept that one form of progress is no more favoured historically than another, surely we should retain some objective moral yardstick for progress? Much of the justification for the Left's version of the old systematising ideal of progress has been provided by the pursuit of equality. It is in the name of equality that the state must intervene in society to order it, to ensure a fair balance of resources. Many fear that without that order there cannot be equality and without a strong sense of equality to provide a moral and political yardstick there can be no sense of progress at all. Yet the times are pulling in a different direction, towards diversity and difference rather than homogeneity and order. The times are throwing up a diversity of claims on resources, indeed on morality. Simple ideas of equality are not capable of reconciling these differences without reducing them to a common denominator. It is in the resolution of this tension between the conception and pursuit of equality and the fulfilment of difference and diversity that the future of left politics lies, in the reconciliation of a diverse individualism with a sense of collective obligation.

This implies two broad possibilities for the meaning of socialism. It may be that a modernised socialism can be born which is more plural, democratic and flexible, more able to accommodate diversity, choice and difference. But it may also mean that we need to make a much sharper break with the past. We may need to move beyond the idea of socialism as the unifying apex for left politics, towards a conception of progressive politics which includes socialism as just one component, one set of values and one constituency.

David Edgar

Novel Approaches:
A Tale for New Times

'Up at the league, says a friend, there had been one night a brisk conversational discussion, as to what would happen on the Morrow of the Revolution, finally shading off into a vigorous statement by various friends of their views on the future of the fully-developed new society.'

'Hey, that's William Morris, isn't it? News from Nowhere?'

'Yes, I believe it is.'

'Well, in that case, we must assume you'll live.'

In front of him, a great grey cloud was coagulating into the recognisable but unexpected form of a member of the Queen Alexandra's Imperial Military Nursing Service.

'Well, I never thought I'd hear a piece of Victorian socialist utopianism quoted in delirium in the middle of a field in Normandy. But then, one lives and learns.'

'A field?' he asked.

'All right. A tent.'

'Go on.'

'You're in a field hospital. A field hospital in a field. Outside Arromanches, off Gold Beach in Normandy.'

He was obviously looking blank. So she went on:

'You are a Corporal in the British 50th Infantry Division. You invaded France two days ago. To liberate the European peoples from the fascist yoke? Inaugurate a reign of liberty and justice? D-Day, does that ring a bell? And you got a piece of shrapnel in your left lung and another scraped your right temple. So it's not surprising that you're a mite delirious, though I'd say that William Morris was pushing it. Are you in pain?'

'In agony. Who am I?'

She checked a list, produced a fiercesome looking syringe and began to swab his arm.

'You're Corporal Thomas Robinson. Now, this will hurt like hell.'

* * * *

The next thing he saw was another face, in its way as surprising as the Nurse's, because it was his wife's. Who was sitting on a bench, in what was clearly still some kind of medical facility. But as the other patients were in large part women and their children, and indeed civilians, and outside he could see not fields but streets (with hoardings advertising Ovaltine, and roadsigns), this was clearly no longer wartime France. But where it was, and who was nestling in Ellen's arms, he couldn't say.

'Why, Tom. Aren't you at work?' asked Ellen, smiling pleasantly.

'Uh, no. I don't think I'm very well.'

'The spam. You'd best sit down. I'm told that there'll be quite a wait.'

'Uh, wait? What for?'

'The doctor, Tom,' said Ellen, quite sharply. 'For Kate's diptheria and the baby's smallpox. I suppose it's people coming here on the first day.'

And as Tom was obviously looking somewhat alarmed, Ellen carried on, reminding him (with exaggerated patience) that if he really concentrated he might recall that today was the Appointed Day, in which the National Health Service had been brought to birth, by that nice Mr Bevan, and that Katey (four) and Richard (two months) were here for their innoculations. And as Ellen was obviously no longer pregnant, Tom worked out that the freckled little girl sat sucking on a lollipop was Katey and his daughter, that the baby boy was Richard and his son, and that somehow he was now in England and in 1948.

'Well, you say that nice Mr Bevan,' said a woman in a flowered pinny sitting next to Ellen, 'and this is all very fine and dandy. But if I was Mr Attlee I'd have devoted a sight less energy to buying off the doctors and rather more to doing something about the rooves over people's heads.'

And all right we won the war, she went on, but three years later she was still living in a prefab, and a young couple next to her countered that *they* were in a back-to-back without an inside wc, and another woman remembered that in the war there'd been all these grand visions of new towns full of great towers set in open parkland, 'streets in the sky' complete with all mod cons, and where were *they?*

And the young husband responded that before we built new towns, we had to win the battle for production, and *he* wanted to know when the Government was going to move on from fuel and transport and take over all of industry in the interests of the people.

And an older man remarked that he remembered, in the war, how managers and workers in the factories had worked together in committees to maximise production and he wished that instead of being run by faceless bureaucrats, the people's industries had been genuinely given to the people.

('Ah, but which people?' someone asked. 'The workers? or the consumers of the products? Or a bit of both?')

But when it was pointed out that, however limited the changes, at least Britain was an infinitely fairer and more equal place than it had been before 1939, then even the most cussed nodded. For, however irksome, the ration book did ensure that everybody reached a basic standard; and while Bevan might have had to concede too much, at least there'd be no return to the really bad old times, when half the population had no form of medical insurance, and the hospitals were financed by whist drives, theatre benefits and flag-days. For despite the difficulties and delays, at least a people's government was bending the machinery of state to create a new world quite unlike the one they'd left behind.

* * * *

'So, Corporal, is there anything you need?' He woke to see the beaming face of an army padré, clutching a Bible to his chest. And once awake, he realised he felt considerably better (not least because of remembering that crucial phrase, in the dream he'd just dreamt, 'although we won the war').

'Well, I don't suppose there's any literary matter. I mean, in the way of a newspaper or magazine or something.'

And the Padré thought perhaps there might be, and pottered back a moment or two later with a copy of the Daily Mirror, plastered with invasion news.

'I'm afraid it's from last Wednesday,' said the Padré.

But Tom said that didn't matter, thanked his benefactor, and settled down to read.

* * * *

It wasn't easy. It was the way the thing was set out, with white print over colour-pictures. And it wasn't helped by the fact the room was lit with candles (was there some kind of power crisis?) and the noise was pretty deafening. So it took a moment or two to recognise the young man (dressed, it seemed, as a Red Indian) who entered, took one look at him, and demanded what the hell he was doing here.

'Richard?'

'Dad.'

And not being quite clear where he was or how he'd got here, Tom put down the magazine (called 'Red Midget' or 'Black Vole' or something equally outlandish) and suggested that in order to avoid the indescribable racket (clearly gramaphone technology had developed *dramatically* in the intervening years), they repair to some local hostelry.

'So this is − student life?' Tom asked, as he noted from the front page of a discarded newspaper that it was 1968, and Richard would be twenty.

'No, Dad,' said Richard, 'this is the revolution.'

They passed rooms full of posters, sleeping bags, duplicating machines, and typewriters; Tom noting that in fact the basic technology of political communication was comfortingly familiar. As was the rhetoric: with placards calling for the smashing of imperialism and power to the people, and Richard explaining how the students were opposing the imperialists and supporting the heroic national resistance against them (the imperialists were the Americans, but that was no surprise to Tom).

But there the resemblance ended. Because, as Richard patiently explained, the socialists the students followed weren't British or even European, but from South America and Africa and Asia; and furthermore, they saw the present Labour government as nothing less than the principle *enemy* of socialism (this as they reached the pub, and clambered out of Richard's apparently hugely popular small German car).

'Because the point is, Dad,' said Richard as Tom bought the drinks (a pint of bitter was *two shillings*), 'that what your generation calls the great achievements of the welfare state like nationalisation and the NHS and stuff − all that did was buy off the revolutionary aspirations of the working class.'

'Yuh, that's right. Repressive tolerance,' said one of three young men with beards sitting at their table.

'And anyway the point now isn't national capital,' said a young woman wearing a kind of oriental smock, elaborate make-up and an alice band. 'Now the central fact is a global system dominated by the American super-state in the interests of the multinational companies.'

'Or, supra-nationals,' said the second beard.

'So you see, dad,' Richard said, 'in one sense, the contradiction is much clearer now − I mean, it's the peoples of the Third World up against America. But in another sense, it's a lot more complicated, in a place like Britain, where the working class has been bought off by capitalist consumerism, and you've a number of new agencies of revolution. Like blacks, and disaffected youth, and national minorities.'

'And women,' said the alice band.

'Yuh, sure,' agreed the Scottish beard.

'Which is why, man,' said the third beard, 'which is why like where it's at isn't nationalising steel for Christ's sake, but confronting like late capitalism with a genuinely revolutionary alternative.'

'Like the San Francisco diggers have abolished money in the Haight. And the Provos in Amsterdam put people without houses into squats and their solution to the transport problem is abolish cars and provide free white bicycles for the people. Like confronting the fetish of like private property.'

And Tom repressed the urge to tell the beards that the principle of squatting buildings had its history, that this wasn't the first generation to take on bailiffs, and that the mass-trespass movements of the 1930s had had a thing or two to say about the private ownership of land.

But it did seem that the students had a point about the state of housing ('private affluence and public squalor, man'), and he was told in no uncertain terms that the great dream of planned housing − particularly when vertical − had all too often come to literal grief.

'But at least there's full employment, isn't there?' he asked. And although there was general agreement that there was, clearly things had moved on here as well, because, as the alice band remarked, that begged the question of whether people *need* to grind their lives away in factories, whose interests it served, and whether the real issue wasn't so much the right to work, as the right *not* to.

To which Tom found himself unable to respond. And so resorted, rather feebly, to a change of subject.

'So, Richard. How's your sister?'

'Kate? She's flipped. She's going to have a baby.'

* * * *

'Well, that's nice,' said a Nursing Major, who appeared above him.

'What is?'

'You muttering something about somebody who's going to have a baby. Now might that be Mrs Robinson?'

'Yes, that's right. Any day now,' Tom said.

(But in his mind there was another baby − a baby *of* the baby as it were.)

'Well, and here's you, fighting to make a world that's safe and free for your baby to grow up in.'

'Or rather, lying in a hospital using valuable military resources in not doing same.'

'Now that's not thinking positive, now is it, Corporal,' the Nursing Major said, and before Tom could raise a matter that was on his mind, a matter about which he was feeling pretty negative, she'd passed on down the line of beds.

So he raised it with the Nurse, who told him that she'd see if there might be a practical solution to his problem, that would preserve his dignity while not setting back his recovery, but for the moment he should lie back quietly and think of England.

Which was, oddly, precisely what he did.

* * * *

'Grandad, why aren't you in your home?'

'I'm sorry?'

And he was standing on a grimy, dismal street, in what was

obviously England, indeed an England nearer to the one he'd
left behind than he had thought — or wished — to see again.
Small knots of angry looking young men stood at corners. In
front of him, a sign said 'Health Centre', with a list of doctors'
names. But the door was padlocked, and the windows boarded,
and on one of them somebody had scrawled 'closed'.

'Grandad, for Christ's sake, get in. The young man had
opened the passenger door of his terrifying car, and was
gesturing. And Tom must have looked blank, because the young
man then reminded him that he (the young man) was his
grandson, William, that he (himself) was supposed to be all
comfy in the twilight home his daughter Kate had thoughtfully
enrolled him in, and if he didn't get in now they'd both get killed.
And indeed the young men on the corner did look threatening,
and realising from a quick glance at his image in the bodywork
that he was now in his seventies, he did as he was told.

'So what's the car?' he asked, to evade the subject of his
apparently going AWOL from his 'home'.

'It's a Porsche,' his Grandson said.

'What, French?'

'No, German. Look —'

'What, like a VW?'

'No, nothing like. Grandad, why aren't you in your home?'

'Oh, I'm on a visit ...'

'What, to Clara?'

'Yes. Yes, that's right, to Clara.'

'Hmmph.'

They had turned the corner, past the young men, into an
equally dilapidated thoroughfare, and Tom was thinking, that if
this was 'Faith St' (as it announced itself), he wouldn't like to see
the state of Hope or Charity.

'So, aren't you well?' young William asked.

'I'm fine. Why, don't I look it?'

'You were looking at the doctor's.'

'No, I wasn't ...' (He was not quite sure what he *had* been
doing, on a pavement in a strange and frightening area of town.)

'No, I was just interested,' he improvised, 'as to why the
surgery was closed.'

'Oh. I'd think, no call for it,' said William.

'No call for it? Round here?'

'Or rather, not so much lack of demand, as lack of viable

supply.'

And Tom teased out of William how the National Health Service had been replaced by an 'independent' sector (for most people) and by coupons (for the rest), which you cashed in with the hospital or doctor of your choice. But as the doctors also had a choice − whether to practise in leafy suburbs with bright young healthy patients or to slum it in a place like Faith St − the consequence was that there were proportionately now seven times the number of doctors in − say − Dorchester as Rotherham, precisely the same differential (Tom remembered) as had obtained between Kensington and South Shields in 1939.

And pointing to obese young women leaning idly against crumbling balconies, on the upper storeys of grey blocks with names like Cripps and Morrison and Bevan, William remarked that one could see their point.

And Tom somewhat tartly asked his grandson, what he had been doing driving through this infernal quarter; and William explained that he driven up overnight from Salisbury, to give a 'presentation' for his company (the advertising giant Haussmann, Yoto, Peele and Eluard) to their clients British Lada (now a wholly-owned subsidiary of Lockheed-Mitsubishi), and that he'd decided to take the opportunity to check out the housing scene. And Tom asked if that meant the company was relocating here from Wiltshire, and William said, of course not, it's a London firm, and he was damn lucky to find somewhere reasonable in Salisbury, half the chaps now were commuting up from Exeter, or down from Nottingham or Shrewsbury.

And at this point they crossed under a great Expressway, via (as it happened) Hope Close, to another group of blocks of flats, but as different from those of Faith St as could be. For a start, to get into the estate you had to explain your business to the barrier guard, who then gave you your parking ticket and allowed you in.

And Tom remarked that this was an odd thing to happen on a public street, until William explained that was precisely what Charity was not (as they parked the Porsche and made their way past Hohenzollern's watchtower and Bourbon's moat to Hapsburg). For this hitherto municipal development had voted to transfer itself to a private landlord around 1990, the subsequent increase in rents driving out the poorer tenants, and the flats then being sold, the freehold being retained by Arnhem Properties. And although the bright 're-cladding' of the buildings was not quite to everybody's taste, and despite the fact that gaining ingress was a little trying (William's tin of sweeteners set off both alarms), once inside the vestibule of Hapsburg (or of Romanov or Saxe-Coburg) with its private shops and indoor pool and sauna club, one felt both pampered and secure.

'So you drive from Salisbury every day?' asked Tom of William, having seen round both the 'Luxury' and 'Sybaritic' scale of residential suite in Hapsburg (not bad, concluded William, except that the panoramic vista took in Beatrice Webb). And as he turned the Porsche back into public streets, William replied, no, not everyday; sometimes he took the train, travelling Eminent or Sovereign or even as a treat Imperial. And as if a little embarrassed by this revelation, and concerned at his grandfather's appalling ignorance of life in the Glorious Fifth Term (didn't the Alan Sugar Sunset Sanctuary subscribe to Newsnight?), he fell silent for a moment, and Tom could look (as they passed by Tawney, Beveridge and Keynes) at the miserable rows of shops, those still in business mostly locksmiths, off-licences and outlets offering 'cut rates' on 'daytime rentals.' And even without being absolutely clear what a 'video' was, it seemed obvious enough that if you lived in Beveridge or Morrison, you spent your evenings behind locked and bolted doors, with your fist clutched round a bottle. And as if he could overhear Tom's thoughts, William explained that the problem was − and what his sister Clara would not understand − that even if there were jobs here the residential population had neither the qualifications nor the drive to take them.

And it being half past twelve, and the city centre being on the way to his sister's unhygienic bedsit, perhaps he could entice Tom into a spot of lunch.

They parked in a multi-storey reserved for the owners of a certain charge card, and passed through yet another security check (reactive, apparently, to 'electronic tags'), and proceeded up an escalator into what was not by any means what Tom thought of as a city centre, but rather what he'd always imagined the back lot of a film studio would look like. Here, there was what was obviously supposed to be some kind of continental piazza, over there a Roman fountain − next to what appeared to be some class of wharf − and at the other end a row of shops decked out in cod Dickensia, with the whole thing roofed in glass as if it was Kew Gardens.

And when he asked his grandson where the *real* centre was, with the library, museum, clock, Town Hall, the institutions of the municipality, William patiently explained that the City Corporation (which offered various environmental and other services, in exchange for a basic all-in charge) had been recently relocated in the suburbs.

And as they sat down to the Mexican Experience, served by a Turkish Cypriot and prepared by two Iranians and a Chilean refugee, Tom realised that from a time when more or less everything was possible apart from shopping, he'd come to a time when nothing very much was possible except.

'You see, Grandad,' said William, as he raised a forkful of beef enchilada to his mouth, 'the mistake your generation made was the obsession with production. Which meant that you defined people not by what they wanted but by what they did to pay for it.'

'You mean, by class,' said Tom.

'That's right,' said William, spooning extra sour cream on to his burrito. 'Whereas we look at people differently. Our firm, for instance, divides people into seven basic lifestyle categories, five fundamental outlooks and four crucial needs. So this morning I explained how instead of targetting their new saloons at hopeful-seeking belonging-aspirant traditionalists, if British Lada went for Mellow Yellow early nesters seeking peer esteem they'd mop the market up in no time.

'Because, you see, Gramps, what most people feel they are isn't trodden proletarians, but home-owners, share-holders, charge-card members, time-sharers, Brits and frankly proud of it. Which is the real reason why she'll keep on winning and the other lot − or lots − will lose.'

And Tom forbore to mention that his grandson worked for what appeared to be a Franco-Japanese conglomerate, that his car was German and the property he thought of leasing sounded Dutch. And a little later William put his hand up for the Middle-Eastern waitress, and when the bill arrived he placed a green plastic rectangle upon the table (next stop gold and platinum), aware that by subscription to a New York charge-card scheme he was a member of a club that had its privileges.

Or so he thought, just as the lightning struck, the glass shattered, and it all went dark.

* * * *

'Phew,' said the Medic. 'That was close.'

(The Medic was a RAMC Lieutenant, apparently not quite yet seventeen.)

'Still,' he went on, 'we're doing very much the same thing to Caen. With a great deal more effect I hear. Now, any worries?'

And through the fug of sudden wakefulness − combined with the more literal fug left by the Luftwaffe − Tom confessed that he did have worries, yes, if he was honest, he was deeply worried.

'What about?'

'The future.'

And as he took his pulse the Medic assured Tom that as far as his own future went, he could be confident (if he took care); and that though things were still pretty sticky in the war *pro tem*, there was surely now no doubt about the final outcome. And beyond that − well, who knew what the future has in store.

'I mean,' he went on, with a twinkle, 'in my ABCA group there's some Bolshie Corporal who reckons that we ought to nationalise the railways.'

The Medic told him that he ought to stay recumbent for another day or two, and Tom − who was getting quite dispirited with at least one aspect of his horizontal state − asked if he couldn't have a go at least as far as the latrines, but the Medic said he shouldn't take the risk.

But later on the Nurse took pity, and decided it would be therapeutic if a group of callow convalescents were to try and do something clever with a canvas chair, two rifles and some bandages − to construct some crude means of conveyance to preserve Tom's constitution and his dignity.

'Because you see,' she said, as this makeshift sedan chair took shape, 'if you apply your mind to it, there is always an alternative.'

* * * *

'Hey, Grampa. Why aren't you in Oxford?'

'Uh?'

A young woman on a white bicycle screeched to a stop beside him, as another woman − of vehement appearance − strode towards him from the opposite direction, said 'hallo Clara' to the cyclist, and marched past a bike-rack into the nearest building, which though still in need of decoration and repair, was inhabited, and announced itself to be 'The Women Well'.

'Faith St,' he said.

'That's right,' said Clara.

'Women Well?'

'It's a kind of pun. You know, as in, 'drawing from the'. It's a women's health centre of course.'

'Of course. So what's wrong with your friend?'

'Oh. I'd think she's here for Basic Plumbing. Every other Wednesday.'

'Plumbing? In a Health Centre?'

'Now, come on Grampa,' Clara said, 'you of all people should know the connection between sanitation and public health. So. Why aren't you in Oxford?'

And Tom − who was becoming something of a dab hand at this − managed to imply that he was visiting the city for a limited time and unspecified purpose, and Clara said she had some visiting to do, and would he like to join her, and he said yes but what about her bicycle, and she said that if he felt up to it they'd ride together. And he said he was perfectly capable of riding a bicycle, indeed he had done so for several years before Clara's mother had been thought of, but, well I never, he didn't seem to have one about his person. And she said, don't be silly, walked into the Health Centre, borrowed something from her friend, and rapidly returned.

'Town Card,' she said, slipping a piece of plastic into one of a row of meters on the bike rack, thereby releasing a bicycle, apparently for Tom's use.

'Bike hire. Among the many rights of membership,' she said. 'Don't they take the newspapers at Balliol?'

'And is the Women Well just for women?' he asked her, somewhat breathlessly, as they peddled along.

'Yes, of course it is.'

'And is there a Men's Well?'

'There's no call for it.'

(They were heading past what Tom recalled were H G Wells and Crosland, but they'd been if not rebuilt then at least refurbished, and renamed.)

'So, men are utterly and completely healthy in every

way?' asked Tom sarcastically.

'No, Grampa,' said Clara, 'in fact, far from it. But they can go to the general Wellbeing Centre just like everybody else.'

'And what's that, please, when it's at home?'

'Oh, Grampa. It's a Health Centre. Where you can go and see your doctor, or an acupuncturist, or an osteopath, or do aerobics or learn first aid or plumbing – or indeed to ride a bicycle. In fact, just like it sounds.'

(They passed the little shopping centre where the locksmith's and the video shop had been: there was still a locksmith, though now obviously expanded to incorporate a general supplier, now called 'Bricks and Mortice'.)

'But it's all 'independent,' I suppose?' asked Tom.

'Well, if you mean 'private', no, of course it isn't,' replied Clara. 'It's all ultimately paid for out of taxes, and it's overseen and regulated by the local Health Assembly. But the healers organise themselves in a variety of ways. Some are fulltime employees, others are co-operatives. And of course your osteopath may well do Mondays at Wellbeing, Tuesdays at Women Well, and Wednesday, Thursday – Grampa, what's the matter?'

For Tom had screeched to a sudden halt, in the middle of the junction between Faith and Hope St.

'There's a road here,' he told Clara. 'A big – what? A big expressway.'

'No, there isn't,' Clara said. 'Do come on, or you'll get killed.'

And indeed there was no expressway, or barrier, and although Romanov and Hohenzollern stood in front of him, they had not been moated, barricaded or 're-clad'. And as they rode on, Clara said that she supposed he was referring to a grand development – put forward by a scratch consortium of British architects and Dutch financiers – upon which an amazingly successful if short-lived alliance between local residents, the Council and the Waterways Association had effectively put the kybosh a few years ago.

'The Waterways Association?' Tom asked.

'Oh, it was a heritage thing,' Clara said. 'It would have meant re-routing some canal.'

And Tom understood that what he was now seeing, dreaming or imagining was not what followed or preceded what he'd seen or dreamt with 'William,' but somehow an alternative, or parallel.

So the erstwhile Hapsburg, certainly less grand, was in the same state of refurbishment as the demonstrably rehabilitated Cripps and Morrison; and although its lobby still had a foodshop, what had been ground floor flats were given over to collective purposes: the concierge's office, Family Room (for playgroups and the like), Health Room (whatever saunas were, they were obviously an essential aspect of all social systems), and a Meeting Room, where matters vital to the block were regularly discussed, including, naturally, its name. (As the blocks were different – as a policy, new dwellers tended to be housed in their own age range – this had resulted in a certain referential bricolage: they were now in Tulip, between Rose and – as a protest by a somewhat younger residential population – Cauliflower; the oldest block was called Sinatra and the youngest Boadicea; and it had been forgotten whether 'Berry' was as in 'Goose' or 'Chuck'.)

Clara had business with a Bricks and Morticer, who was trying to sort out the central heating in a fifth floor flat, and so Tom sat down with the concierge, who told him that the key to the economic revival of the area had been, first, self-management (under a variety of forms of individual and collective ownership and rental, including a kind of licensed squatting for young people, in exchange for renovation work); and second, the insistence that all rehabilitation work that could be done by dwellers was. But, third, the scheme had acknowledged the *limits* of self-management, and indeed, of the democratic process: the agreement with the council stipulated a full-time, paid concierge in each block, so that if attendances declined at block meetings (as has occurred), or if conflicts were irreconcilable by democratic means (as had been known), then there was somebody who was responsible to keep things going.

And the concierges were also partially responsible for countering the trickiest aspect of self-management, which was its tendency to busybodying, intolerance, and age, class, sexual or racial exclusivity.

'But the real point is,' the concierge explained, 'that we're trying to break down the barriers in people's real lives; to challenge the distinction between paid and unpaid labour, work and leisure, 'production' and 'consumption' and 'community.' So for example the estate has places for people to meet safely, and for people who don't want to do that we've our own interactive cable channel, which gives home-bound people a chance to participate in estate affairs. And although flat-owners can make their own arrangements for repairs, the Council has collectively assessed and licensed plumbers, carpenters and so on, and so by-and-large that's taken out of people's hands, although of course people participate in that process by their own assessments and reports.'

'But, surely,' Tom said, 'a city of this size can't survive economically on home repairs and laundries. Or for that matter sticking needles in each other.'

'No, indeed,' said Clara (who'd returned, having apparently secured the temporary loan of thirty 'radio-mikes' for a purpose she seemed disinclined to specify). 'Look, I've got some business in the Centre. Fancy coming too?'

Which Tom did, but he wasn't sure about continuing by bicycle. So they deposited their machines in Tulip's rack (a welcome move, as a short queue was developing) and took the tram.

Clara was warming to her explanatory task (though she made a mental note that the city's strategies were clearly not yet widely enough known). Since Sheffield and the GLC, back in the 1980s, transport policy had of course been central to the strategies of socialist municipalities. The revival of the trams was only partly economic; it was partly to do with the historical associations (some stern critics thought this was a sell-out to the heritage industry – what next, sedan chairs?), but more importantly, it was about the notion that as many services as possible should be pleasing and indeed entertaining as well as functional (after all, a town clock didn't just tell you the time). So the revival of the trams and barges was an agreeable alternative (slightly more expensive) to the buses; and the minibuses that patrolled the city centre were distinctively liveried to reflect the nature of their circuit, like stations on the Paris metro.

But although there had been virtually complete pedestrianisation in the city centres, it was understood that private (or municipally rented) cars could liberate the old, and women, and young mothers. So there were days when they had carparking priority, as part of the city's contribution to the Europe-wide campaign to make cities more responsive to their needs, a campaign of which Tom's summer residential course at Balliol was also an example.

And luckily, before she could enquire how it was going, the tram arrived at what he hardly recognised as the same city centre, and as they alighted he could not restrain himself from asking 'Where's the fountain? Where's the *shops?*'

For what he had come into was a huge transportation terminus; where travellers by rail and tram and bus assembled, coming in and going out, on several levels. And in fact, now he took it in, there were shops, and booths, and stalls, and restaurants and cafes; but looking closer he could see that the frontages were by no means all of retail outlets: there were offices and bureaux and information points; and small workshops too. Because the problem with the great explosion of city building in the 1980s, Clara said, was that the retail revolution had, like cancer, consumed everything except itself, excluding and alienating those without the means to participate, and the aim of the New City was to return to at least an aspect of the very old, the medieval city: of a place of business, commerce, entertainment, travel – but above all, an open place, a place where everyone could come to and feel welcome.

So caught up had Clara become in this that it took Tom some time to interrupt her flow, to ask the obvious, which is what Marks & Spencer, Debenhams, Waterstone and Next (whoever *they* might be) thought about sharing their tastefully-dressed frontages with city information booths and co-op grocers, law centres, book exchanges, video-libraries, union offices and street stalls. So Clara explained how the municipal authorities had realised that while they were not necessarily the best people to run shops or build buildings, they *did* have planning powers over what were after all most attractive sites, which they could use to social purposes. And so the City could insist on equal access to the Terminus and the other public places in the City, it could control the relation between commercial and other public uses, and it could insist (through what she called the city code) that retailers – like any employer or producer in the city – comply with public policy on matters like employment opportunities, product quality (including environmental acceptability), and on what Clara called the 'community contribution' which was a fixed percentage of a company's turnover to be contributed to the city's musical, theatrical or sporting life.

'So this city code applies to manufacturers?' asked Tom.

'Well, yes, of course,' said Clara. And she assured Tom she would be delighted to explain the City's entire industrial and employment strategy, indeed, to *show* it him, just as soon as she had seen a man about some floats.

'Right, Gramps,' said Clara. 'Business done. And it's Hi Ho for Theatreland.'

'Well, good,' said Tom. 'But I thought you were going to show me the city's industrial and employment strategy.'

'Well, I am,' she said. 'And as a treat, I thought we'd see it from the water.'

And so they left the Terminus, and boarded a canalbus, and set forth along the City's waterways. And as they passed what appeared to be a large engineering plant, Clara explained that, yes, there were still such manufacturers, and that the municipality had expended some efforts (and finance) to encourage them to locate or expand their operations in the city. But in exchange for such encouragement (and for the opportunity provided by a highly-skilled and experienced workforce), all enterprises were required to offer equal employment opportunities for groups vulnerable to exclusion from the labour market; employee share schemes or a collectively-held investment fund; a proper means of worker consultation; and the opening up of a company's health and recreational services to the general community.

And Tom felt this system, splendid on the surface, begged a rather obvious question, but now they were passing into a different area, and Clara was eager to explain that this was an example of a phenomenon that had been dubbed (rather unhappily she thought) the 'small industrial milieu'; effectively, a cluster of small enterprises in the same broad field − some commercially owned, some co-operative, some in essence single-person operations − sharing joint facilities and using common services. And there were obvious examples of activities peculiarly conducive to such schemes, from the rag trade of Emilio Romagna in Northern Italy (with their shared suppliers, accountants, catering and training facilities) and the film and TV programme-makers of Sheffield in South Yorkshire (with their cutting rooms, viewing theatres, equipment hire and graphics and design consultancies), to the very quarter they were now approaching, where design and manufacture for the showbiz industries combined with a flourishing network of clothing designers, manufacturers and distributors to form the milieu known to one and all as Theatreland.

'And the interesting thing about all this,' Clara went on, 'is that many of these concerns began life as hobbies, in communities, schools, colleges and homes. So you're turning fashion, music-making and the like from a spectator to a participatory activity, but you're also challenging the division between training and employment, the school and the community, and actually, round here, between the workplace and the home. And you're providing kids — again, especially round here — with alternatives to selling petrol to the rich and junk food to each other.'

And as though to answer Tom's unspoken question, Clara admitted that, in exchange for state support of such endeavours, and the guarantee of jobs or student grants at Youth Wage rates, young people were required to take up at least one of the options offered. 'Which as you can imagine caused some trouble with the Class of '68,' said Clara. 'The Inalienable Right Not To Work brigade, you know.' (Which of course Tom did.)

They reached a jetty, and Clara and Tom alighted, as Clara had *considerable* business to contract in this particular district. And Tom noticed a familiar sight, a sign proclaiming an office of the Transport and General Workers' Union, and he asked Clara what role the unions performed.

And she explained how the unions had understood that the changes going on around them provided the most exciting and challenging opportunities for organisations with experience of collective action and association. So, first, they'd seized the opportunity for a new deal for women workers, and had negotiated flexible working agreements, guaranteed career breaks and term-time contracts. And then they'd begun to organise in the community (as black workers had for years), and had started to provide their members with all kinds of services (from workplace bakery deliveries to health visits, creches and insurance).

But perhaps the key moment, Clara said, had been when the National Union of Mineworkers, understanding that the carnage of the coal industry in areas like Scotland and South Wales was irreversible, had mounted its campaign for the rehabilitation of the former mining regions through the development of what had formerly been dismissed as 'alternative' technology, a campaign that involved community organisations, churches, and local government, but which also saw a significant revival of the alliance between former miners, their wives and urban political activists, that had been such a feature of the last great miners' strike. And it was such people who developed the Productivity Code (a subsection of a cluster of a codicil to the fifth revision of the European Social Charter, but none the less significant for that) which sought to extend the definition of 'productivity' to embrace a company's pollution record, its use of non-renewable resources, the health and safety of its workforce, and its contribution to the surrounding community.

Her business took an hour or so, whereupon Clara asked if Tom felt up to bicycling again, to give them an appetite for lunch at Boadicea's cafeteria. But Tom insisted first that she explain how this remarkable economy got over what seemed its obvious problem, which was that without the complete control and ownership of at least the means of production and distribution, all these exemplary restrictions and controls could be evaded by the simple expedient of employers moving out and setting up elsewhere.

To which Clara said, inserting both her own and her borrowed Town Card, and releasing two white bicycles from the rack outside the T&G: 'Well, as ever, Grampa, you have grasped the nub. That is indeed the problem, and that is where the politics comes in.'

But she refused to go further until they were back at the estate, she had popped into what appeared to be a radio station in the basement of Bob Marley, and they were seated at a table with two portions of a clearly wholesome if somewhat tasteless bean thing.

'Now you will remember,' Clara said, 'that election in the early 90s, with the Tories as the largest party, but no overall majority?'

(Tom nodded, trying to look a little vague about it; after all, he wasn't getting any younger.)

'Well, then, you will also recall the Sellafield disaster, and the Inquiry finding that half the cabinet either had shares in British Nukes, or were responsible for aspects of its safety, or both. And how they lost the vote of confidence, and Labour campaigned on the basis of a two-year, emergency revival programme, whereupon it would resign, and fight the next election on PR. That's proportional representation,' Clara added helpfully, as if talking to a child.

'Yes, yes, I *know*,' said Tom.

'Upon which programme, as you know, it won, or rather was the largest party, with the middle parties and the leeks and leafs but not the deeps supporting. And because of needing to keep the centre and the greens sweet, even its emergency programme got a bit truncated, provoking all that trouble with the True Believers. But there were two elements of the programme that the Government insisted on, and as they looked innocuous, the middle parties said OK.'

And, as Clara continued to 'remind' her grandfather, the first was the devolution of considerable powers from national down to local government, and to its regional tier, which basically consisted of an assembly of the strategic authorities that had taken over from the old metropolitan counties, but which were now directly elected, and formed one of the estates that made up the new upper house (which was – among other things – the first parliamentary body in the world to guarantee 50 per cent of its seats to women).

While the second was the acceptance of a much greater European Community involvement in British economic policy, a shift welcomed by the centre parties as more evidence of Labour 'realism,' but which was much more about the leadership's desire to shape pan-European policy on employee rights.

So by the end of the two years, there was in place a comprehensive Continental Charter, arising from the Social Charter and incorporating (among other things) the codes on women's rights and refugees, and which applied to all EC residents of whatever origin, and so went some way to redress the super-exploitation of Third World 'guest workers' that was such a feature of the 1980s, and did something too to arrest the growth of overt racist parties that had begun (but by no means ended) at that time.

Thus in neither the capital nor the labour market were companies able to evade the policies of progressive national or local governments; and the decline in the importance of the national tier meant that Labour could continue in a state of *de facto* coalition, without provoking the terrible compromises and betrayals that had been predicted.

But the most important thing, Clara said, was that at the local level it was seen that Labour's social policies were working, and that, despite the many difficulties (not least the problem of unequal social distribution and the undoubtedly high failure rate of small co-operative endeavours), the Left could now present a genuine alternative to market enterprise, the image of a truly active citizen, responsible not just to his or her own family, but to all kinds of overlapped (and interlocked) communities.

'Because you see, Gramps,' Clara said, lifting a forkful of what looked like grated radish to her mouth, 'the problem was, that people who were powerless in market terms found themselves increasingly excluded from all social life; if they were poor, or old, or ill; or if they had skills that had no immediate commercial market value.

'But in fact, of course, that view of life is desperately one-dimensional. Because although I work, indeed I've been working hard all day, I'm also about what I eat, and how I exercise, and who I do that with, and where I live and who I sleep with, and my relations with the other people who do all those things, and those who do quite other things as well, and the planet we all live on, and my views about how we should protect it and sustain its future.

'And feeling ultimately that I am a member, of a neighbourhood, of a society, of groups and callings, federations and assemblies, of a locality, and a generation, and a gender ... and that without those various identities I wouldn't in any real way be me at all.'

And Tom's head was beginning to grow light, and the image of his grand-daughter to fade, and he felt that any moment he would slip back to wherever he had come from. But before he went, he wanted to find out what indeed she had been working at, with the Bricks and Morticer, the float-provider, the radio station and the co-operative endeavours of the small industrial milieu.

'Oh, that,' she said. 'Well, it's the fiftieth anniversary as you know of 1945, and the plan originally was to hold a sort of pageant, to commemorate the ending of the war and the aspirations people had for what would follow it. But somehow that didn't seem to fit, with the city as it is now, and people thought it shouldn't be a pageant, more a sort of carnival, and not about the war, but other things. And I'm sort of one of the co-ordinators, and come to think of it, you ought to come.'

'So what *is* it about?' Tom asked, 'and when does it begin?'

And Clara explained that it was hard to answer that, because it was about a variety of things, about the present and the future and the past; and it didn't actually 'begin', in the sense of starting at one point in space and time and moving forward to another; that it was something which began all over, in homes and neighbourhoods and associations and communities, but which she hoped would, as it were, converge: but from different starting points, at different speeds.

'But in the same direction, surely?' Tom asked, as Clara's image ebbed and dimmed before him.

'Ah, well,' his grand-daughter replied, 'that is of course the question.'

* * * *

'O if I could but see it,' Tom announced, rising insistently on to one elbow.

'I beg your pardon,' said the passing Nurse.

'It's what William Morris says,' he went on. 'At the beginning of his book. He says, 'O, if I could but see a day of it.'

'Well, does he now,' the Nurse replied. 'And why d'you think that popped into your befuddled brain?'

'Because, in a way, I have,' Tom said.

Göran Therborn

Vorsprung Durch Rethink

Three concepts are sufficient to sum up a long-term socialist or, if you prefer, radical-humanist project: human life-realisation, universality, and history. Universal human life-realisation is, in a nutshell, what socialism is about, with the addition that it has a location and a range in historical time. It is not a moment, or even a lifetime, of bliss only, but a period rooted in the past and connecting itself with the future.

A *vision* of it may be seen as the outside of a sphere, with open horizons in every direction, some spaces in varying shades of daylight with people peacefully and autonomously going about myriad activities, difficult to distinguish between work or play, not to speak of between rewarding and bare subsistence-yielding activities. Some people are acting alone, others in smaller or larger groups, leaders and led may exist, but are impossible to distinguish from afar. Locales vary seemingly infinitely, but slums, rural holes of misery or concentration camps are nowhere to be seen. A certain clean freshness is hanging in the air and sparkles in the water. Other spaces are in the dark but penetrable to the visionary, who sees well-fed people in safe, well-sheltered sleep, people in the passion of love-making, individuals awake with sleepless eyes wrestling with the demons of creation, or others being born, lying sick or dying, with caring fellow-humans at their bedside. The visionary is looking at Earth from inner space and sees a multi-faceted human life without systematic violence, coercion, misery, and degradation, without sorting mechanisms condemning categories of human beings to having a large portion of their children die as babies, falling prey to famines, preventable diseases, poverty, humiliation, exploitation, lack of care, and to a cruel or unnecessary death.

As this vision is meant to be part of a rational political discourse, it is open to a number of objections. In other words, in forwarding a planetary vision of humanity in daylight and at night, I accept the obligation of a rational reasoner to provide reasons for sceptics to see it as a possible future, and as a future worth striving for. Indeed, I am trying to develop an argument in dialogue with critics.

A Debate With a Liberal Sceptic and a Modern Socialist

Round One: About Evil and Emancipation

Liberal Sceptic: Your so-called socialist vision is little more than a dream of a world without evil. That may be a noble dream, but it provides no indications of how to get there. And, after all, is it worthy of a rational social scientist (politician, writer, activist, citizen – delete what is not appropriate) to promise a world without evil?

Modern Socialist: On this point, if only on this, I agree completely with my liberal enemy, but I would add...

Answer: Wait a minute, let us stop here for a moment. My vision is something significantly different from, or less than, a wish for a world without evil. The world I am talking of is a world without systems of evil, without systematic mechanisms allocating fortune or misery, without, to quote an already half-forgotten Hollywood actor 'empires of evil'. I am assuming no change in the everyday mixture of good and evil in Mr Smith as Ms Jones. And I think I am rare among utopians having envisaged, in a one paragraph summary of paradise, people bed-ridden with sickness, and people dying.

Modern Socialist: All right, but it is still very abstract and vapoury. More than that, even at the level of supreme principles you seem to be fucking things up. The communist and socialist project has always had a clear goal, universal human emancipation. Why are you leaving out the goal of emancipation? Has it become too revolutionary, 'fundamentalist' even, perhaps?

Answer: This is a crucial difference between modernism and postmodernity, which has dawned upon me only lately. I honestly do not think that a socialist or radical project can be summed up in terms of 'emancipation' any more. Emancipation is a key to the politics of modernity, a politics of liberation from the shackles of the *ancien régime*, or of traditional society, monarchical rule supposedly by the grace of God, class exploitation, bigotry, prejudice, patriarchy, racism. Emancipation remains on the agenda in most parts of the world, above all, in the form of women's emancipation, but also of ethnic/national and class. However, the concept of emancipation presupposes that of oppression/exploitation, as a clear baseline from which to move. In advanced capitalist democracies it is difficult, and unconvincing, to conceive of women or workers as generally and unqualifiedly oppressed and as exploited (other than in the accountant's sense of an academic class analysis). Such societies do contain features of oppression and exploitation, and thereby tasks of emancipation, but the former do not hold as general characteristics of life in those societies. *Human life-realisation* has the advantage of not being tied to one linear movement, from oppression to freedom, but of connoting, at the same time, an infinite plurality of life — projects and a universal yardstick, the human life-span universally possible at a given level of world resources and medical knowledge.

Round Two: About Life and the Economy

Liberal Sceptic and Modern Socialist: Your vision seems to entail a biologisation of politics and of social life. Does that mean that you accept the current capitalist economy as the most efficient one?

Answer: No one but a fool would say that the present is the best of all possible worlds. Only hopeless utopians may dream of capitalism lasting for ever. But it is true that I have reformulated the socialist project, from being couched in terms of property, markets, and the state, into basic concerns of human life.

Liberal Sceptic: But that implies a recognition of markets and of capitalism, doesn't it?

Answer: Of markets yes, of capitalism no. The marxist conception of socialism was based on an analysis of capitalism asserting its intrinsic contradictoriness. The development of capitalism would bring about an increasing dysfunctionality between the private relations of production and the increasingly public(ly dependent) forces of production. That did happen, up to about 1950, expressed in the socialisation of mass communications and mass transport, even of natural resources held to constitute the 'commanding heights' of the economy. For another fifteen years there was the establishment of a public management of the economy, of its growth rate and its business cycle. The process of international cartelisation, which culminated in the 1930s, was part of the same tendency. Since then, however, the world market and the multinational corporation have reasserted themselves against both cartels and states although the publicly managed economy remains – and will remain.

Liberal Sceptic: But why don't you then accept the superiority of the capitalist market? Isn't that what is implied both in the reforms of Deng Xiaoping and the *perestroika* of Gorbachev?

Answer: The functioning of the market is dependent on the initial distribution of endowments, and the current distribution of resouces in the world denies the possibility of a decent human life to hundreds of millions of people. That distribution has to be changed. There seems to be no empirical evidence that speculative financial markets have any positive function in what serious liberal economists sometimes call 'the real economy', and often the former have clearly negative effects on production and work. The increasing power of financial capital has to be reversed. The market is furthermore a poor mechanism for dealing with fundamental human questions – for which there are no clear compensatory trade-offs – with choices of rare frequency and/or of special information requirement. The market can function rather well with regard to your choice of consumer goods, but rather badly, for instance, with respect to what old-age care you, as a resourceful prime-age adult, may need in the far-off future as an elderly person.

Intellectually, it is interesting that probably the most popular metaphor of contemporary rational action theory is 'the prisoner's dilemma', which is a sad story of two or more people who cannot communicate and co-operate with each other, and who therefore, as rational egoists, end up much worse than they would have scored if they had been able to co-operate. This example teaches us a lesson exactly opposite to that of the 'invisible hand' of the market.

Round Three: About Socialism and Liberalism

Modern Socialist: But if you hold those views, why don't you present a clear picture of a socialist economy? Instead you are presenting a vision devoid of any concrete institutions. Wouldn't it be more honest to say, in your case, that you are abandoning the idea of socialism for another vision or utopia of a more general humanistic kind?

Answer: The vision I am seeing presupposes a complete overhaul of the distribution of endowments, of property and propertylessness, and a complete change of the relationships between financial and productive institutions. Those changes would entail a universal equalisation of life-chances and a decisive role allotted to productive, in contrast to merely appropriating, creativity. Therefore, my vision implies a number of crucial institutional changes, which are all contained within the traditions of socialism. However, in contrast to classical socialists, I am not sure what the new institutions needed would look like exactly.

Liberal Sceptic: Fine, but isn't that tantamount to civilised liberalism?

Answer: In case you should recognise your liberalism in my vision, or somebody else social democracy, christian democracy, ecologism, or x-, y- or z-ism, I would be happy, because that would mean a broadened support for it. The sectarian preoccupation with drawing demarcation lines is alien to me.

Liberal Sceptic: Thank you, but doesn't that amount to an abandonment of socialism as a specific political tendency?

Answer: There is a basic continuity with modern socialism, in universalism, in historicity, and in concentrating on scrutinising and changing the content of social and political forms, the social human contents of political constitutions and sets of juridical rights, and the structuring of situations of choice with systematic outcomes of affluence on the one side and misery on the other.

Round Four: On History and Historical Tendencies

Modern Socialist: Why do you put such an emphasis on history in your three concepts summary? Isn't that more than anything else a cover-up for the fact that you have substituted a utopian vision for the marxist theory of history?

Answer: No, the reason is an aim at retaining a link with 'scientific socialism', ie, with the location of socialism in actually existing history. But I had also something else in mind, more directly related to my conception of life politics. A vision of a better world must contain a sense of link with, and thereby responsibility for, the future, for coming generations. No generation has the right to destroy life-chances for the next one(s). That is a constraint on universal life-realisation.

Modern Socialist: Talk about 'history' is not enough! The scientificity of historical materialism's conception of socialism was that it analysed how the latter developed out of the contradictions and of the social conflicts of capitalism. But your so-called vision is not derived from any analysis of historical tendencies of contradiction and conflict. You are only holding up a picture, hoping that some people will find it attractive. Do you see any social forces with an interest or tendency to bring them about?

Answer: The most concrete answer to your first question is that my vision involves a universalisation and a deepening of the institutions of the most advanced welfare states. Secondly, it follows up the vital issues brought on to the historical agenda by the progressive women's movement, of gender relations, modes of human reproduction, and of the quality of personal relations in the systems of institutional forms. Thirdly, my vision expresses the actualisation of basic questions of the human environment put forward by the ecological movement. What I see are all tendencies of the new times.

Modern Socialist: Is it deliberate that you refrain from referring to any economic tendencies of contemporary capitalism?

Answer: The welfare state, the women's uprising, environmental concerns, have all grown out of affluent developed capitalism, out of forces and issues generated within it, although the processes have been very complex and are irreducible to a purely economic dialectic. Between these tendencies and capitalism, there are fundamental conflicts, which does not mean incompatibility or impossibility of coexistence, however. After all, life is not incompatible with violence, cruelty, and fraud, for instance. But wouldn't you admit that life would be more pleasant without them?

Liberal Sceptic: Why don't you relate to the rise of the post-industrial knowledge economy with its substitution of information for toil and capital, of networks for hierarchy, of flexibility for rigid rules, of decentralisation for centralisation?

Answer: The tendencies of contemporary capitalism are ambiguous in their social implications. While Taylorist, army-type bureaucracies are clearly on their way out, industrial production is of declining economic weight, and the computerisation of information and of the use of information are clearly of rapidly growing economic importance, no clear pattern is emerging, bestseller ideologies not withstanding. The global centralisation of corporate power is growing simultaneously with decentralisation within corporate organisations. Union busting and idiosyncratic personal management are increasing alongside more and more autonomous personnel involvement. Rent for attractive, increasingly scarce natural estate, and for urban real estate is rapidly growing in importance in contemporary capitalism. The manipulation of, or privileged exclusive access to, information is becoming an increasingly important means of capital accumulation. And so forth. Very significant in these ambiguously contradictory economic tendencies is, I think, the growing role of a large category of qualified employees, overcoming manual/non-manual divisions, the commitment and the sophisticated life-demands of whom productive capital is getting crucially dependent upon. People of this kind are already providing much of the support for new humanistic movements, and given an institutional chance they could also give a new impetus to the labour movement. The counter-strategy of capital and conservatism, however, is to try to segment these employees in corporate and local loyalties and to isolate them from the rest of the population, from the bulk of the service workers, traditional production workers, the unemployed, and the retired.

The two basic institutions of welfare states are (membership) rights and care. As a member of a relevant category, as a citizen, or as a member of some other group, you as a person have a right to certain services and forms of support, regardless of your property status and of your ability to pay the going market price. Secondly, most of what existing welfare states do is to provide care for people, care for the sick, the infirm, and the elderly, care for children to grow up and learn. The rights of persons and taking care of people have a tense, conflictual relation to the principle of exclusion inherent in the notions of property and purchase, and to the production and circulation of commodities.

The women's movement challenged the male particularisms in the prevailing conceptions of freedom and equality, solidarity and socialism. In that respect the movement has been a tendency of universalism. Pertinent in this context is also another feature of the feminist insurrection: its concern with the quality of personal human relations – between men and women above all, but also among women, among men, and between adults and children. Autonomy, dignity, authenticity, concern in human relations, are standards or demands raised in defiance of instrumentalism and commodification. A third aspect of the women's movement, that I find particularly appealing, is its combination of a radical individualism with collective action and solidarity. Feminism challenged the unproblematised collectivity of the family – the hidden cupboard of most bourgeois individualism, a cupboard full of victims of patriarchal power and despotism. It did that pointing towards a more authentic individualism, which at the same time entailed a universalistic concern with and care for other human beings.

The ecological movement has put life environment at the centre of attention. Like all radical movements, including the classical socialist one, it also contains dubious elements, fragile prophecies of imminent doom, puritanical moralisms, and upper middle-class neglect of the work and housing environment of ordinary people. However, ecologists have made invaluable contributions to a new life politics, demonstrating the lethal or seriously damaging, unnecessary threats of pollution, poisoning, and the destruction of nature.

Round Five: The Welfare State and Statism

Liberal Sceptic: But isn't the welfare state a bureaucratic dinosaur which is now being challenged both from the Left and the Right as something which has to be replaced, or at least cut down, by a 'welfare society', of one form or another?

Answer: You are mistaking the current institutional forms for the basic principles of the welfare state, and the current ideological steam around those forms. The core of the welfare state is that the reproduction of the population of a given political entity is a public, political responsibility. Neither Thatcher nor Reagan and their acolytes have been able to challenge the right of people in need to support and to service. Neither has been able to do away with institutions of human care and concern. The development of the productive forces, of science and technology, will require more education, rather than less. The growth of medical knowledge and technology will raise the demand and the supply of care in the future. Ageing populations will need much more care.

It is certainly not inconceivable that the current right-wing tendencies of restricting the services and the care given to the ordinary human being without property or the properly conducted insurance policy to the shoddiest possible minimum, will continue, and even aggravate. But the life politics issues of human reproduction, of the education, the curing, the caring, and the keeping healthy of the population will not go away. Nor will they be buried in families and networks outside common political responsibility and organisation. The traditional socialist Left has lost sight of the meaning of the welfare state through a myopia of economic functionalism and a macho preoccupation with 'high politics'.

Liberal Sceptic: But surely, any serious attempt at new thinking would have to break with the statism of the traditional Left?

Answer: True, that the public corporation and the planning commissariat, even some of the large public health care authorities, no longer inspire the confidence and enthusiasm they once did. But statism or anti-statism is not the real issue. To put the choices in those terms is a diversionary manoeuvre. What is needed is to put the most important social problems into focus, and then to discuss the proper institutional forms. For everybody on this earth to have a chance to realise a decent life, in view of the resources and the knowledge available to humankind today, a lot of public political intervention and regulation will be absolutely necessary. But new forms of public intervention and organisation will certainly be called for. I am no reliable defender of actually existing welfare state forms, but you will never lure me into any statism/anti-statism debate.

Round Six: Social Forces

Modern Socialist: You never answered directly my question about the possible social forces that might be mobilised for your utopia. I also wonder, from what you did say, if you mean that there is a growing contradiction between capitalism and what you call universal life-realisation?

Answer: There has been so much growth in the contradictions of capitalism in past socialist rhetoric, that considerable caution seems proper for a while. I am not saying that the internal contradictions of contemporary capitalism are growing or are likely to grow in the foreseeable future. What I am saying, is that the conflicts between capitalism, even advanced affluent capitalism, and the universal possibility of realising a meaningful, dignified, and reasonably decent and healthy life, do not show the slightest tendency to disappear. And at least in some areas the gap between the potential and the actuality of human life is definitely increasing. We see this in the expansion of poverty in the United States, in the enduring, American-type ghetto-producing mass unemployment in most parts of Western Europe, in the increased pollution of many cities and waters, in the growing destruction of children and youth (visible in addiction, violence, crime, and prostitution), in the glaringly inadequate care for the elderly also in the richest countries, in the increase of misery in large parts of the Third World, and in the persisting threats of ecological disaster.

Life politics has no single or even central subject. That is a handicap in short-term power politics. On the other hand, it can, or might, draw upon a broad spectrum of social and cultural forces, which in terms of long- and medium-term societal transformations is a source of strength.

The labour movement, in so far as it is a class movement rather than an aggregate of interest groups pursuing sectional interests, and the movements of the popular classes or the poor people of the Third World, in so far as they are movements of popular needs rather than merely waves of frustration or objects of demagogy, are certainly necessary forces. Without them, life politics would tend to become concern for the quality of life among the affluent and prosperous only.

Women, not just the women's movement, are and will probably become another major force. Whatever the reasons, women are, and seem likely to remain (as far as we can see), over-represented in reproductive work (paid as well as unpaid) and tend to be more concerned with the quality of the human condition. In the past, family seclusion and confinement to a narrowly religious interpretation of existential issues tended to make women more politically conservative than men. That is now changing, and turning the other way around. Of course, women constitute no one tendency, and they will continue to spread over the political spectrum. But it seems likely that women will have a strong, stronger than men, tendency to support radical politics for universal human life-realisation.

Various aspects of what I have here called life politics is also what various groups of concerned middle-class people, mostly professionals of one kind or another, have already committed themselves to. Environmentalist groups, human rights groups, people concerned with helping victims of famines, disasters, and of persecution. While here there has been an erosion and a demoralisation of the traditional Left, the right-wing politics currently in vogue in several countries does not seem to have extinguished, or even lowered, commitments to specific issues of humanistic concern, does not seem to have lowered the vistas of the whole middle classes to political concerns with taxation rates, mortgage interests, and portfolio trajectories only.

Liberal Sceptic: But if there are so many people and movements of goodwill, why does the world then look the way you say it does? Or do you mean that paradise is imminent?

Answer: My answer to your second question is no, and to your first would be too long to print here. But, as a general point, the people of this world are caught up in a welter of conflicting situations, structured by a starkly unequal distribution of resources, constrained by economic competition and power rivalry, and affected by unintended, unforeseen, as well as by conflicting consequences of action. The progressive forces I referred to above are also entangled in this web. What is needed is to cut a path on which a life politics can stand tall, can see its own vista, and can walk forward. That task of clearance is first a task of re-orienting the political debate, such as we are doing here. How such a re-orientation should take shape in line-ups for power for a change is a later question. And changing the terms of prevailing discussion will already in itself bring about some changes in existing institutions and configurations of power.

Round Seven: A Summing-up of Issues

Modern Socialist: Please, could you formulate the re-orientation you are talking about into an understandable everyday political language? What do you want us to do?

Answer: I am not going to present a party platform nor a blueprint for the next socialist revolution. But I will sum up my argument in a few points. What I am suggesting is, first of all, to take a step behind economic and political institutions and to begin to formulate the tasks of radical (socialist, progressive, humanist, democratic) politics in terms of people's life environment and their life chances, of everybody's possibility of realising the full potentiality of human life, with the constraint that this possibility should be preserved for future members of humankind.

This perspective puts certain issues and political tasks in the foreground.

– Disarmament (not necessarily unilateral), arms control, attemps at preventing or defusing armed conflicts.

– Universalistic human solidarity, fighting racism, sexism and ethnic oppession, overcoming exclusivist nationalisms.

− Health and adequate healthcare for everybody, which means a frontal assault on national, ethnic, and class differences in mortality, morbidity, and well-being; provision of decent care for the infirm and for the elderly.

− Education to enable a full participation in a continuously developing society with a secure milieu of growth for all children and youth, and possibilities for further education for adults.

− A distribution of material resources and rewards egalitarian enough to make a decent human life a possibility for everybody, which means massive efforts at restructuring the material life chances of people within most countries (not least Britain), and the construction of new forms of cross-national support and development co-operation.

− A restructuring of personal and social relations so as to render individual antonomy possible for all women as well as for all men.

− Work, with basic health safety, and potential for human growth for everybody who wants to take part in the economy. An organisation of social time which makes it possible and easy for people to arrange their life-time according to their choice of remunerated work, care for children, kin, and friends, education and re-training, and of leisure and recreation.

− De-pollution of air and water, economic growth and life-realisation only under the constraint of nature conservation. Nature has to be recognised politically and economically for what most of us know privately already, that nature should not just be an object of human conquest, since it is a basic aspect of the quality of human life. Large efforts have to be made at finding out and doing something about the life-damaging consequences of produced substances and waste products, and of various human practices.

− A reorganisation of urban life and of the different opportunities in cities and in the countryside with a view to the abolition of slums and metropolitan congestion and to steering the trade-off between anonymous freedom and, on the other hand, vandalism, violence, criminality, and abandoned despair into more positive directions.

Liberal Sceptic: Beautiful! And who is to foot the bill?

Answer: All of us. This cannot be paid for by the rich only. But almost all of us will also benefit from it, to a larger or smaller extent.

Modern Socialist: You didn't say a word about capitalism, or, for that matter, socialism!

Answer: The gist of my argument is, that the issues of life environment and life chances should be put first, and that the economic institutions most adequate to the former will have to be found out later. The issues I give priority to are certainly different from maximising capital accumulation. Nay, they require a drastic restriction of the sway of capitalist property and capital accumulation. In that sense they follow a classical socialist line. On the other hand, I am quite aware of the dynamism of a market economy and of the requirement of economic and administrative managerial competence. In order to give everybody on this earth a decent life environment and decent life chances we need a very efficient economy and very efficient forms of organisation in all walks of life. Markets and professional management will without doubt be necessary. But for the rest, what organisational forms and systems we should head for, I am not sure. The crucial thing is, in my opinion, that the latter will be geared to the goal of giving everybody the possibility of realising the full potential of a human life in a fresh environment.

Round Eight ...

The Editor: You haven't allowed your opponents to concede defeat or to be knocked out, so this could go on for ever. But, in case you should want to publish these scribbles you had better stop now!

Answer: Yes sir.

Manifesto for New Times

Realignment of Politics

We need new politics for the new times. The new times are changing the character of politics — how it is conducted, what it is about, where it takes place. The transformation of what is 'political' is one of the characteristics of the new times. However politics is also shaping the new times. Thatcherism, Gorbachev, the green movement, are all setting the agenda of the new times, shaping society's responses to the issues which confront it.

The crisis of the Left is its failure to find a role in the new times. They represent an epochal shift in the organisation of society, certainly the most profound set of changes since the second world war, possibly since the turn of the century. Such movements in the geological plates of society inevitably provoke fundamental changes in the organisation of politics and parties. As yet the labour movement has been unable and unwilling to risk the kind of shift that is required to match the fundamental nature of restructuring in society.

The scale of what might be required is evident from the labour movement's history. The epochal changes around the turn of the century led to the creation of entirely new political parties — the modern socialist parties, including the Labour Party. The second world war produced a major realignment of the centre-Left. The Labour Party absorbed a large part of the Liberal Party, assimilated the ideas of Keynes and Beveridge, and for the first time won the support of significant sections of the middle class. A political upheaval and realignment of similar proportions is required by the new times.

The significance of those realignments was not the new relations established between political parties. It was what that realignment in turn meant for society. For those realignments produced new ideas of progress and how it could be achieved. They did not dabble in politics as the art of what was possible. They changed what was possible. They opened up new possibilities for social development.

The central point of a political realignment in the 1990s would be to establish a new conversation between the Left and society. What has happened to the labour movement in the last two decades is the political equivalent of the fate we all dread befalling us at parties. For many years after the second world war the labour movement was the magnetic centre of conversation. But gradually people started to get frustrated that they could not join in the conversation. They wanted to ask questions but were too often ignored. They started to get bored and drifted away to other parts of the room to find more interesting discussions. The labour movement is in danger of ending up in a corner talking to itself. The only way it will re-establish a conversation with its fellow party-goers is to move towards them, start to speak their language, and listen to their views. Above all it has to start saying something interesting, engaging and entertaining – something worth listening to.

The labour movement's gradual estrangement from society has six fundamental causes which are reshaping politics. Thatcherism has been successful because it has responded to these changes much more effectively than the labour movement.

Firstly, one of the forces which has created the new times is the expansion of the realm of politics over the last thirty years. Personal life from consumption to sexuality has been increasingly politicised. Social movements, such as the women's movement and the green movement, have arisen, organised directly around the politics of real life, the politics of social issues as people confront them. Politics is less and less confined to a distinct realm of parties, resolutions, manifestos and elections. The agents of political change have become more diverse and complex – unions, students, women, campaigners over the environment, peace and aid.

The expansion of the politics of society, rather than the politics of institutions, is not confined to the Left. One of Thatcherism's great strengths is its drive to embed its politics in civil society. It seeks to achieve this through cultural change – enterprise culture the spread of Thatcherite personal identities of home-owner, credit-card holder, and share-owner. It has also wrought significant institutional changes in civil society.

Companies have become not merely sources of employment and output, but geysers for Thatcherite values − value for money, choice, efficiency. Private sector employers, for instance through the government's plans for local Training and Enterprise Councils, are playing a key role in delivering Thatcherite policies. The company and the private home have been elevated as key institutions in society.

A vital part of Thatcherism's success is that it has responded to the expansion of politics through society much more effectively than the labour movement, which still has uneasy relations with its natural allies, the social movements.

Secondly, the expansion of politics through society is one force which has changed the role of the state. The labour movement is a creature of the state. The hub of the Labour Party's sense of its purpose is electoral victory in order to form a government. The labour movement is deeply defensive of its main historic achievement − the corporatist, Keynesian welfare state.

This approach to the politics of the state is inadequate for the new times. The corporatist, Keynesian welfare state has low public support. The economic and social conditions it was designed to address have been transformed. The idea of the state managing society, playing an extensive role in delivering solutions and services is being superseded by two developments.

There is a widespread desire for a state which is capable of taking determined, strategic action to sort out problems. Several of the central issues of the new times, for instance the modernisation of the new technology economy, require such a strategic state. It is matched by a desire for a less embracing, intrusive, paternalistic state. People want a more decentralised, open, enabling state, which helps them reach their own solutions to problems.

The labour movement has a conservative approach to the state. It wants to occupy the state, when it needs to be transformed. It supports the current electoral system, it accepts the British union and is conservative on issues like a bill of rights. The labour movement wants to be a respectable manager of the state. It needs to be a radical reformer.

In contrast Thatcherism has much more clearly understood the need to transform the state. It has used it much more strategically and ruthlessly than any previous government. But it also has a much clearer idea of a right-wing enabling state. Much of its legislation, on privatisation, council house sales and trade-union reform, has been aimed at enabling its supporters. Its state works both strategically and in alliance with groups in society.

Thirdly, politics is becoming increasingly internationalised. The labour movement's concentration on the politics of the centralised British state means its political arena is almost exclusively the nation state. That is where the labour movement's politics are played out. However, with the passage to new times, politics and power are becoming ever more international with the integration of the world economy, the power of the international company, the Europeanisation programme and the growing importance of international institutions such as the IMF. Thatcherism is riven with an insular chauvinism which means it will never be able to adjust fully to internationalisation. But the labour movement has responded even more inadequately.

Fourthly, the depth and force of the changes underway in society require radical new thinking, both to understand them and respond to them. During a period of radical restructuring which is taking society through uncharted territory, politics has to have wide horizons. It has to have vision. Developing that vision requires two things: clear values which command popular support and the confidence to innovate new policies and ideas.

Thatcherism has excelled at both, partly through creating a web of right-wing think tanks. The Right has gone through an intellectual renewal since the mid-1970s. The Left has only just started training. Thatcherism has had the confidence to take risks to refashion the meaning of modern conservatism to match the new times. The Left has yet to match its confidence.

Fifthly, an aspect of the new times is the fragmentation of old political constituencies and social allegiances. This has been accompanied by the rise of new collective sources of identity and attachment. The labour movement has been unable to come to terms with the decline of its old constituencies among the male, manufacturing class, and the emergence of new social movements and aspirations. In contrast Thatcherism has much more effectively realigned itself with rising social groups and aspirations – the affluent working class, entrepreneurial businessmen, and the meritocratic private-sector middle class.

Finally, some of the old polarities of politics are being refashioned. Where does the green movement fit into a world of two political poles − left or right? Indeed most of the social movements, the women's movement, the aid campaigns, nationalism, and black politics, do not easily fit within the straitjackets of right and left. They are opening up ideas of progress, forms of organisation, conceptions of politics which differ markedly from the priorities and traditions of socialist party politics.

Moreover, the transition to new times is creating another new point of commonality. There is a vital division between those parts of the opposition to Thatcherism which have shifted on to the terrain of the new times and those who still hanker after the familiar past. The modernisers in different parties may have more in common with one another than they have with traditionalists in their own parties. Thus, alongside left and right, we need a new vocabulary to describe political polarities. That will turn on the line between progressive and regressive politics, modernisers and traditionalists.

Socialism has always claimed to speak for the future. But in the last fifteen years its authority to do so has been thrown into doubt by these six developments. The combination of these six forces has raised fundamental questions about the links between socialism and progress.

What is social progress in the age of the threat of environmental catastrophe? Is socialism just a part of a much wider conception of universal human values and progress? Can it or should it attempt to encompass the different ideas of progress thrown up by the new social movements? Who are the social agents of political change? What is the role of the unions, the women's movement, pressure groups and campaigning organisations? What should be the division of labour between national and international politics, change in civil society and state intervention? Should political parties on the Left aim to unify the diversity of social movements, or should some other relationship be encouraged?

These are central and difficult questions. The lack of adequate answers is at the heart of the historic exhaustion of the Left as a political force. This is not just true of Britain. This exhaustion is evident in the lack of vision of many socialist governments in power in France, Spain, Greece and Australia. It is true of the Left in most Western European countries, where there is debate about the relationship between Socialist Parties, Communist Parties and Greens. It is also true of many Eastern European states where the growth of social movements in civil society is a major force reshaping politics. The resolution of those questions will provide the key to the long-term renewal of the Left.

One of the most striking, hopeful and inspiring examples of how to respond to these questions creatively has been provided by Gorbachev. Perestroika is creative because it is confident enough to take risks with the meaning of socialism. The role of the party, planning and the state are being questioned. Gorbachev talks of a new socialist morality of enterprise, individual responsibility and initiative within Soviet society. He has confidently rejected the old polarities of the cold war. Instead he talks about common human values, self-determination and pluralism. Gorbachev has had the honesty to admit that socialism has suffered from the arrogance of omniscience and the stagnation of bureaucracy. If he came to a party everyone would want to talk to him.

The malaise of the Left is that the old is dying but the new cannot yet be born. We are searching for a new political language. We can imagine it resounding in our ears. But it is not yet on the tips of our tongues. Embarking on this search is risky. But it is inescapable. Social change and political failure are driving us in that direction. But it will almost certainly involve a loss of self-confidence and direction before a new sense of identity and purpose can be found. It is impossible to prescribe in detail how that renewal should take place. But the elements of a new sense of purpose are emerging like fragments of a conversation between people stumbling to learn a foreign language. That must provide the starting point.

Notes on Contributors

Neal Ascherson is a columnist on *The Observer* and author of *Struggles For Poland* (1987) and *Games With Shadows* (1988).

Sarah Benton is the political editor of *New Statesman and Society*.

Rosalind Brunt is director of the Centre for Popular Culture at Sheffield City Polytechnic and co-editor of *Feminism, Culture and Politics* (1982).

Beatrix Campbell is a writer and broadcaster; her books include *Wigan Pier Revisited* (1984), *Iron Ladies: Why Do Women Vote Tory?* (1987) and *Official Secrets* (1988).

David Edgar is a playwright; his plays include *Destiny, Mayday, Entertaining Strangers* and an adaptation of *Nicholas Nickelby*. He is author of *The Second Time as Farce* (1988).

Stuart Hall is professor of sociology at the Open University, co-editor of *The Politics of Thatcherism* (1983), author of *The Hard Road to Renewal* (1988) and is on the editorial board of *Marxism Today*.

Dick Hebdige is a lecturer in communications at Goldsmiths College, London and is the author of *Sub-Cultures: The Meaning of Style* (1979) and *Hiding in the Light* (1989).

David Held is a senior lecturer in social science at the Open University and the author of *Models of Democracy* (1986) and *Political Theory and the Modern State* (1989).

Paul Hirst is a professor in social theory at Birkbeck College, University of London. He is co-author (with J Zeitlin) of *Reversing Industrial Decline* (1988) and the author of *After Thatcher* (1989).

Martin Jacques is editor of *Marxism Today*, a columnist for the *Sunday Times* and co-editor of *The Forward March of Labour Halted?* (1981) and *The Politics of Thatcherism* (1983).

Charlie Leadbeater is the industrial editor for the *Financial Times* and a broadcaster.

David Marquand is a professor of politics at Salford University and author of *The Unprincipled Society* (1988).

Frank Mort lectures in cultural studies at Portsmouth Polytechnic and is the author of *Dangerous Sexualities* (1987) and a forthcoming book on consumption.

Geoff Mulgan is based at the Centre for Communication and Information Studies at the Polytechnic of Central London.

Robin Murray is a fellow of the Institute of Development Studies at Sussex University and author of a forthcoming book on post-Fordism.

Tom Nairn is the author of *The Break-Up of Britain* (1977) and *The Enchanted Glass: Britain and Its Monarchy* (1988).

Michael Rustin is a professor in the sociology department at the Polytechnic of East London and author of *For a Pluralist Socialism* (1985) and (with Margaret Rustin) *Narratives of Love and Loss* (1987).

Gareth Stedman Jones is a fellow of King's College, and the author of *Outcast London* (1976) and *Languages of Class* (1984).

Fred Steward is a lecturer in innovation and management at Aston University and the author of various articles on innovation, and green politics.

Göran Therborn is a professor of sociology at Gothenburg University, Sweden and the author of *The Ideology of Power and the Power of Ideology* (1980) and *Why Some People Are More Unemployed Than Others* (1986).

John Urry is a professor of sociology at Lancaster University and co-author of *The End of Organised Capitalism* (1987) and co-author of *Contemporary British Society* (1988).

Gwyn A Williams is professor emeritus at the University of Wales and author of *Goya: The Impossible Revolution* (1984), *When Was Wales* (1985) and *Madoc: The Making of a Myth* (1987).

For the authors of *The Manifesto for New Times* please refer to the preface.

Index